T0300041

Psychology Revivals

Psychology in Africa

It is now well over a hundred and fifty years since the first celebrated geographical explorations of Africa took place. However, it was many years before there began quests of a different kind – the investigation of behaviour, personality, attitude and ability among Africa's people. Originally published in 1975, this book is an account of that work: the first explorations in Africa of psychology.

In an exhaustive and well-documented report the author, a psychologist who had himself done research in Nigeria, Uganda and who had lectured at Makerere University, drew together the main threads of the research carried out so far, putting the issues in an African perspective but anchoring them firmly within the framework of modern psychological thinking and technique of the time.

Are there any common personality and intellectual characteristics among Africans? How does weaning affect African child development? How have Africans' feelings developed about city life and industrial work? The questions the author considers range from the broad-based to the specific. The challenges which lay ahead for African investigators then moving into the mainstream of the work are also discussed.

But perhaps above all the book made a convincing case for psychology becoming a relevant and finely honed discipline in Black Africa, characterised by practical application to Black African society.

Each chapter covers a defined area of modern psychology of the time and presents a comprehensive survey in a language no more technical that the subject warrants. At the time is was felt this book would be invaluable to students of Africa secondary education whose course included a psychology component and to African students beginning a degree course in psychology. It would also have provided an informative supplement to courses in medicine, development studies, political science, sociology and anthropology.

Psychology in Africa

Mallory Wober

Routledge
Taylor & Francis Group

LONDON AND NEW YORK

First published in 1975
by International African Institute

This edition first published in 2014 by Routledge
27 Church Road, Hove BN3 2FA

and by Routledge
711 Third Avenue, New York, NY 10017

Routledge is an imprint of the Taylor & Francis Group, an informa business

© International African Institute

Publisher's Note
The publisher has gone to great lengths to ensure the quality of this reprint but points out that some imperfections in the original copies may be apparent.

Disclaimer
The publisher has made every effort to trace copyright holders and welcomes correspondence from those they have been unable to contact.

A Library of Congress record exists under ISBN: 0853020450

ISBN: 978-1-138-01786-3 (hbk)
ISBN: 978-1-315-78004-7 (ebk)
ISBN: 978-1-138-01864-8 (pbk)

PSYCHOLOGY IN AFRICA

MALLORY WOBER

INTERNATIONAL AFRICAN INSTITUTE
LONDON
1975

© International African Institute

Paper: ISBN 0 85302 047 7

Hard-back: ISBN 0 85302 045 0

Printed and bound in Great Britain by
Clarke, Doble & Brendon Ltd, Plymouth

CONTENTS

INTRODUCTION

This book is written not only for specialist psychologists, but also for students of any of the social sciences, or of education, who will find a knowledge of what psychology in Africa has accomplished, useful or interesting. Among non-specialists, the book assumes at least some familiarity on their part, with the procedures and questions of psychology, or some ability to connect with the subject matter. The task of explaining what psychology *is* is tackled by other books (e.g., for students in Africa, by Durojaiye, 1972a); this book deals with what psychology has *done*, in Africa, and to some extent *why* psychology has developed as it has.

Psychological research has been carried out in many parts of Africa for over half a century. Some writers (e.g., Levine (1961), Crijns (1962, 1966), Doob (1965), Wickert (1967), Munroe, Munroe and Levine (1972), Armer (1974) and Hoorweg (1974)) have offered short overviews of the whole, or longer accounts of some part of the field. However, the achievements of psychological research in Africa have not yet been surveyed comprehensively in a single work. Yet there are two good reasons for presenting a summary now that tries both to give a wide coverage of what has been done, yet also attempts to be readable and cohesive. The first reason concerns the amount and diversity of work that has been done.

Recently Marais and Hoorweg (1971) have analysed most of the available published psychological research, in Africa. An examination of four-year periods of productivity shows that after a steady growth since the 1920s, the greatest increase in numbers of publications occurred from 1954 to 1961, with a more even development since then. The stage seems set therefore, for a growth of material, both in volume and degree of specialisation, which it will soon be impossible to contain in a single cohesive summary. So this book was started in 1969, in an effort to report on what psychology has done in Africa so far.

The second reason for offering the present summary relates to who the researchers have been, and who they will be, with possible implications of new directions in the development of the science. Overwhelmingly, so far, printed psychological research has been offered by non-Africans, and must embody the different perspectives which such expatriates bring to Africa. It is therefore appropriate in one way for this review to be by a non-African. However, the late 1960s and much more so the 1970s have seen the emergence of African researchers in psychology. Also, this same period has seen in western psychology a growing realisation that the personality and background of the psychological researcher will be bound up with the questions he asks, as well as with the methods he may employ to answer them. So, looking forwards one may see the 1970s as a time in which psychology in Africa turns a corner, in that it will be increasingly in the hands of new people, its own people, with their own outlooks, needs, and directions of enquiry.

The view backwards shows European and American researchers reporting on the psychology of people in colonies, or in the first formative years of political independence. I am reporting on this research for two kinds of reader. The first are the Africans of the future, to whom I say 'this is what has been done', and try to explain why. The others are non-Africans, who may be interested to see what knowledge we may have been able to distil from the past, to present to the people who in future are taking charge of its development.

Two questions of definition concern the scope of that which I will regard here as lying within my field. One question concerns peoples and cultures, and asks who and what is essentially African. I am following the practice of many other writers by excluding the Arabised, the European and the Indian peoples of Africa. The psychologies of these, though doubtless interesting and also interlocked with those of the Africans among whom they live, are nevertheless substantially related to cultures whose bases lie outside Africa.

The second question of scope concerns what we may regard as 'psychology'. Many anthropologists, other social scientists, novelists and other writers have thrown as much or more light on questions of psychology in Africa as have the self-avowed psychologists. One cannot hope to draw any more than marginally from such sources, because of their great extent. So I have concentrated on the work of self-avowed psychologists, or on work published in various psychological journals; but I have also referred to many authors outside this immediate area, and the choice of these references is obviously a more personal one.

Some readers may have an impression that this book is about the psychology *of* Africa, or *of* Africans. Such a book I believe, is not yet possible. For much of the research done is only tentative, and there is some reason to think that some of it may even be misleading. We do not yet have definitively a psychology for most Africans, nor even comprehensively for a few most often studied groups within Africa. Nevertheless, we have to study the available material to try to clarify what may be misleading and what may be valid and to understand the reasons why misleading work may have been produced. In a way, then, I am taking a sociological view of what psychology has been in Africa.

My allowance that psychology in Africa done by outsiders may be different from psychology as it will come to be in Africa, may provoke criticism from those who insist that all science, including psychology, must be objective and pursue paths dictated by the logic inherent in the science. There are certainly some schools in psychology which concern themselves with questions that lend themselves well to such an objectivity. But I am fundamentally a social psychologist, using the view that psychology is a social science. This draws the observer, his interests, prejudices, abilities and cultural background into the orbit of the questions he is studying. This produces, and admits the difficulty that preferences and prejudices are as much in the mind of the reader as of the writer. I believe we have to cope with all this, and can best do so by a combination of vigilant perception and emotional relaxation.

Finally, a writer should try, especially when making a critical review, to leave indications of and room for other interpretations of the material, so that a reader who is sufficiently interested and able can follow references and leads and form his own picture of a situation. I have tried therefore to include both reporting and comment, but as distinct strands of my total account. Overall, I have tried to distinguish what has been useful in past research; and to point to regions in which work seems particularly to need to be done.

I would like to add that I would greatly appreciate copies of any ongoing or subsequent research from workers in Africa. Such material may be incorporated in any later edition of this work.

CHAPTER I

INFANCY AND WEANING

The world into which African infants arrive
Africa's diverse peoples exhibit many forms of social organisation, and there is a corresponding diversity of contexts into which African infants are born. Roy d'Andrade (1967) shows that different forms of economics and of social organisation relate to different ways in which infants are perceived and trained. African societies range from the Dorobo of Kenya, who are hunters and gatherers, to the Fulani of West Africa who are pastoralists with cattle; from the Kpelle agriculturists of West Africa whose rice crops may be stored, to the Baganda of Uganda whose bananas must be consumed directly; from the semi-nomadic Bambuti farmers of Eastern Zaire to the Hausa, the Yoruba and the Edos of Nigeria who developed city life centuries ago in Kano, Ibadan and Benin. With modernisation and political independence, forms of urban and suburban life, similar in many ways to what is found in technologically sophisticated societies outside Africa, including new styles of child raising, have started to develop.

With this diversity of social forms, we cannot point to one world in which African infants are born and in which they are nurtured. We must always remember the variety which exists; and whenever researchers refer to 'Africans', based upon knowledge concerning some particular Africans, we must remember that there may well be other Africans of whom the generalisations we read about are not necessarily true.

Nevertheless, many authors, including Africans, write about 'Africans' as a homogeneous entity; but it does not follow that everything about these apparent stereotypes is totally untrue. As our first example, there is a distinct stereotype regarding African motherhood. An American colleague of Margaret Mead (Newton, 1970) has shown evidence that cultural differences in attitudes can greatly affect the degree of pain felt in childbirth. Other new research (eg, reported in Kaplan, 1972) suggests that what mothers eat during pregnancy, or how much they smoke, may affect the condition of the child at birth, and even later. How then, do African mothers regard childbirth?

Accounts by 37 students from all over Ghana were collected by Barrington Kaye (1962) and contain much material on maternal attitudes. In Ghana, Kaye says there is a 'universally positive' attitude to the idea of having children. Denise Paulme (1963) writes of the 'African woman' (in Francophone Africa) 'that it is only by becoming a mother that she feels truly fulfilled'. Biesheuvel (1959b) based in South Africa also refers to the high value placed on having children, present in most African cultures; and he considers that this may decrease the amount of difficulties experienced in childbirth. Similarly Salamone, (1969) reports that 'no Hausa adult is regarded as an adult until he becomes a parent' and 'a woman's status is determined not by her husband's status but by the number of children she has'.

Not everything is benign about childbirth in Africa however; and it is important to disentangle the positive and negative threads in the complex of conditions which surround the arrival of infants. The negative aspects of mothers' attitudes seem really to reflect their feelings about the importance of everything going well. Thus Kaye also says that, since childbirth is beset by both physical and supernatural dangers, anxiety 'everywhere in Ghana is said to be characteristic of pregnancy'. Margaret Field (1960) who studied the complaints brought to local diviners in Ghana, found that many problems concerned worries about successful childbirth.

According to Kaye, difficulty with childbirth in Ghana is sometimes attributed to adultery. Welbourn (1963) describes a similar belief among Baganda women, that prolonged childbirth is a sign of infidelity, and punishment was traditionally meted out in such cases. Since Welbourn points out that many Baganda women have a pelvic shape unsuitable for smooth delivery, it seems likely that prolonged childbirth and consequent punishment must have happened quite often — with the result of making other mothers-to-be somewhat fearful.

High infant mortality in traditional African societies is accompanied by beliefs and practices which may have functioned to soften the pain of such losses. Such beliefs may also have alleviated anxieties before childbirth — though they may in other cases have stimulated worries. An Akan idea in Ghana was that 'for the first eight days of a child's life, it is regarded as a temporary being, not fully human, not fully spiritual. If it dies before the eighth day it is considered as the exit of a visitor'; sometimes 'when a child is born after several preceding children have died . . the face of the newborn infant is disfigured with cuts . . . it is often given a slave's name and its hair is left unkempt . . . to persuade the spirits that it is unwanted and to lessen thereby the danger of its sharing the fate of its siblings, since the spirits would get no satisfaction from depriving anyone of something that he did not in any case value'.

A Zulu-speaking psychologist (Lee, 1958) related dream imagery among Zulu women to the great desire they had to produce children — though not too prolifically. Lee's interpretation is that there is both a powerful need for fulfilment, and pleasure in motherhood, as well as anxiety about too many, especially later pregnancies. Elsewhere, Occitti (1971) described various taboos and restrictions which pregnant mothers among the Acholi of northern Uganda observe, to ward off abortion or premature delivery. Occitti says that 'childlessness is regarded by most people as the most serious misfortune that can befall a married couple'. But they 'will rarely dream of making any preparations ahead of time for the coming baby' and have a proverb 'a hammock is not sewn without a child'. It is interesting that though the neighbouring Baganda are considered a different tribe for historic, sociological and linguistic reasons, they share similar pre-natal practices with the Acholi.

These few examples, which can easily be supported by similar reports throughout Africa, suggest that parenthood is widely held to be a major goal in life; while the risks that sufficient parenthood may not be attained, makes people anxious during pregnancy and while their infants are still young. Children therefore arrive into a basically welcoming world; though in some cases if over-anxiety has attended the pregnancy, or childbirth has been prolonged, the infant may not perhaps have experienced the best possible start in life. Limited knowledge from western research, though less as yet arising from work in Africa, suggests that pre-natal circumstances are indeed likely to affect childbirth, and eventually to influence childhood development. These possibilities render research on the psychological and social facets of pregnancy and childbirth of considerable practical interest.

Geber's thesis of precocity among African infants
The notion of precocity assumes that there may be a 'natural' schedule of development for newborn babies and infants, which will be followed at least until cultural differences make their effects felt in the pace and directions of growth. Various tests exist with which to assess newborn and infant development; these include the American tests of Gesell, and French versions of them, a newer American test devised by Nancy Bayley, and an English one by J. Griffiths. Apart from two widely separate pieces of research, which will be mentioned later, the story of the now-famous thesis of the precocity of African infants begins in Kampala, Uganda, in the early 1950s. As with many other discoveries in science, the story begins with work going on in some other direction.

Mulago Hospital, Kampala, was one of the research centres where the problem of kwashiorkor had been related to protein deficiency during infancy. Kwashiorkor is a debilitating disease which occurs frequently in Buganda (the central region of Uganda) and where infants around the time of weaning get a low protein diet based on starchy bananas.

The Director of the Medical Research Council's Infantile Malnutrition Unit, Dr R. F. A. Dean, next contacted the World Health Organisation and asked for someone to be sent out to study the psychological effects on infants, of kwashiorkor. Following up a recommendation, when Dean passed through Paris on a cold wintry January in 1954, he called on Dr Geber and discussed the possibility of her coming to Kampala to do research. Dr Geber, who was then Director of the Child Guidance Clinics at Aisne, near Paris, and very experienced in testing infants of all social backgrounds, heard nothing more until June that year, when she was surprised to receive in the post, a return ticket to Kampala. That summer, her African research began.

Geber decided that to understand the problems of kwashiorkor, she should first study the development of normal African infants, starting from birth. In an early article with Dr Dean (1957a) Dr Geber reported on 37 infants tested at less than 24 hours after birth. These newborns were examined using a Gesell-type technique developed in Paris by André Thomas. This involves an examination of reflexes and of muscular tone (tightness) and co-ordination.

Geber writes 'it was immediately obvious that the distribution of muscle tone in the African child differed from that of the European'. In European infants the Moro reflex is observed, which consists of a spreadeagling of the limbs in response to sudden shock. In African infants the Moro reflex was often weak, and absent in infants over four days old. These Kampala infants often had wide open eyes, and 'a lively look' — which Geber illustrates with a very vivid photograph. One unusually precocious action was seen in a child a day old who had received at birth a slight scalp wound and who 'continually fingered the bandage over the wound'.

This early report gives results on 107 infants tested, mostly at Mulago Hospital. Apart from the 37 newborns, there were 48 up to two days old, and others up to eight days old. Sixty were Baganda, the others from other parts of Uganda.

The first idea tested to explain precocity was that the altitude (nearly 4,000 ft), or climate of Kampala somehow influenced the infants' condition. If this was the case, precocity would be found among European, just as with African children born there. Geber and Dean with difficulty found 15 European and 60 Asian infants also born in Kampala. The 'European children gave exactly the same results that have been found in Europe, and the Indian children gave almost similar results'. Altitude and climate as factors possibly causing precocity, were therefore ruled out, and questioning turned to the roles of maternal diet, attitudes, or other unknown factors.

Next, the researchers explored whether aspects of life styles associated with social class might be the ones affecting infant development. Geber and Dean (1958) reported on 60 children from 27 elite families, with professional class parents mostly practising European life styles. They found that up to age two years, motor development among the elite children was precocious, though not as much as among children of poorer families. After age two the performance of poorer families' children fell away, though this hardly happened at all among the wealthier group.

The wealthier familes' children were socially confident and not afraid of white people. They also performed some of the tasks involving mental skills, better than did the poorer children. One item in the Gesell test which was used in examining older infants was a form-board (with different shaped holes, and cut out pieces to be correctly fitted in); while the poorer families' children could not do this at age two, those from well-off families did so, and even with the board turned over (thus reversing some shapes); however, some babies from other poorer families dealt with this task at an earlier age. Geber and Dean attributed this better performance to 'the superior intelligence of the parents and the increased opportunities for education . . . of the wealthier homes'.

Geber and Dean still had to account for the early precocity of the non-wealthy babies, and raised an important hypothesis which still, over 12 years later, has not been systematically studied in Africa. This is that 'the state of the newborn African child may be related to the attitude of the mother to her pregnancy'. The unfortunate occurrence of unwanted pregnancies among schoolgirls, which so many topical magazines currently dramatise as commonplace in modernising Africa, allows an opportunity to study this hypothesis, since mothers of similar social class are now available who have positive, and others who have not altogether positive attitudes towards their pregnancies. Research on these lines remains to be done.

Geber and Dean (1957b) had meanwhile expanded the information on which their assertion of African infant precocity was based to data on 183 infants, aged up to 72 months old. Some of the testing was done in Mulago in a quiet room, some in the hospital courtyard; other children were tested among the families of students at a Protestant theological seminary at Mukono, 15 miles from Kampala; some children were tested in their village homes, while the remainder were tested at dispensaries at cotton plantations. Geber noticed (personal communication) that children tested in a quiet room as in orthodox western professional practice seemed to feel they were in a strange and possibly disturbing situation; while those tested in a courtyard or a dispensary with a crowd of onlookers seemed to behave in a more uninhibited, natural (and developmentally advanced) way.

From this testing 'Gesell quotients' (analogous to intelligence quotients in the way they are calculated, but based on what Gesell found to be normal standards for American white infants in the 1930s) were calculated. For 33 infants aged six months or less, quotients ranged from 100, to 345 (for motor development) and 300 (for verbal, or vocal development). By a year old the highest quotients were around 150; between two and three years old, among 36 children, motor activity quotients up to 137, language development quotients up to 130, and none less than 100 were reported.

The authors acknowledge that their samples were not representative of 'Africans' or even of 'Ugandans' nor even of Baganda. The infants tested in their homes were from families selected 'because the chief believed that they would collaborate well, and they were probably above the other Ganda in intelligence'. The reason for this is that Geber was embarking on a longitudinal study, and families had to be selected who were reliable and settled so that they could be found again over the years. Even if this is seen as a biasing factor in the sampling, it is still remarkable that such high scores, and no low ones were found.

This paper (Geber and Dean, 1957b) mentioned 113 newborns — saying that 'no explanation was offered for the precocity, but it was fairly clear that it had a genetic basis'. Several critics have taken Geber and Dean to task for this statement. It should be realised though that these articles were written by exchange of letters between Dr Geber in Paris, writing in French, and Dr Dean in Kampala, contributing his ideas and translating into English. Dean has since died in Cambridge and so cannot explain this contradiction; but Madame Geber did not intend to offer a genetic explanation for African infant precocity, which probably got published as a result of imperfect communication between the authors.

The question of genetic origins of a supposedly 'racial' characteristic has been, and remains of socio-political importance (see Wober, 1972b). For in 1969 a widespread controversy arose in western countries following an article by Professor Arthur Jensen of Berkeley University, California. It was pointed out by some protagonists that it was a characteristic of subhuman primates that their offspring matured more rapidly than among humans; and the insinuation was made, using reference to Geber's results, that because their infants were precocious, Africans were genetically substandard compared with other types of humans. It is important to note that Madame Geber herself denies this interpretation of her results, which only arose at third hand following a phrase which inadvertently appeared in this one only of her many publications.

Further research in Africa, supporting Geber's thesis

Though the research so far discussed had not provided evidence from outside Uganda, Geber (1958) soon reported on results further afield. She had tested 16 children of between 8 and 21 months old from Alexandra, a village near Johannesburg and 30 others of less than a year old in Senegal. The atmosphere in South Africa was not conducive to collection of results which Dr Geber could feel validly reflected infants' true condition. Furthermore among some South African groups (as in Ghana and elsewhere) newborns were kept in seclusion with the mother, until a week had passed, when they were 'brought out'. Thus it was not possible to test newborns in their own natural surroundings.

The babies tested in Senegal were found with the help of Dr Senecal in Dakar, and also at Popenguine, a small fishing village where Colonel Dr Raoult held a clinic. As well as these, 150 children up to two years old, tested by Dr Solange Faladé in Senegal, provided data which Geber now discussed. Dr Faladé is a Yoruba from Dahomey who had been a pupil of Geber's in Paris. When Geber went to Kampala, Faladé went to Senegal to run parallel studies there. Their discoveries are therefore of a joint nature. Faladé (1955) published her results in a book in France, and later (1960) in a journal article; but Geber discusses these results along with her own, from Kampala.

She says there was 'an all-round advance of development over European standards which was greater, the younger the child'. Photographs illustrate this thesis; these photographs might be mistaken for the ones taken in Kampala, but were actually taken in Dakar. This again provides grist for Geber's critics, though perhaps we should follow the example of Geber's African infants instead, and maintain a straight head and lively gaze upon the point at issue, rather than be distracted by essentially peripheral issues. Faladé found the Senegalese infants scored above the Gesell norms at every age level tested monthly, from 4 to 56 weeks old; locomotion was at first the most advanced sub-set of skills, but at the end of the year manual dexterity was the skill furthest ahead among the Africans. Faladé also pointed out a precocity in language acquisition, with some children of a year old having a vocabulary of a dozen words (cf Griffith's norms of about 3).

The next study from Senegal was published by Bardet, a psychoanalyst, Massé, a pediatrician, Françoise Moreigne, also a psychoanalyst and Senecal (1960), the medical superintendent. They report on the results of applying a French-developed version of the Gesell test, called the Brunet-Lezine scales. These assess performance on three separate types of skills; locomotion/posture, ocular-motor coordination, and the beginnings of language. The Developmental Quotients for various ages are given as follows:

TABLE 1
Developmental Quotients on the
Brunet-Lezine scales,
for Wolof infants in Dakar

Age in months:

	6	9	12	18	24
Number of infants tested:	57	91	144	129	109
Locomotion/posture:	123	103	102	102	88
Ocular-motor co-ordination:	120	105	99	100	84
Language:	–	85	70	77	85

It is only at the earliest stage that infants were precocious, here with respect to a French baseline rather than Gesell's American one. Language performance was assessed by asking mothers what length of words their infants could utter. This interview-type data is fraught with difficulties in specifying what are words (understandable to others, as distinct from noises intelligible to a mother only), and with the social relations between interviewer and interviewee. There is certainly no sign of verbal precocity. The only evidence in support of Geber's thesis lies in the non-verbal skills up to the age of six months. However, these children were from the distinctly disadvantageous slums of Dakar, not from the more relaxed green surroundings of peri-urban Kampala. Overall then, the Senegalese evidence on precocity collected by Faladé, and later by Senecal's group only partly supports the case for precocity.

The most recent research from Senegal (Lusk and Lewis, 1972) was based on the new Bayley test, using both the mental- and motor-abilities scales. They only tested 10 infants, between 2 and 12 months old, so no generalisations are possible. However, both Motor Developmental Quotients (DQs), and mental DQs were very high, most varying between 130 and 150, against Bayley's American norms of 100. Lusk and Lewis tried to relate measures of infant behaviour with observations made on mothers' interaction; but no link could be found between what mothers did, and infants' DQ scores. They therefore suggested that genetic, or pre-natal environmental variations might be responsible for the level of infants' development.

While the Senegalese evidence comes mostly from Geber's colleagues, an independent enquiry was made by a Dr Paul Vouilloux (1959) in the Cameroons. The children he tested were from the Bassa, Bamileke, and Ewondo peoples. Vouilloux used Gesell tests in three sub-scales, and tested three groups of children — 48 healthy ones who accompanied their families visiting a hospital, 25 sick children, and 25 in an orphanage aged from a few weeks, to six months old. The results are as follows:

TABLE 2
Developmental Quotients on the Gesell scales,
for three groups of infants in the Cameroons

Groups:	normal	sick	orphanages
Locomotor/posture	133	114	97
Manual operations	117	103	73
Verbal skills	100	86	65

As in Senegal, any evidence for precocity is localised in motor skills among normal children, and possibly among those who are merely sick. The orphanage children do not receive the close physical attention that family children get; moreover, they are likely to include some who were abandoned for having deformities, disabled mothers, or who suffered other complex negative influences both genetically and environmentally. In spite of this, their locomotion was basically normal by French standards, though their other skills were considerably retarded. So though in this disadvantaged group there is no precocity compared with Europeans, there is an advancement of some aspects of development (those aspects where normal African babies do better than Europeans) over others.

Vouilloux also charted the reduction of precocity with age, among the normal children he tested. In motor (DQ 129) and manual operations (DQ 110) there is evidence of precocity up to a year and a half old. These children moreover, unlike Geber's in Kampala, were not selected for having come from specially stable families. Furthermore, Vouilloux divided his sample into two groups: 21 from poorer parents and 27 from less poor parents, and found that the first group did better (average DQ of 130.7) than the second (114.9).

Several other researchers have lent support to Geber's thesis, with evidence from Zambia, South Africa, and most convincingly again from Uganda. In Zambia Susan Goldberg (1970) a developmental psychologist, was interested in devising a new test of infant abilities, based on Piaget's theories. These ideas suggest that the infant spends his first two years in refining the precision and purpose of his physical movements; eventually he begins to realise that things can be represented by signs for them – ie, words, or thought (that can be put into words). Goldberg's test include three subscales, of *Prehension* (eye-hand coordination), *Space* (ability to follow and predict movements of objects in space) and *Object Permanence* (the notion that things continue to exist on their own even though the child does not for the moment see, or touch them).

The 25 infants whom Goldberg tested fully were from a Lusaka slum. Goldberg found that at six months for the OP scale, the Zambian infants were ahead of results reported from three different sources in western countries; but at 9 and 12 months, on this scale, Zambian babies lagged in their developmental condition. The same pattern existed for the S scale, though for the P scale the Zambian children were well ahead.

Here again, there is some localised precocity, which is remarkable because these Zambian infants were considerably less well fed and in worse health than the western children with whom they were compared. Goldberg reports that infants over six months old can distinguish strange adults, so the situation was not as relaxed as it could have been. The babies' disadvantage in the testing situation 'was particularly acute at nine months when it was complicated by what seemed to be a great deal of stranger anxiety . . . thus we can not really dismiss the possibility that we have been measuring motivational or personality differences rather than sensori-motor development'.

The problem of rapport between the infant, often with the mother present, and the tester, has often been mentioned in this kind of research. Geber and Dean (1958) mention this. Bertha Akim, then a student at Makerere and later a dietician there, with two colleagues Dr McFie and E. Sebigajju, also noticed that with the infants they tested (from 6 to 33 months old) where a European experimenter was present, the child would 'retreat into its mother's lap and whimper . . . among the possible explanations for this . . . one was provided by a mother who said to her child: "go on, build the bricks, or the white man will take you away" '. These workers also point out that when dividing infants into two groups, from more, and from less educated families, even in the less educated group nearly two thirds of the infants were above 'normal' (European) standards of development. Ainsworth (1963), yet another white researcher in Uganda describes the phenomenon in detail; she shows how the infants' fear can be related to the development of their ability to distinguish and respond to their mothers and other caretakers (aunts, sisters) with a corresponding reluctance to respond well to highly conspicuous strangers.

This difficulty in examining infants over six months or so, is likely to be particularly obtrusive when whites study black infants in South Africa. Dr Renée Liddicoat, as a neuropsychologist at the National Institute for Personnel Research in Johannesburg, worked in this area. With Constance Koza (1963), she studied language development in 120 infants from 18 to 36 months old, and remarked on the childrens' shyness and non-cooperation which occurs after about six months old. Their tests were therefore given by African graduates, and were spoken in Zulu, Sotho, Xhosa and Tswana. The tasks consisted of naming objects in pictures, and from 30 months old, giving the use of an object. Performance was well up to Gesell's norms for naming objects, while at and over 24 months the Africans were well ahead of American standards. However, at 30 months African infants were behind the norms for giving uses of objects. The authors suggest that infants reacted with interest to the pictures, forgetting the presence of strange adults; but asking them to give the use of an object brought attention to a questioning adult. This, the authors suggest, produced a shyness and reluctance to cooperate which might relate to the comparatively recent experience of weaning, for the children.

Renée Liddicoat (1969) has also tested 20 boy and 20 girl infants for each month of the first year of age. On six test items concerned with motor behaviour the African infants were ahead of norms for local whites. This testing used the same idea as Geber's, that as a necessary preliminary for a study of malnourishment, standards for healthy African infants were wanted. Liddicoat is very aware of methodological niceties in testing infants, which need to be satisfied if one is to establish the thesis of precocity. So her latest assessment, with Mr R. D. Griesel (1971) is important, that 'testing of African infants has revealed strong indications that they are initially advanced in relation to Western cultural norms, especially in the locomotor field . . .'

The last major study which supports Geber's thesis is by the young American, Janet Kilbride, now at Bryn Mawr College in Pennsylvania; her studies (1969, and with Robbins and Kilbride, 1970) involved 163 Baganda infants who were born in hospital at Masaka, 80 miles from Kampala. Kilbridge used the Bayley test, whose norms are much more up to date and broad-based than are Gesell's. She then calculated Developmental Motor Quotients (DMQs).

A marked early precocity of the Baganda, African infants emerged, compared with both white and black American infants. Taking the age group 4–8 months (to follow an American study) the Baganda had an average DMQ of 126.8, while the lower class American black infants scored 110.7 and upper class, 103.9. In the range of 9–18 months the Baganda had an average DMQ of 118.6, almost identical with lower class American blacks, while the difference between them and the upper class blacks was closing, the latter having a mean score of 110.0.

There were no systematic differences among Kilbride's infants due to sex, or birth order. She points out that her test was different from Geber's, the tester was different, the samples were not drawn in the same way, and society was changing, in that 12 years' influence towards Westernisation had occurred since Geber's original fieldwork. Nevertheless, Kilbride's extensive and thorough work supports Geber's thesis — the African (Baganda) children showed clear superiority to white and black American groups, though the advantage had almost completely dissipated by the age of two.

In addition to her published data, Kilbride (personal communication) says that she has tested a large group of Baganda newborns, who were precocious; and she herself has tested American infants, so with the same tester (herself) an African superiority over western (American) infants has been demonstrated.

Studies still in preparation, supporting Geber's thesis

In support of Geber, Munroe, Munroe and Levine (1972) quote a personal communication they have from Daniel G. Freedman, of the University of Chicago. Freedman tested 24 infants 'majority Hausa' in West Africa; almost all of the one- to two-day old infants 'showed unusual strength as exemplified by the ability to hold up the head when pulled to a sitting position'.

Secondly, in Kenya a pediatrician Dr P. Herbert Leiderman (1970) from America tested 70 Kikuyu infants using Bayley's scales. He reports that there is motor precocity at each of 2, 4 and 6 months old stages, while for the mental DQ there was a slender advantage of Kikuyu infants over the norms for Americans. Leiderman also measured aspects of maternal behaviour, but has not yet reported on any links there may be between maternal and infant test scores. Dr Geber (personal communication) has heard from Leiderman who has now tested American infants and can make a case for African (Kikuyu) precocity based on his own comparison. Finally, the husband and wife team of Robert and Ruth Munroe (1971a) report from a small sample of Logoli infants in Kenya aged between 10 and 16 months, that almost all could walk with some dexterity; for the younger ones, this is certainly precocious.

Evidence failing to support Geber's thesis

Recently Neil Warren, a social psychologist from Sussex University, has attacked Geber's thesis (Warren, 1972), after having done his own research in Kampala, and on the basis of a critical analysis of the literature.

Warren makes many criticisms, but the main points he, as well as other critics seem to be concerned about, include these:

(1) Madame Geber's own articles contain sketchy and in some places misleading reporting, particularly where she deals with statistics.

(2) Geber's samples are not randomly drawn; on the contrary, babies were specially sought from stable, good families.

(3) The Gesell test was standardised (i.e., its norms, or comparative baseline was laid down) in the 1930s. Since then Western populations have improved their own scores, so a comparison with Gesell norms is not really a valid up-to-date one.

(4) Proper comparison requires that the same tester should use the same test, and work at approximately the same period, with the two groups being compared.

(5) Precision in estimating ages of infants is vital, and must either depend on good documentary records of dates of birth, or on checks on gestational age by examining physical signs. (Thus a newborn who is overdue will have long fingernails and other signs of extra growth while in the womb, and it is not valid to compare him with an infant born on time).

Warren also cites studies which do not support the case for precocity. The first important one is an unpublished script by Theunissen (1948) in South Africa. Theunissen tested 232 infants, aged from 2 to 57 weeks old, with the Gesell tests; 66 of the Africans were compared with 66 European South African infants of matched age (in weeks) from birth. According to Warren, Theunissen tested African infants in Durban, Pietermaritzburg and a native village, while European infants were presumably not tested in a native village. In spite of the native village, the African families were described as urbanised or semi-urbanised: Theunissen is quoted as summing up by saying 'a marked degree of similarity in the rate of development of European and Bantu infants' was found.

The second important piece of work is by a Belgian, J. C. Falmagne (1962) who reports no differences between 78 infants of Zulu, Sotho and Xhosa tribes in Johannesburg, and 105 Belgian infants tested in Brussels, all less than six months old. Falmagne provides comparisons for each month of age on each of 20 test items. Aside from items where the two groups were equal, the Belgians were advanced in 42 items and the Africans in 37. Falmagne correctly criticises the comparison of 'African' with Euroamerican norms, and points out that there can be, and evidently are inter-African just as much as inter-European differences or similarities.

Warren mentions a third piece of work, which shows that the question of African infant precocity was mooted as far back as the early 1930s. In this research Langton (1934—5) observed infants in the north western corner of Uganda, and noted the ages at which they could crawl, stand and walk. Langton himself did not consider these infants precocious; but Warren estimated that their results could be 'interpreted as comparing favourably for the African child with Griffiths' norms for British babies'. Warren also previews a study by Melvin Konner (1974) an anthropologist from Harvard who spent time among the so-called Bushmen in Botswana. Konner found the range of reflexes among Bushmen infants was the same as that found in their European counterparts. It is not clear whether Konner did his own comparative testing of Euroamerican infants. Warren suggests also that Bushmen may be of a different 'race' from (Bantu) Africans.

Elsewhere a Canadian (Poole, 1969) tested 90 healthy, full-term Yoruba infants in Nigeria. Equal numbers were drawn from rich and from poor homes, at each month of age from 4—12 months old. Apart from the vocabulary item (very difficult to assess cross-culturally) the Yoruba babies had all reached the Griffiths test norms at the appropriate ages. Statistically, one would expect half to be advanced, and half to be behind if the population was similar to the one on which Griffiths based her standards. But Poole's samples at each age level were so small that the results must be taken as inconclusive. Comparison of rich and poor families 'did not support Geber's claim that westernisation affects the rate of psychomotor development'. There are two kinds of evidence that would effectively refute Geber; one, if African infants are shown to lag behind others in test scores, and secondly, if reliably large African samples are shown not to differ from others. Poole's evidence is certainly not of the first kind, but more resembles the latter, tending if anything, slightly towards Geber's case.

Finally, Griffiths (1969) tested nearly 1,000 African infants aged between 0 and 52 weeks in Johannesburg. Among these urbanised families' infants, the Moro reflex persisted well into the first month of life, a pattern more similar to European than to the Baganda results reported by Geber and Dean. Griffiths also showed that these African infants had similar courses of development regarding extensor and flexor plantar reflexes as in European norms.

Parkin and Warren (1969) themselves compared three groups: infants from poor, and others from well-off African families, and European infants. Using 33 separate test items, and careful criteria to make sure they only dealt with healthy infants who were not premature or overdue, no overall advantages in favour of any one group was shown; very few of the inter-group comparisons on specific items showed any significant differences. Nevertheless, in comparing European with poorer family African infants, four significant differences were found in the Africans' favour, including the famous holding up the head while sitting; while on only one item were the European infants advanced.

Two other technical details seem to render Parkin and Warren's own data less clear as evidence against precocity than they, and later Warren himself, claim. First of all, the rich family African infants were significantly older at test (in hours and days from birth) than the poorer group. Thus the poor family infants whose scores were so similar to the rich family infants', can be said to be precocious, because they were younger. Although this is not a European-African comparison of precocity, it is in the same direction as findings by Geber and Vouilloux, which were that the poorer families' infants they tested were more precocious.

The second detail is this: Parkin and Warren estimated gestational age for the poor-family African infants, from physical characteristics which must have been established as normative for European samples (e.g., skin texture, Lanugo hair, nail length and texture, etc). Parkin and Warren acknowledge that 'the validity of this method has not been determined for African babies'. It is possible then, that if African infants are precocious with regard to some of these physical signs, this would mean that samples which Parkin and Warren take to be of equal gestational age, might in fact have comprised a younger group of African infants. If then the groups were found to perform at similar levels of development, it would mean that the Africans should be considered a precocious group. It would seem that it really requires exact dates of conception to be known before any valid comparison of newborns can be made, and this is almost impossible with poorer African families, as with poorer families anywhere.

The difficult problem of what defines the normal birth weight and term for African infants has been tackled by two doctors who examined over 2,000 premature infants in the Congo (Vincent and Hugon, 1962). They considered that the African infants showed a superior maturity, for equal weight, to European children, and that a criterion of 1,800 gm is a suitable one to consider as a normal birth weight. We saw, however, early in this chapter that various aspects of maternal behaviour can affect the development of the foetus, so if cultures differ specifically on maternal behaviour, we could expect 'normal' birth weight and 'normal' maturity to be different in one culture, from another.

The questions then emerge, do African cultures show similarities in mothers' pre-natal behaviour and in infant condition and do westernised Africans show results more similar to that which is found in western communities?

The controversy assessed: Have African infants been shown to be precocious?

First we must realise again that the English expression 'African infants' is ambiguous. It can be taken to mean all African infants or it could mean some, who happen to be African. Certainly in the first sense, of a blanket generalisation, no supporters of the precocity thesis would insist that all African infants were precocious. We merely have to consider whether it has been demonstrated sufficiently often, and with sufficient care, that various groups of African infants score higher on development scales than we would expect from European or American ones.

Warren's first criticism, that Geber's articles contain imperfect statistical treatment, must be conceded. It must be remembered though, that articles in psychological journals are passed by referees, who judge by the standards of the day whether the facts have been shown with enough numerical exactitude.

But apart from such defences, the lack of conviction that parts of Geber's papers convey to some English-speaking readers is linked with two sources of difference in style. Geber wrote within an earlier tradition of French social psychology, where there was more trust in a writer's assertion and interpretation of 'facts'; while Warren, and those with a similar view now have keen demands for clear quantification. The second difference in style is between that of a clinical psychologist like Geber, who trusts to skilled reporting of personal interpretation of human situations, and that of a statistical social scientist who mistrusts the ways in which personal bias can affect an account. On balance perhaps, Warren's criticism is fair, since Geber must have had the figures which she could have presented in detail alongside her more clinical observations, which would have satisfied both camps. Geber does give some figures, but for those for whom science requires numbers, perhaps no figures would be better than just a few which seem incomplete.

The second point, that Geber's samples were drawn from special groups is also true. But Kilbride's later work in Uganda did not use such well selected samples of infants, and precocity was still found. So perhaps though this criticism of Geber's procedure is valid, it may not matter in the end.

Geber's use of Gesell's norms is also a weak point in her work. But this is not a grievous mistake; Gesell tests were the principal ones available in those days. Moreover Gesell's tests were chosen for the variety of their tasks and the opportunity these allowed for clinical observation about how the infants dealt with them. Again, though Geber's African scores are held up against Euro-American baselines that have by now shifted, when Kilbride used very recent norms, precocity was still demonstrated. And when Brunet-Lezine scales were used in Senegal, again with more up-to-date French standards, early precocity was still found.

The requirement that the same tester should use the same test on the two groups being compared, was met by Geber and Dean (1957a). Warren discounts this because the European and Indian results were reported in just one sentence. The question really is, whether Warren suspects that the scores were not recorded at all, rather than that they were not reported. To be sure, it would have been much better to have had the numbers to satisfy everyone. But more recently, authors offering detailed statistics, who have themselves tested or supervised testing of both groups being compared, have come forward; and they support the case for precocity. These authors include Renée Liddicoat (1969) in South Africa, Janet Kilbride who has tested Americans as well as Baganda; and Drs Freedman and Leiderman, whose results are not yet generally available.

The final caution, about making sure that infants being compared are of equal age, may also be accepted. But there are so many differences between peoples, including for instance the fact that many Baganda women have small pelvises (Welbourn, 1963) and a low red blood cell count compared to the pastoral Karamojong, or Europeans (Stanier, 1953), that it would not be surprising if Baganda women had a different normal length of pregnancy from

Europeans; and if they produced infants typically in a different condition from those in Europe or America.

The two studies by Theunissen and by Falmagne, which Warren finds methodologically best, and which revealed no precocity, took place in South Africa. The psychological conditions which black Africans experience there are difficult to quantify; but they must be recognised to be adverse, and as such, we may not feel sure that the 'true' abilities of these South African babies were expressed, and hence measured. There are thus doubts with these negative findings just as Warren finds others with the positive evidence.

Recently, an American (Werner, 1972), has reviewed studies on infants from around the world. She is not critical of methodology, and accepts conclusions that authors offer. The African reports of precocity are not found to be unique, as Latin American and Asian infants have also been found advanced compared with European groups. Unless there has been experimental error on a global scale, reflecting some unaccountable bias that for some reason wishes to depict 'third world' infants as advanced, it seems reasonable to accept the precocity thesis. The causes are not yet identified, but presumably are linked somewhere with the broad socio-economic and cultural differences that distinguish peoples in 'developed' and 'developing' nations. In the African data, the precocity applies more strongly the younger the infant, and particularly for test items which involve motor coordination.

What factors may cause infant precocity?

Geber and Dean ruled out a possible effect of altitude on infant precocity, even though it had once been thought that reduced air pressure on mother's abdomens could benefit infants (Heyns, 1963). One obvious difference between most African mothers and Europeans, is that the former breast-feed their infants on demand, though this is changing among the small proportion of westernised families. Several authors have speculated whether such feeding, as well as regular handling which it entails, has promoted precocity.

In South Africa, Salber (1956) examined 185 infants fed on demand; during the first three days before full milk flow developed, these lost more weight than regime-fed infants; but after the first week the breast-fed infants overtook the others. Welbourn (1954) pointed out that breast feeding traditionally would continue well after six months, and unless there is supplementary food, the milk diet may wane in quantity, quality, or both. Welbourn's Baganda babies were heavier than Europeans at three months, but by four months old were losing their weight advantages. Also from Uganda, Mary Ainsworth (1963, 1967) supported Geber's impression that early motor development was precocious; but she also shows how in some cases, where maternal milk supply reduces later, this may contribute to fretfulness and strained relations between mother and child.

Geber says (1958) that breast feeding is but one part of the entirely different way in which traditional mothers bring up their children, compared with westernised methods. She points out that 'a few children who were being brought up in the European way, passing most of their lives in cots and fed at regular intervals ... did not show similar precocity after the first month'. Vouilloux suggests similar reasons for precocity: 'the Cameroon baby experiences in the months following birth a very gradual transition from the intra-uterine to the autonomous life . . . the generously physical behaviour of the mother, her steadiness and cheerful emotions give the child extreme security'.

Taking a more detailed approach, an American, David Cox (1971) who had taught at Haile Sellassie I University in Ethiopia, polled 152 students on their knowledge about current child raising practices. 92 per cent said mothers suckled their infants to pacify them if they cried and that the child is picked up if he cries at night; 94 per cent said the infant has considerable bodily contact with the mother. Similarly, the Munroes (1971) studying the Logoli in Kenya found that in households where there are more people infants were held more, even if it was not by the mother but by someone else, and they were also responded to more quickly when they cried. This supports Ainsworth's idea of the 'multiple caretakers' who are the sources of maternal care, and who may include several people other than the mother.

Whether close physical affection can enhance infant motor development indirectly through a beneficial climate of security, or directly through systematic motor stimulation, is not known. Faladé had suggested that Wolof mothers' practice of massaging their newborn infants daily, might facilitate motor development; while Ainsworth discusses similar customs among the Baganda, in whose case it is the mothers who massage themselves during pregnancy, while infants are encouraged to sit up at an early age by being propped up with cushions (in more modern families) or by being sat in basins or in padded holes in the ground (traditional families). Barrett (1971) has discussed recent research on how pre-natal experience of the foetus may affect infants' neuropsychological condition after birth; and it is entirely plausible to expect infants whose pregnancies have been managed in a certain way, to be precocious compared to others.

Kilbride (1972) also points out that Baganda — and many other African mothers carry infants on their backs, which may promote postural control. Further, Baganda babies are often picked up by a hand around the chest, with the head left to support itself; they are held out to urinate, and propped up in a sitting position to defecate. Such practices are observable elsewhere in Africa too, and may contribute to precocious motor developments. In one example given by Goldberg (1969) Zambian mothers showed more physical contact with their infants than did American mothers; Zambian mothers vigorously handled their infants, picking them up by an arm and swinging them over a shoulder to be placed on the back. Indeed, it would be difficult to explain why all these different ways of handling infants had no effect, if we were to accept Warren's argument that the case for precocity has not been proved.

On the other hand, where African children suffer malnourishment or disease, this may handicap psychological development. Professor Philip Vernon (1969) says firmly that 'the infant brain is particularly vulnerable to dietary deficiencies . . . say from three months to six months after birth . . . damage occurring then may be irreversible'. Bertha Akim and her colleagues (1956) in Kampala had earlier on looked into the possible effects of mild malnutrition. They categorised as malnourished any child 'whose rate of

growth has been interrupted', though none of these children were actually
diseased. Gesell tests with 45 children revealed no differences between the
mildly malnourished and the well-fed children. Unlike Vernon, Akim and
company suggest that since nervous tissue (the brain) has a higher metabolic
rate than other kinds of tissue, it has 'first call' on available nutrients; so
nervous tissue may be less susceptible than other parts of the body to mild
malnutrition.

In South Africa, however, Stoch and Smythe (1967) studied children who
had suffered severe malnutrition in the first two years of life. These were
compared with adequately fed children, of similar socio-economic level; the
malnourished group were later found to have over 15 IQ points lower scores
on average. Further, the patterning of results on various test items, as well as
records on an Electro Encephalo Graph ('EEG' or 'brain wave') resembles the
patterns for brain damaged people.

Recently the effects of malnutrition have been explored, yet again in
Kampala, by Jan Hoorweg who is a Dutch social psychologist, and Dr Paget
Stanfield (1972). They studied three groups each of 20 Baganda children; the
groups differed according to the age at which they had suffered malnutrition
(by 15, 16−21 and 22−27 months). Within each experimental group there
were similar proportions of severe and mild cases, with a control group of 20
children who had not been malnourished. Children with other severe or
chronic ailments were excluded. These children were tested when they were
14 years old, with a variety of psychological tests.

Comparisons were made between malnutrition cases and controls; and
within the malnutrition groups according to the severity, or the time of their
undernourished episode. The principal difference lay between controls and
the malnourished groups taken together, and on five out of ten psychological
tests the control group were significantly better. The psychological deficit,
moreover, lay in tests involving geometric patterns and relationships rather
than verbal problems. Comparisons based on severity, or the onset of time of
the malnourished episode were much less clear cut.

Overall then, evidence exists that malnutrition in infancy is related to
poorer performance in later childhood. Thus management of infant feeding is
of the greatest importance, not only perhaps to infant, but to later childhood
development.

Aside from nutrition, two attempts have been made to relate the quality
of care an infant receives, with his state of psychomotor development. Susan
Goldberg in Zambia used a 'Home Stimulation Inventory' − a checklist which
the researcher fills in with 'yes' or 'no' to several dozen questions. These
assess whether the house is dark and boring, the quality of the mothers'
speech, the toys they buy, and a whole range of other items. One might have
expected the H S I score (which measures westernisation really, as its
standard of stimulation) to correlate with infant test scores; however, no
significant correlations (except one chance one) were found. Probably the
scale misses out a good deal of the type of stimulation (physical and social)
which is typical for Zambian slum dwellers and which is importamt for their
development.

Goldberg raises an important distinction regarding efforts to link maternal

behaviour with effects on infant development. H S I scores in American
research did not relate to infants' development scores at any one time; but
H S I scores related to whether infants' development improved, or fell behind
over a period of months. So African research waits for someone to devise a
measure of material, physiological and psychological variables, which may
predict the development rather than the status of African infants.

An attempt to do this has recently been made by Janet Kilbride (1972)
using data she collected in 1968. She first examined fathers' occupation, and
mothers' education to see whether these would link systematically with
infant performance. They did not, though there were pointers suggesting that
the less westernised the fathers' jobs, and the less educated the mothers, the
children in such families would have *higher* scores. Questions were also put to
mothers, which tried to assess whether they were broadly rigid and rejecting
of the infant on one hand, or permissive and accepting on the other.

No differences were found of infants' developmental scores, based on
mothers' answers to any of these questions. So although we have already seen
that Kilbride suggested that Baganda mothers' physical treatment might
account for their motor precocity, her attempt to link infant development
with sociological and psychological variables was not successful. Neither for
any one of her questions separately, not for material scores based on a group
of three, or a set of twelve questions, was there any relation between
maternal permissiveness measured in this way, and infant development. Poole
also (1969) had failed to find socio-economic differences for infants'
developmental rates in Nigeria.

Research efforts to identify what it is that brings about infant precocity,
are therefore as yet inconclusive. People have suggested that feeding methods,
maternal attitudes, and maternal physical care may contribute to precocious
infant performance. No systematic efforts have yet been made to see if the
physical things mothers do, affect their infants' condition; but two attempts
to trace possible links between parents' status, or mothers' permissiveness,
and infants' performance, have not succeeded.

Weaning, and the end of infancy
In the late 1920s, European psychoanalysts were working out their
theories of infantile foundations of adult personality. Trauma, or
psychological shock had a large part to play in these theories, and in
particular, it was theorised that a severe detachment from the mother at
weaning would be a blow to the development of a secure personality.
Africanists could see that there might be something relevant here for Africa,
as severe weaning methods are commonly reported there. The anthropologist
Audrey Richards (1932) was one who brought this idea into the African
context. Her early data concerned the Thonga, Ba-Ila and Bemba peoples of
Southern Rhodesia, and though she considered it possible that 'weaning has
actually to be enforced in a primitive society', she did not generalise that it
was always done harshly, nor about its effects.

Later, Dr Simon Biesheuvel (1943) set forth the supposed course of events
experienced by African infants, in careful terms: 'during the lactation period
... the child is given every possible indulgence, but it is an indulgence of a

negative kind ... it provides that loving care which appears to be so essential for adequate development of innate potentialities; but ... the positive stimulus which alone can cause this atmosphere to bear fruit is lacking'.

' ... the factors which count most heavily in stimulating mental growth are those .. providing it with suitable perceptual stimuli ...'. Biesheuvel thinks that African mothers do not have time, wherewithal , or even the feeling that it is necessary to provide such positive stimulation. He goes on to say of weaning that 'a new pattern of parent-child relationships is imposed, in which the main emphasis is on respect and obedience ... hence, from the second or third year onward, the African child grows up in an environment which ... lacks that active sympathy between adult and child which is the *sine qua non* of optimum intellectual and emotional development'.

To Biesheuvel, then, weaning (harsh or otherwise) appeared to be a milestone separating two very different ways of parents' dealing with their children. In this view it is the later parent-child relationships which are responsible for whatever cognitive and personality development occurs. Other observers however, saw harsh weaning as a millstone, not just a milestone. They saw it as playing an active part in damaging a child's chances of healthy development.

The clearest exponent of this second view was Ritchie (1943, 1944) whose experience was based in Rhodesia. He says 'because of the indulgent first year, the child gains a feeling of omnipotence. After weaning ... (the child) ... is overwhelmed by feelings of hostility and impotence because he can no longer have the attention and nurturance of the first year ... This high contrast in feelings of acceptance makes him dependent on a mother or mother-surrogate all his life. The individual personality is never liberated and brought under conscious rational control and self-realisation is thus unknown ...'. These are very serious allegations and imply a very active role of harsh weaning (if this occurs — and in Africa it often does) in a person's life.

This theory of weaning continued to attract support. J. C. Carothers (1953), a doctor working for the World Health Organisation in Kenya, wrote in a similar vein. Carothers' observations were among the Kikuyu who not only have (or had) harsh weaning practices, but also had severe adult initiation rites. The dramatic view of the effects of weaning was also current among French-speaking scientists. Vouilloux wrote 'the child is king until weaning; this comes late, between 18 months and 3 years ... from this hypergratifying and oral Eden ... the child is plunged into the darkness of rejection'.

Since Ritchie wrote, 'psychological anthropologists' had suggested that in cultures where there are harsh weaning practices, for the very kind of reasons Ritchie put forward, there would also most likely be severe adult initiation so as to sharpen, define and harden the initiates' grasp of their roles in the adult society. Whiting, Kluckhohn and Anthony (1958) checked this theory in a large number of cultures, and confirmed it. Carothers did not take the phenomenon of initiation, and its function, into account but even if severe adolescent initiation can resolve the difficulties that Ritchie suggests will beset adult personality, it is not likely to affect child development of intellect or personality.

There is a third, intermediate type of theory concerning the effects of weaning, between Biesheuvel's and Ritchie's. P. Verhaegen (1960) a Belgian who had considerable experience in the then Belgian Congo saw harsh weaning as done in the Congo as a 'brutal dispossession' of the mother from the infant, with severe psychological consequences. Not only weaning, but as Biesheuvel theorised, the switch from early infant indulgence to relative independence from the mother and casting off the child into his peer group of children, could have effects on later personality. Verhaegen considered though, that later healthy adjustment could be, and often was made through schooling and contact with a 'so-called universal' culture. Vouilloux had a similar view.

Ramarasaona (1959) reported from the Merina people of Madagascar that harsh weaning could be performed without immediate psychological shock. Though weaning was abruptly performed by applying quinine to the breasts, since the child had been sleeping with both parents, he was not being displaced in his mother's bed by the father, and both parents gave the child special help over the difficult period. Thus the infant did not find itself at the distant apex of an emotional triangle. This supported Biesheuvel's early view, that it was not an abrupt weaning in itself that might be a blow to a child, but the social context in which the weaning occurred that was important.

To what extent in any case, are practices of harsh weaning widespread in Africa? And does this apply for westernised mothers and infants? There are many accounts which show that severe weaning practices occur in many places (though not everywhere) in Africa. Cox found in his Ethiopian students' poll that 61 per cent said punishment was used in weaning, though only 23 per cent said weaning was by sudden withdrawal rather than by gradual stages.

Barbara Levine (1963) writing on Nyansongo, a Gusii community in Kenya says that the word for weaning is *ogotacha*. This means 'to stamp on' and reflects people's awareness of the painful aspect of weaning. But the short term effects can not have been too severe, as Levine later says 'there was no indication that the resumption of parental sexual relations was experienced by the child as a deprivation or replacement by the father'.

Margaret Read (1959) reported from Malawi that all Ngoni realise that weaning is a great shock to the child; a senior woman might hold the child near the breast and say 'leave it alone, this breast is now bad' and then spit in disgust. Chilli paste might also be put on the breast. However, Read says young children are 'happy, busy, friendly, helpful, endlessly inventive and full of initiative' which does not suggest that harsh weaning has been damaging.

Barrington Kaye reported that in Ghana nursing is a source of pride 'and the flabby breasts of the experienced mother command respect rather than pity'. Weaning is done gradually if possible, though sometimes bitter herbs are applied or threats of bogey men are made. Often in weaning the child is old enough to be spoken to to explain, or console him over the event. The modal time for weaning in some African communities used to be much later than it is now. For instance Roscoe (1911) writing about the Baganda said that weaning occurred typically between two and three; but Hebe Welbourn (1963) wrote that the event has now been brought forward to a year old — and recent accounts, especially of more westernised parents show that weaning can be done much younger still. Any psychological effects of weaning would probably depend on the age at which it is accomplished. But no clear research on this question has been done.

Furthermore, Ainsworth (1967) disagrees that one can describe the current Kiganda weaning practices as abrupt. She also distinguishes the process of gradually shifting from a mother's milk to other foods, and the event of the last feed at the breast. The transfer process begins many months before the final breast feed. Only Ainsworth's oldest informants spoke of using chilli powder on the breasts; and even then, the child might accept the chilli, so one informant said that the mother might tell the child the breast was covered with faeces (which a two-year old would understand). Weaning is certainly becoming a gradual process in Buganda — though the final suckling might in some cases have to be signalled by a social act of rejection.

Occitti (1971) makes exactly the same case for the Acholi in northern Uganda, while Abrahams (1967) also says the same for the Nyamwezi and related peoples of Tanzania. Of West African practices, Dawson (1963) considers the weaning practices among the Temne of Sierra Leone to have been very harsh; but Okonji (1969) who is a social psychologist writing about his own people says of the Ibo that their method of weaning is a gradual one — and he makes no mention of any harsh methods of marking off the different mother-child relationshio before and after weaning.

Finally, E. E. Bam (1969) of the University of Botswana says that traditionally weaning in South Africa occurred between one-and-a-half years and three years old; 'the only reasons for weaning that are accepted are that a pregnant mother's milk is harmful for the child . . . it is an abrupt process which of necessity has to be accompanied with deterrents of various kinds and strengths . . . other known methods to effect weaning are to bandage the breasts, to offer substitute food . . . to ridicule him, to ignore his crisis or most drastic of all, to take him to live with a distant relative — a geographical separation'. Bam says that weaning may be distressing for the mother also. Some mothers 'used "Matekoane" to intoxicate the child and spare themselves, even if temporarily from the heartrending cries of the child. Weaning manifests a serious crisis in a child's life . . . emotional conflicts that result from the rejection period have been reported to lead to jealousy, hatred, querulousness. Traditional family control may prevent it from being overtly expressed'.

Bam's research comes from the same part of the world as one of the very few studies of the effects of weaning as such; yet it seems to accept what we might call the 'folklore of weaning', rather than relate itself to what are admittedly the few known facts about its effects.

The study in question (Albino and Thompson 1956) is concerned with weaning Zulu children. The Zulu live next to the Sotho whom Bam described within the South African regime. Albino and Thompson studied 16 children in Polela, a reserve in Natal; none of the babies were markedly undernourished, though all showed some signs of mild malnutrition. Weaning at Polela was found to occur from as early as three months to as late as 36 months.

The study used unstructured interviews, with a Zulu interpreter, though the authors also knew Zulu. All the infants were tested one day before, one day after, and one week after weaning with a modified Gesell scale. Before weaning, infants were comforted or fed on demand, receiving a great deal of physical contact. The paternal grandmother decides the date for weaning, and the breast is smeared with bitter juice of aloe and given to the child. A charm is tied round his neck 'to encourage him to forget the breast' and some substitute food, usually chicken or some delicacy is also provided.

In the first two hours after weaning, children are seen to be 'negativistic, aggressive, and fretful'. Every child showed a change in social relationships to others in the home, of which the relationship with the mother was most affected. Some children attacked the mother and, later, everyone and everything, especially rival siblings. Contrary to the theory that frustration produces regression (to more infantile behaviour) Albino and Thompson noticed an increased maturity, manifest in speech, helping with housework, and venturing further from the home. There was also an increase in naughtiness, playing with water, fire or food and mischievously messing up things. Nocturnal disturbance increased, including bad sleep, dreams and terrors; there is a change of bedfellows (from sleeping with the mother, to sleeping with brothers or sisters); but though 10 out of 16 were still disturbed five weeks after weaning, there was no change in enuresis.

Testing showed no changes in developmental quotients before and after weaning; but there was a great difference in approach to the test. Albino and Thompson concluded that 'weaning involves, after a preliminary disturbance, a series of adaptive changes in the organism, and may, at the age of about 18 months, be a most powerful stimulus to ego development'. Their description of weaning itself, resembles Bam's account; but instead of just pointing towards supposed harmful effects, Albino and Thompson followed up and found that weaning played a dynamic and even creative role in children's development.

Conclusions
Several studies have found that African infants are precocious in their development when compared with American or European norms. A few studies have not found systematic differences; but none have found normal African infants in any way inferior. Obviously, tests for infants do not pertain to intellectual performance, if by this we mean any kind of symbolic mental activity; but the tests do concern learning, and so can be called 'mental' and do not merely pertain to unconscious reflexes.

It is most curious to observe that many researchers who found evidence of precocity in various ways, were women: Geber, Faladé, Bardet, Massé and Moreigne, Liddicoat, Goldberg, and Kilbride; while those so far who found no precocity, or who argued against it, were men: Theunissen, Falmagne and Warren. Whether this reflects some active difference in the testing situation or not, cannot be ascertained; but this possibility must certainly be borne in mind.

Kilbride (1969) remarked that the mortality rate among Baganda infants is 160 per 1,000, compared to the American rate of 26 per 1,000. Operating over many generations, this might serve to select a type which has high skills of neuromuscular coordination, since in Buganda as elsewhere in Africa, babies were traditionally carried on mothers' backs, and while being walked about, had to learn early on to hold their heads steady and adapt to maternal movements. Faladé (1955) wrote 'only the children who have a particularly fine neuromotor equipment survive and can be followed by similar types in turn. This could explain the overall superiority of these infants'. This kind of argument was only mentioned by Faladé as a possibility; but both she, and especially her mentor Marcelle Geber, laid emphasis on the social environmental circumstances, so different in Africa from those in Europe or America, which are more likely to have brought about infant precocity.

Apart from this evolutionary kind of possibility, and from some few signs that infant performance is better in traditional than in more westernised families, it is chiefly descriptive accounts such as those by Ainsworth, Vouilloux, Geber (1960, 1973) and Kilbride (1969) which have pointed to the ways in which mothers deal with their infants, and which are possible causes of precocity. These pointers include very positive attitudes towards pregnancy, massage and exercises both pre- and post-natally; close physical contact with the infant; positive steps to encourage motor development; and especially for the first few months, breast feeding on demand.

Two efforts have been made (Goldberg, 1970, Kilbride, 1972) to demonstrate statistically how aspects of maternal behaviour or home conditions may have affected child development. Goldberg's attempt was perhaps an inappropriate way of looking at the problem in Lusaka. Kilbride's attempt was more appropriate to Buganda, but both attempts failed. Kilbride is currently working on measures of Baganda maternal behaviour, specifically developed for their ways, and hopes to come closer to demonstrating statistically what are the factors which promote precocity.

For some decades western observers have speculated on the view that harsh weaning practices, widespread in Africa, might be a damaging shock, not just a milestone, and that this shock could be the cause of inadequate personal and intellectual development. Only one study has specifically focused on this problem, and its results do not support the academic folklore. Harsh weaning is not universal in Africa in any case, but even where it does occur it is often softened by special social attention to the episode. Moreover, it can play a role in switching the infant from a mother-centred infant role, to a child-directed phase of identity. As such, weaning can be a stimulus to new maturity. It remains then to be see how African children fare when they grow up among their peers, and how their parents may, or may not continue to contribute to their psychological growth, which had been set along such a favourable course up to and including the time of weaning.

CHAPTER II

PRIMARY COGNITIVE GROWTH

Introduction

We have seen it shown in most research studies, that infants in African societies have started well in mental development. Certainly this seems true in their first six months or so of life. Thereafter, the measured DQs are not often so much ahead of European levels. In some cases, as with those in an orphanage, or other impoverished conditions, DQs have, as in Europe, fallen low. Where malnutrition exists, and this is common, mental development suffers. Some theorists have supposed that the widespread practice of late, and harsh weaning is also damaging to mental development; but the only substantial direct research on this question points to the contrary, that weaning may be a spur to ego development. Probably then, adult performance depends on how children are dealt with in the years following weaning.

The perspective in which perhaps most of the current research on this area of primary cognitive growth has been generated, is that of Piaget (see Flavell, 1963). Piaget has set out a scheme of stages of mental growth, and two 'rules' are associated with these stages. One is that development must go on in the order he has described; this is not strange, since the order he has set out is a logically, more than a psychologically necessary one. The second 'rule' is much more controversial and holds that the progress of the stages depends on biological or neurological development, and that the various milestones will pass by at the same age ranges, regardless of cultural or educational variations. Some investigators have tried to devise their studies so as to support this 'maturational' hypothesis, or to refute it.

After the 'sensorimotor' stages of growth, lasting to approximately 18 months or 2 years old (dealt with in the last chapter) Piaget outlines a 'preconceptual' phase — up to about four years old, during which children develop symbolism, acquire language, and coordinate their systems of imagery with experience in play activity. Next there is an 'intuitive' phase — up to about six or seven years old, in which the child begins to link his control of his own behaviour and of his environment in an intuitive way. A watershed follows, at ages six or seven (perhaps later) after which children begin 'operational' thinking; they develop a detached point of view, can 'see' chains of cause and effect, though they do not gain command of abstract thinking until later.

This chapter deals mostly with research on the conditions affecting the development of operational thinking in African children. This research concerns real and important policy questions: should countries with meagre resources put a great effort into primary schooling? or pre-primary schooling?

or concentrate on changing parents' ways of bringing up their young children? Our knowledge is by no means clear yet in this area. Good research with young children is extremely difficult to do, and demands the best conditions of rapport which foreign workers find hard to develop. Nevertheless, it is worthwhile to examine the pioneering and often ingenious work that has so far been achieved.

Early studies of normative trends

One of the first psychologists to tackle the problems of studying development in 'pre-operational' young children was the Nigerian, E. T. Abiola. He used tests based on standard western ones, to explore how normal Nigerian children developed (Abiola, 1965). He studies one group of elite children (from well-off families following westernised life styles) and one from the poor Oje section of Ibadan (from urban, traditional families). There were 15 children at each year of age, from one to five in each group, making 150 in all.

Abiola took two kinds of items from the Gesell, and Merrill-Palmer developmental scales. One set of items (form boards, building towers, paper folding and finding hidden objects) was perceptual-motor in nature; the other group of items he called 'conceptual-verbal' (giving in Yoruba, the names and uses of objects, or the names of animals from their sounds; giving commands, or identifying things when one is told what they do, or are for). Testing was done with children's mothers present. Abiola wrote that 'most children who completed the performance tests remained mute for long periods of time at the verbal stage of the test' and 'children who were ill or who refused to do the tests were replaced by others'. It seems likely that illness and refusal might occur more among the Oje children, and the resulting group would be self-selected for being able to deal well with the test. Such possibilities mean that one will not really be able to establish results for a 'typical' traditional group. However, the results are a starting point for later work, and deserve attention.

On the perceptual motor set of tests, over all ages from one to five, the poor Oje groups scored an average of 39; the elite groups averaged 53. Abiola calculated the overall scores as not significantly different between elite and Oje children — though at certain particular ages the differences were significant. On the conceptual tasks, the Oje groups recorded an overall average of 20, while the elite result was 28. Again, the overall averages are not significantly different, though at certain particular ages Abiola finds the social class groups are significantly different.

Apart from the way in which the children were partly self-selected, two further difficulties impede clear interpretation of these results. One is that the data are not longitudinal, with the same children being tested at one, then at two, three, four and five; thus the sampling at age three, for example, may be biased in a different way from the sampling at age two or four. Secondly, several test items produced scores which were negatively correlated to scores on the complete scale. Thus, for example, a child who scored poorly on building the 'little red tower' might have a high score on the perceptual test as a whole — which is strange since the whole scale score consists partly of scores on which the child has done badly. Four items out of 14 had substantial negative correlations with the whole scale score, but Abiola did not discuss this fully, merely saying that 'special factors were involved'. Abiola however, discounted that any possible innate, or nutritional differences between the groups could account for the pattern of his results.

Two valuable leads did arise though, from Abiola's research. He found that after similar levels of performance at age one, a gap widened between the social classes towards age three, and then ability levels converged again at age five. This might support an argument linked with Piaget's work, that development depends more on inner maturation with time, than on cultural differences. The second valuable point was Abiola's observation that in both groups the children's 'reinforcement values' to their mothers were similar, but that the mothers' 'reinforcement values' to their children differed. This focuses on how mothers behave towards their children, and what consequences their behaviour may have. So although Abiola's normative data and implications run counter to an environmentalist account of development, his clinical insights tend to support it. Edward Abiola unfortunately died, years before the end of a full academic career, so he could not add to his first contribution.

The question of 'convergence' was taken up by the American psychologist, Barbara Lloyd (1969, 1971a, 1971b) who also studied Oje and elite children in Ibadan. She wrote (Lloyd, 1969) that it is 'the spontaneous recovery of (Abiola's) Oje children or the precocious then failing intellectual growth of the elite children which presents such a challenge to contemporary theories of intellectual development'. Lloyd used three types of tests: form M−L of the well-known American Stanford-Binet scale; Piagetian tasks of conservation, and 'oddity problem learning', in which a child plays a machine which shows him five pictures of objects at a time; if he presses a button indicating the odd-one-out of the group, he gets a sweet (mechanically presented) and the pictures change, giving him another turn.

Lloyd's younger group was three-and-a-half, so it was only between this age, and five, that her data related to Abiola's. On the Stanford-Binet test the Oje children scored level with western standards, but the elite group were ahead (aged four-and-a-half to five-and-a-half, elites showed a mental age of six-and-a-half). By age eight, with Oje still level with western standards, the elite appear very advanced at a mental age of 11 years and 1 month. Lloyd suggests that this opening gap between abilities of the two groups refutes Abiola's convergence hypothesis. However, detailed examination of her data (Lloyd, 1971a, Table 5) shows that between three-and-a-half and five, Abiola's findings of convergence are not refuted.

At least two other difficulties attend this report of Lloyd's. Like others, she expects the Stanford-Binet to be at least a little culturally strange for Nigerian children. Yet the underprivileged Oje children scored level with western norms, and the elite were far ahead. Now even though the elite may be socially, and even genetically a select group, they would nevertheless not be expected to score so well as they did. Lloyd does say however, that her two student test assistants were 'anxious to help the children reach optimal performance'; since testing was in Yoruba, even though Lloyd was present supervising, it would have been difficult to prevent fair encouragement from becoming prompting, or hinting at the correct answers, thus inflating scores.

On Piagetian tests and on the oddity learning task, the elite children were clearly ahead of the Oje group. Elite children showed conservation abilities (evidence of Piaget's 'operational' stage) by age seven-and-a-half to eight; but Oje children at this age were two years behind. Lloyd had expected the differences between the groups to be greater on the Stanford-Binet test than on oddity learning, because the former should be more culturally biased; in fact, if anything the reverse was true. All this argues against a strictly maturational view of development, and that education and culture probably contribute to the noticeable differences between the groups.

Lloyd's work in Ibadan is longitudinal, with the same children being re-tested years later, and points to different normative trends of development in different social classes. Some French language contributions also exist in the normative sector, which explore trends in development in different groups.

First Marcelle Geber reported (Geber, 1960) that at ages two to three, three to four, four to five and over, children from better-off Ugandan families *all* had DQs above 100 (the western average) on Gesell tests. Among children in poorer families, a majority at each age were above DQ 100 (except aged two to three). Interestingly, Geber's data mirror Abiola's quite well; below one year old, most poor and well-off children were over DQ 100; at age two to three only 45 per cent of the poorer group were over DQ 100, but at age five again, 87 per cent of the poorer children scored over DQ 100. Unfortunately, Geber and Dean (1964) afterwards showed a graph which appears to use the same data as in Geber's earlier paper; but here, the 'traditional' group children from ages four to six are shown as having DQs below the Gesell average, instead of above it, as in the previous paper. The details of this work are therefore equivocal; but the broad indication is that levels of scores compare well with western norms (admittedly, on the outdated Gesell tests) and that well-off families' children do better than poorer children.

From Senegal, data are also available on three to six year-old children, on the French adaptation of the American Terman-Merrill test (Moreigne and Senecal, 1962). The children were all from lower-middle class families in Dakar, living in crowded conditions of five or six to a room. Some of the children were tested longitudinally, that is, in subsequent years. Overall, the DQ score at age three was 96, which fell steadily to 88 at age six. These scores are unlike Geber's in that they fall steadily further behind Western norms. If one supposes that an elite group of Dakar children might keep closer to western norms, the scores would counter Abiola's hypothesis. They suggest that educationally disadvantaged children are falling behind. Moreigne and Senecal were able to show correlations between DQ scores at various ages; from three to four, scores correlated 0.68 and between five and six they correlated 0.79. This indicates that the testing was probably reliable; those children who scored well at three, did well at four (and vice versa). Also, the DQ levels were becoming increasingly stable with age. The moral of this is that educational measures, if they are to have any effect, should take place earlier rather than later.

Previously, Bardet, Moreigne and Senecal (1959) had tried out a test about which claims had been made that it was 'culture-fair'; this was the Goodenough Draw-a-Man test, in which children simply draw a figure, which is scored for its maturity of representation. Over 700 good drawings were finally collected, 503 in Dakar and 247 in a village called Khombole. The people were mostly Wolofs, with a few Toucouleurs, and the youngest were aged seven, in their first year of school. At this age, the village children scored slightly better, though at later school years the Dakar children showed increasingly to advantage. The data are mainly of interest in that they show that environmental effects are very likely to be important in affecting cognitive developmment.

Factors which affect early cognitive development: 1. Direct studies of parent-child interaction

There is fairly good evidence that there is something which causes children from one background to develop more readily than those from elsewhere. What are the factors which promote development? They could include mothers' (and fathers, and caretakers') attitudes; their behaviour; children's nutrition; broader cultural traditions, and other factors.

A start in studying how parental behaviour might affect children's cognitive development, was made by Nancy Graves (1970). She focused on how maternal attitudes might interact with maternal actions towards their children. Graves observed 20 Baganda mothers, and the attitude she explored was called 'mother efficacy' (what the mother thought might be the success of her methods — a sort of confidence); the behaviour measured was 'future-oriented methods', or what we might call 'planfulness'. Another measure of mothers' behaviour was of observed 'immediate-reactive methods'. Graves did find a barely significant correlation between 'mother efficacy' and 'future-oriented methods', but not with 'immediate-reactive-methods'. Mothers living in Kampala tended to have less confidence, but more educated mothers were more confident. Of course these latter mothers were in families better placed to give their children good careers, so it is not clear whether the mothers were judging the likely effects of their actions, or of their status. Graves herself was very cautious about any relevance or generalisations from her work. Nevertheless, it was a start, and did suggest that it was not going to be easy to find dramatically obvious correlations between mothers' behaviour to their children, and children's abilities.

Another American woman, Mira Schiff (1970) took research further into this field. She did not directly observe mothers' behaviour, but only through what mothers reported. However, she did base her tests of children on what she directly observed, in carefully devised situations.

Schiff studied 94 female 'caretakers' (including 64 mothers, but also aunts and grandmothers) near Kampala, who had children between three and five. There were three scales of mothers' attitudes. The first was a 'stimulation scale', based on questions such as 'how often do you tell (the child) stories?'; the second was a measure of attitudes towards passivity, using questions such as 'should a child play in front of visitors'; the third was a 'self reliance' scale, with questions like 'do you ever send (the child) somewhere alone'.

The children were tested in their homes, aiming for a natural situation (as much as this could be achieved with an exotic visitor) but using certain novel apparatus. One procedure used a basket of toys (a rattle, ball, abacus, etc) given to the child who was observed and rated for 'curiosity' behaviour. There was a 'curiosity box', a wooden box with catches, bolts, springs and holes on it and in it.

Overall, the measures of maternal attitude or behaviour correlated sensibly together; and substantial correlations appeared between one measure of child performance and another. What was more elusive was any regular or convincing set of relationships linking maternal attitude and child performance. The self reliance scale correlated with one of the performance tests among boys, but not for the girls. One major omission from Schiff's scales was any mention of styles or practices of punishment; such a variable has had relatively less attention (than reward) among western psychologists.

It is notable that two African psychologists have more recently turned their attention to this topic. Olayinka Fisher (1973) dealt with physical punishment and ridicule, examining how these methods were used in preference by fathers and mothers respectively, in Yoruba society. Fisher did not present any data on how such parental behaviour links with child development, except to report that children of both sexes felt that ridicule hurt them more than physical punishment. Fisher has however newly joined a research unit at Ibadan University and has time to turn to the question of specifying parental effects on children's early development.

Durojaiye (1973b) investigated punishment within a broader context of parental behaviours, influenced by culture. Durojaiye asked parents of pre-school children aged 0-5 in Ibadan, and Kampala about feeding, handling of aggression and curiosity, reward and punishment, and other matters. There were marked differences between Ibadan and Kampala practices; in Ibadan, elite and traditional subgroups differed on each of the sub-sections of child-rearing practices identified, but these social class differences did not appear in Kampala. All this suggests that there are more variables which may have to be tied in before we can adequately understand how the actions of parents affect their children's performance, in Africa; and further, that cultural and social class differences are considerable and will mean that each system will have to be understood in its own individual way.

On the other hand, from their observations of individual societies, writers have been tempted to generalise that it is 'African' to insist on filial obedience. Klingelhofer (1971) asked Tanzanian secondary school pupils what they intended to teach their children, and a dominant theme was (Kiswahili) 'Heshima' — obedience. Obedience is prominent in a trans-African survey of research published by Doob (1965). Recently Munroe and Munroe (1972a) studied obedience among Kikuyus in Kenya. Eighteen children between five and nine years old were given two tasks by their own mothers and the same tasks by another mother. Overall obedience was very high, as much to their own as to others' mothers. One task was to pick up blocks which had been scattered and to put them in a box; the second 'task' was not to touch a toy — which was perfectly complied with. These 'tasks' demonstrated that obedience is certainly practised, but they do not help to explore the positive limits of a child's potential performance.

A further step however (Munroe and Munroe, 1971b) was taken among the Logoli group of western Kenya. Children do various tasks including herding livestock, and this may take them varying distances from their homesteads. The Munroes measured how far from their homesteads each child ventured; they also gave children three tests — copying a pattern made up of blocks, drawing a copy of a single geometric figure, and solving a maze puzzle. They found that children who ventured further tended to have better scores on the tasks involving thinking about spatial relationships. We do not know from this though, whether venturesomeness brings about cognitive competence, or vice versa; nor whether adult behaviour or attitudes affect the children's level of performance.

The Munroes then began to tackle this next question (Nerlove, Munroe and Munroe, 1971) indirectly. They repeated their Logoli study among the Gusii of south-western Kenya; Gusii children are expected to perform more chores, at a younger age, than are Logoli children. Comparison of Gusii and Logoli children's performances might therefore throw some light on the effects of the different influences brought upon them by adults in their societies, parents included. In general, distance from home was greater among boys, than girls, although Gusii children were slightly more likely to be further from home; the sex difference was significant, but not the cultural variation. A majority of Gusii children scored better on the block test than the Logoli children, though the difference was not statistically significant; but there was absolutely no cultural difference in the test of copying geometric figures. In all, there was scant evidence of how child rearing standards, or conditions, might affect performance.

An opposite type of study was pioneered at Makerere University by Okonji (1971b) who reported his material after similar work by Durojaiye (1970) at Ibadan. Both worked in the laboratory, aiming for controlled conditions in which they could observe and measure the styles and effects of mothers' behaviour with their children. Okonji tested children of pre-primary age; their mothers gave their children a task, and the latter's performance was observed. Mothers also answered questionnaires, in their own language, about their stress on obedience, strictness, use of physical punishment, praise, or material reward, their anxiety about the child's whereabouts, and other indices. Several of the indices of mothers' approaches correlated well together; and the child's reported aggressiveness correlated with greater maternal permissiveness. Okonji also gave the children tests of spatial ability and reasoning (see Chapter V). Here was well conducted research, exploring in detail many of the variables raised in other studies; but the expected links between maternal behaviour and attitudes on the one hand, and children's test scores on the other, did not appear.

In another study, Durojaiye (1970) tested 20 illiterate Nigerian mothers, and 20 elite-class mothers in Ibadan. Mothers and children were observed as the latter played with certain standard materials; an adapted Griffiths test of development for children under two, and the American Stanford-Binet (L–M) test for those aged two to five were also given. Results showed a slight advantage for the elite children; but when results were compared according to patterns of mother-child interaction scores, significant differences were found. Here then, is research which shows that maternal behaviour links with children's development of abilities. It is possible that Durojaiye's use of tests spanning a broader range of abilities than Okonji's concentration on one special kind of ability, allowed the links to show up. But a caution is appropriate; Durojaiye's report on this work is only a brief initial one, rather than a full account of it. It is also possible that the ratings of mothers' behaviour may have been affected if the observer already knew of the child's intelligence.

Further laboratory work by the Canadian, Beatrice Ashem (1972) in Lagos, found limited evidence of links between mothers' behaviour and children's abilities. These early difficulties should not, however, be taken as too discouraging. At the University of Zambia Donald Munro (1967) reviewed many foreign, mostly American, studies on parent-child interaction; he could not readily conclude exactly how parental behaviour might affect childhood cognitive development, though he considered broadly that the two areas were linked.

Factors which affect early cognitive development: 2. Retrospective studies of parent-child interaction

Curiously, a few studies which take a very distant perspective of child-raising practices, claim clear effects on children's cognitive growth, while research involving the actual parent-child interaction has had less convincing success. Leading the way was Dawson (1967b) who asked adults in Sierra Leone whether their parents had been very strict, fairly strict, or not so strict. His data are thus secondhand generalisations by people likely to be biased observers of their parents' behaviour. We might not expect such a design to have worked well, but, surprisingly enough, it did.

Dawson assessed cognitive development with Koh's test of copying geometric designs using patterned coloured blocks. Mothers who were said to have been very strict were found to have sons who scored lower on Koh's Blocks in adulthood. However, with other tests (see Chapter IV) of three-dimensional picture perception, and of finding embedded figures, there was no such direct relationship; instead, the best scores occurred among those who said their mothers had been 'fairly strict'. Dawson also compared two tribal groups, of Mende and Temne men. The Temne were observed to have harsher behaviour towards their young children than the Mende; Dawson expected the latter therefore to have better scores both on Koh's Blocks and Embedded Figures Tests (E F T). Instead, the expected difference emerged only with the latter test.

Dawson's work has been taken by some as good evidence for the effects of style of parental behaviour on cognitive development. It is strong in parts, but not consistent; since Koh's Blocks and the E F T are very similar tests, they should produce similar patterns of results; but they did not. It is perhaps best therefore, to regard Dawson's results with caution.

A study similar to Dawson's was done by Okonji (1969a) in Mid-Western Nigeria. Okonji did not compare groups of people on the basis of their assessment of their own parents' strictness. Instead, he pointed to the obvious differences (based on other researchers' views) between rural and urban people in methods of bringing up children. He used the Rod and Frame Test (see Chapter V), which is closely related in American Measurements to the E F T, with villagers, and with students at the University of Nigeria, at Nsukka.

Urban-bred undergraduates had better R F T scores than rural-bred students; but the difference on the E F T which Okonji also used, was not significant. (E F T had shown up a difference, for Dawson). Among the villagers, men scored better (as expected) on a version of the E F T than women; but no difference was found in the R F T. Further analysis showed that the amount of schooling villagers had had was also related to their test scores. Overall it is not easy to use Okonji's results to pinpoint exactly which aspects of parental practices may affect cognitive development.

More recently, an intermediate-scope study was done by Kasimbazi in Uganda (Kasimbazi and Wober, 1972), with children aged 12–14. Among 37 children tested with Koh's Blocks, 27 mothers were interviewed. Among these 27 families, only 18 had their P7 exam results released by the Ministry of Education, and it is possible to compare these results with mothers' interview data. Mothers answered an attitude scale reflecting strictness or leniency with their child when he or she was under five, they also answered on their practices of independence training (allowing the child to go alone to shops, etc). In the end, the correlations between children's exam performance, Koh's Blocks scores, mothers' attitudes, birth order, and weaning age, were all insignificant. The only correlation closely approaching significance was between mothers' attitudes and weaning age – the stricter mothers weaning their infants later.

The failure of this memory-based research to pinpoint which parental practices relate to good cognitive growth suggests that the best field in which to look will be that of direct mother-child studies. These might ideally be naturalistic, covering a wide range of parental behaviour and children's abilities and should be longitudinal. Thus observation and testing should start on parent-child interaction when the child is two or less, and continue until age five.

An encouraging start to such studies by Munroe and Munroe (1975) reports their test among 12 five-year-old Logoli children, who had been studied with their mothers as infants in 1967. The Munroes focused on only a few measures of mothering behaviour and dealt with three ability tests. Nevertheless, within this small scope for comparison they found that where mothers had held their infants more, there were lower scores on a learning test; and where mothers had seemed to be the cause of infants' crying, there were poorer scores on both learning and the E F T. On the other hand, where mothers had taken longer to answer infants' crying, children aged five did better on the E F T. Most of these findings could fit a genetic hypothesis, that infants with less ability potential needed closer mothering; but the time to answer infants' cries suggests that it is more likely that maternal behaviour

does affect cognitive development and in ways mapped out by Witkin, *et al.*
(1962).

The processes and course of early cognitive development
We come now to a larger group of studies which are concerned more with
the processes of early cognitive growth. These studies explore ages at which
qualitative changes (usually described within Piaget's system) occur. Several
of these investigations do explore whether environment affects cognitive
growth, but the focus is less on what parents do, more on schooling,
'urbanisation' (which presumably works indirectly, through influencing
child-raising practices), or variations in the nature of tests. Aside from studies
using tests Piaget devised, of conservation of mass, number and area, some
researchers used sorting tasks, others used learning procedures, and a few used
a whole collection of tests.

1. Sorting tasks
In Euro-American work, children sort objects first by colour, then later by
form, or function of objects. Rosslyn Suchman (1966) tested 120 Hausa
children aged from 3 to 15 in Zaria, northern Nigeria. Her materials were
cards each bearing three emblems — square, circle or triangle, either large or
small, and coloured blue, red or green. Not only the younger, but all ages of
children first used colour as a basis for choosing an odd-one-out. Among the
12 cards are four in which the colour of all three emblems is the same, and
thus cannot be used for sorting; between these, difference was more often
based on shape than by size of the emblems.
In a second test based on pointing out similarities, the first criterion was
again colour, with no difference according to age of children. In America,
Suchman observed that by primary school age (say six or seven) children
begin to attend to shape as well as colour, as a sorting criterion. The Hausa
children attended Koranic school in which there is little visual material but
mostly verbal learning. Probably the nature of the schooling has something to
do with the non-emergence of shape, among these children, as a sorting
criterion.
Next Serpell (1969b), in Zambia, showed that for any given age the
criteria used in sorting could depend on the extent of colour differences, and
on the familiarity of the forms used. Serpell also showed that among rural
children years of education were more important than chronological age in
relating to sorting methods. Serpell (1969c) found however, that even when
'equated' for level of education in school, Zambian children picked on colour
to much later ages than European or Asian children, and the effect was
more pronounced for the more rural children. This suggests that quality of
school, as well as of home experience, for example with toys and games,
might affect methods of sorting which children use.
Very recently Jahoda, Deregowski and Sinha (1974) compared Zambian
with Hong Kong. Indian and Scottish children on a task of choosing which
one out of three shapes the subject considered different. Shapes were either
round or with corners ('Euclidean' properties), hollow or not ('topological'
properties), or with some combination of the two (called 'unrelated'

responses). Zambian children had the most 'unrelated' choices, which the Indian research showed was related to low scores on a test of 'spatial ability'. This is almost certainly a special kind of 'spatial ability' involved with representing positions and distances pictorially, and leaves untouched another facet of space which is to know how one's body is placed relative to gravity and other objects (see Chapter V). Jahoda *et al.* mention one possible reason for their findings, which relates to the availability of words such as 'corner' and 'hole' in a language.

It makes it easier, if one has to sort objects, if one has convenient names for categories of things. Benjamin Whorf, an American engineer, based his view of the effect of language on thinking, on an extension of this idea. Guided by Whorf's hypothesis, Serpell (1969b) discovered that seven to nine-year-old Zambian children had no standard agreed names, or words for a triangle or a square. They had names for a fish or a boat; so when pictures of these familiar named objects were used for sorting, the children more often sorted by form, or shape. Serpell also tested English children aged between three and eight, and Zambians between 6 and 15. He was able to match English and Zambian children, who had approximately the same levels of certainty in naming geometric forms; but still, at each stage, Zambian children tended to sort by colour rather than by form. This weakens the effectiveness of an explanation of Zambians' sorting behaviour along Whorfian lines; but Serpell suggests there is a difference between 'perceptual familiarisation' with geometric shapes, and the ease with which they are named. This is a bit like saying that though people may know the names of bananas, tomatoes and egg-plant, if asked to sort out vegetables, they might still do so by grounds of colour, since this is more 'obvious'.

The question of how children recognise and sort objects into categories, and whether development proceeds from colour, to form, to function is pursued in several more studies. Davidoff (1972) found in Ghana that children aged between three and five often used form instead of colour in a matching task, which is evidence 'at a very much earlier age than other studies in Africa'. This was achieved by subtly changing the question asked to point to the possibility of using form as a matching characteristic. Nearby in Liberia, Irwin and McLaughlin (1970) pointed out that previous studies have confused *ability* to sort by colour, or some other way, with *preference* to sort by colour. Irwin had 65 elementary Mano schoolboys and 80 illiterate Mano adults do the tasks. There were eight cards bearing geometric emblems, differing also in number and colour; there were also eight bowls of rice differing in size of bowl, type of rice and cleanliness of grains. Manos are rice farmers and different kinds of rice are important in various ways in their culture.

People were asked to divide eight objects (cards or bowls) into two groups in such a way as to 'make sense'. With card sorting, colour was preferred to form by both schoolboys and adults. Upper grade boys more often sorted by form than illiterate adults, strongly suggesting that this is a result of schooling. Even the first year of school experience increases the ability to sort by colour and number, while further schooling improves ability to sort by form.

Adults did much better in sorting rice; they could divide the eight bowls in an average 2.1 ways out of the 3.0 possible ways (they had only managed 1.4 ways on average with cards). Three quarters of the adults sorted rice bowls by cleanliness or type of rice, both being functional criteria. The authors reject Professor Bruner's idea that people sort by colour because there is an early stunting of the capacity for abstraction; they say this because the illiterate adults certainly did abstract the functional qualities of rice, excelling schoolboys in speed and ability to describe their basis for sorting. The authors believe that where there is an interest, or cultural relevance, abstraction is performed; where abstraction is not being performed, we should enquire what interests are being awakened, or not.

Irwin and McLaughlin's work is an advance on previous studies such as that by Kellaghan (1968) in Nigeria, or part of the extensive work by Gay and Cole (1967) in Liberia. These investigators allowed their subjects to sort a set of objects in various ways, but only reported the first way used. This misses the fact that subjects may be able to sort in other ways which may not at first seem apparent. This possibility arises in work done by Greenfield (1966a) in Senegal. Three sets of three pictures each were the materials. In each set of pictures two could be paired by colour, two by form, and two by function. Schooled and unschooled groups of children were to sort which two pictures out of three they found most alike. They were then asked 'why *do you say* these two are most alike?'. Unschooled children did not answer the question; but when they were asked 'why *are* they most alike?' they could reply. This suggests that children become shy when put in a position of *telling* an adult an explanation; but when asked to state it in general, they do so. So the actual form of question, and the social relationship it puts a test subject into, may influence what replies are given out of the range of replies of which the children are capable.

A second recent study which is culturally sensitive is by Deregowski and Serpell (1971), again in Zambia. They tested Zambian grade three children (aged between 8 and 14) and Scottish grade three children, aged between seven and eight. Objects to sort were a set of four motor car models and four animals (all differing in colour and 'type'); and photographs showing the toys. The authors expected Zambian children to perform less well than Scots on sorting photographs, but equally with Scots on sorting the actual objects. Following Serpell's earlier work (1969b) they thought Zambian children would sort more often by colour than did Scots. Finally, they felt that sorting by colour would in both groups be more common with pictures, where shape cues are less prominent than is the case with models.

Only the first expectation was supported clearly. The second produced inconclusive results, and the third was dismissed. The results suggest that we cannot draw fair generalisations from results found from one type of coloured objects, to another type. The use of more complex criteria of sorting depends partly on the objects used, and on their importance in the culture — a conclusion similar to that drawn by Irwin and McLaughlin.

The same point was in fact made by Price-Williams (1962) in one of the first pieces of research in Africa on this question of sorting. Oddly enough, Price-Williams recognised that the language of the people he tested, the Tiv in

Central Nigeria, provided for dealing with 'concrete' and 'abstract' categories. Thus an abstract word distinguished animals which were clawed from those which were hoofed; another word distinguished domestic from wild animals. Recognising that the language catered for abstract categories, Price-Williams set out to discover at what age children began to use such categories.

Test materials included model animals, two dead black beetles, fish and leaves. Children were asked to group objects which were similar; then the criteria of similarity were ranked on a scale for 'abstractness'; criteria such as colour, are 'sensorily immediate', ranked bottom, while higher ranking was given for sorting by function. Children were also asked to choose 'the one which is different' from an array of objects. Price-Williams was particularly interested in how many different criteria ('shifts') children could (or would — if we accept Irwin and McLaughlin's point) use in grouping objects for similarity.

Older children showed more 'shifts', sorted more correctly, and used more abstract criteria than younger children. Interestingly, illiterate children had just as 'abstract' a performance as literate children; familiar plant materials evoked a more abstract level of sorting than the toy animals.

Price-Williams' work broke new ground. In his time, westerners (like himself) used the word 'primitive' to describe people like the Tiv. Many observers repeated the view that Africans 'could not abstract'. However, the mere fact that children learn to speak the language, and can produce sentences they have never used, or heard before, shows that they work on the principle that verbs differ from nouns, and have to be — and are used correctly. In other words, if they can sort words, by the same token they can sort things, according to functional principles. It should not have been necessary for western observers to demonstrate all this with an experiment; but in fact it was necessary. What psychologists should concentrate on are the circumstances in which people use abstract conceptual behaviour, and where people do not develop, or are hindered from developing habits of such behaviour. For instance, Price-Williams could have read about the Ibibio (neighbours of the Tiv) whose abstract symbolism was used in coding certain messages. Ekandem (1955) describes how plants were twined, placed in the ground or shown in other ways to signify war, peace, boundary claims or social messages of various kinds.

We see now that psychologists in Africa were not quick to realise that the use of abstract thinking does occur among children, but that cultural circumstances determine its areas of application. Price-Williams brought the question into systematic study, and over the next 10 years various people repeated his point, in various ways, and in various places. Thus only recently Janet Fjellman (1971) found among Kamba children in Kenya that using animals for sorting experiments, instead of geometric shapes, produced better results. The research in this area has perhaps been most extended by Okonji (1970, 1971a) who reports experiments in Nigeria. Twenty Ibo children aged about 11 and 12 from primary classes P5 and P6 were matched on a task of sorting familiar toy animals (goat, dog, etc) and on socio-economic status, with twenty other children. Two weeks after the pretest, the experimental group received over two-and-a-half hours of training; children were shown plywood pieces varying in colour, shape and size, and were shown how to label (verbally) various classes of objects (e.g. round things, red things, etc). Okonji 'tried to combat their easily observable compulsion to sort the objects on sight on the basis of attractive and readily perceivable features of the objects'. After training, children could sort on average in 8.4 ways, whereas before they only managed 2.7. A month after training, both groups were tested again on animal sorting, and on Koh's Blocks.

The trained group sorted animals in more ways, and gave more abstract reasons for their classifications. But they did not show a transfer of training to the skill involved in Koh's Blocks. The experiment is constructive, in that it taught a skill to half the subjects (a benefit very rarely found in other research). And the lack of training transfer should not be too discouraging, as Koh's Blocks involves very different skills from sorting toy animals. Moreover, Biesheuvel (1943) describes an experiment with 48 boys aged 13—14 in a Johannesburg reformatory, where after three-quarters of an hour training for each boy, Koh's Blocks scores were higher a week later for an experimental than for a control group.

Okonji also found that in comparing 138 Ibo with 105 Glasgow children from working-class families, where the test materials comprised household objects more familiar in Nigeria, the Ibo children gave more abstract reasons for the classifications they made. Also, the Ibo and Glasgow children sorted animals in a similar number of ways and used abstract concepts equally often.

Where it has been culturally sensitive, the research in this section has generally shown African children, even though they only normally have very poor schooling, to be on a par with the abilities of comparable groups of European children.

2. Piagetian tests of conservation

In Piaget's conservation tasks, or games, children say whether two sets of materials, one of which may have been physically transformed in some way (eg split in half, put in a different shaped container, etc) remain equal, or not. When a child sees a tumbler of water poured into two shallow containers, and says that the two 'flat waters' are together the same as the 'tall' water then the child must have abstracted the notion of quantity, and have 'conserved' in his mind this attribute of quantity which has not changed, even though external signs, such as shape of the container have changed. Conservation tasks essentially parallel to this exist with questions of number, volume, mass and area. They are really ways of examining the turning point at which children begin to use abstract principles (without knowing it openly) — the age of 'concrete operations'.

Price-Williams (1961) was again a leader in this type of testing in Africa. He learned to speak Tiv, and tested children aged from six to eight (approximately, for here, as elsewhere in Africa, age is not marked by a precise system of years) for conservation of discontinuous quantities. This involved nuts poured into tumblers and levelled up, or strung out in rows or placed in crowded lines. He found that conservation began to appear commonly in the group aged between seven and seven-and-a-half, which is on a par with developmental progress recorded in Europe. Tiv children were active in these tests, taking their own initiative in pouring nuts back into a glass to check equality, or rearranging nuts which the tester had spaced out differently, in equal rows to show one to one correspondence.

This work was soon followed up by Patricia Greenfield (1966b) in Senegal. She learned Wolof and tested nine groups of children representing three levels of urbanisation and three ages. One group of children was rural, attending a Koranic school (learning without books, by rote), one went to a village school, and the third group attended a town school. Greenfield asserts unconvincingly that because curricula are very closely defined in Senegal, the schools can be considered equal in quality. This assumes that the quality of teachers as also of equipment is equal in village and town, which is most unlikely. Greenfield wants to assess the effects of schooling, and also separately, of experience of urban life in affecting cognitive development. She also innovates by studying the reasons given by children for their judgements.

Unschooled children (who actually go to Koranic schools) include about 50 per cent who conserve at ages 11 to 13, which is similar to performance at ages eight to nine. Thus half the non-schooled children do achieve use of conservation concepts, just as do nearly 100 per cent of the schooled children; but half do not, which means that at ages up to 13, their thinking in some respects resembles that of a six year old.

At the younger ages, the rural schoolchildren had a higher proportion of conservers than the urban schoolchildren. Greenfield thinks this may be because in the city Wolof has become much simplified, almost a pidgin language, and this makes for 'poverty of perceptual description'. City children used fewer adjectival comparatives (e.g. 'this glass is thinner, taller' i.e. *than* something else), but just said 'it is thin, this water is less'. Since schooling is in French, there is also a possibility of bilingual confusion, but this should apply just as much in village schooling.

Greenfield says rural Wolof schoolchildren are developmentally similar to American or Swiss children, and very different from the unschooled children. But what is meant by 'similar' (is it ironic to have to ask this question about the work of a conservation researcher)? Greenfield writes 'in terms of grade level the Senegalese figures are close to being identical to the western ones, although Wolof children are behind in terms of chronological age'. But developmental quotients are based on chronological age, and it is with such figures that other researchers say that African children lag behind in development. There are of course, very clear probable reasons for such a lag, including a late start with formal schooling, and problems of bilingualism. Possibly also, had Greenfield used more familiar materials — the lesson demonstrated by Price-Williams, and other workers discussed previously — levels of conservation might have been better.

Three kinds of reasons for their decisions appear in children's replies. *Perceptual* reasons refer to the visual features of the display; *direct-action* reasons focus on the act of pouring water; and *transformational* reasons are the product of mental (abstract) processes. The most important kind of transformational reason is called the identity reason, which realises the constant identity of something regardless of how it is reshaped. Both groups of older schoolchildren show fewer perceptual reasons, but older unschooled children show more perceptual reasons. Greenfield mentions that a few children used direct action reasons for non-conservation decisions ('there is more in this glass because you poured it'), explained as 'magical thinking', in which natural phenomena are explained by attributing special powers to intervening human agents. Evidently school experience removes this type of thinking, as nobody who had been in school for seven months or more showed this kind of reasoning. Incidentally, Barbara Lloyd (1971b) used similar tests with Yoruba children but did not find transformational reasons given for non-conservation decisions. Thus there was no confirmation for the 'action-magic' hypothesis.

Greenfield knew that pouring the water from one glass to another without allowing the child to see the exchange, in American experiments led to more conservation type replies. This was not found to work with Wolof children. Why was this? Greenfield suggests (whatever this may mean) that 'the symbolic representation substituted for the perceptual image and designed to serve as a guide for organising their perceptions in a new way actually organises these perceptions by means of a conceptual framework foreign to their thinking'. This would appear to suggest that (my paraphrase) 'their thoughts are not *their* thoughts'; but we would do best to consider this matter as unresolved.

Greenfield next wondered if her subjects did their own pouring of water, they might be less likely to think in terms of 'action-magic' or the direct-action of the 'powerful' experimenter. Sure enough, even rural unschooled children aged six to seven who did their own pouring included more who conserved than a comparison group for whom the experimenter poured; but these did better on a second trial. This improvement on retesting throws doubt on the notion that certain children '*are not* conservers' (my italics). This raises the issue of test reliability, and how much we should believe the results of a first encounter with a test (see Chapter III). Greenfield mentions another problem, of possible 'contamination' between subjects, the first of whom may gossip to their friends about what they did. Other researchers, for instance Segall (personal communication – on behalf of Evans and Segall, see below) discount that this problem exists; but Greenfield acknowledges it and tried to reduce the contamination.

So far, Greenfield's results suggest that schooling is very important in affecting the course of cognitive development; she also thinks that because pouring the water themselves affected rural and urban children differently, urbanisation is also important in cognitive development. However, we cannot be sure of this, as urban children probably also attend better schools and it may be this, rather than the complex demands of city life which stimulates development.

A further correlate of schooling emerges from Greenfield's sorting experiments (1966b), reported above. In saying why two pictures are similar, the incidence of abstract reasons was low among unschooled children, and even diminished with age. Among schoolchildren the use of abstract reasons increased with age; and the Dakar school results are better than the rural school results at all ages. This undercuts Greenfield's belief that rural and urban schools are equal in quality; for if the pupils in one school are more advanced, they constitute a more stimulating environment.

Greenfield believes that one important contribution of school is that it teaches 'European' habits of perceptual analysis. School provides an arena also, in which pupils have to talk and think about things without those things actually being present. Greenfield's complex analysis of how school can help cognitive development, finds echoes in several other Piagetian studies done elsewhere in Africa.

In one of these studies, Heron and Simonsson (1969) in Zambia tried out a non-verbal method of testing conservation. The test involved scale weights, equal and unequal balls of plasticine, non-representational (ball, rings, discs) and representational toys (a snake) which had to be judged for equivalence of weight. European children produced results very similar to those recorded by other conservation tests in the USA. The test was therefore reckoned 'to work'. Then 225 Zambian children, aged probably from 7 to 17 were tested in a poor school. The Zambian children were equal to or better than European children up to age eight (Primary four in school); but in P5 the Zambians showed fewer conservers than in P4, and older children slipped behind the European standards.

This work shows that age and the early experience of schooling are linked with a higher score on this test. But the study has three drawbacks. The non-verbal procedure lacks much of the material which Greenfield's work suggests is of major interest. For historical reasons, the background experience of the older Zambian children was less favourable than that of the younger ones. A third question, not discussed by the authors concerns how the Zambian children may have reacted to a toy snake among the test materials. Nevertheless, the most interesting part of the results is the satisfactory state of development among the youngest Zambians. It may also be that more years spent, often repeating grades, in a poor school, can be cognitively stunting.

In Nigeria, Poole (1968) varied the Piagetian approach. All his tests were on paper using pictures, with items on conservation of solids and fluids. Poole had his instructions played on tape (presumably in Hausa − he doesn't say) to 10 and 11 year old children drawn from schools in a city, in a village, and in between. City children scored better than the peri-urban and village groups, but did not quite reach the levels of scores found in England. As with Greenfield's comparisons, the results probably reflect differences in quality of school; but quite possibly other factors also contribute − thus more capable people migrate to the town which itself may be a stimulating environment socially and linguistically.

Most recently in Nigeria, Owoc (1973) tested over 400 children from 8 to over 18 on conservation of quantity. Up to ages 8 and 9 schooled and unschooled children showed an equal proportion of conservers (63%); afterwards schooling increased the proportion of conservers to almost 100% at 18, but non-schooled youths still included 30% of non-conservers at 18 or over.

Earlier, in South Africa, Cowley and Murray (1962) tested Zulu and white children, five from each group at each age level from five to twelve. The tests

involved copying from sight simple geometric figures, or feeling with the
hands while blindfolded solid shapes and then either pointing to comparison
ones, or drawing copies thereof. The Zulus showed a similar sequence of
cognitive development as among white children, but Zulus' scores were lower
for each age. In view of the differences in school quality (see Chapter III)
between English and Zulu schools, this again is probably the strongest
explanation of different scores; but Cowley and Murray do speculate about
genetic differences, unsurprisingly, as South African observers. The results
from elsewhere on the Continent, as we have seen and will see, belie such
ideas.

Nevertheless, much backward performance remains to be explained.
Okonji (1971c) tested children in the Ankole area to examine their ability to
conserve length and angular measurement. Two flexible wires of equal length,
one of which could be bent to appear 'shorter' explored length conservation;
while wooden forms of angles one arm adjustable, were used to copy a given
angle. As a third test, children had to mark a point on a piece of paper as
nearly in the same position as a mark on a test card, and could use a ruler or
other instruments available, if they wished. Schooled and unschooled
children, from 6 to 16 years old, in all 358, were tested, making this probably
the largest survey of its kind in Africa to date.

While school-children showed more conservation of length, with age,
unschooled children showed no more length conservation at 11 than they did
at 6. School-children gave 'identity' reasons for conservation after age 7,
while others tended more to give simple affirmation ('it is equal because it
is'). Reproducing angles, and locating a point on paper, produced very poor
scores, except among a handful of school-children aged 10-11. Okonji
emphasises the importance of school experience rather than of simple
'maturation', which in the absence of suitable cultural ways will not
necessarily promote cognitive development along Piagetian lines, at least with
this kind of task.

Next to Ankole, in Ruanda, Pinard, Morin and Lefebvre (1973) gave
training to 6 and 7 year olds on conservation of quantity tasks. Retesting
showed better standards of performance independent of differences in
schooling or urbanisation. All groups came to give predominantly identity
reasons for conservation decisions leading the authors to emphasise not only
that schooling, but that good teaching can remove cultural differences in the
rate at which children acquire conservation principles.

Adding a fresh Piagetian test in Uganda, Barnabas Otaala (1971) tested
children from his own Teso people on conservation of number, mass, and
area. Two sheets of green blotting paper simulate 'fields'; small blocks
represent 'houses' and the child is asked whether a cow (toy model) will have
more to eat in one field (when the blocks are placed close together) or in the
other (when the blocks are scattered apart).

Schoolchildren, from P1 to P6 grades, 282 in all, were tested, and many
gathered enthusiastically at the windows of the testing room to peer inside.
Difficulties of 'contamination' thus exist, but Otaala does not discuss them.
Conservation did increase with school grade, but was not yet complete at P6,
with children aged about 12. Otaala accepts that 'this group's progress seems

to be much slower than Piaget's theory would suggest'. Conservation of number was best established (100% at P6), but with area, only 16% of P6 pupils showed conservation. This supports Okonji's finding, of a particular weakness in tests involving questions of spatial relations – a situation we will find very commonly reported throughout Africa (see Chapter IV).

Simple Piagetian studies are easy to do, and form suitable exercises for those on education courses. We should now, therefore, expect more sophisticated work from professional researchers – for example to examine how cognitive development might be accelerated, or promoted without or before schooling. Yet disappointingly, some studies have merely repeated the basic demonstrations. Thus the noted Professor Vernon from England (1969) gave children in Kampala a large variety of tests. Their conservation abilities were even less in evidence than among Otaala's subjects, possibly, as Vernon suggests, because they were tested in English and 'much of the difficulty may be one of communication of ideas'. Unfortunately, Vernon's reporting seems to share communication difficulties as with his testing. Thus with an English vocabulary test Vernon reported a quotient of 57, nearly off the bottom of the scale. Vernon said 'the notion that words can be isolated and defined in the abstract was unfamiliar, except to the most intelligent'. But on another subtest of sorting, the quotient was 88, leading Vernon to write that his subjects had 'no special difficulty in "abstracting" and naming classes'. It is surely difficult to accept these explanations together. We do have to look for careful interpretation, careful testing, as well as useful topics to investigate, from now on.

It is therefore disappointing to note that Teachers College, Columbia, sponsored conservation studies in Kampala, which got no further than raising questions that were already in the air. Thus Millie Almy (1970) tested Baganda pupils from P1 to P3 in Kampala, and felt their thinking was 'impressionistic and unsystematic, untroubled by logical contradiction . . . beguiled by the appearance of things, interested in small details . . . more interested in colour than form'. This study told us nothing about how such things might have come about, and whether, or how they might be altered.

More useful perhaps is work by Birgit Roloff (1970) and her 35 students, who tested between them over 200 children in Zambia. Most children were in P1, 2 and 3, and did tests of conservation of mass, liquid, and number. By age 10, though half the children showed conservation in each of the three subtests, the number of children who showed 'total conservation', i.e. on all three tests, was quite small. Roloff examines the idea that children attain conservation principally 'as a result of maturation'. But she comes round to the view that the conservers 'probably reflect the effect of schooling' where the child is 'exposed to more systematic and guided experiences of numbers and discontinuous quantities, whereas he is not so exposed to experiences of masses and liquids'. In fact conservation of number was attained by more pupils than who showed it on the other two tasks.

The idea that conservation relates to cultural practices is supported in a recent report by Durojaiye (1972b). Testing was done with 60 schoolchildren (boys, and girls, aged 5 to 9) from the following cultural groups: Yoruba, Edo, Nupe and Hausa (all Nigerian) and Baganda and Karamojong (in

Uganda). They all did conservation tasks with water, beads, clay, area, pieces
of string, and tests of number. On conservation of amount of beads, girls did
better than boys in every group, possibly related to interests girls may have in
beadwork. Karamojong children were generally behind, on most tasks, except
the beads. Conservation of area was the most difficult task in all the cultures.
This work shows that cultural differences probably affect the pace, as well as
the directions of cognitive development.

    Finally, in this section, Ogbolu Okonji (1972) has again opened up a new
direction of enquiry: studying how children between 3 and 6 can form classes
of objects. In all, 128 children in Zambia were given plywood shapes, varying
in colour and size, which they had to thread together on cords. Piaget expects
children at these ages to be unable to assemble a group of objects,
representing *all* available of that type. Instead, they often make 'graphical
collections', being guided by pleasure in how the assortment looks together.
In a sense, they function like some modern artists (and might we say that the
reverse is true?). Okonji found that the early, unclassifiable groupings gave
way to collections basing their likeness on colour; but that 'graphical
collections' were rare. The children were not able to explain how they
grouped things, as 'the exercise was for the children a mere physical game'.
No real difference was found between children who had some nursery school
experience, and those without. The study tentatively suggests that such
schooling is ineffective, but this may well be due to its limited quality.

3.   Studies based on learning
    A number of useful studies set children actually to learn a task or a skill,
and derive their contribution from studying how learning occurs, and what
can or cannot be learned. An early example of this approach is by Evans and
Segall (1969). They had 20 sets of four pictures each. In each set, two
pictures were of the same colour, and one was 'functionally related' to the
third (e.g. both showed clothing, or food, etc.). The task, done by over 300
children in Uganda, was to 'put two together which are alike'. Alikeness could
be decided by colour, or by function. The experimenter decided which of
these two principles would be the task for a particular child; when the child
sorted by that principle he was rewarded by being told he was right.
Eventually, the child would learn that the task was to sort by colour — or by
function.

    The overall result was that children required to learn the colour criterion
took an average of 7·5 trials, while those who had to learn the function
criterion took 11·3 trials. Children who were not in school learned to sort by
colour as easily as those in school, but failed completely to learn the function
concept. Similarly, amount of school experience did not much affect the ease
of learning to sort by colour; but function sorting was learnt most readily by
those with most school experience, in a Kampala school. The advantage of
five years in a rural school was only half that of being in the corresponding
form of the city school. Adults tested, with less than P4 education, failed to
learn the functional sorting criterion. All this strongly suggests that neither
biological ageing, nor experience of life in the community such as is found in
and near Kampala, is as useful as formal schooling in promoting certain

learning abilities. Also, factors of school quality, migration of more capable people to town (in unknown amounts), and possibly the stimulus of the pace and variety of urban life may all affect cognitive development, and scores on such learning tests as these.

Richard Kingsley (1968), another American working in Uganda, used another approach which may turn out to be very useful. His 'apparatus' was simple: four white cards. Two cards bore circles, one red, one blue. The other two cards bore squares, again one red, one blue. The game presented to children was to guess which was the 'right' card of the two the experimenter would show him. As with Evans and Segall, the experimenter would fix on colour, or shape, as the 'right' solution to this particular game. He merely 'rewarded' the child by telling him so when he guessed 'right', took the cards away, and presented them again, sometimes with the position reversed. So far, this is simple.

The complication arises when the subject has learned the first correct solution. The experimenter then changes his mind, and the child has to learn the new solution. If the rule has been *colour,* and the exact solution, blue, the new rule could still be colour, but this time, red. Such a 'shift' is called a 'reversal shift'. The colours have been reversed in the experimenter's mind. On the other hand, the new rule could be *shape,* and the child would have to pick only the circles, of whatever colour. This, going to a new 'dimension' is called an 'extradimensional' shift.

Over 50 children, aged between 4 and 12, were tested, near Kampala. The youngest children found the shape idea easier to learn than the colour one — against the impression from other research which suggests that colour is usually more easy to deal with. Older children made reversal and extradimensional shifts equally well, although American children found the latter task more difficult.

In a slightly altered experiment (one of the cards with a square was changed to one with a triangle) it was found that Baganda subjects made less than half the errors than the quicker American children made in a comparable experiment. Kingsley thinks the Baganda children were using an effective strategy of 'win, stay; lose, switch' — which works in tasks of this sort; while American children might have been 'overclever'. However, Kingsley did not claim any more than that this was an interesting beginning, and resisted any firm conclusions.

Very closely related work appeared from Zambia, not long after, by Phillip Kingsley (1973). He asked: does improved ability to cope with learning tasks just occur at about primary school entering age, and do so regardless of school experience? Or is school experience necessary for the development and *use* of particular learning tasks?

Kingsley tested over 100 children in a less-well-off area of Lusaka, aged from 5 to 10 years old. First the child had a memory task — to look at 20 common objects in one room, then to see photographs of them, finally, after a short interval, to fetch six of the items which the experimenter had earlier mentioned. It was noted whether children made lip movements, indicating some rehearsal of the list of six objects to memorise them. Older unschooled children showed no further sign of rehearsal than the younger ones; but the older school-children were more likely to show rehearsal. Also, the Zambians produced as good memory scores as did American children of similar age.

A second task used a set of 32 blocks, each of which was different from every other one by a combination of factors; shape, size, colour, and geometric signs painted on it. The experimenter selected one block, and asked the child to pick another that was similar. Neither older non-school children, nor older school-children did better than the young ones. Probably the task was too difficult, and schooling at this stage was not enabling children to tackle such things effectively.

School-children were found to be able to count up to 10, earlier than non-school children; but the latter can finally do this. Counting is a basic skill one learns in life, even outside schooling then. Children were also asked to estimate how many small 'bricks' had been used to build each of nine, variously shaped 'houses'. Children who were observed to tackle this systematically, by counting, got better answers than those who merely looked and answered. Here again, schooling made no difference; for though the school-children were *able* to count, no greater proportion of school-children *did* count. It is one thing to have a skill, but another thing to put it into practice. The kind of schooling involved here, was not getting children to apply their skills.

Finally, Kingsley had the children guess the number of coloured beads in five different glass jars. Here, the strategy was analysed, rather than the correctness of answers. Did the child systematically guess for the jar obviously having most (or least) beads, and relate his other guesses to this first one? Here, the older non-school children did better than the younger ones; but schooling did not produce a still better range of performance. It seems here that when it comes to applying basic cognitive skills or strategies, the schooling provided does little better than everyday life. However, schooling may promote certain basic skills (like verbal rehearsing), which, if they are applied, can help raise performance in certain tasks.

We now come to the major work by Michael Cole and his colleagues (Cole, Gay, Glick and Sharp, 1971) among the Kpelle people of Liberia, which includes many learning-based experiments, as well as sorting and classification studies. They showed, for instance, that school-children could sort cards using more criteria (Price-Williams' 'shifts') than illiterates; but that sorting pictures of locally familiar animals was not particularly easier than sorting geometric shapes; thus in this case, culturally familiar materials did not significantly help classificatory behaviour. Children were equally ready to use number, or colour as a basis for sorting, and almost equally ready to use shape or form. This does not support the suggestion by some (e.g. Suchman) that there is a strong and lasting preference to sort by colour.

In a concept learning task using geometric shapes as the concepts to be learnt, Kpelle school-children performed similarly to New Haven (U.S.A.) first graders. However, non-school children, and illiterate adults were much slower to learn such concepts. These two studies support the effectiveness of schooling for cognitive development.

Another concept-learning experiment used a successive series of two unequal piles of stones. The subject had to guess which, of the relationships 'more than', or 'less than', the experimenter had in mind. People more quickly learned the concept 'more' than 'less'. Investigating multiplication, Cole and his colleagues showed cards for brief intervals in a viewer. The cards bore neat rows of dots, and anyone using the principles of multiplication could easily say, for example, that four rows of three dots each altogether contained twelve dots. It would be more difficult to estimate twelve dots if they were scattered unevenly. But Kpelle subjects did not estimate patterned rows any more correctly than scattered dots. The authors say that 'the Kpelle do not recognise multiplication and division in visual situations'. This is perhaps an over-generalisation, as one of their own later experiments may hint.

Ten different piles of stones contained from ten, to one hundred stones. Subjects were asked to guess the number of stones in a pile. Adult Kpelle were more accurate at this task than American students, though when the latter were given a hint, namely the number of stones in the pile of 60, their performance improved to equal the Kpelles'. This suggests that what is culturally familiar and functional (more so than pictures of animals on cards) will be well organised and dealt with mentally. It also suggests that a study of Kpelle's ideas of multiplication using stones, might be more successful than one using rows of dots on cards.

Scribner and Cole (1973) had presented evidence of a link between levels of formal education and the ability to transfer one's ability with familiar problems to deal with unfamiliar ones. In later work among the Mano, neighbours of the Kpelle, Irwin, Schafer and Feiden (1974) found that Mano sorted rice better than U.S. undergraduates did, while the latter sorted cards better. The Americans' performance dropped more than Mano's did when sorting objects unfamiliar to them. This suggested a limit to the idea that more education increased the ability to transfer one's abilities; namely education may not help where the new problem, however structurally similar, involves culturally strange materials. It is possible that the problem lies with the culturally familiar connotations of any problem ingredients, which may constitute a 'comfortable mental environment' for cognitive operations.

We are still left with a picture of a restriction of ability to use their abilities, among Kpelle (as among several other groups in this chapter). We must confess ignorance on this matter, especially in the face of what we are told about the use of metaphor among Kpelle. We are told that Kpelle has no word for zero, but sometimes expresses the idea in a metaphor (here: 'let's enter old-town site' − i.e. an abandoned place where the number of people living is now 'zero'). The use of a metaphor (literally 'same shape' in Greek) acknowledges that the essence, or shape of one situation is the same as the shape of another one. Thus to use a metaphor, is to use what Greenfield called a 'superordinate concept'. It seems that in Kpelle, as in other African cultures, the metaphor as a more vivid and interesting way of communicating an idea was preferred to an emotionally neutral, shorter, 'more efficient' way. This leads to the idea that the unfamiliar and perhaps uncomfortable metaphoric possibilities surrounding problems using culturally unfamiliar materials may be part of the difficulty observed in shifting abilities.

Cole *et al* also used shift in concept learning tasks like those that Richard

Kingsley used. They suggest that if learning is 'concrete' and based on how things look, without thinking in words about what one sees, it should be relatively easier to 'shift' to a new concept rather than change within the concept. Thus older children should do better with 'reversal shifts', younger children with 'extra-dimensional shifts'. This was found to be the case. Also, Kpelle learned quicker than American children on all variants of this experiment. The authors suspect that it may be 'a mistake to dichotomise learning (or thinking) into the categories concrete and abstract . . . Kpelle use generalising verbal labels in their solution of simple problems'.

Cole *et al* pick up the oft-repeated charge that 'a concrete way of thinking in the African' prevails (e.g. see Carothers, 1972). If this is so, then if one showed Africans a series of objects, instead of just telling them a list of names, verbally, they would recall them better. Also, if the object list is 'clusterable', or the objects belong to easily recognisable classes (e.g. animals, minerals, etc) then the list should be easier to learn − unless one is merely 'concrete' or perceptually-dominated in his thinking.

In fact, a list was more easily learned if it was clusterable and schoolchildren learned better than did illiterates. However, while American children tended to give their recall in clustered groups, this did not happen with the Kpelle. Interestingly, when objects were shown to educated children, they recalled them better than when just a word list was used, whereas uneducated children performed similarly with both methods of presentation. One may suggest that school-children when shown objects, use visual as well as their own verbal imagery; while non-school children use either their own visual images, or the verbal list they are given and cling to by rote, neither situation being more advantageous for them.

There is much to be learned from Cole and his colleagues' work. One thing is that we must do more work to uncover appropriate conditions for eliciting the classificatory, and learning abilities that are evidentially there in African children. Also, we need to know why there may be restricted ability, or tendency, to use their abilities among children, and more so among unschooled adults.

It seems that Kpelle adults do not consider it so important to solve problems, but consider it clever to be able to construct unanswerable arguments. They may be thinking less about how to answer a problem but more on how to construct a metaphor with which to describe a situation. School education in a western style may therefore introduce an entirely different direction to the development of cognitive ability about which we know, as yet, but little. The German Afro-linguist Diederich Westermann (1939) reported ' . . . proverbs belong to the sphere of men. They are a mental exercise and sharpen the wit . . . A Twi saying is: "a clever child is told proverbs and not stories" '. Cole's work gives further details of possible cultural differences in direction of cognitive development.

Perhaps the latest available major piece of research in the present area is by the American Charles Super (1972) from Zambia. He wanted to explore whether the transition to a new stage of cognitive development, at about ages 6 or 7, happens as a result of normal biological growth within the ranges of experience provided by most cultures; or whether culture, or schooling might contribute major effects towards advancing, or delaying the transition in cognitive development.Super tested urban and rural adults and children. The children were aged 4-9. The urban group included members of 28 tribes, but the villagers were all Chewa. Super used over a dozen psychological tests — and two physical checks on age. The first was an examination of teeth; the second, used in colonial times in several African countries as a test of school-entering age (minimum, 6) was to see if the child could touch his right ear lobe with his left hand stretched over his head.

Ability to count numbers, and to repeat strings of digits, increased with age, with urban children doing better, even before school-going age. In a test of classifying cards, there was less of a tendency to use form as a criterion than is reported for European samples (thus resembling Serpell's 1969 findings in Zambia). In the Bender Gestalt test, in which the subject has to copy on paper designs he is shown, urban children did better than rural ones, but the main differences were associated with age. Among a variety of further tests, was one of sensitivity to contradicting oneself. Children were shown two cutout shapes, in which one looks larger, by the operation of a visual illusion (see Chapter IV). The positions of the pieces are then reversed and the question repeated, Super took it that sensitivity to contradiction would occur alongside with transformation in cognitive growth to 'concrete operations' which begins the road towards a self-aware view of the world. In his urban group, Super found a dramatic decrease in the tendency to allow self-contradiction, between ages 6 and 7; but in the rural sample the change occurred between 8 and 9.

A simple but important sensory test was also used. In this a touch is made simultaneously on the subject's hand, and face (two soft, rubber 'ticklers' were used, the child shut his eyes, and 'guessed' where he was being touched). Super reports that previous researchers found that good performance on this test depends on biological integration of the brain mechanism, and that children under six fail to notice two touches, reporting only the one on the face. Two other sensory tests were used. In one, the child wore earphones and listened to two voices simultaneously; one voice told him to point to one object on a sheet of eight drawings; the other voice told him to point to another. The child's task was to attend only to one of these voices, against the distraction of the other. In American research, the ability to do this rose rapidly between ages 5 and 7, but gradually thereafter. Super found a more steady growth from 4 to 9.

The final sensory test involved 'delayed auditory feedback' (DAF). The child speaks into a microphone, and through suitable electrical apparatus hears his own voice through headphones approximately a fifth of a second delayed — thus upsetting his normal awareness of the timing of the sound of his own voice. This usually disrupts speech, but American research showed that disruption in children between 4 and 6 was much *less* than that in children between 7 and 9. In other words, this suggests that the child begins to take into account awareness of his own performance (and false awareness will disrupt him) as he develops cognitively. Super found that after age 5, both rural and urban children increasingly showed reactions to DAF; urban adults learned to cope with the disruption, but rural adults did not.

Several important general points emerge from Super's work. Tests involving visual analysis and integration improved steadily with age, and independently of schooling or experience with pencil and paper. In the urban sample, changes are under way substantially before the children enter school. With tests of what Super calls 'cognitive maturity and logical thought' (e.g. absence of self-contradiction, and consistent sorting on the colour-form task) there is 'important growth around the age of 7'. With the more sensory tasks, such as delayed feedback, which are said to reflect changes which stem from physiological developments of brain organisation, there is evidence of distinct signs of development at age 5.

Super's data show a generalised advantage for the urban children, probably due to a number of reasons including familiarity with the kind of social challenge involved in the test situation, as well as having to be able to cope with the more complex life of the city. Above this, Super points to a relatively large increase in cognitive and verbal scores at ages 7 and 8, as evidence of the stimulus provided by schooling. Overall, Super convincingly presents his material as evidence that the reorganisation of cognitive structure which Piaget pointed to, at ages 5 to 7 in European children, is going on in Zambian children 'at about the same time and in a similar manner'. There are clear cultural differences which bear upon the rate and order of the changes, but Super suggests that these merely overlay the basic similarity of humans everywhere.

4.   An 'action study' from French-speaking Africa

The mass of work reported here, has been in English. But there is one study in French, from the then Belgian Congo, that is worth including as an end-piece. It picks up the question, left aside by most writers in English (except, perhaps, Okonji) of *how* cognitive changes can be intentionally brought about by the investigator. Maistriaux (1960) used techniques inspired by Piaget's testing methods which involved 'active' teaching, centering around a shopping situation, using a great deal of apparatus (boards, signs, goods, animals and plants to look after). Maistriaux wanted to avoid separating thought and action, to 'bring thought into action rather than thinking of an action'. This approach is opposite to that of Greenfield, who suggests that schooling promotes cognitive growth by forcing the child to detach his intellectual operations from physical reality.

Maistriaux noticed in the shopping situation that several children who had not played 'seller', were shy to do so, and could not do calculations efficiently until they were in the role of 'buyer'. He says 'this rigidity is very common among African children'; it may relate to Greenfield's data, where children placed in an unfamiliar social role become shy and unable to perform properly. At the end of the year, Maistriaux found that the experimental group were better than the controls not only in test results, but also in social behaviour. They were more active, forward and alert. Maistriaux deals with the then common belief of the backwardness of African school performance saying that 'after 2 or 3 years of special teaching, young Africans can catch up with their European counterparts, and then compete with them on equal terms'.

Summary

A few early studies tried to answer the question of what is the 'normal' course and level of cognitive development after infancy, and towards the years of schooling. Abiola suggested that children from different social backgrounds start (at ages 1 and 2) at a similar level of ability, grow apart, and then converge to a similar level at age 5. Lloyd challenged this verbally, but her results do not dispel Abiola's thesis; and Geber's data agree with it to some extent.

Research has gone on to discover what it may be in maternal attitudes, or maternal behaviour, that might bring about certain patterns or speeds of cognitive development. Oddly enough, a few studies such as those by Dawson (1967) and Berry (see Chapter VIII) which assess parental behaviour by recall over a period of over fifteen years, suggest that patterns of parental severity may link up with the development of certain of their childrens' abilities. But as Kasimbazi and Wober pointed out, a repeat of Dawson's study in Nigeria failed to confirm his findings; and studies closer to childhood have only recently begun clearly to identify what it is that parents may do, to improve their childrens' development.

Many methods have been used to study cognitive development at this age range, including sorting tasks, Piagetian tasks of conservation, and learning problems. Several studies point out that African cultures differ, and this appears to affect the patterns and speeds of cognitive development (e.g. Durojaiye, Dawson, Price-Williams, and Greenfield). Some studies suggest that African children lag behind somewhat in their pace of cognitive development — particularly in tasks dealing with spatial relationships (e.g. Okonji in Ankole, Otaala, Cowley and Murray, Suchman, and others). Other studies point out very similar levels and ages of cognitive developments (e.g. Cole *et al*, Super, Okonji in mid-west Nigeria, Price-Williams) among African and European samples. Only one study (Barbara Lloyd, in Ibadan) suggests that Nigerian developmental levels are considerably in advance of European rates, but even she has not emphasised this point, and the weight of numbers of other studies casts doubt on Lloyd's findings.

The question has been seriously raised among African psychologists and educationists, that children enter school (even when they are fortunate enough to do so) inadequately prepared to benefit from the experiences that school can potentially give. Okonji (1969b) has suggested that the school entering age should be drastically brought forward, with children starting some form of organised education as early as 2, or 3 years old. This view is supported by the correlations given by Moreigne and Senecal (1962) which show ability levels settling down already by age 5. Durojaiye (1970) reflected the administrative view that such a step would be infeasible, and suggested an approach via adult education, to improve the ways in which parents can develop their childrens' abilities.

Most studies certainly show that schooled children do better than non-schooled ones, and the difference is often apparent within the first year of schooling. Maistriaux also demonstrated that an energetic, devoted and involved teacher can greatly help development. Super suggests that too much concern may be being devoted to the pre-school and early school age development problem; perhaps biological maturation and ordinary life experience, especially as urbanisation and westernisation spread, may bring about just as useful a course of cognitive development. However, there is a distinction between developing ability, and developing the ability or inclination or enthusiasm to use one's abilities. It is in this latter area, of applying their abilities to these kinds of problems posed in modernising cultures, that African children may have most progress to make, and there is reason to believe that it is schooling which enhances the ability to express and use the child's potential.

There is no reason, from the evidence in this chapter, to suppose that African children are constitutionally at a disadvantage. Far from this, in several cases there is a remarkable flowering of potential, even in ill-equipped surroundings. The tasks for further research are now to look more closely into parental behaviour and cultural influences that can enhance development; and to clarify further how various facets of the school experience may also contribute to development. This information can then play more part in influencing policy on the allocation of scarce educational resources.

CHAPTER III

FURTHER COGNITIVE
DEVELOPMENT
AND ITS MEASUREMENT

Introduction

The last chapter reviewed how children may develop into Piaget's second 'stage' of 'operational thought'; in this stage, usually reached from 6-8 years old the mental operations are 'concrete'. In Piaget's scheme, at about the beginning of adolescence, children develop into the third stage of 'formal operational thought'. Here the mind deals in concepts directly, without need of real props or reminders to act as landmarks in thought. While much ingenuity has been spent in exploring children's arrival into the second major stage, there has been much less work, especially in Africa, on how the third stage of formal operational thought is reached. This is perhaps an omission which future research will put right.

Instead, investigation of the ways in which people do use, or can use (this is an important distinction) concepts, has been done in terms of 'intelligence tests'. Intelligence is sometimes explained as the ability to educe relationships, and then to deduce correlates; but Alfred Binet, the French innovator of intelligence tests included initiative as part of his concept of intelligence. This question of initiative perhaps emerges in the work in Africa under the label of 'general adaptability', to which I will return later. Much of the work in Africa has used imported tests, sometimes adapted to local situations; and the very idea of a standard test was also strange to many Africans. Most testers thus expected to learn about the abilities of the 'testees'; but sometimes the data have been more informative about the tests, or even about intelligence and adaptability among the testers themselves.

The early history of testing in Africa

For the first third of this century, most of the reported testing came from South Africa, where western-type educational systems had probably first taken root. C. T. Loram (1917) tells us that a racially segregated educational system had begun to develop in the nineteenth century. Sir Langham Dale told the Cape House Assembly quite clearly in 1889 that education would be planned to ensure white supremacy, 'with the majority of the natives, at best, qualified to do the work of rough artisans.' Loram shows that in 1913 the annual expense of European pupils was £4.12.8 each; for 'natives' it was £0.2.1. This disproportion of effort would inevitably be reflected in test results recorded then, and most probably also set deprived standards whose inertia would be felt for decades afterward.

In 1915 and 1916, Loram, who had returned from training at Columbia University in America, tested European and 'Native' (I will follow his term here) pupils in Natal. The natives came from 'permanent and reputable schools'; but teaching was less efficient there, and the overextensive age range in classes (newcomers of fourteen might be put in Kindergarten classes) promoted a vicious circle of congestion in lower classes, increased failure rates and non-promotion. Loram's tests were of what we now call 'achievement'; that is, they assessed the results of what had been learned, rather than some supposedly inbuilt capacity to learn.

Blacks excelled whites at a handwriting test (they had to copy the sentence 'Natal is the most beautiful province of South Africa' as often and as well as they could in five minutes). Among several sub-tests of verbal composition, and arithmetic, (measuring speed and accuracy) Europeans did better. However in two arithmetic subtests (subtraction and division) among sixth formers blacks had better accuracy scores, while on a third subtest (multiplication) accuracy was equal. Loram points to slower performance among the Africans; but since he mentions that many entries on the records said 'left school—tired', it seems likely that a nutritional or health factor was affecting alertness.

Loram also tried to test abilities which might exist apart from skills which have been acquired. Tests were given to explore 'logical memory', rote memory, digit symbol matching and cancellation; and also one of 'free association', which must have been one of the earliest uses of what are now called 'divergent' tests. All these tests were given to about 300 white, and black children, each. On logical memory and symbol-matching tests the wide gap between white and black groups at age 9 was virtually closed by age 18; on free association the groups at 9 were more similar than they were at 18. Since this test assesses fluency in language, one might have expected the 9 year old black children, less used to English, to have been at a particular disadvantage. This was not so, and the reason for this finding is obscure.

Loram pointed to some evidence of a pause or levelling off in development reached at age 12. He reported a belief among whites in Africa, that Africans' abilities stagnate around the time of early puberty. This belief probably related to some Victorian missionaries' fears that adult initiation rites, which occurred among some peoples, led to too much preoccupation with sexuality which they considered detrimental to intellectual growth. Loram sent a questionnaire on this to 48 missionary teachers, but over half the replies denied that there was evidence of any such arrest in intellectual growth.

Loram's results implied that 'the Native is considerably inferior to the European, but there is no evidence that this inferiority will be permanent'. Loram thus acknowledged that these tests did *not* measure inner potential, but the results of education; he insisted that test differences mainly pointed to the inferior education provided for black children. He proposed reforms, but unfortunately most black children probably still receive inferior education to whites, both in some newly independent African states as well as in South Africa.

Two similar pioneering efforts on test development were made in South Africa, alongside Loram's work. Martin (1915) adapted the French

Binet-Simon tests for Zulu children from 4-18 years old. Tests involving memory and observation were coped with best. Loades and Rich (1917) also used the revised Binet-Simon test with 211 Zulu pupils at a missionary school — the eldest being 27. They considered that 'post pubertal development of the mind is different in Natives than in Europeans' (p.383). The reason for this is most likely to lie with the point that Loram underlined, that of educational quality.

In the next decade, Endemann (1927) again tried to assess 'the intelligence of the Native'. Endemann's original contribution was to point to a range of special abilities which few others had then, nor many have yet, explored (see Chapter V). Next, MacCrone (1928) tested 87 South African schoolchildren, with Porteus' maze test (see below). MacCrone compared his results with some recorded by Cyril Burt among London children, unfavourably; he also found that scores rose from ages 9 to 13, then dropped away among older children. The causes of this were still left unexamined.

Porteus himself (1937) repeated his maze test with 182 adults from all over Southern Africa (as far north as Mozambique) and determined their 'mental age' at 10½ years. Bushmen from the Kalahari desert appeared even lower, at 7½ years. Porteus interpreted his results (and clung to this theme over the next 30 years) as evidence of genetic differences. But most psychologists now consider Porteus' comparison of his African data with western standards to be inappropriate, just as much as a Bushman testing Porteus on desert lore might evaluate his 'mental age' as something startlingly low.

The 1930s saw two substantial reports from South Africa, as well as a start in investigations elsewhere. First of all Lawrence Fick (1929, 1939) set forth his evidence, and argument. Fick used, among others, the American Army Beta Test, developed during World War I. Results from 293 Zulu children were compared unfavourably with those from other ethnic groups in South Africa. Fick was criticised for using verbal tests, biassed against those outside the culture where the tests had been devised. So (Fick, 1939) he then used a variety of non-verbal tests, which at that time were thought of as 'culture fair' with 557 African School children. Fick still concluded that the mental age of South African blacks was substantially less than that of whites.

A more sophisticated study than Fick's was done by Jansen Van Rensburg (1938). He gave three types of tests to Zulu Africans and to Europeans, and attempted to control for factors such as language, attitude towards speed of working, attitudes towards a tester, and socio-economic level. Van Rensburg still found differences between the groups which he took to show that the Zulus could not 'compete on equal terms with the Average European' and that 'the difference in ability is partly innate'.

In South Africa itself, two acute criticisms were directed at this kind of work, especially Fick's. Dr. Simon Biesheuvel (1943), then busy as an Air Force Officer made a special effort to publish a critical analysis. He pointed out errors, internal inconsistencies, and basic flaws in the assumption that black and white groups in South Africa could be found who had experienced equivalent social conditions or opportunities. Later J. M. Winterbottom (1946) in a review of Biesheuvel's book wrote more scathingly that '. . . Dr

Fick has rushed about South Africa giving Intelligence Tests and drawing conclusions from them, without having any idea of what Intelligence Tests actually measure. . . and with a control group of incomparable material. . . His offence is made worse by the fact that many of the faults that mar "The Educability of the South African Native" (1939) were pointed out to its author . . . in 1934. His own educability would therefore appear to be nil, which seems to be a serious disqualification for assessing that of others'.

Clearly, claims like those of Fick and Van Rensburg could continue on a basis of similar data which were fairly easily available; but the conclusions offered by such people were beginning to be met with cold and detailed, as well as with heated argument. Though Fick withdrew, similar studies subsequently appeared, and have been reviewed by Arthur Crijns (1962) who himself believed that 'intelligence and intelligent behaviour are culturally specific', and therefore that simple comparisons of two groups of people from different cultures, were meaningless. Crijns agreed with the French writer Wintringer (1935) who believed that certain cognitive skills were well developed in one culture, while other skills were better developed in another.

A pioneering study of specialist cognitive skills was by Oliver (1932a, 1932b). He was the first, and perhaps the only worker to have tried out tests of musical abilities in Africa, in this case with Kikuyu pupils in Kenya. Apart from two subtests which clearly depend on western taste for 'correct' answering (e.g. judgement of the 'goodness' of harmonies) the Kikuyu pupils scored better than a comparison American group. However, with tests of the letter and digit substitution type, the Kikuyus scored less than younger European schoolboys.

Several writers have reported prodigious memory among illiterate Africans; examples include Bartlett (1932) and from Francophone Africa Bourdel (quoted by Crijns). One who had evidence for this was Augusto (1949) who compared 849 Africans in Mozambique on items from Binet and Terman-Merrill scales, with 100 Portuguese soldiers there. Augusto found the soldiers scored better, but the Africans were superior in certain tests like free association (compare Loram's evidence), interpretations of pictures, and memory for figures. Augusto did not merely want to dramatise African inadequacy by European standards. For he did point to a difference in the cultural patterning of abilities; he also showed that African women scored much lower than men. In contrast, Heuse (1957) tested 93 soldiers from French West Africa and compared their scores with those from various white groups. He found the Africans' memory ability was about 80% that of the western samples, and considered that the Africans showed a lack of concentration and speed in dealing with the problems set.

Higher male scores were also found by Gonzales (1952) in testing Africans in Spanish Colonies (e.g. Equatorial Guinea). He tested over 400 Africans aged from 7 to 20, and compared them with a white 'control' group of merely 15 people. This attempted inter-cultural comparison is therefore absurd. But of interest was that the average performance of Africans decreased with age; there was a slight superiority of urban over rural Africans, while people of mixed race did not score better than Africans.

Two studies follow, whose findings do not so much shed light on the cognitive behaviour of the people tested, as throw up a question on the thinking of the testers. One of these studies may be the first ever American venture into Africa on this subject. Nissen, Machover and Kinder (1935) first wrongly supposed that Loades and Rich had been the only pioneer testers preceding themselves. In Guinea (then a French colony) they gave 50 Sousou children aged perhaps from 5 to 14, twelve 'white man's games' (their term). The tests involved the principles of recognising patterns, and exercises of part-whole identification. For example, with cube-tapping, the tester taps a row of four cubes in a given order, and the subject copies this.

One of the jigsaw tests particularly astonished the experimenters. A set of pieces making up a human profile, was often not rearranged to make a flat picture, but the pieces were piled up upon each other. The Digit Symbol test was not understood at all. The whole episode in fact seemed to be full of misunderstanding, not only on the subjects' part, but evidently on the experimenters' side as well. Instead of showing the vaunted western intellectual quality of adaptiveness, which would have led them to change their tests long before boring the 50th child, the experimenters persisted and thought it worthwhile to work out 'quotients' on their data. With this obviously unrepresentative and inappropriately tested sample, they compared these quotients with others from St Helena, and America.

Philip Vernon (1969), considered to be a major authority on cross-cultural testing, still did not think the episode had been fruitless, and told of another even less successful study, conducted by an Egyptian. Vernon wrote 'Nissen et al were fairly successful in 1935 with Sousou children' because 'at least they did score on all tests except Digit-Symbol'. In contrast to this 'M. Fahmy, who gave a similar battery to primitive Nilotic Skillak (sic — probably Shilluk) children in Southern Sudan was unable to get scorable responses to half the tests'. Vernon continues somewhat limply 'such studies nowadays seem to have gone out of fashion'. Fashion of course, is not the point, as though the vogue may return again.

The second enterprise which raises questions about the investigator, came 20 years after Nissen et al wrote their piece. Robert Maistriaux (1955a) for the Belgian government, used non-verbal tests with illiterates and schoolchildren, in the then Belgian Congo and Ruanda-Urundi. Illiterates in Kivu and Kasai (Congo) scored similarly to a group of mentally retarded Belgian children; while African schoolchildren, aged 13 to 20, scored similarly to Belgians aged 6. Separately (Maistriaux, 1955b) he studied patterns of errors on the test he gave, and considered that they 'show that the human mind reacts qualitatively in the same manner, in spite of differences of race and civilisation.' Though his title refers to 'The Unity of Human Intelligence,' he has insultingly chosen to compare normal Africans with Belgian retardates, well after the demonstration by Biesheuvel (1943) that it is inappropriate to assess people in one culture by the standards of another.

The studies in this section cover the first attempts to assess the abilities of Africans. They first tried out standard Western tests, then 'culture-fair' western tests, to measure the average and distribution of something called 'intelligence', which was thought of, like soul, or human rights, as being qualitatively the same in any humans. First it was pointed out that cultures can be so different, that the measuring instruments devised in one culture are not appropriate for measuring qualities in another, no matter how one tries to balance age, wealth, or nominal education. Then it was suspected that cognitions might develop towards an end product that is qualitatively, as well as quantitatively different according to cultures. In spite of this, some investigators still contrasted Africans with European standards, finding, or implying some inferiority, without exploring a contrary implication, that Africans may be good at some mental tasks which Europeans are not.

Exploring what tests and their results might mean

Overlapping with the previous section, we find a large group of studies whose aims have been to use tests to explore cognitive development among Africans as a topic in its own right. These studies have not aimed primarily to produce some IQ, or score from a group of Africans to compare this with European scores. This kind of comparison has, however, sometimes come as a by product. The tests have nearly always been imported and adapted from Europe or America, but they have been used to explore the patterns of abilities which have been fostered, or not, in various social and educational conditions in Africa.

For example, Barbé (1946) studied young people with and without schooling in French West Africa, using Burt's and Pieron's scales with the former, and Koh's Blocks, and jigsaw tests with the latter. Though the literates did well with Pieron's test, they did poorly on Burt's scale. The illiterates found particular difficulty with the jigsaw and blocks, almost irrespective of their age. As in Augusto's and Gonzales' research, females did worse than males. Barbé also found that people of mixed race did better than the Africans, and this is most likely to have been due to their better educational and socio-economic position.

In South Africa, Hunkin (1950) set out to 'validate' Goodenough's Draw-a-man test. Over 2,000 children aged from six to 13 in Durban were tested. Both age, and school standard related positively to test scores, and this is as far as the validation went. We do not know from this whether the test measures some inner ability which in turn determines school performance, or whether (as is more likely) school experience helps confer the ability to score well on the test. Hunkin found Africans superior to whites on grasp of general outline and gross structure of figure. However, overall the Africans scored less than whites, and the discrepancy increased with age; Hunkin says these differences are probably culturally determined.

Difficulty with tests involving diagrams and drawings is a recurring theme of many reports from Africa. Many non-verbal tests, specially brought in to try to avoid the more obvious cultural bias of verbal tests, proved especially difficult. Clarke (1948, 1949) who tested 261 Nigerian students with tests such as assembling scrambled sentences, block designs, and cube construction, put forward a possible reason for difficulties with non-verbal tasks. He felt that the strategy often used was of a trial and error nature, and thus inefficient. But if the element of strategy was the basic reason for poor scores, it would produce these on any kind of test, not just particularly on non-verbal ones. It would be more fundamental to enquire why some kinds of tests in particular provoked the use of inefficient strategies.

That testers should themselves follow useful strategies was the concern of Professor André Ombredane (1951). The first Director of the CERP (Centre d'Etudes et Recherches Psychotechniques) in the Belgian Congo, Ombredane laid down principles to follow in testing in Africa which were widely read by French-speaking scholars, though not always followed by them, or others. Ombredane wrote: 'it is indispensable ... to (1) determine the delicate balance of factors which can affect the behaviour of the Africans studied and (2) as one does his research, make one's observations accurately ... before jumping blindly into a testing programme and then comparing without doing any more, the results that one obtains with those that one obtains from whites. Any such results, which disregard situational differences, mean nothing'.

One scholar who followed Ombredane's advice was Berlioz (1955). He tested 80 men, recently in employment, on behalf of a vocational training centre in Douala, Cameroons. His main test was Raven's Matrices (see below p. 65) on which he found that certain kinds of error were particularly common. This meant, unlike Clarke's conclusion, that people were not just behaving in a random, trial and error way. This implies that people are using some consistent approach (though a wrong one by the test's requirements) and it is our research job to discover what the strategy is. Analysis of errors, particularly on Raven's Matrices test, has preoccupied many Francophone workers, but oddly enough (Raven having invented his test in Britain) few Anglophone ones.

Another suggestion that has been made by several researchers is that Africans approach tests very warily, or slowly. Dent (1949) maintained that Zulus were not interested in individual speed at work; and with intellectual puzzles he felt they did not like to take risks and used 'safe' strategies. Heuse (1957, see above) also commented on slowness. Ombredane, Robaye and Robaye (1957) mentioned slowness, and presently, (Ombredane, Bertelson and Beniest-Noirot, 1958) explored the matter further. Members of a group of 159 adult Congolese mineworkers were matched with individuals among 190 Belgian schoolchildren on a basis of equal quality of performance; but 83% of the Belgians did the test faster than the time taken by the average Congolese. Slowness arose more from 'a general lack of interest in speed performance rather than by a slower operation of mental functions'.

That 'African' subjects need longer to work on tests has been accepted by a Nigerian researcher (Yoloye, 1971, see below), while the question of whether people believe intelligence implies quickness has been explored by Wober (1974a). Here, Baganda and Batoro villagers in Uganda were asked to associate each of a list of adjectives, strongly, or weakly, with the concept 'intelligence', as they felt fit. Whereas an educated group of medical students associated the concept 'intelligence' (given in English) with the word 'fast', villagers associated it with the word 'slow'. Anecdotal reports from elsewhere in Africa were quoted, to the effect that there seemed to be a frequent idea that intelligent behaviour is that which led to respect of and compliance with society's ways. This point was also made from the opposite end of Africa by

Bisilliat, Laya, Pierre and Pidoux (1967). Recently too, Serpell found in Zambia that adults' ratings of childrens' intelligence did not correlate with their scores on three tests. He suggested that intelligence as conceived in Chewa culture emphasises qualities of co-operation, which are not sampled by these tests.

Returning to cross-cultural comparisons of test scores, we find work by Marc Richelle (1959), who tested 310 children in Elisabethville in the Katanga region of the Congo. Richelle used a test devised by Rey, in which a series of eight transparent plastic boxes each contains a coin, which has to be extracted by the subject who must cope with various obstacles within the apparatus. The subject can use a piece of wire, or other available aids which can be poked through holes in the sides of the box, to get at the coin. As in other research, girls scored less than boys of equal age. The Congolese were less successful than one comparison group in Switzerland, but were better than another group of poor Moroccan Jews. The Congolese were slower, but showed fewer failures than the Swiss, and far fewer than the Moroccan Jews.

Robaye, Robaye and Falmagne (1960) next discovered a way in which inter-racial test differences could be minimised. Using a complex psychomotor task, they tried three different testing procedures, including getting the subjects to memorise the verbal instructions and to demonstrate to the examiner that they understood them. Under these conditions a group of Congolese apprentices and white school pupils achieved similar scores, making the same numbers of errors.

While most cross-cultural comparisons so far discussed have contrasted Africans and Europeans, Nelly Xydias (1963) working for the Prohuza organisation (Centre d'Etudes et d'Information des *Pro*blemes *Hu*maines dans les *Z*ones *A*rides) in the Sahara contrasted four different tribal groups given Raven's Matrices, Seguin's form-board, wire bending and other tests. On the Matrices, the people of the small town of Laghouat did best, and the people least exposed to western influence, the Touareg, did worst. Since the Laghouati were unschooled, Xydias concludes that 'schooling certainly accelerates acculturation, but the latter can also occur in other ways'. Unexpectedly, the nomadic Reguibat did substantially better overall than the Touareg, also nomads. Xydias wrote 'can one suppose that the mode of life of the Reguibat, little known, gives its members more possibilities of development than the mode of life among the Touaregs? Or that Reguibat who seek work are a select group? Or that they are a gifted race? . . . personal experience . . . leads us to opt for the last idea . . . but we know this comes from personal sympathy rather than any objective considerations'. Here is honestly admitted an important possibility, that the shape of a researcher's results may stem partly from the quantity of her sympathy with and for her test subjects. Since researchers, even Africans, usually come from different cultures than the people being tested, this is a considerable problem to ponder.

Alongside efforts to discover more about people, researchers continue to try out new tests. For example, Gustav Jahoda (1969), whose work we shall also follow in subsequent chapters, tried out a Perceptual Maze Test, in which a testee has to join up a maximum number of dots which are scattered throughout a maze. Testing with 280 male students at the University of Ghana gave a normal distribution for most of the sample, except for 8%, who scored nothing, after getting the first item correct. Jahoda questioned some of these people afterwards and put the difficulty down to a misunderstanding of instructions. This echoes the point repeatedly made, from Ombredane (1951) first of all, through the Robayes and Falmagne (see above), again by Silvey (1963a) in Uganda and Wober (1969) in Nigeria, that it is of paramount importance that instructions are understood. This may seem a simple point, but it cuts across the orthodoxy of western testing methods, which has it that instructions should be read out in a 'standard' fashion, just once, and not gone over again. Jahoda also found that this test correlated well with a version of Koh's Blocks, making it a speedy alternative to that test. Students from literate families did better than those from illiterate ones, suggesting that there is something in family background that affects later cognitive performance; however, science students did not do better than others on this test.

In a very different area of Africa, and of cognitive ability, Joel Davitz (1970) of Columbia University investigated 'divergent' skills among children in Uganda. His tests were such where there is no one correct solution; rather, the tester explores the testee's fertility and quality of ideas. Children had to suggest alternate uses for common objects (banana leaf, knife, etc.), find as many ways as possible in which pairs of objects are alike, suggest meanings to rather bare line drawings, and so on. Some children were tested in English, others in the vernacular, Luganda. Neither language afforded a consistent advantage, though the range of scores was greater among those tested in English, than in Luganda. Older children tested in Luganda had better scores on verbal tasks, but showed no improvement over younger ones with the graphic items. This repeats Loram's and Augusto's pointers to healthy abilities in verbal fluency, and echoes several other instances where difficulty with diagrams or drawings have been found.

Columbia University was also an academic base for two Nigerian test researchers. One, Christopher Bakare (1971) used the Draw-a-man test (see Hunkin, above) to explore the relation of social class differences to test performance, to validate the test, and to provide local norms. Bakare tested 204 upper class Nigerian, 189 lower class Nigerian, and 106 American and English children. He gave the test 'in strict accordance with the instructions provided in the . . . manual' — a procedure which we have seen, is likely not to bring out the best in the lower class children. Not surprisingly, at every grade level, upper class children scored better than lower class ones. Unlike the South Africans, the Nigerian upper class scored equally well as the Americans and Europeans, grade for grade. Though Bakare quotes other research findings that girls often do better on this test, he found (as in several other studies discussed here) a sex difference in favour of the boys. His validation consisted in finding a low but significant correlation between test scores and teachers' ratings of mental ability. The test scores did not correlate with overall school achievement marks, though an information test did correlate significantly with the test among lower class children. The test thus shows yet again that class differences somehow interact with intellectual development, though the scores would not be much use for selecting pupils for further training.

The second Nigerian psychologist from Columbia, Ayetunde Yoloye (1971) studied how bilingual students cope with intelligence tests after years of schooling. Yoloye expected that scores on both verbal and non-verbal tests would increase with school grade; and that as pupils became more at home with the language of their education (English) so their verbal scores would increase more rapidly than non-verbal ones. Yoloye tested over 500 adolescents, 85% Yorubas, in three secondary school grades; he used a 'new multi-level edition of the Lorge-Thorndike intelligence tests', but allowed longer times. Verbal IQ levels did in fact rise, so that by the fifth form they stood at average American levels; while the non-verbal IQ levels actually slipped slightly back in the higher grades, though not by a significant amount. Verbal and non-verbal test results, though acting in partly different ways, clearly also measured something in common, with a correlation of 0.66.

Finally, Durojaiye (1972c) gives results of testing 540 secondary school pupils, in three grades, in Uganda. They did Raven's Matrices, a maze test, a scholastic aptitude test, and several questionnaires on home experience, class, and their own aspirations. Teachers' attitudes to education, their ratings of pupils' behaviour and estimated academic progress, and parents' attitudes to child raising practices were all measured by the questionnaires and interviews.

Pupils' ambitions, and 'attitudes to the school situation', and parents' attitudes all correlated significantly with good academic performance. The Matrices, and Maze test results only barely yielded significant correlations with performance, among urban school boys and girls. Most interestingly, in every group (rural boys, and girls, and urban boys, and girls) the more wealthy parents produced children whose scores were worse than those of less well-off families' children. This is very surprising, given that richer parents usually afford better quality schooling, and since other research suggests both that good schooling and well equipped homes make for good intellectual performance. However, it may be that wealthy families in Uganda often relied on traditional modes of bringing up children, and sometimes patronised poor quality private schools. Durojaiye emphasises that it is attitudes rather than status in itself that determine academic performance. Nevertheless, this is still a surprising set of findings. Its value lies in cutting down to size the imported notion that psychological tests offer a direct route to measuring latent ability, and in focussing on parents', teachers', and especially pupils' attitudes to education.

Test reliability

The evidence now leaves us uncertain as to what mixture of present performance, and innate ability it is that a test measures; this is the question of 'validity'. But there is also the question of whether the test score produced at a first testing is a 'reliable' estimate of a person's ability. Possibly at a subsequent testing the score may be different from the first estimate. In western countries it has widely been accepted that established tests are reliable, and that they will be so anywhere. Yet work on the speed at which tests are often done in Africa, and discussion of the need for more than the standard explanation when administering tests, all suggests that the topic of test reliability needs particular study in Africa. The contention at issue is that in many situations in Africa, the score produced on first testing a candidate may well not be a true estimate of his ability.

Ombredane pioneered the exploration of this question. First, (Ombredane and Robaye, 1953) he realised that 'a test like the Matrices is equivalent to a test of culture rather than a test of intelligence'. The idea introduced here, which comes out more clearly in most of the studies we shall examine, is that as testees become more used to the tests, they will reveal more 'ability' by getting better scores. (And of course, they must have had this ability in the first place, which initial testing often does not reveal).

Ombredane (1956) first explored this thesis among the Asalampasu who 'had for long been considered as exceptionally fierce and redoubtable, head hunters and cannibals, merciless to the black and white stranger who ventured into their territory'. Only by the late 1920s had they taken up jobs with the Forminière company with whom 'they show a particularly remarkable performance — in three months they become heavy tractor drivers, handling 8 ton machines which lay bare the soil to get at diamond beds beneath'. In other words, they show considerable adaptability.

Ombredane used ten tests, including the Matrices which he 'applied' three times. Results from 693 subjects are shown as means of the three successive testings. Up to ages 12 and 13, unschooled children and those with two years of schooling did equally, but after this unschooled children showed reducing scores. Thus contrary to the impressions of MacCrone, Fick and Gordon (1934) a cognitive stagnation at adolescence is not inevitable and progress depends on education. Ombredane also noticed that errors occurred in systematic ways, suggesting that testees might have misunderstood what were supposed to be the 'correct' solutions. Over age 12, those with more schooling showed a better gain on their first retesting, while by the second retesting those with most schooling may have reached their ceiling, so those with medium school experience showed the best gains.

Extending the project, Ombredane, Robaye and Plumail (1956) found that test results correlated with a rating for work efficiency (0.38), better at the second testing (0.48) and finally the third testing gave scores correlating quite substantially with rated efficiency (0.51 — all for 78 men).

Ombredane, Robaye and Robaye (1957) next tested the more westernised Baluba with the Matrices, and noted scores achieved at 20, 30, 40 minutes, and at an untimed period to allow completion of the test. Both school experience, and time allowed for testing bore considerable relation to test scores. Ombredane noted that these testees were slow with their work, suggesting that 'they are inclined to observe each other and one waits for the others'. A small positive correlation between time and test scores (0.23) showed that those who worked longer got better scores. In Belgium, normally, slower workers would score less. Again, the greatest gains were found with people who initially had medium scores. Ombredane's interesting verdict on the Matrices is that it is 'a badly constructed test, but it is because of this ... that one is able to unravel important phenomena ... and this is not its least merit'.

One of Ombredane's last papers (Ombredane, Robaye & Robaye, 1958) dealt with another well known western test, the Minnesota Form Board. Here again, children with schooling showed fewer errors through and after adolescence; while those without schooling showed more errors after adolescence. Retesting produced much less increase in scores than with the Matrices.

Not all researchers, or all tests revealed increased scores on retesting. Verhaegen (1956) tested various groups of adults in the Congo, with Matrices and other tests. The Matrices gave quite stable scores, with first and second testing correlating very closely (0.83) when there was an interval of 'a few weeks', though this dropped to 0.55 after a year. The tests gave more stable results with more westernised adults. It seems likely that retesting after a year yielded many scores above the previous ones, but Verhaegen did not discuss this or isolate the improvers to analyse their results further.

In the same year, Gustav Jahoda (1956) reported testing over 300 Ghanaian schoolboys with the Matrices three times; whereas at the first testing only 4% scored over 40 marks (the test has a maximum of 60), at the third session 30% got over 40. The average overall rise was 6.5 points. Jahoda says that contrary to other research findings in England, the best improvement among Ghanaians was in the middle range of scores.

Further studies came from all over Africa supporting this finding. Lloyd and Pidgeon (1961) in South Africa tested 300 children from the African, Asian and European communities. Each group was randomly split into experimental and control subgroups. All were tested with a National Foundation for Educational Research non-verbal test; experimental groups received half an hour of coaching on each of two weeks after the test. On the third week, groups were retested, Africans gaining most (7.6 points) Eutopeans less (3.2 points) and Asians not at all. The African's average scores thus overtook the Asians'.

An even clearer example of improvement with coaching was reported by Schmidt (1960) who was a pupil of Lloyd's. The same numbers of children as in the above experiement were given an IQ test, tested again after practice, and a third time after an hour's coaching. Zulu children responded to coaching with an average gain of over 14 IQ points, which was not found in other groups and which left Schmidt 'astonished at its magnitude'.

In Uganda, a doctor John McFie (1961) gave 26 boys entering a training school verbal tests, and a Block Designs (adapted Koh's Blocks) test. After two years' technical training, scores on Block Designs and related tests had improved, while verbal tests had not similarly shown gains. This suggests that relevant cognitive experience, though not necessarily focussed on the test itself, can produce significant changes. Far across Africa, in Sierra Leone, Dawson (1963a) showed that a similar group of trade apprentices made large gains on being coached specifically (as in Lloyd and Pidgeon's experiment) on a task of three-dimensional style of picture perception. A combination of practice effect (i.e. where there is a repeated encounter with the test, but without teaching) and coaching was shown by Jonathan Silvey (1963a) in Uganda to be very effective. With practice, secondary schoolchildren showed an increase of 15% on their test scores; 7% was gained by coaching alone, but

22% by a combination of practice and coaching. Silvey next varied his procedure, some pupils receiving coaching for only one third of the range of problems in the Matrices, and a second subgroup having explanations for all sub-sections of the test. The section receiving fuller instructions showed a gain of 5 points on average scores on retest.

A different type of improvement, not in the same individuals, but in members of the culture, was reported by Gisèle Dormeau (1959). She tested three separate groups of Balubas, each of the same age and nominal educational experience, but in three successive years. The group tested last scored more than that tested first, the difference being attributed to widespread improvement of general educational standards and to greater 'acculturation'. Dawson (op. cit.) reported a similar finding in Sierra Leone.

Further French language studies have explored the effects of repeated testing, in much more detail than the English work. J. Laroche (1959) gave the Matrices to over 200 children in Katanga using a mixture of Swahili and French instructions, retesting them up to a fourth time, at 2 day intervals. The biggest gains were made at the first retest, then again significant gains occurred at the third testing, with a small rise to the fourth. Among the lowest form tested, however, there had still been room for significant improvement at the fourth testing. Laroche noted a change in the type of errors being made, from rather mechanical mistakes at the initial encounter, to what he calls 'intelligent errors' at repeated encounters with the test. At no stage in his programme of testing, did Laroche find any good correlations between test scores and school performance at French, or arithmetic. Evidently the skills required to do Matrices well, and improve at it, were not the one determining performance in these two school subjects.

Laroche (1960) next presented results from 189 children of workers in the Union Minière company in Katanga, and compared them with similar tests given to children at the same school level (Primary 6) in Belgium. There were 18 tests altogether, and Laroche reports that the patterns of correlations were largely similar in the two cultures; one or two discrepancies he attributes to Katangese childrens' strong superiority in mental arithmetic, and their relative unfamiliarity with French. He carried out retesting, after one week, and nine months later. Most tests, except those involving 'spatial visualisation' and 'abstract reasoning' (as with other researchers) gave stable results; but here most children made significant gains on retesting.

A third report from the Congo was by Erpicum (1959), who used a battery of tests including the Matrices, and a numerical analogue of it. We can illustrate what a Matrix test is, by an example of the numerical analogue. The candidate sees a pattern of numbers, such as this:

38	56	40
46	30	58
50	48	—

The gap is to be filled in, with whichever the candidate thinks is the correct item of: 40 58 38 48 46 36.

The correct answer is 36, as it contains the digits 3, and 6, which appear in each complete row, and in each complete column. Raven's Matrices proper used this kind of problem format, but geometric diagrams and symbols instead of numbers.

Erpicum coached experimental groups, with special attention to the difficult features of each test; these experimental groups, with control groups, were tested twice in three months. P.4 pupils in the experimental group showed better correlations between the Matrices and two other tests, suggesting that this 'trained' Matrices performance was the more valid measure of their ability. Similar advantages did not appear for a 'trained' Matrices performance in P.6 pupils. Erpicum considers that these had already become familiar with the kind of skills involved in Matrices performance.

A slight contribution from the French is also of interest because it contains evidence from adolescents tested in Mauretania. Rerat (1963) repeated the French fascination with the Matrices, and found that coaching produced substantial gains in scores on retest.

Finally, in favour of the proposition that retesting reveals previously unrevealed potential, comes evidence from 86 industrial workers tested in Southern Nigeria (Wober, 1969). Without coaching, and a six month interval before retesting, there was a significant gain in scores. The amount of education a man had received was not related to the Matrices gain; but scores on the EFT were related to Matrices improvement. The point of this study is that it dealt with mature adults. Without schooling, or maturational experience that may improve adolescents' approach to a test, the improvement among mature men suggests that pure familiarity can also help.

Two studies support the idea that initial test scores are reliable, particularly with Raven's Matrices. Vernon (1967a) tested Tanzanian schoolboys on Number Series, Classification and Matrices tests, each in two parallel forms. He used five different conditions of test administration (printed or spoken instructions, blackboard aided instruction, class, and individual coaching), and two languages, Swahili and English. Vernon claims that it does not matter whether the Matrices are explained in Swahili or in English, as this test is 'almost self explanatory from its sample items'. Elsewhere though, (Vernon, 1967b) he allows that Africans may have criteria of what constitutes a 'correct' answer, that differ from European criteria. Vernon nevertheless emphasises that 'practice and coaching effects . . . are no larger than three to eight standard score units'. The pupils he tested had recently taken their primary leaving tests, which are not unlike 'intelligence tests'. So they may already have made their principal familiarisation effect gains in the first testing Vernon gave. He himself suggested this (Vernon, 1969), commenting 'it is probable that they were able to transfer their familiarity with printed tests to new intelligence test materials'. Further, Vernon does not calculate if the gains shown in his groups are significant.

Vernon is keen to say that test results are reasonably stable (1969) and that retest gains are not large. He mentions Ombredane's and Silvey's work, and the latter's idea that the amount of test gain might itself be used to predict academic ability, but dismisses this 'for various technical reasons. . .' Thus, if the top scorers at the first testing made small gains at retest, while the medium-range scorers made larger gains, leaving both groups roughly equal, it would be awkward to argue that the second group were better than the first, because they made greater gains. Vernon's own result was that scores on retests were not any better related to school gradings than were scores on first testing. He did not however calculate the correlation between the amount of test gain individually achieved, with school performance, which would have directly tested Silvey's suggestion.

The second investigator contending that testing methods were relatively unlikely to affect the reliability of initial test scores, was E. L. Klingelhofer (1971). He did not work on familiarity by practice, or gain of insight by coaching, but on differences which might result from giving instructions either in the vernacular, Swahili, or in English — which pupils had been using for only two years by the time they had been tested. Klingelhofer found similar scores when the test was given in either language; nor did individual examiners (he used two) evoke different levels of scoring. Klingelhofer tested in schools of widely differing quality (urban and rural) and said that school quality was not strongly reflected in test scores either. The study argues that provided the standard instructions are used, a single testing with Matrices may give a good estimate of pupils' abilities. But no figures are given in Klingelhofer's paper; he only tested Standard VII children, and he did no retesting. These facts weaken his and Vernon's advice that we can trust in the outcome of Matrices scores derived in an orthodox western way.

Finally, showing that the social psychological conditions of the test occasion may affect speed, if not directly power scores, comes a project from Botswana. Cook and Molomo (1971) investigated whether incentives might affect performance of primary schoolchildren. They gave a verbal test, and one of marking letters (a test of speed and accuracy) to seven groups of children; one was a control group, and six had motivations based on tribal rivalry, own sex pride, knowledge of results, money, praise for an outstanding scholar, and threat of punishment. On the power test, there were no significant motivational differences, but different motivations did affect speed. Lower speed scores occurred with knowledge of results, while a money incentive accompanied quicker performance. Cook and Molomo realised that primary school children take all tests with near-maximum enthusiasm, believing that they might affect their lives in case they are not 'just experiments'. Also (though the differences were not significant), pointing to tribal comparisons did reduce scores, while threat of punishment increased them. It may then be that, if motivational conditions can affect speed of work, they might also affect the quality of results, especially if a test is retaken, and testees have some knowledge of their previous results.

In this section we have looked at Anglophone and Francophone African evidence that a first test score for a person with limited education by itself is not likely to give a fair estimate of the person's potential ability. Western psychologists had thought of IQ as something like height; measurement of such things could be accurate, and should not be very different on one week from another, nor should it be affected by the social setting of the testing session. But psychological test scores have been shown to be quite unlike height. Various procedures have been shown to affect test scores, and recommended as ways of test administration. Such procedures include simple repetition of a test ('practice'), coaching on the test material itself, going beyond the strict adherence to instructions (which were mostly devised for use in western countries) to make sure they are truly understood and training people in skills not identical, but related to those which the test involves.

Several investigators found it worthwhile to repeat testing three times, to draw out candidates' real potential. Most studies used Raven's Matrices, but gain in scores has also been found with other tests such as an IQ scale (Schmidt). Some studies suggested that initial test scores were reliable, but this evidence is not extensively convincing. Verhaegen found test-retest correlations dropped markedly over a year; Vernon claimed only small gains occurred, but did not say if they had been statistically significant, and did no third testing. Klingelhofer did not do any retesting, and Cook and Molomo found some motivational conditions affected speed of working, which might well affect quality of results on retesting, if done. Overall, it seems unwise to accept initial test scores complacently, in most situations in Africa.

Tests in selection

Some workers see tests not as academic devices, but as practical ones. They want to use scores to judge which candidates may be better for one or another type of training. Selection is a problem that arises in education and in industry, and tests have been devised for, and used in both fields. But we shall look principally at the educational field here.

The first, and one of the largest projects of this sort in Africa was by MacDonald (1944) working with British forces in East Africa. Scores from nearly 2000 men on 14 tests were examined alongside ratings of the men's military performance. Though success in military performance is hard to define and express numerically, MacDonald found a correlation of 0.43 between his tests, and the criterion. MacDonald's report is not publicly available, but his material has been re-analysed by others, including Irvine (1963), who felt that the tests could be of practical use. There is not much sign in the academic literature though, that any useful application has been directly made of MacDonald's work.

In the Sudan, Scott (1950) also worked singlehanded on an educational selection test, based on the Gabbani-Ballard test which had been developed in Egypt. He soon found (as did others in Africa) that test scores had virtually no correlation with age, as they are expected to have in western countries. Scott then produced new items, such as sorting out jumbled sentences, finding opposites, and analogies. He advocated the use of demonstrational gadgets, and ways of explanation to achieve good humoured rapport. This time Scott found a reasonable correlation with age, and a very high reliability correlation of 0.9; this was, however, an individually-given test.

Next, Scott devised a printed test, useful for giving to people in groups. Among grade IV pupils the group test correlated only 0.4 with the individual test; but in higher grades (V-VII) the correlation rose to 0.8. This suggested that the process of education produced a qualitative change in the nature of abilities: 'Sudanese children . . . find great difficulty in realising that the object of writing is to convey meaning . . . partly because some teachers still tend to teach "classical" Arabic as material for correct recitation rather than as a vehicle for ideas'.

Biesheuvel (1952) worked in South Africa on a similar task, for the National Institute for Personnel Research. Recruits were being selected from all over Southern and Central Africa, for jobs in the mines, some of which were more skilled and some involving supervisory responsibilities. Biesheuvel's General Adaptability Battery (GAB) was the result of this work. Administered by filmed instructions, the GAB used considerable apparatus, which was cumbersome. Nevertheless, perhaps because profits were directly involved, the GAB has seen more application than have many tests in the educational field.

After a lull of about a decade, during which there was fieldwork rather than publication, the American W. H. Cooper (1961) described the use of the California test of mental maturity and the Otis Self Administered Scale in Nigeria. Cooper worked with Technical school students and found correlations ranging from −0.24 to 0.74 between test results and success on various school subjects. These were not, however, true predictive correlations, for the tests occurred after the students had been selected and partially trained. They were thus a somewhat specialised group. As often happened though, Cooper does not tell us if his tests were either refined, or used later on.

In Francophone Africa meanwhile, Verhaegen (1962) studied selection procedures at the Union Minière du Haut Katanga (copper mines). He gave several tests including Matrices and Koh's Blocks, to people in the first year of a technical school. It was clear that those doing well on the tests overall, included several doing well in class, and none doing poorly; while those doing poorly on the tests were mostly doing poorly in class. By the second year of technical school, various tests correlated from 0.49 to 0.85 with progress in training. Verhaegen points to a difficulty that can arise in selection experiments. If entrants are selected who do well on a test that is valid for the types of ability required, very few will do badly; thus scores on test, and on criterion will all be bunched up at the top ends of the scales, and significant correlations may not appear. Ideally, one should admit to training people who have scored poorly on pretest, to verify that they will train badly. Of course, for humanitarian, as well as economic and social reasons, it is not easy to do this on purpose. So the efficacy of selection tests may often be difficult to demonstrate.

A French study next tells of work in Mali, a country which has seen relatively little psychological research. Fontaine (1963) tested over 2,000 pupils with Matrices and similar French tests, a mechanical aptitude test and locally devised achievement tests. Correlations between Matrices scores, and pupils' place in class were generally higher in the higher forms (up to 0.93), supporting the idea that the more educated pupils are, the more their abilities display themselves equally in tests and in classroom achievement. Fontaine describes the Mali educational system in which large numbers of pupils compete for small numbers of places in secondary and technical schools; tribalism is said not to be a problem, and therefore selection gives scope for tests to be used as pointers to ability, though not immediately on entering school.

At the same time Brimble (1963) presented a paper based on work for an

MA Thesis done in Zambia several years earlier. He gave 760 school-children six tests. Results correlated well with scores of attainment on English and Arithmetic tests, but as the psychological tests were done after the training effect of schooling, the correlations were concurrent rather than predictive. The same problem therefore occurs as with several other studies in this field; he did not know if these tests can be used for predicting an ability to benefit well from education, at an early stage.

Also in this year, Schwarz (1963) reported on test construction in Nigeria for an American Aid for International Development project. Schwarz made an ambitious claim that 'the first major effort to develop such (ie selection) tests was begun in 1961 as part of the United States foreign aid programme'; this discounted the work of MacDonald, Scott, Brimble and Fontaine. However, Schwarz's project was certainly a large one and began by collecting not less than one million words uttered in Nigerian schools, to analyse which were frequent and which were rare. Using the most familiar vocabulary, twenty subtests were developed, and tried out on 15,000 examinees. The tests required a certain amount of apparatus and visual aids for their administration, a feature for which Schwarz had, however, criticised Biesheuvel's GAB. Schwarz's programme seems to have been planned as an on-going study, but regrettably no follow up papers by himself are well known (though see Silvey, below).

Schwarz's work probably influenced a project by Taylor and Bradshaw (1965) who also worked in Nigeria. Whereas Schwarz had had to devise elaborate ways of administering tests so that they might be fair to candidates with limited, or no schooling, Taylor and Bradshaw intended to cater for primary school leavers, who should be fairly familiar with the idea of tests or exams. Six subtests of tasks common in western tests were produced, though using contents familiar to Nigerians. These tests were given to 240 pupils, and more among the higher scorers were later found to have gained admission to secondary schools. This then, was a genuinely predictive finding.

Another true follow-up study was contributed by S. H. Irvine (1969a), who dealt with 1,842 pupils tested in Rhodesia and Uganda. Irvine showed that his tests could predict later performance in school; he also pointed to the fact (which it is the purpose of tests to try and counteract) that school quality would contribute to pupils' performance afterwards in exams, and this would affect success in careers. Irvine (1966) had already shown this phenomenon before, in Central Africa. He had found that a grading of primary school quality gave as good a correlation with future success as did Raven's Matrices results, while primary schools' Head teachers' ratings of pupils were still more predictive. In such a situation the strictly pragmatic approach which aims to produce 'high level manpower' in the most efficient way might decide to do without tests; but where a goal is also to give a chance to talented pupils from poor schools, the purpose of the test comes into its own. For example Pillner (1964) found in West Africa that teachers' evaluations varied in their quality; he considered that a combination of test results as well as knowledgeable ratings of pupil quality would be the best predictive combination.

Extensive research on the use of tests in selection has been done in Uganda. The New Zealander A. C. Somerset (1968) started by collecting results of the Junior School Leaving Exam (JSLE) done in 1960. Pupils had been selected by this for secondary schools, in which they took the Cambridge School Certificate (CSC) in 1964. Somerset showed that the JSLE was not an efficient predictor, in that people with borderline JSLE passes were equally likely to do poorly, or very well on CSC. However, pupils with good JSLE passes were likely to do well, not badly, at CSC. School quality influenced which ones of the poor JSLE pupils would do well, or badly, later on. Somerset correlated parts of the JSLE with success on different subjects in CSC, and drew policy recommendations from his results. He pointed out that a low priority given to elementary school development could reduce performance at higher level. But a broader policy issue to which this leads, is whether primary education and selection procedures should be improved in order to lead to good performance in higher education, or whether these primary educational facilities should be designed as ends in themselves. The point is, that for the present and the foreseeable future, over 90% of the population work on the land, and an educational system designed to produce industrial expertise may bypass socio-economic realities of the pace and nature of development, and even aggravate problems (see Chapter V).

Very similar questions were tackled by Jonathan Silvey (1972), who had been working in Uganda since the early 1960s. He had measures of pupils' abilities and school performance at the end of primary school, further tests at the end of Form I and even more at the end of Form IV of secondary school; Silvey was able to supplement Somerset's study by giving his own tests as well as having examination results. Silvey used Schwarz's tests for his S IV groups (taking CSC exams), with Matrices and other tests used at the primary leaving stage.

A test of Mental Age at Primary leaving was the best predictor of CSC performance, JSLE being closely behind, while Matrices scores were not related to CSC performance. Even when three primary leaving measures were statistically combined, the overall predictability of CSC remained low, with Matrices adding nothing to the predictive power of the other tests. Silvey examined how four sections of his sample fared on Schwarz's and other tests: those who were high on CSC and on JSLE, those who were low on both; those who were low on JSLE but high on CSC ('improvers'), and vice versa. Certainly the pupils who were better at both the JSLE and CSC stages, tended to score better on Schwarz's tests. But discriminating best in this way were tests of reading comprehension, scientific information, and clerical speed and accuracy. This measure of speed as a predictor of exam performance reflects the suggestions of Ombredane, Wober, and others, that a different approach to speed may be important in the ability to score well on Western tests. Silvey found that the 'better' schools probably did not influence success over and above the quality of the pupils they received, since as many of their better entrants declined, as their poorer recruits improved. In other words, the 'good' schools may not be good particularly because of their methods, but more because they recruit pupils of a better range of ability.

This section shows that tests are available which will predict which pupils are more likely to perform well later on. Correlations, hence predictive power, have not been high; particularly children tested early in the educational process can often show a surprising improvement over, or a disappointing failure to fulfil their early promise. All sorts of factors of health, family background, and school quality may upset predictability. One of the difficulties, as the previous section showed, is that an early test result is often not a good estimate of a pupil's potential abilities, which can be developed and disclosed better by more education, or even just by specific practice on tests or on related work. For this reason, ongoing studies like Silvey's are particularly important.

It is also important not to be misled by the argument put forward by Verhaegen (1967) who examined the percentage of pupils passing exams at the end of their first primary year, depending on their exact age of entry. He found that those aged 5 years and 9 months had the least proportion of success, which increased with age of entry, until 52% of those boys entering at 6.6 passed their exams a year later. Verhaegen inferred from this that it might be wise to increase the school-entering age; and in Tanzania, for politico-economic reasons this has been done, raising it to 7. But Verhaegen's own result also showed that there is no better (in fact slightly worse) a pass rate among those entering school aged 6.7 and 6.8. Thus it seems that 6½ is the best age at which to start school; but the other results in this section suggest that later academic success can not be predicted well by performance at an early age. Therefore policy based on Verhaegen's arguments would seem unwise. In fact the opposite case, that primary education should start as early as age 3 to combat the discouraging effects of many child-raising practices on cognitive development, was made by Okonji (1969b), and has considerable developmental, if not administrative, appeal.

The overall impression from selection tests is that though some degree of prediction is possible, the final outcome for pupils is still open to a considerable degree. Thus educational systems might ideally remain as flexible as possible, responding to the emerging needs and performance of individual students, rather than aiming for rigid procedures based on selection and allocation of pupils, which work best when potential can be accurately assessed early on. This last condition is far from being the case, as yet, in Africa.

Factor analysis of patterns of abilities

At their most sophisticated level researchers use tests to map out the patterns or structures of abilities which exist in people. For this purpose, researchers give people 'batteries' of tests (usually at least a dozen), and then apply a statistical procedure called 'factor analysis' to the results. This basically picks out whether certain sets of tests correlate well with each other, and poorly with the rest. These sets of tests thus form into 'families' of tests, or 'factors'. The researcher merely looks at each of such groups of tests, and gives a name to the aptitude which seems to be required by those tests as a group.

The statistical demands of factor analysis have meant that not many people have carried out such projects in Africa. Added to this, there is some doubt about what factor analysis can tell us. The implication is that the factors revealed are discoveries about people, and correspond to major directions or ways in which ability can be developed. However, Silvey (1963b) warned: 'one limitation of factor analysis must be pointed out at once. Factors ... are more useful in describing tests than in describing persons'. Silvey was suggesting that if a factor analysis is done in two cultures, based on the same tests in each, and if the results reveal the same factors in each project, this may not mean that the patterning of cognitive development is the same in both cultures, but merely that the tests were the same ones. No doubt Silvey's caution is not completely true; but it is certainly worth noting.

The dozen or so studies whose results are available for our consideration, are summarised in the Table.

One of the principal controversies in western research on abilities has been about whether one basic and general ability ('g') underlies each special skill, or whether the cognitive equipment consists of a set of largely distinct abilities (even though they may overlap somewhat). Most of the African studies have shown a general ability in some guise; Irvine's re-analysis of Brimble's work even points to two general type factors. This illustrates a negative aspect of this section of research literature. Investigators have challenged each other's work, not only in points of minor detail, but also as regard the major structural aspects of their findings. Unfortunately, the method of factor analysis is one that is not likely to appeal to a layman, as apparently very abstract technical treatment, and almost whimsical interpretation are mixed together. Thus Vernon (1950) analysed MacDonald's data and found three factors; one of these was a set of tests which just did not seem to tap similar abilities; so Vernon discarded this as illogical. El Abd also (1971) says at the outset of his report that his collection of eleven tests represented 'five mental abilities'; but his results pointed to seven factors, each of which, by implication, represents a 'mental ability'. Whether then the intellectual structure of East African post-graduates is supposed to consist of five, or of seven kinds of abilities is not clear.

Irvine (1969c) replaced Brimble's own analysis of data indicating two factors, with a new interpretation showing three. Two of the new factors, though not closely related in the mathematics of their results, nevertheless suggest a similar type of ability. It would be understandable therefore, for a lay reader to be sceptical of some, even though not all of this work. One untidy fact is that factors are not always discovered in similar orders of importance. Thus although several of Irvine's analyses reveal 'g' as the most important factor (as presumably, in its nature it should be), sometimes V:ed is more important than N:ed, and vice versa; while in Clive Jones' data from Kenya, Irvine finds 'g' only third in importance.

One of the factors Irvine demonstrated, he termed 'male educational information aptitude'. This means that boys tended to do better at most school subjects than girls; the phenomenon has been linked by Dawson (1967b) to a personality attribute termed 'field-independence', which he claimed to measure with tests like Raven's Matrices. Unfortunately, Raven's Matrices in Irvine's results appear to have no link with 'male educational aptitude', and this leaves a conundrum for further research to resolve. Other

TABLE 3

Summary of Results of Factor Analytic Research on Abilities in Africa

	Biesheuvel (1952)	Murray (1956)	Grant (1969)	Vernon (1950)	Vernon (1969)	Durand (1960)	Claeys (1972)
Author							
Country	South Africa	South Africa	South Africa	East Africa	Uganda	French West Africa	Zaire
Details	2 groups of: mineworkers motor workers. Tested with GAB (five sub-tests)	MA Thesis 119 workers tested with 19 tests	90 mine recruits given five new tests, and GAB (five sub-tests) elaborate inst. ensure overlearning	Analysis of tests by MacDonald. Calculations showed three factors, but one discarded as illogical	Mainly Baganda primary pupils. No 'g' factor appeared	475 subjects four separate analyses.	102 primary school teachers.
Results (Factor names)	both studies find: 1. General factor 2. Doublet for Sorting Tests	Three factors appeared, but reduced by simple statistical examination, to one factor. Study challenged as inadequate by *Grant*.	1. Pattern analysis and synthesis. 2. Speed of perception	1. General adaptability (*not* identified with 'g', as this factor includes dexterity). 2. A Bipolar Cognitive ('g') – physical manipulative factor. *reanalysed* by Grant: 1. 'g' 2. Dexterity	1. Verbal: educational ability. 2. 'Induction' factor (abstraction, Matrices, Piaget tests). 3. Resourcefulness 4. Perceptual-practical ability. ('Quite distinct from educational attainments')	1. General efficiency. 2. School knowledge. *Reanalysed*, without school tests: 1. General ability. 2. Speed. *Reanalysed*, school tests only: 1. Knowledge. 2. Mechanical-spatial ability. *Reanalysed*, with school exam criteria. 1. Speed. 2. Acculturation. 3. Perceptual ability.	1. School skills 2. General ability. 3. Perceptual analysis ability. 4. Abstraction ability. 5. Impulsivity. 1, 2, and 4 considered as facets of 'original general ability'. 3, and 5 seen as cognitive westernisation.

TABLE 3 *(continued)*

Summary of Results of Factor Analytic Research on Abilities in Africa

Author	*Country*	*Details*	*Results (Factor names)*
Irvine (1969c)	Zambia & Rhodesia	1615 (R) & 684 (Z) Standard VI pupils.	1. Reasoning (g) 2. 'N:ed' (numeracy learnt in school) 3. 'V:ed' (verbal skills taught in schools) 4. 'Male educational aptitude.' 'Both analyses show the extraction of four factors, accounting for 64% of total variance.'
Irvine (1969c)	Zambia	Mine youth (failed to enter Secondary School) 72 young men.	1. Reasoning (g) 2. V:ed 3. N:ed 4. Perceptual ability. These four factors account for 66% of the total variance.
Irvine (1969c)	Zambia	Form 2 School Children.	1. Reasoning (g) 2. N:ed 3. V:ed 4. Mechanical spatial ability.
Jones (in Irvine, 1969c)	Kenya	Forms 2, 3, and 4 185 boys.	1. N:ed 2. Clerical Perceptual ability. 3. G. 4. V:ed
MacDonald (in Irvine, 1969c)	East Africa	Military Recruits (1855); 13 tests.	1. General reasoning 2. Mechanical spatial ability. 3. 'Physical factor with a strong manual dexterity component.'
Brimble (in Irvine, 1969c)	Zambia	Brimble himself indicated two factors, but Irvine points to three.	1. Reasoning A. 2. Reasoning B. 3. Perceptual ability.
Somerset (1968)	Uganda	Not a true factor analysis, but a similar treatment of a set of correlations.	1. g 2. Numerical Sciences. 3. Descriptive sciences. 4. Arts-evaluative studies
El Abd (1971)	Uganda	'Eleven tests representing five mental abilities' 32 Post-graduate Students.	1. g 2. Verbal Comprehension. 3. Numerical facility. 4. Perceptual Speed. Three other factors also claimed.

anomalies also remain to be resolved or explained. The major criticism of factor analysis however, is Silvey's point, repeated also by Grant (1969a). The factors got out depend considerably on the tests put into a project. Grant despatches an attempt by Murray to infer that a simple factor solution reflected a simple structure of mental abilities among the subjects. More likely, this reflected an over-simple research approach.

The over-all conclusion therefore seems to be that abilities among Africans tested seem to be underlain by a general ability factor, as well as to manifest themselves in special ways. A few investigators point to motivation or speed as a factor discovered (e.g. Durand, Grant, Claeys), while some also mention westernisation through education (Irvine, Durand) as characterising factors of ability.

Overview

The question intriguing most early investigators in this area was whether African groups were less intellectually developed than people in Western cultures. Previous chapters mentioned how intellectual limitation was thought to relate to harsh weaning, or to inadequate stimulus from parents in the early pre-school years. This chapter mentions the folklore that intellectual damage, or blockage might commonly occur at puberty, linked with initiation rites. The puberty hypothesis was already old when Audrey Richards (1932), the anthropologist was probably one of the first to raise the harsh weaning hypothesis; while early childhood experience has more recently been studied as the foundation of cognitive development. All these ideas have one basic element in common however. This is that there is something to explain, and that is that African adults seemed often not to shine with what westerners observed, defined, and measured as 'intelligence'.

African psychologists such as Otaala (1971) and Yoloye (1971) acknowledge the broad evidence that most African groups have not scored well on western tests, and this evidence is referred to in the first section of this chapter. Fick and Van Rensburg tried to infer that low scores meant that Africans were inherently inferior; but Biesheuvel and Winterbottom exposed the false reasoning here. Not only was it not possible to have 'culture-free' tests of any really intellectual task, it was also not really possible to have 'culture-fair' tests.

Testers later looked at results in a more diagnostic fashion, as indicators of the ways in which abilities developed and were applied to tasks in life, among the kinds of peoples tested. Dent, Heuse, Ombredane and others all pointed to slowness in dealing with tests (not to be confused with error); Wober, and Irvine indicated that certain African cultures may have a conception of how best to apply the mind, that respected slowness (much as the Romans respected 'gravitas'), while Serpell pointed to an interest in cooperation as an attribute of mental ability. What few psychologists have pointed out, or sought, are tests appropriate to the abilities that certain cultures do specifically develop.

Other factors determining the development of abilities have included social class (as in Bakare's study of the Draw-a-man test) while Durojaiye's work in Uganda has pointed to the role of parental behaviour and attitudes. One important facet of the home environment concerns the languages used; each language probably registers an influence of the culture with which it is associated. Davitz found no overall differences between Ugandan boys tested in Luganda and in English, but verbal performance was better when they were tested in Luganda. Yoloye found that pupils in higher classes, knowing more English, showed much more improvement in verbal tests than had occurred with non-verbal tests.

A basic question that concerns any test is whether it is reliable. Many researchers have found that, unlike among western groups in whom these skills are 'overlearned', among African groups, retesting often reveals substantial gains in scores. This has been seen with coaching, with special instructions, among youth and among adults. Eventually, however, even strange tests measure real differences in personal abilities. This knowledge is then useful; it can help predict which pupils are likely to do better in further education. Though pupils from good schools may do better overall, nevertheless tests may be fairer measures of abilities than are measures of school attainment, such as exam results in various subjects. It has been shown, for example by Taylor and Bradshaw, Irvine, and Silvey, that tests adapted from well-known western ones can be useful in selection; others, especially Schwarz, and Scott, have shown that tests based on local ideas and ingredients are particularly likely to be good measures of real ability. It is therefore technically possible for African countries to improve the efficiency of producing 'high level manpower', even though there are powerful pressures which work to get around objectively defined systems, in the interests of special factions. This is not a strictly psychological, but a sociological and political problem.

Finally, factor analysis has been used as a pure research procedure. It appears to show that there is a general factor of ability that underlies other special directions of cognitive development; but that some of the latter are also discernible. The more educated the groups tested, the more the factors discovered resemble what has been found, in testing in western countries. One reservation to this tentative conclusion that Africans' patterns of abilities resemble Europeans', is that the tests used in these studies have nearly all been verbal or visual in their modality (see Chapter V). Thus since the researchers have not been really looking for structures of cognitive development patterned differently than in Western cultures, it is not surprising that such specifically African patterns have not been found. The topic is a controversial one, as there are strands of opinion in Africa which seek to assert a universalistic philosophy, that mankind is equal and Africans are basically like others in potential; while others wish to confirm that Africans have their own nature, which may include specific structures of patterns of abilities. The available research results do not disturb the first kind of assertion, while the next chapter certainly suggests that several researchers have thought that such specific structures may be there to be found.

CHAPTER IV

SPECIAL DIFFICULTIES

Introduction

The last chapter has shown broadly that on many western tests, African groups, even educated ones, have tended to score lower or work slower than western adult groups. As to explaining this phenomenon, some have pointed out that it is invalid to compare scores in one culture, on tests devised in and for a foreign culture, and comparisons of scores between cultural groups are fairly meaningless. Others have held (a recent exponent being Carothers, 1972) that notwithstanding the strangeness of tests, the level of scores often shown by African groups gives some cause for concern. It remains to discover the cause of low scores, and efforts to link it with lack of schooling, or other environmental difficulties have been described.

The chapter has also described the paradox in which the tests which western scientists thought might be 'culture-free' sometimes turned out to be the opposite; they were even more sensitive to cultural factors evidently common in Africa, which made it particularly difficult for Africans to do well on these tests. The western assumption had been that since verbal tests refer to objects and processes familiar in one culture but not necessarily in another, such tests were culture-bound. It appeared to follow that non-verbal tests, using diagrams or drawings as symbols for elements of problems, might be more culture-fair. This is one reason why tests like Raven's Matrices were so widely used. But for some reason which is still not well understood, many Africans found the 'language' of visual symbols to be particularly awkward to work with.

Factor analysts have suggested that the 'structure' of abilities among Africans is similar to that among westerners. However, the similarities have been demonstrated only at a very general level; that is, the same ingredients have been found among Africans' abilities as among westerners'. But two further complexities may arise. First, among Africans some abilities may be more or less strongly developed than among westerners. Second, the tests given may have totally ignored particular special abilities that may exist among Africans, and therefore these ingredients or 'factors' have not appeared in the results of research so far. This second possibility is quite plausible; for if certain abilities have not been well developed in western cultures, then appropriate tests for them will not have been devised either.

It seems therefore, the western psychologists in Africa may have concentrated on testing for certain abilities which are not strongly developed among African cultures; and possibly, they have missed out research on abilities which may be well developed in Africa. There may be two types of reason for this state of affairs. The first is that western psychologists have learned to seek out those special abilities which foster quick progress in developing a technological society. Secondly western psychologists may have reflected the perceptions of the colonial situation; by concentrating on tests on which Africans do poorly, and ignoring tests on which they might do well, westerners have provided data which appeared to justify western colonial power. This may have come about through sub-conscious preferences for looking for suitable evidence. But a problem arises for Africans here. This is that even though it may have suited westerners to document certain weaknesses, these will not simply vanish or become irrelevant because colonialism has ended. African psychologists have been extremely realistic about this problem and have concentrated on working on ways to remedy any areas of special difficulties. So work should continue to develop on what has gone before. Most 'hard' evidence we have, concerns the areas of difficulty or less well developed skills. The area of specially well developed abilities is more a question of reasonable hypothesis so far. Therefore we shall deal first with the difficulties, and then come to the unprospected assets.

Difficulties with visual representation
   The psychologist who introduced the questions we shall consider here, was W. Hudson, in South Africa. He declared that 'western culture is primarily a visual culture' (Hudson, 1962a); by this, he meant that a great proportion of communication is provided for the eye to receive and then the brain to interpret. A great deal depends on understanding the symbols which constitute writing, and much also depends on being able to use pictures, diagrams and illustrations.
   Early travellers in Africa realised that pictures impressed people who had never seen them before in a novel way. Verney Lovat Cameron (1877), travelling in Tanzania reported of a chief whom he met that 'he recognised some pictures of animals which we showed him, but invariably looked at the back of the paper to see what was there, and remarked that he did not consider them finished since they did not give the likeness of the other side of the animal'. Hudson (1962a) noted that western artists (and photographers) mostly show what they *see* and not what they *know* about an object, or scene; he also reported (Hudson, 1962b) in drawings from Africans, that some African artists showed details of the unseen side of an object – or even of its insides (in the case of one who drew the intestines of an elephant). These people, like Cameron's acquaintance, expected pictures to show what they *knew* about an object, and not be restricted to what one could *see* at any one moment.
   Franke (1915) studied drawings from 233 subjects in the Congo and Tanzania, finding that they did not reveal the same conventions expected in western pictures. Such differences unfortunately led other western observers to generalise too far, and we see for example Dudley Kidd (1925) writing that 'the natives are frequently quite incapable of seeing pictures at first and wonder what the smudge on the paper is there for. When they see that it represents something they are very excited'. The same impression, of the strangeness, and sometimes the incomprehensibility of pictures is described by Herskovits (1950), an American anthropologist with West and Central African experience. Herskovits' most celebrated example, of an old woman who evidently failed to recognise her own son in a photograph, was however

encountered in South America. Africans themselves have sometimes referred
to difficulties with picture interpretation: a Cameroonian novelist, describing
his hero's visit to a village mentions that the villagers 'begged me to teach
them to read, write, do sums and understand the pictures in their books'
(Mongo Beti, 1957).

This loose conclusion, that Africans might not be able to recognise
pictures, was not, however, universal. Adolphe Cureau (1915) a French
administrator in Central Africa wrote 'the Negro perfectly understands any
engravings or photographs which one shows him'. There was plenty of
evidence, also, to support this conclusion. As reported in Chapter I, Geber
(1958) described an infant who obviously recognised, and tried to grasp a
bowl shown in a photograph; Cowley and Murray (1962) also successfully
used pictures which infants recognised. More systematically among adults,
Brimble (1963) prepared two sheets of drawings which he showed to 1,648
uneducated people from 45 villages on the Great Barotse plain in Zambia.
Among the 670 women, 94% correctly identified all the 40 itmes shown on
one sheet. The men showed an even higher incidence of correct answers.
Pettigrew, Allport and Barnett (1958) showed photographs of faces to
uneducated Zulus in South Africa, and made no mention of difficulties in
using these materials.

Most recently Jan Deregowski, a British psychologist of Polish origin, with
American colleagues (Deregowski, Muldrow and Muldrow 1972) showed that
among 35 people of the remote Me'en tribe of Ethiopia, there was little
difficulty in recognising that a picture was a picture. Some were, however,
nervous about the properties and perhaps the potency of the strange object.
Did the impression, then, that uneducated Africans could not tell what a
picture was arise from chancing upon atypical subjects? To begin to clarify
the issues, Deregowksi (1968a) distinguished between *detection, recognition,*
and *identification* of elements in pictures. Detection consists simply of
realising that one is not looking at meaningless blotches on paper, but of
realising that they represent something meaningful. Recognition means that a
person can match a picture of an object with the object; identification goes
further and means that the viewer can name the object which the artist or
photographer has pictured. It is not now believed that Africans, however
uneducated, cannot detect what a picture is. But a mass of work does exist on
the many conditions in which Africans misidentify pictures; that is, they may
not interpret pictures in the same way that the artists or photographers have
intended.

In the late 1940s, Biesheuvel in South Africa, while trying to use pictures
in tests, came upon examples of misinterpretation. In one picture, a speaker
outside a factory harangued a group of workers. In the background, shown
small, stood the factory with three smoking chimneys. On paper, the
speaker's hands were shown outstretched above the distant chimneys. Several
factory workers said the speaker was a madman, who had climbed to the
roofs to warm his hands at the smoke. Hudson (1967) realised that a
difficulty lay in interpreting the conventions of showing perspective, and
distance in pictures, and took the useful step of constructing a test to study
how people interpret depth shown in pictures. Line drawings of scenes

involving an African hunter (with spear about to be thrown), an elephant, an
antelope, and a tree were drawn. The figures always appear in the same
positions on the paper; but outlines of hills, a road and the horizon can be
put in as desired in separate drawings. Answers to questions about the
position of items in the picture (e.g. which animal is nearer to the hunter, or
which one is he trying to shoot) 'were taken as self-evident indications of
two-dimensional or three-dimensional pictorial perception'.

Figure 1.

Figure 2.

Figure 3.

Three of the Figures devised by Hudson, for his
test

Hudson's original paper on this (Hudson, 1960) presented results from a group of different races, ages, levels of education and occupation. African secondary pupils, and even some graduates did not all interpret the pictures in the conventional western three-dimensional ('3-d') manner. Hudson therefore believed that apart from education, a western 3-d style of perception might be related to 'other cultural factors in the environment'. As white labourers (Mundy-Castle and Nelson, 1962) also 'saw the pictures flat', however, Hudson says this style of interpreting pictures 'cannot be explained away on ethnic grounds'. It can hardly be supposed that style of picture interpretation is somehow genetically linked with bodily physical differences; therefore a non-3-d perception must be due to educational, or cultural conditions, or both. What we must note, which Hudson has not made clear, is that it is possible for non-3-d interpretation to occur not only because something is *absent*, but perhaps also because something may be *present* (i.e. particular cultural factors, as yet unclarified, among Africans).

Two attempts were made by non-psychologists to explain Africans' own style of appraising pictures as something positive from Africans' cultures, rather than resulting from an absence of western influence. Du Toit (1966) suggested that linguistic structures might enable people easily to deal with questions like what? why? and how? concerning things, rather than where? This is not much different from Hudson's comment about Africans seeing pictured objects for what they are, rather than how they look. However, Hudson (1967) dismisses Du Toit's idea because it fails to explain why white labourers, who did not speak African languages, nevertheless got low scores on the 3-d test. We are not, however, told about the nature of the labourers' errors. If Du Toit is correct, white labourers might get low 3-d scores, but for different reasons than the Africans; they should thus show different kinds of error. Unfortunately, Hudson does not provide the details to clarify this issue.

The second idea was raised by Littlejohn (1963), which Hudson does not mention. Littlejohn studied the Temne of Sierra Leone and found them to have an organised, meaningful but non-western way of comprehending the space they inhabit. They, and similar people therefore, should naturally expect pictures to 'work' in a different manner than is conventional in western culture.

Littlejohn writes that 'the space Temne inhabit is neither homogeneous or isotropic,' (ie it is not of even consistency or extension, like still water, or air, but that it is 'lumpy'). He continues: 'it is divided into regions with some differing qualities ... the first which is open to human perception and the other three which are not ... ordinary Temne space is neither arithmetically measured nor geometrically analysed... For us the cardinal points (ie N S E W) are co-ordinates for establishing location ... their cardinal points contain meanings which qualify activities and events in various ways. . .'.

Littlejohn continues: 'Temne space is not the featureless container of things it is for us ... instead it falls round them in meanings read off from the physiognomy of landscape and the human body, combined with images embodying notions of good and evil'. Littlejohn seems to be saying that whereas for westerners, *space* consists of extension in three 'dimensions' each of the same quality of distance, but not of time, or spiritual or social elements, for Temnes, space is a concept integrated with social and spiritual dimensions. This may be very difficult for westerners to grasp, or even accept without grasping it. By and large, however, western psychologists have not been open to this line of enquiry, even though it clearly suggests that Temnes would have different ways of looking at the significance and meaning of pictures, than westerners have.

Numerous studies have extended Hudson's work in other parts of Africa. Mundy-Castle (1966) tested 122 primary school children in Ghana, with four pictures from Hudson's set. He found that correct identification of items was most likely with objects with familiar names (like locally common animals); identification was least likely with a depiction of a more abstract concept, such as the horizon. Mundy-Castle found only minor differences in interpretation among children of different ages (hence school classes) and concluded that cultural stimulus in the home and society is crucial for prompting a western style of depth interpretation of pictures. It could also be, of course, that schooling was of a poor standard, particularly in this special skill, so that simply spending more years there is not likely to be of any effect.

Edward Abiola (1966) tested children in Nigeria with Hudson's pictures; boys had higher 3-d scores than girls, and European and Nigerian professional families' children had higher scores than poor families' children. Abiola says his samples were matched for 'intelligence and final educational standard'; he does not explain how they were matched for intelligence (and the previous Chapter should suggest how hard this would be) but one may assume that the groups were composed of children who had similar scores on a verbal test. Abiola's work is important for at least two reasons. As he was a Nigerian, it is less likely that his results might be criticised for having failed to explain the test or to understand children's replies properly. Second, if children of similar verbal intelligence score very differently on a pictorial test, it suggests that the latter involves a very specific skill; and that since the schooling which produces equal intelligence has somehow failed to promote 3-d interpretation, 3-d style is indeed culturally influenced. Something in indigenous culture (mostly Yoruba, in Abiola's research) does not hamper verbal intelligence, but does keep western 3-d interpretation from developing.

The husband and wife team of Ruth and Robert Munroe (1969) showed Logoli children in Kenya a short test based on two of Hudson's pictures. Logoli primary school leavers had results similar to those of American pre-school children (aged 5 and 6). The Munroes point particularly to the greater number of Logoli boys using a 3-d inference style, and add that both education, and cultural experience of pictorial materials are probably important in determining inference style.

Several studies have observed the distinction between the problem of recognition, and that of 3-d inference. Sometimes these issues overlap; Hudson's, Mundy-Castle's and other subjects have named a line intended to be the outline of a hill, as a snake; a road receding into the distance has been called poles, or a ladder, or an elephant trap. As Mundy-Castle pointed out, such 'errors' (which are not errors in the subject's view, but the artist's) are partly due to the attention the child gives to constructing a dramatic account of what the picture shows him. So it is important to distinguish how far recognition can be accurate, if it is not mixed up with questions of three dimensional space *between* objects. For we must accept, before going any further, that if children can identify solid, three-dimensional objects in pictures, we are not dealing with a total failure to realise that a 2-dimensional picture on paper represents 3-dimensional space.

Deregowski (1968a) showed 27 schoolchildren and seven adults both models of animals, and photographs of the models. Six models were of animals familiar in Zambia (eg zebra, elephant), while the others were unfamiliar (eg camel, polar bear). Subjects had to point to a model which each photograph showed. First, there was no trouble in *detecting* pictures; if some people could not detect that photographs were pictures, they would make errors randomly, but this did not happen. Secondly, unfamiliar animals were more difficult to *recognise* than familiar ones. This is not a question of naming them, but of matching the photograph image with the solid object.

Part of one of the 'Hidden animals' pictures used by Wober for his test
(see p. 86)

Deregowski (1971a) returned to this question of pictorial recognition, this time in an experiment with 80 women living in a poor district of Lusaka. There were ten toys (animals and cars) and two photographs of each toy. Subjects were given either a toy, or a picture, and asked to point to a corresponding picture. More errors were made when women had to match a picture and an object, than when they had to match two pictures. Deregowski therefore does not think that there are substantial difficulties in detection or recognition of what pictures show. He considers that errors arise at a more abstract level: 'difficulties stem from the very fact that ... subjects were requested to cross the boundaries between two radically different sets of objects'. Why this may be so, remains for further research to clarify.

Other data from Nigeria deal with *identification* of pictorial items (Wober, 1966c). Drawings of animals were 'hidden' in the convoluted forms of two forest-scene pictures. Subjects were industrial workers, who named as many objects they saw, including animals, as they could. Strictly speaking, the detection being examined here, was different from Deregowski's concept; for workers were not pointing out that a whole collection of marks was a picture — most of them took that for granted. They were however, detecting hidden items; correlations show that men with more education, or who had high scores on Raven's Matrices and other tests, also detected more animals. Correct identification happened with two thirds of the items detected. Errors of identification included one which called a tortoise a flower pot, though a tortoise is a locally familiar animal. The giraffe, unfamiliar in West Africa, was often called a horse, antelope, or goat. The size of an object as drawn on paper was often not a guide to identification. Just as we do not require the word 'chicken' to be smaller than 'lion', so people need not require a drawing that they will call a chicken to be drawn smaller than one they will call a lion. That is, unless there are recognised rules of size and perspective; but as we are learning, such rules do not readily apply in many situations in Africa.

Misidentification, then, can be readily found, especially with less educated observers, and with pictures that involve distracting elements, camouflage, or unfamiliar pictorial conventions (such as the horizon line). Una MacLean (1960), working on health education in Nigeria, found that printed handbills were a more efficient means of communication than pictures. The latter were misunderstood, but literate people were pleased to show their skill and explain texts to eager listeners. Wendy Winter (1963) found much misidentification of industrial safety posters, especially of unfamiliar western symbols such as a skull and crossbones for danger, and the colour red which has a particular social significance in Zulu society. In some cases depth cues actually misled some people. The more educated workers understood the pictures better. Holmes (1964) found similar difficulties in Kenya, and that the amount of detail in pictures influenced their comprehension. More detail does not always help identification, as Chaplin (1969) reported from Uganda. She presented line drawings, each one with a little more detail added, and found that a 'house' consisting merely of a square with a triangle placed over it was identified by the whole sample as a house; but a 'house' drawn in perspective, with window, door, and boarded roof shown converging to the far end was recognised by fewer children as a house.

A pair of 'psychological anthropologists' (Kilbride and Robbins, 1969) set out to examine Hudson's case that 'the critical threshold (for determining how people interpret pictures) is cultural, and not educational'. They showed that Kampala residents identified objects more correctly overall than did rural people. When rural and urban groups were subdivided according to amount of education, it was the rural members in each who made fewer correct identifications of pictured objects. This itself does not clearly separate effects of education and culture, because the rural people who have a similar 'level of education' on paper, have been to much inferior schools. However, when taking the rural people only, there was a tendency for those with the habit of wearing the *kanzu* (a traditional gown, very characteristic of a less westernised approach to life) to identify fewer pictorial items correctly. This is a pointer only, in favour of Kilbride and Robbins' argument; for it is quite possible that *kanzu* wearers had received a lower quality of western education, than non-wearers.

Chaplin too, used 20 of her pictures to form a test, given to 118 children aged from 3 to 13 in Kampala schools. Correct identification scores were weakly correlated with socio-economic status (0.22), likewise with tests of verbal fluency and teacher's rating of the child's intelligence; but a very large correlation (0.84) appeared with educational level. Children were asked in Luganda *why* they identified certain drawings in the way they did; 50% 'could not answer the question at all' and Chaplin infers that 'the differences (in pictures) must have been noticed only in a subconscious way and could not be described in terms available to them'. Whatever this means, it does point to the difficulty of trying to identify reasons why people misidentify picture items. Probably the best way ahead is by ingenious experiment, rather than by asking children questions which make them socially uncomfortable, and which they then may answer in ways which are not entirely related to how they see the actual pictures they are shown. This idea has been expressed in French by Francine Robaye (1959) when discussing Professor Ombredane's experiments on Congolese adults' perception of films. Robaye found that the Africans'

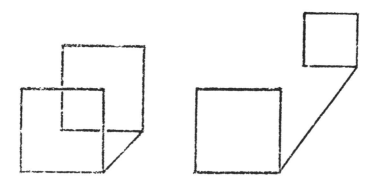

Two of the diagrams used by Deregowski in his construction task (see p. 88)

understanding of what they saw was direct, and related to their interests; she wrote (my translation) 'the misunderstandings of the Africans are most often a function of our incomprehension of their motivations and of their defenses in their encounters with the whites. . '.

The most extensive series of experiments on picture perception in Africa is probably that by Deregowski, in Zambia. In one study (Deregowski, 1968c) groups of schoolboys and of domestic servants saw geometrical drawings, and were asked to 'build what you see on the picture with bamboo splints.' Preliminary construction tasks had accustomed candidates to making models (including a triangle, and 3-dimensional pyramid) with the splints and small pieces of plasticene. While in preliminary tasks, subjects made models to copy models, the experiment consisted of seeing how they would copy diagrams. The resulting models were judged to be 3-dimensional if all the splints did not lie within two parellel planes ½ inch apart. Since splints were at least 5 inches long, a person would have to be quite determined if he really intended to make a 2-d model.

While very few people gave 3-d interpretations on Hudson's test, over half made models which were judged as 3-d. Now since Deregowski as an afterthought distinguished between 'correct' and 'incorrect' 3-d models, this seems to acknowledge the possibility that people built 3-d models sometimes by mistake, or because it is really harder to make a 2-d model. Deregowski infers that 'a subject can not be classified as a 2-d perceiver . . . merely because he is a 2-d perceiver as far as Hudson's test is concerned'. This is certainly a wise caution, even though it does not emerge convincingly from this experiment. For example, Hudson's test explores subjects' tendencies to interpret the space which a picture suggests exists between separate objects; while Deregowski's construction test explores people's ability to construct a model of a single continuous object. Deregowski also claims that his results have 'thrown doubt on Littlejohn's suggestion that misperception of depth cues in pictures is a result of a different concept of space'. Deregowski argues that if people have a certain conception of space which leads to low scores on Hudson's test, then it should also lead to 2-d and not 3-d models on his construction task. However, it is not clear whether people made 3-d models because of the conception of space, or for other reasons, such as that it was more difficult to make 2-d models. Thus Littlejohn's idea probably survives Deregowski's attempt to dispose of it.

A later experiment (Deregowski, 1969) also threw doubt on his interpretation of his construction test. The method was to show an 'impossible figure' (a two-pronged trident) and ask people to draw a copy of it. People who got 3-d scores on the construction test were expected to notice the ambiguity of the figure, and have more difficulty in copying it. However, 3-d and 2-d scorers on the construction test made drawings of similar quality. This could be because, as suggested here, some people who make 3-d models do so accidentally, since it is more difficult to make a 3-d model; such people would react similarly to the impossible figure, as those who made 2-d models.

Another experiment by Deregowski (1968b) used a toy Land Rover, mounted on a card and photographed from three different positions, in turn. Primary schoolboys from a 'high density suburban housing estate' were

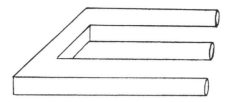

The 'two-pronged trident' shown by Deregowski
(see p. 88)

shown the pictures, and asked to place the toy car in exactly the position shown in each picture. They were best able to do this when the picture had been taken from the same position facing the board, as that in which they were sitting. Otherwise, large errors in positioning were found in a direction which made it seem as though subjects took their angle of view to be the same as the camera's. Deregowski likens this to Piaget's idea of 'egocentrism', in which the observer assumes that other eyes (and cameras) see the world from the same position in space as that which he himself occupies. This is essentially a view which is 'embedded' in its concept of space, rather than detached from it. A variation of this experiment used a model of a cowboy ('hunter') and buffaloes instead of the Land Rover. Deregowski suggests that the meaningfulness of the scene has more effect on pupils when they place the hunter, than occurred in the case of the car. This curiously implies that the Land Rover was less 'meaningful' to urban children than a scene involving cowboy and buffaloes. It is clear however, that errors in positioning photographed objects have been demonstrated.

A 'chain-type' drawing of elephants,
used by Deregowski
(see below)

An uncertainty concerning the angle of regard of the artist, or viewer of a picture, occurred in Hudson's (1962b) report of drawings showing both sides of an animal at once. Deregowski (1970) supported this by showing drawings of elephants seen either from the front, or the side; others were 'chain-type-drawings' (see illustration) which could be understood as showing two sides of the same elephant. Deregowski wrote: 'rural Zambian women . . . were found to prefer a chain type drawing to a front view drawing'. A difficulty in interpreting this is that some highly educated people also prefer such drawings, whose style has been popularised by Picasso and other famous western artists.

Recently, Deregowski and Byth (1970) tried to measure the extent of 'depth perception' with a piece of sophisticated optical apparatus they called 'Pandora's Box'. The subject looks into the apparatus, and sees the experimental pictures 'as a network of black lines against a pale green luminous field'. A spot of light can be brought to focus on any line chosen by the subject turning a knob. From the mechanism, the actual distance from the eye at which the spot exists, when focussed, can be read off. Zambian servants were shown the man, elephant and antelope of Hudson's pictures, and their relative distances were estimated from the focussed positions of the light spot as 0.95 cm separate in 'perceived relative depth'. For Europeans the elephant and the antelope were 1.14 cm separate likewise. Neither of these depths, even though they may be different from each other, approaches zero. Therefore it is surprising that Deregowski and Byth write that 'depth perception as measured by Pandora's Box does occur in the European sample but not in the Zambian sample,' who remain 'solidly 2-d'. What indeed could be inferred about the depth perception tendencies of people who use the literary contradiction 'solidly 2-d'!

Two investigators have explored links between educational experience, other abilities, and the ability to interpret depth in pictures. Philip Kilbride (1970) made up his own test of 3-d pictorial interpretation, using locally taken photographs, in Uganda. His test was given to nearly 200 people, while no less than 720 people did Hudson's test. Kilbride also devised an index of 'phenomenal modernisation', which counts physical evidence of westernisation, such as possession of gadgets (eg TV, camera), also pastimes such as cinema attendance, and occupation and amount of schooling. One notion often put forward by testers in Africa was somewhat discredited by some of Kilbride's evidence; this is, that uneducated Africans usually have no pictures in their homes. But Kilbride reports that one peasant farmer had:

> Four photographs (of self or friends), calendar pictures of Pope Paul
> and another, one polychrome painting, magazine or colour cutouts of
> Gina Lollobrigida, a Blonde girl, a Black girl, the British Royal Family
> and a civet cat.

Results showed that 3-d style of inference as well as correct identification of elements in photographs, correlated strongly with the modernisation score. This is all straightforward, since modernisation as defined overlaps considerably with formal education. A more penetrating task is to try and find whether education operates on people who are ready to form whatever style of inference is being taught; or whether education has to work against a positive tendency, embedded in the cultural context, against interpretation in the 3-d style conventional in western pictures.

Elsewhere, Kilbride, Robbins and Freeman (1968) showed that among Baganda school children, education and Hudson's test 3-d scores were significantly correlated. More usefully, they noted that the cue of object size (a smaller shown object is assumed to be further away) became used for 3-d inference somewhat later in educational experience than the cue of superimposition (overlap suggests that a hidden object is further away from the viewer than the one obscuring his view). Kilbride and Robbins (1968) alone gave data from 523 Baganda aged from 4 to 75; they showed that use of the perspective cue (like roads, or railway lines which are in reality parallel pairs of lines, but shown on paper as converging into the distance) is also correlated with educational experience. In both these studies, even when results were studied for people of similar ages, the relationship between pictorial inference style, and education still existed. This showed that education itself is a potent influence on style. However, having tested such large numbers of people, another comparison could have been made, to more purpose. They could have analysed results for people of equal levels of education; if now, age had no relation with 3-d scores, then education would be seen as a principal element in determining style; but if Littlejohn's hypothesis is correct, then, for a given educational level, the older people, who have absorbed more traditional culture, might have lower 3-d scores.

Phyllis Ikua (1971) in a new approach asked primary school children in Kenya to put sets of pictures, like simple comic strips, into the right order. Children had to say what was in the pictures, and also to make 2-d or 3-d inferences. Ikua, who conducted the testing herself, in Kikuyu, found that the largest improvements in correct identification, and in setting pictures in 'correct' story order, occurred between non-school, and PI children. Inference of pictorial depth began to change later, between P II and P III.

Training of 3-d inference style was one of the important contributions by John Dawson (1967a, b). First of all he showed, among several groups of Temne and Mende workers, that 3-d inference style (on Hudson's test) was correlated with tests which he claimed measured an entity called 'field independence'. Thus the 3-d scores correlated (for 99 males) 0.41 with a

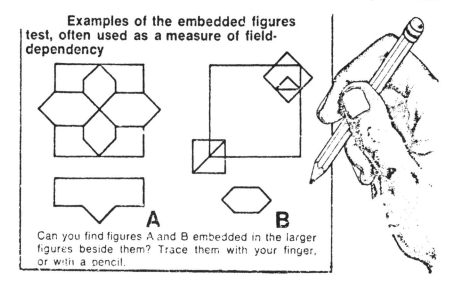

Examples of the Embedded Figures Test (EFT) — used by Dawson (see p. 92)

verbal measure of intelligence, 0.64 with Koh's Blocks, and 0.66 with the Embedded Figures Test (EFT). There was also a correlation of 0.88 between EFT and a retest score on 3-d inference. All of this supports two themes discussed in Chapter 3; one concerning certain patterning of abilities, and the other holding that retest scores are more valid measures than first tests. Now, observing that 3-d inference style had its roots in the matrix of social and perceptual experience (since he had shown that field independence was related to reported parental strictness), Dawson tried a training experiment. Twelve trade apprentices were matched on Koh's Blocks, and 3-d test scores, with a second group. The first, experimental group received eight weekly, one hour training sessions using a variety of aids of photographs and films. The experimental group later had significantly higher 3-d scores, while the control group did not alter. There was not a complete switch from one inference style to another. The experimental group had an average, after training, of 3.8 out of 9.0 possible points. Thus while some researchers have referred to people who 'are 2-d in pictorial inference', such blanket statements are misleading. If they were strictly correct, people would score 0 out of 9; or 9 out of 9 if they were '3-d in inference style'. In fact, most people score in between, showing that in some cases they make 3-d inferences, while in other cases they do not.

Since Dawson supplied a plentiful amount of training, but still did not alter pictorial inference style to be predominantly 3-d, this suggests that though education is effective, it has to work against some cultural complex of attitudes to space and how it 'works' and is filled, that has not been adequately studied by psychologists. One indirect psychological approach to this question was made by the Ghanaian social psychologist, Susan Gilbertson (1970). She tested Accra children from three socio-economic levels, divided within each class into half who watched television and half who did not. She found differences in attitudes towards cultural questions posed in a questionnaire, but no differences in 3-d inference (with Hudson's test) between TV watchers and non-watchers. Thus experience with TV may first interact with attitudes, but familiarity with moving pictures does not in itself enhance 3-d inference. It may therefore be that it needs a combination of cultural change, and purposive pictorial training to produce complete 3-d inference style.

Two studies which partly weaken the role being attributed to culture, here, were done by the South African, Schepers (1969) and his student Miss C. J. Hyde. Schepers used a figure showing a grid of lines, and with diagonals leading from the corners to the centre. Over 100 African labourers were asked how they saw this grid, by an African psychologist. Any interpretation such as room, tunnel, or box was counted as 3-d. Only 3% did not make some such 3-d inference. Miss Hyde found that about half her subjects with the same picture made a 3-d interpretation, and over 60% of the remainder did so after suggestions (which we can liken to a minimal version of Dawson's 'training'). Only a small handful did not make a 3-d inference, and amount of schooling experienced made little difference. One important difference between this test, and others must, however, be pointed out. Here, as with Deregowski's drawings for his construction test, the subjects see one set of interconnected lines at a time; these they interpret as a single object — usually solid. In fact there are few 2-dimensional objects apart from sheets of paper, that could look like these geometric grids. With Hudson's, and similar tests, people are asked to interpret pictorial depth *between* separate objects, and it is here that the real difference between inference styles seems to exist.

It may well be asked if 3-d inference is the grand goal of cultural development, and obviously it is not; Hudson and others have pointed out that this style is necessary for advanced technical education, and this is why so much research has been done on it. It may also be a well-trodden field because intriguingly 'non-western' results are easily available. This is, unfortunately, a fruitless temptation, and efforts should now be made not to merely repeat, but to extend research on this topic.

One useful development has been from South Africa, where Duncan, Gourlay and Hudson (1972) reviewed the literature and reported their own success in training people to be much more systematically 3-d aware in interpreting pictures. Methods and apparatus are both described so they can be used elsewhere.

What does this picture show?
Can you give names for the people whom you see, and write a short story describing what is going on in the picture.

Pictures devised by Wober (see p. 94)

In another new departure, Wober (1970) mentioned that 'some Africans may even infer time as an added fourth dimension in their perception of pictures'. This was because some Nigerians had interpreted three birds in one picture not as three birds, but as one bird flying along. Two new pictures were therefore prepared (Wober, 1974b). A western 'camera style' assumption with pictures would be to interpret the first picture as showing three boys. But a 'poly phasic' inference (PPP) would allow several moments of time to be seen in the same picture, and people could thus say they saw only one boy, in three episodes. The pictures were shown to various school groups in Uganda, and in England. In general, children with more, or higher quality education showed camera style inference (CPP); but there was plenty of evidence of poly phasic inference.

To confirm the phenomenon, Deregowski and Munro (1974) reported results from 654 Rhodesians and Zambians and 306 Canadian children. Nine pictures were used, varying the backgrounds and the order in which the pictorial episodes (left to right) were shown. In general, a similar level of PPP was found in Rhodesia as in Uganda. This occurred regardless of variations in positioning of the trees (bunched in two groups of two, or spaced evenly apart) or of sequence. However, bringing in background cues (a horizon — as in Wober's second picture) did reduce PPP in one Rhodesian class. In both Canadian and Rhodesian groups, PPP responses were more 'stimulus bound' or tied to immediate pictorial details, while CPP were more imaginative. Deregowski and Munro are not satisfied that 'stimulus boundness' justifies calling polyphasic stories 'perceptually' linked. Instead, they suggest that, since African pupils were answering in English, PPP may not be 'perceptual' but may reflect cultural influences.

Evidence on this question exists in an unpublished study by Acayo in which Acholi primary pupils in Uganda were given PPP pictures and 3-d items based on Hudson's test. These pupils were unable to speak English so answered verbally in Acholi. Again PPP was found, as in the Rhodesian samples, more in P7 than in P6. Acayo suggested that since P7 classes often contain more 'repeaters' (making several efforts to enter secondary school) these can perform poorer overall in some ways than P6 classes. PPP was unrelated to 2- or to 3-d pictorial inference. Thus the cultural patterns affecting perception may do so in different ways to produce 3-d or CPP styles of picture interpretation.

These findings generally support the original assertion by Hudson and later by others that 'the African depicts what he knows and not what he sees' (Hudson, 1962a). To this, it may be added that people sometimes see what they want to see. Nadel (1937), an Austrian-born, but British-based psychological anthropologist, learned the Nupe language in Nigeria, and wrote a very thorough study of that kingdom. He also did an experiment showing pictures to Nupe and Yoruba teenagers, and found that they interpreted details to match certain motivational conditions and attitudes which he linked to their cultural backgrounds. An art critic when discussing the artistry of West African bronzes (Underwood, 1949) wrote 'the artist drawing from nature does so by a conscious intellectual effort which cultivates his judgement of relative measurements and proportions ... the ancient or pre-classical artist sees things in proportion to their subjective meaning . . . anything which might be added to their intensive vision by relative measurement would only weaken and obscure its expression'.

We have therefore, independent views that there is a positive culturally-linked tendency to want to use pictures in certain ways, among certain people. Few people now think there is a serious problem about detection of pictures; recognition also presents few problems, unless perspective cues confuse the viewer, when identification (or naming objects) often reveals errors. At all events, people see that pictures represent real solid 3-dimensional objects; but they do not always infer the distances between objects (and hence also the relative sizes of far and near objects) according to the conventional western rules of perspective. Specifically directed education on this can still make a significant difference, but may still not accomplish a radical change in pictorial inference style.

The perception of time

We have mentioned that time is not necessarily 'ruled out' of pictures by some African observers, in the way in which it is according to western technical conventions. This in itself does not tell us how time is perceived in general, by one sort of people or another. There are a few experiments however, and many descriptive reports that do try to explore how Africans in a few cultures perceive time.

Some observers, like Pierre Etienne (1968) who studied the Baule, report that the psychological processes relating to time, like memory and prediction exist in African as in western cultures. People must cope with seasons, crops, hunting patterns, milestones of human life and other time-structured events. Other writers emphasise differences. Bekombo (1966-67) reported that the Duala of Cameroon emphasise the present quality of existence rather than the extensive perspective to time. Thomas and Sapir (1967) analysed, also considered that the Diola of West Africa feel comfortable in the present and lack an analytical or measured view of time past, stacked with temporally ordered memories. Erny (1970) generalises to 'Africa' and evaluates the commonly reported emphasis on present awareness as infant-like behaviour. Erny also sees concepts of space and time overlapping in his description of traditional Africans as men of 'limited horizons'.

Professor Mbiti (1969) of Makerere University, bases his analysis on linguistic considerations. He believes that East African languages reflect in the tense structures of their verbs, certain attitudes to time. Mbiti suggests that the future as a philosophic notion, as a verb structure, and as a psychological experience, is one thing for a speaker of such an East African language, and another for someone whose mother-tongue is English. Mbiti says that time is experienced as a consequence of events, which in a sense created their time instead of it being a constant progression. Time moves from the now to the past, while the fluidity of events is their removal from the *Sasa* sphere of present time to the *Zamani* realm of historic events. There is no experimental work directly arising from Mbiti's ideas yet, though some investigations do examine how Africans may be differently oriented towards impatience, which can be seen as a person's relationship to the future (see Chapter VIII).

Professor Doob (1960), of Yale University asked some survey questions in Uganda, and elsewhere, on how long people were prepared to wait for expected rewards. The Ugandan results were somewhat untidy; on one question men seemed to be more patient ('future oriented'), by saying they would rather wait a long time for a greater reward, than have a small benefit without delay; on a similar question the results were reversed. Wober and Musoke-Mutanda (1972) found that boys who had boarding school experience were more future oriented than day school boys or girls. It was suggested that experience of boarding school life is highly structured with regard to time, and boarders are made very aware of the strict passage of the hours, and to wait for their gratifications.

A similar idea, that cultural experience of time may affect how it is perceived, underlies an experiment by Deregowski (1970b). He had urban school boys and rural women listen to a story. The story contained details of times, and other numerical details of numbers of objects, distances and so on. The rural women had poor recall of the time details compared to the boys, though their recall of other numerical facts was better. Deregowski points to the very vague practices of time keeping among the women, compared with the more time-marked experience of urban boys. Unfortunately, Deregowski included no educated rural people, or illiterate town ones, to disentangle whether this factor, or sex, rather than just cultural ways of dealing with time, was what principally affected attention to, or ability to recall time details. Kemigisha (1973) repeated Deregowski's experiment in Uganda, using groups of rural and urban women, thus ruling out sex, or age as possible factors affecting correctness of remembering time-items. She found, as expected, that urban women remembered more time items (4.39 out of 8) correctly, than did rural women (2.85). However, urban women were still better with non-time items (5.35, compared to 3.20 for rural women). It was previously thought that rural women would be at less of a disadvantage on non-time items, as they have to buy and sell, and know the distance to market. Thus their lower scores on time items (than urban women) could relate to their low level of education which leaves them without a precise attitude to numbers in general; and the indigenous ways of dealing with time need be no more handicap in learning to use precise clock time, than in learning other technological skills.

Gay and Cole (1967) experimented in Liberia, on whether tendencies exist to underestimate or overestimate time intervals. Inferences can be drawn from such results as to whether people are considered patient ('future oriented') or hasty. However, the technique of doing such experiments appears to have considerable effects on the results. What is clear is that this remains a wide open topic for future research, in at least three ways. The experimental techniques need investigation, and comparison against each other; we need to know about time perception for itself; and we need to know how, if at all, ways of perceiving time relate to cultural or to other psychological factors.

Attempts to understand cognitive processes by studying perception through behaviour

Unhappily, though psychologists have the separate terms perception and cognition, which should presumably have fairly precise meanings, these often overlap. Perception refers to events between and including the arrival of information at nerve endings in sense organs(e.g.the retina of the eye) and the delivery of impulses to a central area in the brain, ready to influence action. Cognition refers to the ways in which percepts are given meaning in awareness. For example, the way in which the optic nerve delivers the information to the brain, from the retina, may depend on a person's cognitive processes or development. Some believe that whatever the history of the person, the nerve delivers the same information to the brain, and 'percepts' are therefore psychologically equivalent, for a given stimulus perceived by two people. Others hold that learned habits, attitudes or cognitive structures influence perception. One way in which this could happen might be by some selective process affecting how a person pays attention to things that come before and upon his senses.

One approach to understanding cognitive processes is then to discover more about what happens at the stage of perception. Yet how can we know about how a person perceives something, unless we ask him about it? In answering, he processes his percept, for report, through his cognitive apparatus of deriving and presenting meaning, to himself and to others. This would mean we are denied access to the stage of perception, free of the process of cognition. However, there has seemed to be a way around this difficulty. If we present something for perception and see what a person does with his percept almost without thinking about it, then we may have 'behavioural' evidence which could be a valid pointer to how the percept has occurred and how it has been dealt with by the cognitive system. The chief example of this approach is the study of visual illusions. Another area of research has dealt with the phenomenon of 'rotation' (see below) and whether this may be influenced by some factors of attention; the phenomenon is still not properly understood. We can survey what has been done on rotation first, before turning to the larger question of illusions.

Rotation

As Deregowski (1972b) pointed out, Europeans have for many years observed that house servants appeared not be influenced by the concept 'straight' in such things as setting pictures on the wall or carpets on the floor. Nissen *et al* (1935) first noted, in psychological testing, that designs were copied according to the same shape as the models, but were often set at an angle different to the original. A square might be copied as a diamond. Biesheuvel (1949), Maistriaux (1955), Jahoda (1956) and McFie (1961) all noted this 'rotation' of copies of designs, the latter suspecting this revealed a 'fundamentally different attitude towards perception'. We can use rotation here as an introduction to various ways in which cultural influences lead subjects to construct something different out of stimuli they perceive.

Shapiro (1960) was the first to devote a study to this matter, testing Malawian street sweepers in Southern Rhodesia, ordered to do the experiments by their foreman. He duly found that designs were copied rotated, and considered three possible causes. One is based on a lack of ability, in this case 'to make an adequate integration of the directional properties of the visual world'. Such a lack of ability could occur for reasons of culture or education. Secondly, Shapiro noticed that rotation occurred more often with some figures than with others. This might be because subjects preferred to 'set right' a design in a rotation which pleased them better. We can see how this phenomenon has been handled as an experiment in perception and behaviour, and not in cognition, as Shapiro did not ask people why they set designs in different orientations from what was provided. This second explanation does not assume any lack of ability, but infers a positive (cognitive) preference. Thirdly, Shapiro thought rotation might occur through 'gross disorientation of attention in the testing situation as a result of wild fears about the purpose of the experiment. . '. This third possibility is not, however, likely to have accounted for all the examples of rotation reported by other researchers.

Apart from one anecdotal report from Nigerian data (Wober, 1967a) which suggests that rotations are probably due to some positive preference rather than an inability, most of the work has come from the University of Zambia. Robert Serpell (1969a) tested school pupils to explore two ideas as to why rotation occurred. First was the concept of 'monitoring tolerance' which appears to mean that people notice the shape they are shown, but simply pay less attention to 'which way up' it is. Serpell soon rejected this possibility however, as he found that subjects did place their copies 'in a particular orientation different from that of the standard being copied', thus they were 'rotation errors rather than disorientation errors.'

Serpell's second idea was that a person first notices some outstanding feature of a shape, then other parts of it; when making a copy, the 'focal point' of the shape is put at the top and the person works downwards to complete the pattern. Some of his evidence, in six experiments he did, does support this notion. Such sequential copying behaviour was found more often in younger pupils, and more schooling was associated with making more copies in the correct orientation. Serpell extends this hypothesis to see what it would have predicted in detail about Shapiro's, and some of Deregowski's results; but because the detailed information is not available with which to examine all these questions, he remains cautious about suggesting that he has successfully explained how and why rotations occur.

Serpell (1971) next asked whether Zambian children may perhaps just like it better to see shapes a 'particular way up'. This was indeed so. Over 90% of pupils asked quite simply preferred a vertical to a horizontal line. Other shapes, lines and diagrams evoked distinct preferences when they were a particular way up. This strongly suggests that cultural influences cause children to associate some sort of 'connotative' meaning, or 'atmosphere' to diagrams which on the face of it one may suppose to be meaningless. Two previous studies in Africa also show this to be true. Jahoda (1956) in Ghana found that before puberty boys preferred some kinds of figures and girls preferred others; after puberty, preferences altered. Jahoda suggested that certain kinds of figures are reminiscent of male qualities, others of female;

while people do not consciously say a square is male and a circle female, they deal with such figures as though such as idea was subconsciously at work. In a remote part of Tanzania, Davis (1961) showed substantially the same thing. Children were asked which of two nonsense words they associated with a curvy, and which with a jagged figure. The fact that preferences did exist shows that there is a shadowy or subconscious 'meaning' to figures. Such a meaning can presumably affect, in ways we do not yet understand, how figures are copied.

Deregowski has also worked on this problem. He showed (Deregowski, 1972a) that Zambian adults and children both tended to reproduce patterns so that they were symmetrical. This evidence seems to conflict, as Deregowski pointed out (1971), with the findings of Tekane (1961). Tekane, an African psychologist working in South Africa, first reported his results with a *Pattern Completion* (PATCO) test, in which subjects are invited to complete a figure as they wish, so long as the result was symmetrical. Tekane found that the solutions were systematic in certain ways, though a majority were not symmetrical. This was not because subjects were unable to produce a symmetrical figure, but because they placed pieces down untidily. There need, of course, be no contradiction here. Tekane's subjects were from peoples thousands of miles away from Deregowski's, with different cultures and education. There is no need to assume generalisations about psychological functioning in Africa, until and unless the evidence points to them. However, Tekane (1963) later reported that subjects 'completed the patterns in a regular way in approximately 97 percent of all the responses'.

In further work Deregowski (1971) found that while Zambian children made more errors than European children in copying designs, there was a 'qualitative similarity' in the types of error made. Later (Deregowski 1974 and Deregowski and Ellis 1974) he showed that the nature of symmetry or of asymmetry of stimuli affected the types of errors made in copying figures. In particular, designs which are symmetrical both about a vertical and a horizontal (like the letter O) are best remembered, then designs symmetrical about a vertical axis only (eg the letters V, W), then horizontal symmetry (eg the letter E), then diagonal (eg the letter Z) and, finally, asymmetric designs are least well remembered. These findings do not directly explain rotation of copied figures, but support Serpell in suggesting a preference for some orientations over others. Increased education reduces errors, but the possibility remains that cultural influences lend hidden meanings to diagrams which influence the ways, including orientation, in which such diagrams may be copied.

A fresh study on this link between culture, and copying designs was done by John Berry (1969) in Sierra Leone. He showed simple figures which might be thought to resemble common objects such as pots, axes and so on, in a tachistoscope (a device which one looks into through an eyepiece, and which allows a momentary glimpse of what is on display). Temne drew and described what they saw, in a large proportion of cases calling them by the names of objects common in Temne culture. This 'assimilation' occurred much more among the 64 Temne tested, than when the same figures were shown to Eskimos in Northern Canada. Berry interprets his finding in terms of Witkin's (1967) concept of field independence; he considers that Temne culture, incorporating strict child raising methods and a low emphasis on independence, is more 'context dependent'; thus Temne 'see' things in terms of objects which are familiar to them.

Berry's thinking here must be examined carefully, as it is at odds with other theories dealing with illusions, which we shall consider below. Berry is saying that field-dependent Temne are more likely to make pictorial inferences about diagrams and shapes they are shown than are field independent Eskimos. Field independent people, he infers, are more likely to accept shapes as shapes, rather than assimilating their meaning into a familiar cultural context. In any case, a possibility other than the factor of field independence may be affecting Temne copying behaviour. This is that there may simply be a greater variety of physical objects in Temne culture to act as visual analogies, than there are in Eskimo culture. What is lacking in this experiment of Berry's, is a comparison between more and less field independent Temne.

However, Berry found further evidence to support his theory. He showed Temne a photograph taken in their own surroundings – to one eye – while the other eye was simultaneously shown a foreign photograph. In this procedure the subject is asked to describe what he sees and it is known that many people tend to see either one scene, or the other, and to be unaware that two scenes are being shown at the same time. Temne were found to be more likely to say they were looking at an own-culture photograph, than were Eskimos.

Previously Berry (1966) also explored the range of words and terms available in Temne language for spatial ideas (such as 'horizontal', 'upside-down' etc). He found that Temne had only 39 direct equivalents in word or phrase for 100 English spatial words, and that a further seven words were derived from the English. Thus the Temne word for 'horizontal' was one borrowed from the English. If then, the concept was not sufficiently frequent to have acquired a Temne name before it was borrowed, this might have some connection with the possibility (if it is true) that Temne might be like other Africans (at least this has been reported in Ghana and Nigeria) and be uncertain about the orientation of drawings they are asked to copy.

Our final evidence on the question of copying forms comes from Serpell's latest work, briefly reported (Serpell, 1972). Serpell followed a train of thought that crystallised from earlier work in Nigeria (Wober, 1966b); this suggests that the efficiency with which people deal with perceptions may depend partly on the primary sense from which the perception comes. People who from an early age deal mostly with visual perceptions and cognition based on this source, may deal more efficiently with such material later. Western psychologists, it so happens, use visually presented material in the vast majority of their tests. On the other hand, people in a culture in which 'proprioceptual' inputs (the sense of body position and movement, used in dance and athletics) are common as well as visual perceptions, may have a different history of cognitive development. Serpell first devised a task of mimicry in copying hand and finger positions. Zambian and English children did equally well on this. Next, there was a task of bending wire to copy shapes. Here, Zambian did better than English children, though there was the usual sex difference within the culture, Zambian boys doing better than Zambian girls. Interestingly, when almo'st the same shapes were presented as drawings to be copied using pencil and paper, English children did better than Zambians. Children also did the copying tasks blindfolded. This greatly impeded good performance, but Zambian boys were evidently still better at bending wire than English children, even when blindfolded. This illustrates the paramount importance of visual information, probably in both Zambia and England; but it remains possible that the tactile skills or sense of positioning body parts (fingers) or physical materials (wires) are better organised among Zambians, than among English children.

Overall, the material on copying designs and figures does not point clearly to a single pattern of cause and effect. There is some evidence that attention to outstanding details in a pattern may influence that these are put at the top of a copy – whether they originally belonged there or not, and then the copy gets built up rightly, or wrongly as the case may be. Other evidence is that people may prefer patterns to be a particular way up and to have a certain symmetry, or to resemble objects familiar in the culture. When a tester asks a subject to copy a lopsided pattern, he may mark as an error a copy rotated to 'look better'; the misunderstanding may be in the received meaning of the word 'copy'. The psychologists take it to mean 'carbon-copy', while many of the testees may have taken it to mean 'produce a version that is meaningful or pleasant to you'. The evidence then, is strongly in favour of effects of nurture in determining how perception is organised and used.

Illusions

The first relevant work was by Beveridge (1935) in Ghana. He dealt with the question of 'size constancy'. If one shows a person a dinner plate close up, and asks him to chose which of a number of different cardboard circles is most nearly the size of the plate, the subject can make a fairly accurate choice. One then takes the plate to a distance, and now it appears as small as a coin, though since one knows it is a plate, one could still estimate its size fairly well. If a person has high 'size constancy', he will make an accurate size comparison, no matter how small the distant image is to the eye. Beveridge found that West Africans have high size constancy compared with Europeans. This could be interpreted in line with later ideas on picture cognition, that African subjects have often tended to make inferences about things they see, interpreting them as they know them to be, rather than as they see them.

The next attempt to explore cultural influence dealt with the perception of movement, and was reported by two Americans, Allport and Pettigrew (1957). They used an apparatus called a rotating trapezoidal window. Its wooden window frame has one side much higher than the other. The top and the bottom consequently slope inwards from the wide end to the narrow one. This frame is mounted on a short upright pole, and rotated, but the physically longer edge always produces a line which is longer on the retina. This is very obvious when this side is actually closer to the observer, but it is still true when it is at the other extreme of its circuit, away from the viewer. A normal rectangular window rotated would have its edge produce a longer image on the retina when close, but a *shorter* image when far. When the trapezoidal window is rotated then, it can produce an illusion that it is not rotating, but merely appears to be swinging to and fro, with the longer edge always appearing closer to the observer.

Allport and Pettigrew expected that Zulus from a country environment where round houses have no windows, might not receive this illusion. Zulus were tested at Nongoma, and Ceza, both villages over 200 miles from Durban. Subjects were also tested at Polela, 100 miles from Durban, and in the city. When viewing the apparatus with one eye, a majority of subjects in all groups saw the illusion. This shows that whether they had experience of windows or not, the country subjects had developed expectations about the size and distance of the physically longer side of the trapezoid. If, like the West Africans Beveridge tested, and the Malawians reported by Myambo (1972), Zulus also had greater size constancy, they would more accurately relate the lengths of the edges to their distance from the viewer; thus, with less illusion, they would see the frame as rotating, not swaying. However, looking with both eyes shows a very different pattern of results. Here urban Africans and Europeans have almost identical results, with a majority still seeing the illusion; Polela Africans were intermediate, while the most rural subjects had a clear majority who did not see the illusion. Allport and Pettigrew say that binocular viewing provides added information, and this is a less favourable, or 'marginal' condition for exploring illusion. In marginal conditions, effects of cultural background, in this case the visual environment, do appear to relate to differences in illusion susceptibility.

We come now to the compendium work on the topic. Marshall Segall, an American psychologist who had been interested in Uganda since the mid-1950s was the principal author, along with Donald Campbell and the anthropologist Melville Herskovits who seems to have lent his name to the enterprise, and died before the book was finished. Segall, Campbell and Herskovits (1966), or 'SC & H', report on several different illusions, presented to nearly 20 different populations, mostly in Africa, but also in America and the Philippines. They also summarise work by the French language authors Heuse and Bonté, who tested the same illusions though not with S C & H's standard materials. In these, subjects are merely asked to say which of two lines on a page is longer, a red, or a black one. These choices could be called 'behavioural responses to perception'; on the other hand, it may be thought that the response of choosing which line is, or seems longer, is a cognitive decision drawing from an applied use of the concept 'longer'.

Statistical analysis has shown that of the several illusions SC & H used, there are two which are most important, and work in ways independently of each other. One is the Muller-Lyer (ML) illusion (see p.103). The illusion is that the line with outgoing fins appears to be longer than the one with ingoing fins, even if the two lines are in fact equal. Drawings can be made in which the ingoing-fin line is actually 5%, 10% (etc) longer, but subjects will continue to say the other line seems longer. The percentage at which the ingoing-fin line really is longer, when the two lines are judged equal, is a measure of the strength of the illusion for that person.

To explain the ML illusion, SC & H (analogously to Allport and Pettigrew)

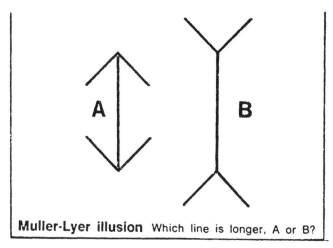

The Muller Lyer Illusion (see p. 102)

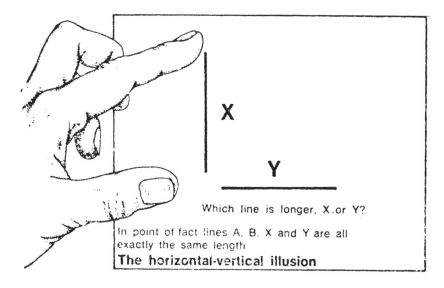

The Horizontal-Vertical Illusion (see p. 106)

argued that people living in a 'carpentered world' with many manufactured objects having straight edges and right angles, subconsciously learn to associate a line with outgoing fins as the distant inside edge of a ceiling; they associate the line with ingoing fins with the near edge of something like a table. If a line with outgoing fins is thought of as though it represents a distant object, that object would be a big one. Similarly, the line with ingoing fins would represent a small object. By association then, the first line has more length to its appearance than the second line. If we accept this theory, then some further predictions become possible. People who live in 'more carpentered' environments would be more susceptible. This hypothesis is of considerable interest, because it suggests that aspects of the physical environment which we take for granted, may have deep-rooted effects on how we see things. Furthermore, SC & H conclude that these effects are accomplished by the age of 4, since children have been found to be more susceptible than adults.

SC & H did not attempt any precise measure of 'carpenteredness' of environment; they merely compared non-western, and western samples. Certainly, the Americans and South African whites were more susceptible to the illusion; but so also were two groups, of Zulus, and of Senegalese. The Zulus, though described as 'moderately Europeanized' had their cultural roots (up to age 4 certainly) in the so-called 'circular culture' of Allport and Pettigrew's description. Senegalese were tested in small villages and described as 'slightly Europeanized'. Apart from these, the other African samples did not vary greatly in susceptibility. SC & H claim this western/non-western difference as support for their theory; but this is to ignore the two unfitting cases. At best then, one might consider the theory unproven at this stage, if one does not wish to face that it has been rejected. Other evidence also does not neatly support the 'carpentered environment' theory. Jahoda (1966) tested two Ghanaian groups who differed clearly on carpenteredness, but the expected effect on illusion susceptibility was not found.

Berry (1968) pointed out that another process might be at work affecting M-L susceptibility. As people acquire more education and become more 'perceptually developed' (which Berry proposes to assess by Koh's Blocks scores) they become less field dependent, less likely to be illused by the effects of fins going one way or another, and more able to concentrate their judgement on the lines themselves. Thus more educated people (like Westerners) should be *less* susceptible than less educated people (like non-Westerners). This theory works in exactly the opposite direction to the SC & H idea; unfortunately it greatly reduces any force their analysis has, because they made no mention of the educational standing of their samples. Berry's method did cope with both theories.

First, he collected from his files, results from Temne who lived in a 'moderately carpentered' environment, either in a small town, or in the more carpentered houses in a village. With the degree of carpentered environment therefore similar for everyone, it was the group who had higher Koh's Blocks scores, who were less susceptible to the illusions. This is support for the theory that 'perceptual development' decreases illusion scores. Berry was able to find Eskimos living in a very carpentered environment, who had equal Koh's Blocks scores with other Eskimos living in a less carpentered situation. This time, with Koh's Blocks scores equal, there was a higher susceptibility among the more-carpentered environment group. This supports the carpentered world theory. Berry's work shows, however, that the cross-cultural comparisons that SC & H have made are rather risky to interpret. Berry presents results of two Temne, and one Eskimo group ostensibly all in a 'moderately carpentered' environment. One Temne group has very low Koh's scores (6.6) and high illusion susceptibility; the next Temne group has better Koh's scores (15.6) and less susceptibility (fitting the theory); but the Eskimo groups have tremendously better Koh's scores (89.8) and instead of having *very* low susceptibility, it is back again at the same level of the first Temne group. It is clear therefore that we do not know fully yet, how 'perceptual development' interacts with visual environment, or other factors unknown, to affect illusion scores.

A short resumé of further work on the M-L illusions will confirm that our knowledge in this area is still in a state of chaos. Segall's friend Clive Davis (1970) reported from Uganda that more 'perceptually developed' people (measured by Koh's Blocks) tended to be more illusible, runs counter to Berry's evidence. Davis also found that a different set of illusion drawings, types of instruction and practice, all affected levels of illusion scores. Bonté (1962) tested Bambashi, Europeans, and Bambuti pygmies in the Congo, though not using SC & H's test materials. Bonté found that the Bashi, who live in round houses ('non-carpentered') have very high illusion scores, and so do Europeans. The difficulty here is not the direction of the difference between the two populations, but the absolute size of the illusion scores. These suggest that when SC & H say about a population group that their illusion level is x%, this statement does not refer simply to an attribute of a group of people, but is just as much a measure of the qualities of the test instrument. Davis and Carlson (1970) reinforce this doubt. They say that illusibility is 7% among southern Ugandans, and 6% among Americans – while SC & H had given figures of 16 and 19% for similar groups of Americans.

Jahoda and Stacey (1970) more recently tested Ghanaian students who had at least two years' training in drawing or related skills (T) and others who were untrained (U). The T Group did not differ on M-L scores from the U group; nor were there significant differences between Ghanaian and Scottish groups, which could be expected unless one assumes that Ghanaian and Scottish environments are equally 'carpentered'. There was no actual measure of carpenteredness used in this study, and only one other investigator since Berry has attempted to quantify this variable.

The largest study on illusions after SC & H, was by a Canadian student of Campbell's, Mary Stewart (1971). She tested five separate African samples in Zambia who differed on education and on visual environment. The least schooled had the least carpentered surroundings, in the Zambezi valley; while the most educated also had the most carpentered environment. There is therefore a confusion between ecology and education. Overall a slight increase in M-L susceptibility among the more educated groups was found. But Stewart admits (p.68) 'when just the schooled Zambian African groups who differ only on carpenteredness were compared, the statistical significance of the effect disappears. . .' This does not prevent her from summing up that 'the ecological hypothesis was generally upheld'. A more careful evaluation would surely accept a 'not proven' verdict.

Finally for this illusion, it should be noted that the SC & H theory initially assumes that people make (subconscious) interpretations that one line is *far away* and the other *closer to* the observer. In other words, some

3-dimensional inference process is taken to be at work. None of the above investigators has reported a comparison of illusion and 3-d test scores. Wober (1967a) showed, however, that among 50 Nigerian clerks there was no significant correlation between M-L and 3-d test scores; but among 173 manual workers there was a small though significant negative correlation (−0.16). This suggests that making 3-d inferences about pictorial material went with lower M-L susceptibility. This runs counter to the reasoning behind the 'carpentered world' theory.

The second major illusion is the Horizontal-Vertical one. Simply, a vertical line is judged to be longer than a horizontal line meeting it which on paper is of equal length. To explain the illusion, SC & H offer an old idea that a person infers that a vertical line represents (pictorially) a pathway extending from the observer to the distance. A horizontal line cannot be interpreted this way. Thus the vertical line has a 'lengthy' meaning to it and is judged longer, even though on paper it may be equal to or even marginally shorter than a horizontal line. Deregowski (1967) pointed out that the T form of the illusion included a mixture of effects, part being due to what he called 'dichosection' (or bisection). He showed that it was correct only to examine data for the L form of the illusion.

SC & H suggested that for people living in environments of open rolling plains or wide vistas, there would be greater HV illusion. This would be because they *might* be more accustomed to associating vertical lines on the retina with the sight of paths, or ploughed furrows extending into the distance. People who live in cramped cities, or forests are not thought to have such opportunites for inferring ideas about verticals.

Two severe points of criticism have to be made about this straight away. One is that a visit to the South Uganda region of Ankole, (which Segall cites as a prime case) shows that it is extremely rare for vertical lines upon the eye to come from straight paths running to the horizon. Railway lines are uncommon, and people do not walk upon them. Paths are curved. There are no furrows. Retinal verticals more commonly arise from people standing, trees, or sides of houses. Thus the reasoning based on verticals simply does not accord with fact. Further, it is most likely to be in towns (especially American ones) that the vertical on the eye will come from a road going into the distance, since many American towns have rectangular grid road plans. Secondly, the reasoning depends on inferences said to be made about the vertical line; it has nothing to say about cognition of the horizontal line, which is surely a serious omission.

SC & H emphasise that urban samples from America and South Africa tend to have low susceptibility; results from Toro and Ankole (open rolling and hilly country in Uganda) show highest susceptibility to the illusion. They do admit (p.193) that 'unfortunately, other groups who live under similar conditions were not so highly ranked' (on HV scores); these other groups include the Basonge of the Congo (whose territory is characterised 'primarily as flat, open savanna') and the Zulu, whose culture is supposed to be 'circular', and whose paths we may presume therefore to be winding. SC & H seem to be influenced with tortuous ways too; they say that if anyone might expect that their data should fit their hypothesis, that 'we plead, this might be asking too much'; but they comfortably 'conclude that . . . the relative standing of the samples . . . is quite in accord with predictions. . .' The main illusion here, ironically, seems to have afflicted the psychologists in their zeal to assimilate data to patterns with which they felt familiar and comfortable.

Two later studies cast doubt on SC & H's theory of the HV illusion. Wober (1970) argued that if SC & H were correct, people associating a vertical line with distance, should also have higher scores on inferring 3-dimensional depth in Hudson's test. Among two groups of Nigerians, manual workers, and clerks, though, the correlations between HV scores and Hudson's 3-d test were not significant. Secondly, Wober (1972a) reasoned that if SC & H's reasoning was valid, a greater illusion would occur when the vertical was contrasted with a horizontal at its 'foot' than when contrasted with the horizontal at its 'top' (supposedly distant end). This was tested with subjects in Uganda, but results with the two versions of the illusion were much the same. Both studies would seem to result in crucial rejections of SC & H's theory. An alternative to SC & H's environmentalist theory was suggested by Jahoda (1971) with some evidence from Malawi that illusion susceptibility related to retinal pigmentation. However, though this might explain some of the differences between 'races', it has little power to explain differences which exist widely enough between Africans.

Jahoda and Stacey (1970) also gave the HV illusion to their Ghanaian and Scottish students. Among the U groups, the Ghanaians had higher illusion scores than the Scots. This is interpreted as supporting SC & H's theory 'since there is more flat, open terrain in Ghana'. Stacey himself pointed out though (personal communication) that the Ghanaians came from the coastal plains 'or the central forest belt' — neither apparently more flat and open than countryside which is common enough in Scotland. In all, Jahoda and Stacey's results are really equivocal and neither prove, nor disprove SC & H's theory.

Stacey has however, raised a new line of explanation which seems worthy of future study. This is the idea of Kunnapas, a Finnish psychologist, that the visual field is an ellipse with the longer axis horizontal, and that a horizontal line is judged shorter than a vertical, because it is related to the width of the visual field. Stacey did not, however, see how the shape of the visual field might relate to cultural differences in HV susceptibility. We can suggest here, however, that if peoples' eyes are set wider apart, their visual field will be a flatter ellipse; they would then be expected to have greater illusion susceptibility. Sasieni (1962) reported that the 'pupillary distance' — PD, or the width apart of the eye pupils, is greater for 'Negroes' (68mm or more) than for Europeans (63-64). Babalola and Szajnzicht (1960) report PDs of 69.6 for West African students, and 64.6 for Europeans. I myself recorded PDs of 67.6 mm for Batoro, 67.9 for Banyankole and 68.3 for Baganda males; Europeans had an average of 64.1 mm PD. It is possible then, that the width the eyes are set apart, and the resulting shape of the visual field, may have some bearing on HV illusion susceptibility.

The outcome of all this work on illusions is unfortunately closer to chaos than to order. The question at issue, though, is not a trivial one. It is whether there are characteristics of the sensory environment which, before formal education starts, very profoundly influence how we interpret what we see.

When we see a bird soaring in the air, or hear a tantalising phrase hover slowly about a climax in some music, do we feel about these things as we do because it has been consciously taught to us, as part of our upbringing? Or do we feel as we do partly at least because of visual or auditory characteristics of our surroundings, which have not been purposely organised for the intention of teaching us, but which nevertheless structure the architecture of what experience we can build with our perception? These are the kinds of questions which illusionists have been approaching in their experiments.

The evidence though is quite inconclusive. Neither of the major illusions (M-L or HV) have shown any consistent relationship between visual surroundings and measured illusion susceptibility. This therefore lets us for the moment allow more weight for educational experiences, influences on cognition that are more clearly part of how the culture intends to influence its new members. Such influences can include the provision of visual experiences (via toys, books, TV etc.), auditory experiences (via stories, songs, music), kinaesthetic or proprioceptual experiences (through attention to movement, bodily grace, dancing), other sense experiences (e.g. smell) or mixtures of all these, in proportions unique to each culture.

Summary

Hudson (1960) early on distinguished between cultures that are 'visual', which develop precise and storable symbol systems (writing and pictures), and those which are 'non-visual'. Hudson was not very clear on what the latter kind of culture did encourage, or depend on, but McLuhan (1962) and Wober (1967c) have offered ideas on this. Visual cultures involve their members in reading, needing quietness and privacy to be able to concentrate on visual inputs; non-visual cultures, with more use of conversation and singing, story telling and dancing, music, metaphor and parable, lead to more social forms of interaction. Thus perceptual circumstances may have social and cultural consequences — and vice versa.

Following Hudson's invention of an experimental tool, much work has been lavished on the question of interpreting depth in pictures. It is fairly clear now that simple drawings of single objects are both detected as representations, and usually correctly labelled. Thus even completely illiterate rural people can and do infer three-dimensional reality from two-dimensional marks on paper. It is thus wrong for writers (as Dawson did) to describe Africans as 'two dimensional in perception'. However, perspective built into an object, for example, narrowing of a train seen along its length, or the modified size of an object (e.g. a distant elephant shown very small, compared with a close-to dog) can lead to misidentifications. Further, illiterate people very often do not interpret the space between objects indicated in pictures or even in photographs, according to the rules of perspective representation. Ability to interpret pictures in conventional western ways increases with education, and with special training; but there are clear signs that cultural factors are at work which restrain a simple switch into using western conventions of picture interpretation.

Cultural conventions which influence styles of picture interpretation probably differ across Africa, and are not yet well understood. An exploration of polyphasic perception has begun, which points to new complexities and links with the ways in which time is conceived; as well as time, anthropologists have suggested that spiritual and linguistic factors may affect conceptions of space. This all means that the possibilities are too complex to permit an easy definition of psychological research questions; so relatively little work has been done on these broader questions.

Instead, ingenious efforts have concentrated on smaller questions, such as why copies of designs are often rotated with respect to what respondents are shown. A large body of work has also dealt with visual illusions. These are not deficits of skill, such as pictorial interpretation phenomena may seem to be. Indeed, many African groups are less susceptible to certain illusions than are westerners. Various possibilities to explain illusion susceptibility have been explored. These range from the kind of educational experiences which can relatively easily be changed, to ecological settings which are less alterable, to genetically determined physical properties which are out of reasonable human control. No firm conclusion has been reached, but the educational and ecological causes currently have most support.

While nobody has suggested that Africans be trained to have greater illusion susceptibility, there have been efforts to find how best to teach western conventions of perspective. It is important to realise that what modern psychologists have implied is an area of special difficulty, is only so because people now have to function in societies making increasing use of western-style technology. Traditional representational styles were not any handicap in their own time, but were the great credit of sculptors all over Africa, whose work has impressed and influenced modern western artists.

CHAPTER V

SPECIAL ABILITIES

The previous chapter dealt with difficulties in interpreting pictures according to modern western conventions, and with whatever the study of illusions may reveal as to physical, ecological or cultural influences on perception, interlinked with effects on cognition. Now we can explore evidence of positive directions of development in perceptual and cognitive skills, directions which are strengths and functional in traditional terms, and which may still be so, possibly with modifications, for modern purposes.

First there is evidence on skills of visual symbolism. It is certainly true that without formal education systems of writing and prolific production of pictures have been largely absent in African cultures. These, or other symbolic uses of visual patterns have, however, not been entirely absent. For example, some people get to know the stars of the night sky by identifying and naming patterns among them. Beyer (1919) tells us that among the Suto (Sotho) of South Africa, major constellations (Orion, Gemini, and others in Arabic-Western astronomy) have been recognised and named. Stars' regular movements have been noted, and used for determining the calendar. Dunn (1960) reports on Ghanaian fishermen that 'lying off shore in their canoes . . . the heavenly bodies have interested them and have led them to some attempt at classification . . . apart from the fishermen, other Fante people know nothing of, and have little interest in the stars'. Dunn describes at least 10 large constellations in the Fante astronomy. He also says that, like the Greeks, Fante treat stars as having personality. They say 'the stars are fighting' (for place in the crowded sky). Hausa on the other hand refer to 'the conversation of the stars'. These examples are enough to show that some visual pattern organisation regarding stars has been devised, and in some cases used for social purposes.

Another use of visual symbols is in writing. Evidence of some sort of writing has been found in many parts of Africa. Amaury Talbot (1912) tells of the Nsibidi writing of the Ekoi and Ibibio peoples of Southern Nigeria. Several hundred characters were said to have been discovered, though not translated. Mrs. Kathleen Han (1959) reports that the neighbouring Bini culture probably used written characters before there had been any contact with the first western (Portuguese) explorers who reached there. Dr David Dalby (1966) of the School of Oriental and African Studies in London, discusses one of four indigenous scripts recorded in the area of South Sierra Leone and North-West Liberia. The earliest example was that of the Vai people, reportedly devised around 1930. This was well after both European and Arabic literacy had affected the region, though it was not a copy of either. The French writer Zahan (1950) reports that further north, in the

Sahel the Bambara people had 'a system of writing and that its use is more widespread among the population than the Dogon system . . . there are extremely few Bambara who are not familiar with the direct symbolism of signs. . '.

Zahan explains: 'every pictograph stands in the first place, for an inanimate object, a living being, a natural phenomenon, or an abstract quality. Each sign has at the same time a varying number of secondary meanings. . . This capacity of a single sign to evoke more than one idea derives . . . partly from the fact that each of the ideas represented can be viewed as a component part of some other idea, and this in turn of a third and so forth'. Then: 'a sign may have different meanings in different geographical areas . . . often again, two or more people in a single region will interpret a given character differently, . . . the variety of meanings . . . tends only to enrich the signs. . '. This system lacks the precision of a writing based on an alphabet representing each spoken word. This precision in turn has implications for such things as the practice of law, and the development of technology in a society. The advantages or disadvantages of any culture with its systems of recording meaning, of law and of science are not in discussion here. We should merely recognise that the stereotyped idea that other cultures had writing, while African cultures did not, is not entirely correct.

Psychological testing in Africa has suggested that there is an area of weakness, namely with visual analysis and processing of diagrams and relationships of objects in pictorial space. Sources in cultural anthropology suggest that African cultures have developed skills in this very area; but it seems that these skills may have been rare, or highly specific, and have not helped in impressing western psychologists. To bridge a gap in the research effort so far, Hopkins and Wober (1973) call for research on African board games, which require both speed, and accurate analysis of spatial patterns as well as psychological understanding of one's opponent, in order to play them well. Griffith (1956) describes one version of the game, in Nigeria, called Dare. Similar games are called Owuare in Nigeria, Warri in Sierra Leone, Coro in Northern Uganda and Omweso in Southern Uganda. In Dare the board has 36 'houses' in lines of six. One player has 12 twigs, the other 12 pebbles. They alternately (and swiftly) throw down their counters, the first aim being to get three pieces in line (as in noughts and crosses). Since this may not be achieved, players cast their pieces also with a view to later strategic advantages. When the pieces are all cast down, individual moves are made, and the game then involves speed and spatial strategy.

Apart from pointers to visual skills as yet untapped (though for some reason they do not generalize themselves to being able to do well on certain psychological tests), there have been for several decades noises among psychologists that another area of skills may exist. This area concerns music, and the integration of aspects of music (particularly rhythm) with movement.

First Endemann (1927) in South Africa wrote of pupils at the Bothsabelo training school 'night after night we hear them singing, but only in two parts . . . they say that the girls are singing the other two parts and so they need only sing *their* two. . . That it is possible . . . to do this shows that he is capable of representing imaginally the voices which are not sung. . . Nearly every native is an amateur composer . . . one of them hits on a tune . . . after a while the simple tune becomes a part song. . . Sometimes in as many as five parts'.

Biesheuvel (1943) took this further: 'in the auditory sphere, ability to work out, remember and create intricate new relations of a most abstract kind is by no means inferior to that displayed by the European in the visual or conceptual sphere'. Two French language authors also echoed this idea. First, Ombredane (1956) wrote 'I will contrast the intellectual organisation of the African with that of the white, saying that the first is built basically on musico-choreographic structures, while the latter consists of arithmetic-geometric structures'. Maistriaux (1960) added another implication by pointing out that 'African civilisation . . . depends more on musico-rhythmic than on spatial-visual structures. And it is these last which underlie the conceptual and abstract activities which characterise western civilisation'.

Maistriaux implies clearly that a culture which may have prominent 'musico-rhythmic' structures will produce certain skills which by all present evidence do not help a person progress easily in a culture built around 'spatio-visual' structures. To develop the new skills may then require one to break away from many of the cultural patterns which interlock with their traditional skills. Such a break involves the problem of knowing what the basis of self-esteem is to be (see also Chapter VIII). If one has not yet fully developed the skills of the new culture, one may not (unless one deludes oneself to a degree) have self-esteem on new criteria; yet one may have abandoned old ways in the attempt, and thus given up the opportunity to evaluate oneself in these old terms. The position of people bidding for success in a new culture (on Maistriaux's model) is precarious; often it might be safer to return to the safety of being a man of the traditional culture. It may of course be possible to learn new skills without sacrificing identity in the old context. But existing research on picture interpretation skills suggests that this possibility is not strong, since there does seem to be a cultural entity which expresses itself variously in a person's actions and skills, and affects the shape in which these skills can develop.

We can select four reports (from several others available) which point to the existence of a 'musico-rhythmic' design in African cultures, with the development of associated skills. Professor Balandier (1965) in his history of the ancient Kongo kingdom, quotes the remarks of a monk called Pigafetta, who wrote in 1591; 'from words to the rhythm of music and dance there was no discontinuity in the traditional society of the Kongo; they were all language, whether of sound or of gesture. The drums had a voice; they transmitted messages that were governed by a code . . . the lute spoke an agreeable language and notably that of the heart. . .'; of this lute, Pigafetta wrote: 'admirable phenomenon, by means of this instrument they express their thoughts and make themselves understood so clearly that almost anything that can be said with words they can render with their fingers by touching this instrument'.

An English writer, Rattray (1923) explains further about what western writers liked to call 'talking drums'. Among the Ashanti people of Ghana, Rattray says there were certain drums called *ntumpane*, treated almost as having a life of their own, with a room in the Chief's house assigned to them, Another kind of drum called *fontomfrom* was used only for transmitting proverbs. Rattray tells us 'the drum only gives us the tones, number of syllables, and the punctuation accurately ... the repertoire of Ashanti drummers consists of certain holophrases which are in constant use ... should another drummer ... strike out on his own, drumming at fancy, new phrases ... another drummer who heard these combinations for the first time, could not ... read his message with any accuracy'.

From the Cameroons, comes this enticing account of musical skills by Griffith (1951) who wrote of 'a pipe play called Ndong which the local farmers used in dances and public festivals ... some twenty men will take pipes made from bamboo ... each player carefully chooses his own pipe ... as each pipe gives out only one note each person must blow at the correct moment in order to achieve the proper effect. With twenty pipe men, or twenty notes, some magnificent tunes can be played'. This method of making music must require a high degree of social sensitivity ('team work'), of ability in auditory pattern recognition, and a skill of auditory-muscular co-ordination.

Finally a musicologist, Gerhard Kubik (1964) from Austria, describes certain Ugandan music, pointing to aspects of it which western students and psychologists have not previously easily grasped. Kubik is describing music played on the *amadinda*, a large wooden xylophone which is played jointly by several players at once, sitting in rows opposite each other across the instruments; he refers to 'inherent rhythms ... patterns which are not played by the performers but arise in our ... imagination directly. . . It is somehow like a crossword puzzle, where every letter is at the same time an ingredient of two different words; only a little more complicated'.

'. . . inherent rhythms are certainly not merely rhythm patterns. They are rhythms and melodies in one gestalt. . . To make all the inner dimensions of these musical picture puzzles gradually visible to yourself the total pattern must be repeated again and again. . . If there were no repetitions, if the Uganda musicians had tried a horizontal development of their art of the kind found in European music, there would be no time for listeners ... to enjoy the music in its highly developed vertical dimension'.

'Listening to African music demands different abilities from the listener than hearing European music. . . A listener to African music has to direct his attention more to the inner dimensions of the composition, which are so manifold that they cannot be perceived all at once in a split second. The listener has to change his own 'position' gradually just in the same way that one looks at an object from different sides'.

If Kubik is not just imagining all these complexities (and Nketia (1961), puts forward similar observations from Ghana) it is intriguing to speculate on the possible links between skills involved in attending to such music, and those which result in 'rotation' of pictures and diagrams so often reported. These independent reports do lend weight, however, to Maistriaux's and Ombredane's theories.

From quite a different direction comes a hint of a 'special ability' which was actually first reported as a difficulty. Peter Fraenkel (1959) studied comprehension of radio programmes on the then Central African Broadcasting Station. He found that 'only a very small proportion of listeners' understood some programmes. One difficulty was that listeners took statements as metaphors. Thus 'the fly, though small, is dangerous' failed as a health message but was taken as 'though the Europeans are few they are powerful ... we'll never be able to drive them out.' Though such broadcasting problems have been overcome their psychological implications are interesting. Some Africans seem to expect pictorial statements to show things as they know them to be, rather than at face value or how they appear in a simple perspective. So, sometimes, verbal statements are not taken at face value either, but are subjected to considerable cognitive transformation.

Illustration of the situation during administration of the Rod and Frame Test (RFT) here, both the subject and the frame are tilted
(see below and p. 116)

Psychologists have been extremely slow to devise any tests of such auditory skills and of their intellectual implications, if any. However, I used Witkin's Rod and Frame Test to explore a very similar idea, in Nigeria. There,

infants were carried a great deal on mothers' backs, therefore perhaps learning
the feel of walking motion in an upright position at a very early age; children
danced well at an early age; choral singing and childrens' bands were also
widespread, and of a high quality. Yet dealing with the visual patterns
entailed in Koh's Blocks and Raven's Matrices test often produced poor
results. Clearly, some other combination of skills should be explored. An
auditory pattern recognition test was tried out, but did not develop far.
Witkin's RFT (see Chapter III) was already available, and was therefore used.

Two broad patterns of results emerged (Wober, 1966b, 1967b). Nigerians'
scores on the RFT were not nearly as 'behind' western standards, as they
were on purely visual tests. In fact, for certain conditions of the test (where
the subject had to resolve bodily sense of direction in conflict with visual
information about the 'true' vertical of gravity) scores were better for
Nigerians than for Americans (in results published by Witkin). Where the task
was to a greater degree a visual one, the Nigerians did not do as well as the
American results. The second pattern in the results concerned the relationship
between RFT and Embedded Figures Test scores. Witkin (1967) asserted that
the RFT and EFT measured the same thing, and that scores on these tests
correlated well — in America. This was not repeated in the Nigerian testing.

All this was interpreted as support for Biesheuvel, Ombredane, and
Maistriaux's concept, which was now also given a name of 'Sensotypes'. It
was suggested that westerners, and to an extent also western educated
Africans exemplified a 'visual sensotype', since the pattern of sensory
information with which their cognitive processes had to cope with since
infancy was primarily visual. Certainly, they have auditory and
'proprioceptive' experience; but these modalities are not so used as is vision,
in communicating symbols which have to be penetrated for their meaning.
The less-educated Nigerians were held to exemplify another sensotype
(unnamed); their accustomed pattern of sensory information included much
less visual symbolism (writing, pictures and diagrams); it included more
auditory meaningful material, since languages are tonal, which means that
syllables are 'sung' in the appropriate pitch, and differences in tone entail
differences in meaning. The Nigerians also seemed to express a greater 'poetry
in motion' that westerners — though this is an extremely subjective matter to
evaluate, and quite possibly this is a figment of the observer's imagination.

Subsequently a few researchers have tried out the RFT in Africa though
none have really vindicated the idea of sensotypes. Okonji (1969a) showed sex
differences in certain samples — men score more than women; he also
repeated Wober's finding that RFT and EFT did not relate well together. Du
Preez (1968) was interested in inter-sex differences rather than in
cross-cultural ones, and used only part of the RFT in which proprioception
was not so important. Durojaiye (1971) mentions his RFT study in Nigeria,
using the tilted chair condition and having tested 540 people; this partly
supports the sensotype idea, but his report is too brief to allow a thorough
assessment of the results. In particular he found that illiterates were better at
judging uprightness of the rod when they were themselves tilted, than were
literates; manually skilled people were better than clerical, and also than
unskilled men. Durojaiye points out that the variety of his results makes it

difficult to say that there is one particular level of RFT response which is a general 'African' characteristic.

The most thorough RFT study was reported by Gerda Siann (1972), who tested children in Zambia. Siann analysed and disagreed with Witkin's method of test scoring, which simply records how far from the true vertical a subject sets the rod when he believes he has got it upright. Siann found that EFT and RFT did not correlate well even for European children; there was slightly more indication that EFT and RFT correlated, among the Zambians; but still, EFT scores had a closer resemblance to scores on a verbal test, than did RFT. This tends to support Wober's (1966) contention that the RFT is tapping some skills other than those measured by EFT among uneducated Africans. Siann also analysed her results to check the sensotype hypothesis. The Zambians' average error was 20 degrees for the 'visual' part of the test (where the chair is not tilted, but the square frame around the rod, is) while the non-Zambians scored 6.5 on the visual test. The Zambians were thus much weaker than the Europeans on this part of the test. On the 'proprioceptive' part of the test (when the subject's chair is tilted) Zambians scored 1, while non-Zambian children scored 0.7. On this basis, that the Zambians did not do better than non-Zambians on the proprioceptive test, Siann says her results refute the concept of sensotypes. A less rigid interpretation could, however, be taken. This would point to the Zambians' proficiency on the proprioceptive test, and not just disregard it because the Europeans did as well; secondly, it would recognise that a radical difference between the chair tilted, and non-tilted conditions does exist, that requires interpretation (which Siann does not offer). It is very surprising that the chair-tilted condition produced such extraordinarily low error, and it is noteworthy that the non-Zambians did so much better on the 'visual' task. The results perhaps point best to a modified sensotypes concept.

A more precise experiment exploring a question similar to that of sensotypes has also been done in Zambia, by Okonji (1974). Okonji points out that his experiment differs structurally from the ones involving RFT. In the latter, as Okonji puts it, 'the experimenter introduces conflict between the inputs to different sensory modalities and observes how the senses . . . resolve the conflict'. Okonji instead chose a method where 'the experimenter requires subjects to use information obtained from one modality to solve a problem presented through another'. Okonji tested well-off and poor-family Zambian children, as well as European children. The children heard tapped-out sequences varying in rhythm (auditory inputs) and had to select which pattern of dots on one of several cards correctly represented the pattern as heard. European boys had a very significantly better score than poor-family Zambians and were also better than well-off family Zambians. Okonji cautiously sees no help here for the sensotype notion; but the results do not falsify it either, since what is being examined here is intersensory integration, rather than a more sophisticated treatment of one sensory source than another. But he does recognise that differences between people from two communities may exist in their respective rates of development of sensory integration. Okonji points out that more research of this sort can be very useful, in helping to surmount difficulties found all over Africa, where children are taught in school in foreign languages – e.g. English and French.

Finally, Poortinga (1972) interpreted the sensotype idea to imply that Africans would have 'relatively higher scores on auditory tests than on visual tests when compared with Europeans', even though this ignores the fact that most claims have pointed also to the importance of proprioception. Poortinga tested ability to differentiate loudness of pure sound tones and intensity of lights. Europeans did better in judging loudness while there was no difference on brightness judgements. As with Okonji's later work, this is not a direct test of sensotypes since it focusses on the qualities of simple stimuli rather than on the ideas which such stimuli can evoke. Nevertheless, this finding is not encouraging for the sensotype idea.

Summary

The observations of some psychologists from Endemann to Maistriaux, and further evidence suggest that African systems of abilities explored by factor analysts (Chapter III) have not been fully mapped. Without invoking the 'nonsense in – nonsense out' warning needed for interpreting all factor analysis, it is obvious that if skills are neither suspected nor tested, they will not figure as part of a factor analytic solution of the 'structure of abilities'.

There is evidence that however 'non-visual' their emphasis may be, African cultures nevertheless had several examples of visual symbol systems. These included star names and constellations, and systems of recording messages, instructions and ideas by visual signs. Zahan explained that where visual systems existed, they were restricted in scope of what they dealt with, or as to who could unequivocally understand them. In some ways this can be a virtue; but one possibility it allows is that for the same person, a symbol may have different meanings at different times. This non-specificity might relate to phenomena such as 'rotation' or polyphasic picture perception, questions which are open to further research. Perception of time, both in terms of accuracy and of attitude (such as patience) may also be explored further for anything it might tell us about slowness in working at tests.

The great skills in Africa of artistic and cognitive achievement in sculpture and music, and the cognitive areas of parable and public administration ('lore and law') have escaped qualitative study and certainly quantitative measurement by pscyhologists. Yet we surely know enough to realise that traditional systems, before it is too late to study them, offered plenty of challenges to such investigation. Unfortunately, psychologists have but recently worked free of a centri-cultural approach, and this chapter is short because there is so little research in the area to report.

The sensotypes hypothesis, while still lacking respectable empirical support, remains, with Witkin's concept of field independence, capable of linking perception, cognition, social behaviour and socialisation procedures which in turn may affect perception. We may have to realise that educational attempts to break into such a circle are likely to affect all parts and processes in the chain, rather than to remain specific in impact. Some of the links between skills and attitudes are now examined in the next chapter.

CHAPTER VI

VOCATIONAL ASPIRATIONS

Introduction

The previous chapters have discussed something of what has been found out about the processes of cognitive development. This chapter, and the next two, discuss the broad question of what kind of adult does the young person want to, and eventually, become. Most likely the amount and kind of education received will have had the major influence on the state of people's abilities. But together with abilities, at least three other factors determine what kind of people the new adults are. These three factors include economic development and opportunities, with which we are not directly concerned in this book; 'social facilitation', or the operation of the network of friends and relatives which helps a person find his place in society – and again, this is primarily a concern for sociologists; and thirdly, personal aspirations, or ambitions.

Aspirations have interested sociologists and educationists, as well as psychologists. Sociologists and planners have wanted to compile job status ranking systems to help anticipate where people will demand education and training, so that these can be provided sufficiently to supply workers in numbers and at levels fitting in with the general development plan. We can also see where people should be encouraged to direct their interests, so that unknown sectors, or unpopular levels of the job market receive recruits who are suitably fit, in their abilities and attitudes, for such jobs.

In particular, planners have been worried that aspirations far outstrip the available possibilities. Reactions of frustration and hostility were already reported by Devauges (1965) in Togoland, replacing the earlier uncomplicated enthusiasm for schooling. P. C. W. Gutkind (1969) is clearly alarmed that unless such unrealistic aspirations are somehow abated – and he does not point to this as a serious possibility – there will result a tremendous amount of misery in frustration and poverty; occasionally too, this 'constituency of the unemployed' will be rallied by a politician who seeks to change society – at least by placing himself in power. However, Gutkind suggests that modern African governments understand this aspirational tinder well enough, and usually take firm steps to keep the political sparks well damped down. The size of the problem has been indicated by Angi and Coombe (1969) who write about Zambia that 'in January, 1970 about 75% of the 1969 primary school leavers will be unable to find places in secondary schools', and 'it is obvious that Zambia's problem occurs in almost every other African country'. They continue 'although government has urged youth to undertake a career on the land, it has failed . . . to implement a programme of action to satisfy these conditions'.

Numerous other observers have added to this alarmist view. In Uganda, Kamoga (1965) wrote that 'the majority of school leavers have an interest in clerical work and think that menial tasks are beneath their dignity'. Kamoga's allegation reflects a major finding reported in previous chapters, that education has a large effect on cognitive development. It also points, probably unintentionally, to a fundamental problem; for if middle class observers consider some jobs 'menial' then other people may also be likely to consider these jobs menial; and it is hard to see why one should expect anyone to want to do such jobs. In a fair society — and few leaders have yet pointed to this particular aspect of such a society — no work would be considered menial, and more people would be willing to do all kinds of jobs. Philip Foster (1968) whose fieldwork has been in Ghana and Tanzania, points out that efforts to provide 'rural oriented' courses in primary schools have not been successful in arresting 'the flight from the land'.

Aside from the alarmists there has recently grown up a less-well-known, but more optimistic view. The work here has been primarily social anthropological, but it implies that most people are not unrealistic in the way they apply their attitudes. Some who have contributed here include Polly Hill (1970) and Keith Hart (1970), who studied small scale enterpreneurism in West Africa; and Tina Wallace (1972) who has studied youth in Uganda. These observers have pointed out that alarmist calculations of numbers of unemployed are based on the notion of 'formal employment' — that is, of jobs which are properly specified and contracted by public bodies. There is, however, another range of 'informal employment', in which farming, retailing, manufacturing, repair and service activities provide useful and sometimes lucrative rewards. To recognise this 'informal sector', and the extent to which its world overlaps with the formal sector, is to realise that the situation is less cut and dried than that which the alarmists fear. This social anthropological perspective allows us to look at the psychological question of whether people are 'realistic', in a different light. Already a few studies which have brought the investigator closer, in the fieldwork situation and in the depth of questions asked, to the people studied, have found evidence of realism.

The intellectual demands in this area of study are limited. There are only two or three main concepts to grasp about what is going on. One is that there are two available ways of assessing prestige, or status of jobs, and hence their possible desirability. The first way is to ask people how they think *society*, or *other* people evaluate jobs. This method does not tell us directly how individuals themselves may respect, or not respect certain jobs. The second way is to ask people how *they themselves* value particular jobs; but strictly speaking, unless there is a large and representative sample, this does not tell us how jobs are ranked 'in society'. Nevertheless, some investigators have appeared to use the second type of question for the first purpose. Another idea to grasp is the one that jobs with high status may attract aspirations in like proportion. This is perhaps too often taken for granted as true, when sometimes it is untrue; and not enough questions are asked in some studies about why people want to attain certain jobs, or not. Also, it is as well to remember that psychologists (and others) are well aware that attitudes do not always correspond to actions, and thus a person's felt ambitions and attitudes towards education and careers do not always mean that appropriate action will be taken.

The material in this area falls fairly neatly into three sections. We can consider pupils' aspirations for the type and extent of education they hope to attain, and the reasons for such aspirations (often taken for granted by investigators). Then we can see what is known about job prestige, with an accent on what, if anything, is known about how prestige may affect people's personal aspirations. Thirdly we look at job aspirations, or the kinds of jobs people hope to, or feel they can attain. Finally, one important psychological assumption remains an undercurrent beneath all this. This is that the kind of job a person does, has a powerful shaping influence on the kind of person he has become. To name a person's job is to begin to tell us a great deal about him as a person. The ways in which this assumption is true, or untrue, remain to be investigated; but it seems to exist as a reason why psychologists are interested in this broad area.

Educational aspirations

Early work in this field was reported by Remi Clignet (1964). He drew from his own fieldwork in 1959 in the Ivory Coast, and from that of other workers in the Ivory Coast, Mali, Gabon and Senegal, involving over 6,000 students in all. Clignet draws a conclusion that 'in general, the desire to achieve an occupation determines the level of studies which the pupil proposes to undertake'. Clignet brings out clearly that education is not usually wanted principally as an end in itself, but as a means of making a living. Of course, we have seen that pupils cannot always attain what they 'propose'; but if their outlook is dominated by practical considerations, as Clignet says it is, we would expect them to have realistic ideas of what levels of education they will be likely to attain.

Neighbouring Clignet's results were those of Philip Foster (1965), who questioned secondary school boys in Ghana. Nearly all wanted to continue education after Form V, if possible; but only about 40% were sure that it would be possible for them to continue. In spite of this evident caution among the greater part of his sample, Foster knew that many even of this 40% would not find the places of which they were so sure. He generalised this concern, making it appear to apply to everone, when he wrote 'the hopes and expectations of students are by no means realistic in terms of the actual educational opportunities open to them'. Miller and Bibby (1969) found a similar picture among Accra Form V schoolboys.

In Nigeria, Abiri (1966) questioned 250 grammar school pupils, and found, like Clignet, an opinion of education as a means to an end. Girls particularly prized the utilitarian over the interest value in education. There may well have been a reflection here of local traditional divisions of work role. For example, Yoruba women do much trading, while men cultivate more social roles and are actively working in some cases for relatively short parts of the year when cash crops are harvested. Also in Nigeria, Durojaiye (1970) found that at the International School in Ibadan, over 60% of pupils wanted to go to University. Pupils at this school related the type of education desired to the exact type of jobs they wanted to do. Probably more confident of their well-being, and given an amount of vocational guidance, they could relax from the more pressing view of education as being principally a means to the end.

A strong desire for further education is also found in Nigeria at a lower social status. McQueen (1965, 1968), a Canadian, interviewed about one thousand primary pupils, and school leavers both employed and unemployed, in the then Eastern Region. Though 90% of primary leavers would not find secondary places, 84% did want some further education. Among those who managed to find work, the proportion still wanting to continue their education dropped to one third – a strong indication of realism (or defeatism?) among the majority. Unlike Clignet's and Abiri's, three quarters of McQueen's interviewees wanted education for self-improvement, as well as to get a better job; only 15% mentioned they wanted education for altruistic reasons – to provide a living for the family or simply for access to money and prestige. Since many of these conclusions will depend on the quality of interviewing and comprehension it was possible to have attained, it is wise to seek support for such results from other investigations.

Jonathan Silvey (1969) in Uganda, asked over 500 secondary school pupils 'what do you hope to do after completing senior 4?' Though some pupils might have taken 'hope to do' as meaning 'expect to do', the majority wanted university education, felt their chances of attaining it were good, and knew what they wanted to study at university. Only 1% actually wanted to leave school after O level exams and find middle-rank jobs in society. At that time in Uganda, with subsidised places available at a growing University, it was hardly sensible, once well into secondary schooling, to want to drop off the ladder. Silvey reported, like Clignet, an emphasis on seeing education as the essential step to good jobs, rather than as an end in itself.

At a lower level, in Kenya, Koff (1967) asked primary pupils what they considered to be the purposes of their education. From a country-wide survey, he selected randomly over 600 responses to analyse. Among rural pupils, four times as many saw education as a means of social mobility, as those who said they were interested in knowledge for its own sake. Among urban pupils, the proportions were five to one for the above two motives. Over 80% would study hard to help their parents eventually, or send their siblings to school; over 50% wanted to study hard to become 'a government leader and help rule the country'. Pupils completed the sentence: 'a man without education . . .' from their imagination. Over half mentioned unemployment, about a fifth mentioned lack of knowledge, and 12% referred to being unable to help one's parents, or turning criminal. Thus different questions investigating the same area, can produce a different picture of the priorities in response. Koff concludes broadly that, while people do realise education's maturational benefits, the main perception is of its giving social mobility. Also occupations resembling educational activities like desk work are favoured, thus clerical work is preferred to farming.

The researcher who has probably achieved most in this field is the New Zealander, Tony Somerset who worked in Uganda (Somerset, 1968) and later in Kenya (Somerset, 1970). The Ugandan study showed the strong competition for secondary schooling, with over three candidates for each available place, but dealt mostly with psychometrics, or predicting progress in secondary school from primary leaving performance. Pupils' attitudes were studied mainly in the Kenyan research.

Here, over 1,000 pupils in 24 secondary schools indicated how much more education they wanted, and how much they thought they would get. Nearly nine out of ten pupils answered the two questions with equal estimates of personal and of attainable ambitions. Just under a third thought University education would be available, which in real terms is itself an overestimate, and shows moreover, that many who (unrealistically) said they would be able to go on to further education also realise that suitable places are not available. The abler pupils had a stronger desire to continue education, and school quality and socio-economic background factors were also linked with educational aspirations. In the elitist, 'National Catchment' schools even the major portion of those with poor academic performance had University aspirations. Against these signs of unrealism, is evidence that in the best of the 'Harambee' (self-help, community initiated) schools, which only tap local populations from which the best has been creamed off, there is a smaller proportion who aspire to levels which they most likely will not reach.

At the same time, Kenneth King (1971) also used Somerset's aspirations questions in Kenyan schools, finding that biographical background factors also link up with aspirations. Thus schools set up by government for the pastoral Maasai, were being filled with Kipsigis and Kikuyu pupils; those who had moved into these districts to get school places included some who may have failed to advance scholastically elsewhere, and among these 'outsiders', was a smaller proportion of those with unrealistically high ambitions. King also found that over 45% of Form IV pupils in the schools he sampled wanted University education, while Somerset found just under 30% likewise. These differences appear to be significant and may be regional variations.

Two precautions need to be remembered in dealing with this kind of research. First, if 40% of people in one place say they want to go to University and 60% elsewhere likewise, it is common enough to read, or to think that the second set of people 'are more ambitious'. But strictly speaking, the second group simply has more people who are equally ambitious as those in the first group. Secondly, if a person is first asked about his ambition, and discloses it, he may feel ashamed to answer the next question by saying he does not believe he will realise this ambition. This kind of difficulty is sometimes, though probably not in the above surveys, met by 'rotation' (half the people are asked one question first, the other half the other).

Nevertheless, Somerset (1970) produced further, very useful work. This focussed on vocational guidance and its possible effect on aspirations. According to psychological theory, and common sense, increased knowledge will affect attitudes towards an object; in this case, pupils get knowledge from sources ranging from well designed talks, to pamphlets handed out without any personal exposition. Although quality of vocational guidance in a school was not the major determinant of the levels of aspirations, it was clear that better guidance did link with a smaller proportion of pupils having unrealistic attitudes. Further, there are signs that even as little guidance as reading a careers pamphlet may have had an influence on the aspirations of significant numbers of pupils.

Building on this possibility, Somerset devised a careers information sheet that would in future be supplied with the application forms that Form Four leavers fill in ('Form A') for further education opportunities. Meanwhile, Somerset showed that, as so often, attitudes are not always reflected in actions. For among nearly 18,000 'Form A' documents completed in 1970, there were only 5,830 actual applicants for 3,300 places. Thus the mere act of filling in Form A apparently served as a 'reality test'. One sensible goal for careers guidance is to even out imbalances which exist between desired, and available jobs. For example, at Kenya Science Teachers College there were only 1.5 applicants per place, while enthusiastic careers talks for the latter, produced 15 applicants per vacancy at a Health Inspectors Training College.

Somerset concluded that 'pupils, by and large, set realistic aspirations within the limits of information available to them'. Hopefully, a similar realism may be found among educational and manpower planning authorities. This is not always forthcoming; for instance, the Government of Zambia maintain an Educational and Occupational Assessment Service whose Director, Mary Allan (1973) stated that the aim was to see that 'Manpower Utilization within the public, private and para-statal sectors of the Community is reasonably efficient'. This may be a realistic goal, but she ended her paper unrealistically by saying 'it is too early to forecast how efficient (the school leaver service) will be in getting the bulk of school leavers fixed up in jobs'. This latter aim cannot be the responsibility of people involved in careers guidance, if the bulk of jobs required do not exist.

In summary here, though there is a reasonable worry that the enthusiasms of youth might and sometimes do stimulate widely unrealistic educational ambitions which could easily turn sour when not satisfied, other research suggests that pupils also come to realise this. Clignet found that young people were mostly dominated by practical concerns in their attitudes to education, and McQueen in Nigeria and Somerset in Kenya have shown that when students meet the test of 'real' life outside school, or are adequately informed in school, many do form realistic attitudes towards themselves and to their chances of educational advancement. Though it is the task of political scientists rather than of psychologists, it would be rewarding to see if a similar realism infused the policies and actions of politicians and planners of manpower development.

Job prestige

Psychologists are interested in attitudes towards jobs, and in how job prestige may affect aspirations. It is not to be taken for granted, however, that job prestige is the main, or even an important influence on individual choice of jobs. One youngster may want to be a social worker, and another a priest; both may say that these jobs have lower prestige, or status than those of the doctor, or judge; but this recognition of relative status may have no effect on actual career choices. So for psychologists there are two parts of this concept to investigate: first, the prestige hierarchy, with a related, social psychological question, namely how the hierarchy varies according to the personal status and background of the perceiver; and second, how if at all, the hierarchy may affect personal aspirations.

Nelly Xydias (1955) made an early contribution with a study in the then Belgian Congo. She asked secondary, and technical school pupils to assess the prestige of occupants of various jobs illustrated in photographs. This was a useful technique suitable for use among uneducated people, though there is little sign that Xydias' example, or methods have been followed. Xydias also recorded a group of clerks' ideas on job prestige. Two basic findings were that the two groups of subjects have extremely similar perceptions of job prestige; but there is some slight sign of a tendency to upgrade one's own, or similar occupation. Xydias' study did not include jobs such as healer or diviner, which emerge from the traditional society.

Soon after this, Mitchell and Epstein (1959) published the first of several studies from Zambia and Rhodesia. Over 600 replies were analysed from 'scholars at three educational institutions near Lusaka' to questions on the prestige of 32 occupations. Overall, occupations 'were ranked in roughly the same order that we should expect from a group of European youths'. However, for some jobs the 'don't know' responses ran as high as 51%; and there was a closer agreement about jobs at the bottom end than for those at the top end of the scale. Mitchell and Epstein did not explain this, but it could be that more information was available, from relatives and friends, about lower than about higher prestige jobs. Though there was a remarkable overall agreement in rankings between sets of people with different backgrounds (correlations all over 0.90), Mitchell and Epstein did point to a few differences in how jobs were perceived. These they related, as Xydias did, to a tendency to rate jobs more like one's own intended one, higher than other people did.

Mitchell and Irvine (1962) then reported very similarly from Rhodesia; only very slight differences in job prestige rankings were found between people of different social classes, or ethnic backgrounds. They repeated the same findings again in Zambia (Mitchell and Irvine, 1965). Three groups, again of young trainee workers and scholars showed remarkable agreement in their perceptions of a job hierarchy not only amongst themselves, but also in comparison with Mitchell and Epstein's 1959 results. A later study by Hicks (1967) however, comparing Zambian and European boys' prestige ratings, showed slightly lower correlations than in Mitchell's work. The Africans rated certain technical jobs such as engineering and electrical trades higher than did Europeans, while the latter rated cultural-arts jobs relatively more highly. Hicks (1969) again reported that secondary school pupils accorded certain jobs stated as done by a woman (e.g. lady doctor) somewhat lower prestige. However, boys' and girls' ratings of prestige correlated well.

These similarities continued to emerge in studies over the Continent. For example, the anthropologist Gamble (1966) interviewed adults in their language, Temne, in Lunsar, an iron mining town in Sierra Leone. People placed fifty cards, each bearing a job title, on a tilted board divided into five sections. Gamble points out that 'prestige was not an easy concept to translate into Temne ... the basis on which the rating was done was deliberately left as vague as possible to avoid imposing western concepts'.

Furthermore, 'prompting by friends and spectators was also common . . . if an individual's opinions were really decided by his wife or his colleagues, it seemed reasonable to let this be taken into account'. With this 'contamination' it would have been impossible, even if Gamble had wanted (which evidently he did not), to tease out differences in perception that might exist between, say, clerks and manual workers. Nevertheless, he concluded that 'the main trends find parallels in other surveys. . .'; importance to and of the self were also said to have influenced judgements. Thus, for 'thirsty manual labourers the palm wine tapper, despised by the greater part of the population, was a man to be valued. A trader who employed a watchman to guard his shop ranked the position higher than did others'. However, not every provider of services is magnified in prestige, as people also employ leather-workers and 'night-soil men' (sewage disposers), but do not rank them highly. In combination however, 'when an individual's own occupation occurred in the list there was a strong tendency to overrate it, overrating occurring in 80% of such cases'. Gamble also observed that older men upgraded traditional occupations, and holders of authority.

While Gamble had begun to study prestige of traditional occupational roles among low-status people who had strong links with traditional culture, Morgan (1965) questioned Ibadan University students about such occupations in Nigeria. As usual, his list of 41 jobs was ranked in much the same way as elsewhere. Traditional occupations of diviner and herbalist ranked very low; but traditional cultural authority roles of Oba, Emir and Obi (Yoruba, Hausa and Ibo terms respectively) were ranked high. Morgan thus showed that some traditional positions can retain prestige in modern society, in the eyes of high-status observers. It still remains to be more fully explored though, how low-status observers, or people with strong traditional cultural ties, would see the prestige of a wider variety of traditional occupations. McQueen (1965), also in Nigeria, found that students ranked occupation broadly as people did eslewhere; but he did not shed light on the question of how traditional occupations are perceived.

The American, J. M. Armer (1968) did, however, explore this question among nearly 600 seventeen year olds in Kano City, Northern Nigeria. They were interviewed in Hausa, using a picture of a hill divided into five levels, and asked to point to which level they thought corresponded to how 'all the people in this city' saw the prestige of each of 16 jobs. As usual, the rankings were broadly similar to those found elsewhere (in this case, American comparisons). However, the traditionally-rooted praise singers and drummers were seen as very low in prestige; farm owners were also low, but Mallams (Muslim clergy) were ranked high. Armer found that 'primary school teacher' was ranked lower by the more educated than the uneducated segments of his sample. This goes against the findings often reported (see above, from Zambia, Sierra Leone and elsewhere) that 'ego-involved' occupations are upgraded; but Armer offers no comment on this.

The next step was to divide the sample according to how they identified themselves on a scale of 'traditional or modern self-identification'. Correlations between subgroups were again very high. These findings add to Gamble's to show that prestige rankings are broadly similar not only in western countries and in westernised sections of African nations, but also in some more traditionally-linked sectors of an African nation. Armer's contention that 'a common occupational prestige system is shared . . . across all societies, whether industrialised or not' is perhaps premature; for it still needs to be seen whether a thoroughly rural and uneducated African sample would see prestige, in rural terms, likewise. Armer tried to cope with this, as an afterthought. He compared the job rankings from boys who came from farm-families, with those from boys from non-farm families. There was an extremely close similarity. But this was not a true test of the question; for the farm-family boys were still tested in or near to Kano City, and were asked to rate jobs as they thought people in town would rank them. They were not asked to rate jobs as they thought people in the countryside would rank them.

Further evidence on traditional occupations and their prestige, was provided by Foster (1965) in Ghana. He had pupils from 23 schools rank each of 25 occupations on a 5-point scale. The traditional occupations present were Chief (ranked fourth) and Chief's counsellor (ranked fourteenth). In other respects the results were, as usual, like those elsewhere.

Foster added a new angle to his study. He asked subjects to rank jobs on perceived levels of income. Correlations of around 0.9 linked perceived prestige with perceived income rankings. Foster feels this throws doubt on 'the frequent observation that "prestige" factors largely govern the assessment of jobs by educated Africans'. We can perhaps accept Foster's doubts, even though his reasoning is not irrefutable. For prestige may still determine job choice on the one hand, even though on the other hand it is linked to perceived income levels; it is not necessary to assume that income has any causal link with job choice. It is better to establish this, as Clignet did, with direct questions on peoples' motives for job, or educational aspirations. One way would be to ask whether people will prefer one of two jobs with different prestige but equal pay, and the same for two jobs of similar prestige but different pay.

To study how job prestige might affect job choice Nelly Xydias (1960) explored six possible reasons which could make jobs attractive, and found that 'well esteemed work' came third in importance only, after 'work which one enjoys', and 'a good boss'. Xydias' subjects were already working, which no doubt made the topic of the bosses' qualities more salient. Interestingly, 'good money' was ranked after esteem as a factor of job attractiveness. This does not, of course, disprove Foster's suggestion that money is a principal motive, since Xydias questioned a different sample in a different country. Nevertheless, it supports his distrust of prestige as a principal factor influencing choice of training and of jobs.

We come now, to a few studies which explore how prestige is made up, or what it is about jobs which gives them their esteem. Hicks (1966) was one of the first to explore this question, in Zambia. He questioned men at a Railway Training School about 12 jobs ranging from Cabinet Minister, to domestic servant and about why jobs were esteemed, or not. Not unexpectedly, he found that prestige was a compound of several attributes including pay, responsibility, intelligence needed, service rendered to others, working conditions, and power wielded.

Similarly Irvine (1969b) asked secondary pupils in Rhodesia to tick any of the items they liked, in a list following the question: 'would you like a job in which you. . .?'. The most popular choice was 'lived in a town', then 'spent a lot of time helping people'. At the bottom were 'lived in a reserve or purchase area' and last of all 'worked in a store selling things'. This last item shows that though helping people is prized in the abstract, one way of doing so by serving in a shop is not a popular way. Irvine also asked the students to say which jobs, from a list of 26, they would like to do; and which they would not like to do.

In a section titled 'job preferences and prestige', Irvine treats the rank order of popularity of jobs as if it was equivalent to prestige. This makes two assumptions: that high prestige would relate to wanting to get such jobs; and that one can infer prestige from individual opinions among a sample who do not represent a cross-section of the population. After some discussion, Irvine realises that his assumptions need to be substantiated. He shows that the job preferences he has found, correlate closely with prestige rankings in other studies, for example by Hicks (1967).

Irvine now presents a factor analysis, in which the first statistical grouping, or 'factor' is labelled by Irvine 'Indoors: Office/Clerical'. This is because readiness to work as a clerk, grocer, telephone operator (and other indoors jobs) all tend to come together. One would have expected the job condition 'worked out of doors' to have had a strong negative correlation with this factor; but this was not found. This can only be because a sufficient number of people who do want jobs which happen to be done indoors, may also have said they would like a job where they 'worked out of doors'. This first factor is not, therefore, a 'clean' one. In contrast, a third factor (third because it is less clear-cut statistically) was logically more consistent. This contained the job characteristics 'often got rather dirty', 'worked out of doors' and at the same time had a negative correlation with 'worked in an office'. This tells us that some people would like open air jobs where they do get dirty; these people include very few, if any, who also make the illogical preferences for working in an office. Unfortunately, though this factor is logically consistent as regards this indoors/outdoors question, it is untidy in other ways. Such people who show a taste for outdoor and dirty jobs, also would like to be research workers, or cashiers. Irvine thinks this is because they are attracted by the 'upper end of the white collar job scale in terms of wages'.

Unfortunately, such research does not appear to advance knowledge much further than what we knew after Hicks' work. Irvine concludes that 'prestige would depend' on what an individual 'most clearly associates the occupation with and whether he identified, in himself, the qualities he associated with success in the occupation'. Also 'the single social prestige rating seems an extremely complex concept'. Here, Irvine points to an interesting psychological question, that of the self-concept, which has been an undercurrent in several prestige studies. It remains for further work to investigate how the ways in which people think of themselves (eg I am a kind person, I am a competitive person, etc) might relate to how they think about, or may want to do various jobs. Prestige would presumably relate better to job preference, among people who agree that 'I like to be a person who is respected or admired,' than among those who 'like to be liked'.

Jonathan Silvey (1969) generated a simpler, and perhaps clearer picture of the issues of job preference, and prestige. In his Ugandan study he asked 'when it is said that certain jobs have very high prestige and respect, what do you think are the two main things about such jobs that give them this prestige?' The most favoured reason was 'it is an essential service to the community'; next came 'it needs intelligence and ability', while 'it pays so well' came only fifth out of the nine available characteristics. As the most important aspects of a job they would hope to enter, 62% had specified 'interest in the job', and 49% chose 'abilities and personality well suited', but 'highly respected job' was only among a residual group netting just 5% of replies. Thus prestige may not always relate well to job preference, while the occupational psychologist's ideal of 'fitting the man to the job' is not uppermost in respondents' minds either.

Silvey pointed to the results of Clignet and Foster (1966) from West Africa, where security and stability were preferred as reasons for seeking jobs, over prestige; income, and promotion chances were well down the list. Similarly, McQueen (1968) found in Nigeria that very few people said they wanted education so as eventually to gain prestige, or wealth in themselves. Silvey concludes that 'we cannot therefore equate prestige with an incentive to recruitment'. Silvey criticises Clignet and Foster for the interpretation that if income levels are altered, then prestige will alter accordingly, and that people will seek jobs according to the new levels. Ugandan results suggest that both salary and prestige are well behind more 'psychological' aspects of job interest and suitability in influencing how students think about their careers.

Finally, Silvey listed the 28 jobs in his questionnaire, in order of prestige as perceived by secondary students. While students had answered that 'essential service to the community' was what made a job prestigious, it appears that essential service did not confer prestige on all jobs; for bus driver, carpenter and primary school teacher were all very low in the prestige hierarchy.

Though Silvey says his was a 'co-ordinated parallel study' with Irvine's, he does not show the correlation between the prestige ranking he found, and that which Irvine recorded. If we take the 15 of Silvey's jobs which are almost identical with those in Irvine's list, the correlation between the two ranks is 0.79, which is as usual, very high. In an unpublished enquiry of my own, there was an even better correlation for the same 28 jobs, between the rankings derived from Silvey's secondary pupils, and those from university students. High correlations also related the job aspects of income, social esteem, responsibility, and the like. Notably however, the pattern of correlations differed somewhat between men, and women students.

It is not always easy to see why researchers have explored the concept of prestige. There is an implication that if we know the prestige hierarchy (which is thought anyway to be basically similar in all societies, even in those with relatively little modernisation) then we will understand better how people are going to compete for places in the new society. However, the results have suggested that prestige is a result of several aspects of each job; and that in any case, prestige is not usually the focal aspect which determines how people will desire a job. Probably most people are sufficiently realistic not to say to researchers (even if not to themselves) that they all want the most prestigious jobs. People know which jobs have most prestige; but their choices are likely to be for less prestigious jobs.

This brings us to the question of what jobs people do wish to attain.

Job aspirations

Job aspiration studies are most likely to be done among students. A few studies (e.g. by McQueen, 1969) have been among unemployed youth, but these are more difficult to find and to question. Unemployed people are usually so keen to get any kind of work that their ideal aspirations become blurred; and employed adults answer about aspirations, partly in term of how their present job suits them. Such status effects, of whether people are in school, unemployed, or employed would be questions of major interest for study; however, it is hard to find research that has looked at this kind of variable.

In connection with his work on educational aspirations, Clignet (1964) studied the overall level of jobs aspired to, as well as the types of jobs wanted within any level. Differences in aspirational level varied with the education of pupils who were asked; thus in the Ivory Coast more secondary pupils (quite reasonably) had higher level aspirations than primary pupils had. There were also inter-national differences, between Mali, Gabon, Senegal and Ivory Coast groups. In all these countries, technical jobs, teaching, and medical jobs were most sought after, while politics and agriculture were of little attraction; in fact, the latter field was 'totally devalued'. Using as rather a blunt measure of occupational knowledge, the number of jobs known and chosen among a group, he found that this 'knowledge' about occupations was 'effectively the same among primary and secondary pupils and for the different countries'. However, in some countries (e.g. Gabon) pupils of urban origin had higher level preferences; elsewhere, (e.g. Senegal) urban and rural origin pupils had similar preferences; but in general rural pupils did not want high level jobs any more than did urban pupils.

Clignet adds that 'traditional social organisations and the positions of various ethnic groups impinge upon the aspirations and professional motivations of the school population'. For example, 'in Senegal, Wolof pupils look towards a political career more than pupils from other tribes. Inversely, they are less attracted towards medical professions'. Clignet gives other examples of occupations that have become associated with particular tribes; thus 80% of the Attie children questioned in Ivory Coast came from planters' families, against 54% of Agni children. Such links between tribe and types of work are to be found all over the continent. Wells and Warmington (1962) explain how immigrant Ibo were the largest group among plantation workers in the Cameroons, having different aspirations from the local people. Similarly in southern Nigeria (Wober, 1967) Urhobo in a sawmill town, as landowners, at first felt detached from the hurly burly of an industrial society, but then decided belatedly, after being overtaken in wealth by immigrant workers, that they did now have similar industrial aspirations.

In East Africa, King (1971) found that 50% of Kipsigis pupils wanted to become teachers, with only 20% of Kikuyu pupils in the same schools saying likewise. On the other hand 35% of Kikuyu boys wanted technical jobs, but only 3% of Kipsigis. This probably mirrors the fact that Kipsigis live in rural areas, where teaching is one of the commonest professions; while Kikuyus live nearer the city of Nairobi and may hope to join the industrial life there.

Clignet offers us at least three more major points. First, 'the majority of children asked intended to choose different professions from those of their parents'. This does not mean that a student's overall social background, including family occupations, does not affect his job aspirations. A youngster may wish to work near his family, but at a higher status than his father. Parents too, may agree in this: 'among 400 planters asked ... only 30% wanted their children to follow in their footsteps'. While European children in Senegal (mostly middle class) wanted to follow their parents' example, this was not so among the Africans, possibly because most Africans were not yet of middle class or elite status, and wanted to better themselves.

Further exploring desires for social mobility, Clignet asked 'where do you want to live later on?', and 'why?'. Four fifths of the Senegalese sample wanted to live in town; but more city pupils wished to live rurally (33%) than did pupils already in rural schools (16%). Clignet concludes oddly that 'education is thus established as a technique of urbanisation'. Though education is not chosen chiefly as a road to city life since 'the final purpose of education is ... to support the family' Clignet believes the pressure for urbanisation is increased as a result of education. Clignet's evidence that a host of factors affect job aspirations parallels his view that job prestige is not the main influence on aspirations. Thus though Ivory Coast students wanted medical careers for the prestige involved, those who chose engineering were thinking principally of the pay. In Senegal 'pupils choose their jobs according to job-related criteria ("I like this work", "I can do it well"etc) in 39% of the answers'. Reasons for aspirations also varied with level of jobs wanted; thus 61% of students wanting high level jobs gave 'personal' reasons for their choices, compared with 49% of those wanting medium level jobs.

Though acknowledging the variety of causes and motives influencing job choice, Clignet's work supports the psychological observation increasingly manifest through the 1960s, that more education fuelled higher aspirations; in turn, these aspirations could only be met by seeking opportunities in towns and cities. In cities, where there was insufficient rewarding employment, as Callaway (1963) put it, unemployment would become 'perhaps the most serious long-run socio-political problem facing African countries'.

Near Clignet, Foster (1965) studied ideal and expected job predictions among Ghanaians. Among middle school pupils the most popular ideal choice (of 51%) was for jobs as 'artisans and skilled workers'. Only 21% gave, even as an ideal, that they would like professional jobs. Less than 1% said they wanted to teach. These data gathered in 1959, illustrate how opinions change, in contrast with Margaret Peil's finding (1968) also with middle school boys in Ghana, that the most desired types of work were teaching, skilled manual jobs and the services.

Foster also asked Ghanaian middle school pupils what they thought was 'the best reason for choosing a secondary school'. Over three-quarters gave good exam results as the favoured reason. Foster ranked the schools on five objective criteria (of exam results, staffing ratios, etc) and found that the pupils' ranking of worthiness of schools closely resembled his own. Among secondary school pupils nearly 20% hoped ideally to have jobs in medicine or law; but none *expected* to enter these professions. Clerical work was only hoped for by 7% though expected by 52%; and primary teaching was also less wanted than expected. Foster compared the family background of pupils with various aspirations and concluded that 'teaching in Ghana as in most countries constitutes the principal mode of occupational mobility for lower status groups'.

These two major pieces of work show that pupils' ideal hopes and their real expectations differ markedly. Clignet sees education functioning as an agent of urbanisation. Foster sees education as a means of social or occupational mobility. The gist is the same. People get as much education as they can, to equip themselves for as rewarding jobs as they can get — most of which are based in towns. Foster is much more alarmed about the consequences of all this than is Clignet; and Foster's alarm is, perhaps unfortunately, expressed in terms that appear to apply to the whole population of young people; whereas his results show that lack of realism is only found among a minority.

Support for Clignet's position comes from McQueen (1965, 1968, 1969) and his work in Nigeria. With 65 other questions, he asked 'what would you most like to be in life?' and 'if not able to be what you would most like to be, what will you do?'. Here again, more secondary pupils allowed themselves high ideal aspirations than did primary pupils; and there was a substantial drop in expectations from ideals. McQueen (1969) found that neither primary nor secondary pupils expected to get professional jobs; while 24% even among secondary leavers (and 40% primary leavers) expected to find themselves farming or doing unskilled work. McQueen says this argues for 'a pragmatic and somewhat flexible approach to careers'. Wallace (1972) showed likewise in Uganda that though people try to get 'formal' jobs, they realise this will happen for only part of the population, part of the time, and fill in with other useful 'informal' occupations. McQueen found that four fifths of employed respondents were optimistic about 'how does the future look during the next five to ten years', and even over half the unemployed were optimistic. Like Wallace, McQueen found that formal unemployment is a harsh stimulus to realism. For among secondary leavers who were unemployed for under a year, 70% hoped for professional and white collar jobs; but only 39%, who had been unemployed for over a year, still had these aspirations.

Silvey (1969) advocated vocational guidance to diversify aspirations and help people make decisions with better knowledge both of the real opportunities available, and of themselves. He wrote 'contrary to received opinion (although in line with the evidence from Ghana and Ivory Coast), general commercial and administrative posts are not popular, nor is the desire to teach commensurate with the needs of the country'. Silvey also tried to answer the question whether expectations represent ambitions scaled down in the same occupational area, or move into totally different fields of work. The answer was the latter; 'only teaching and scientific work would hold a substantial proportion' at a lower level. Klingelhofer (1967) was another researcher concerned at the lack of jobs at suitable levels to satisfy pupils' greatest ambitions. He foresaw harmful effects, not this time just among the unemployed, but in terms of inefficiency and in application among people who unwillingly enter jobs which are very unlike what they would really want to do.

Two somewhat more optimistic studies were also done in East Africa. In one, Koff (1967) asked 'what is the best job to have in Kenya', and found that cash crop farmer was top choice, with primary teaching next. However, both urban and rural pupils personally hoped to do clerical work. Koff also analysed reasons why jobs were thought 'best to have', or were personally wanted. Choices varied with the background of respondents; but overall among rural pupils the commonest reason for choice of a job was its income (not its status), while a close second was the service-to-the-nation type of reason. Curiously, only 39% of rural pupils thought that farming *would be* their work, as against 51% of urban pupils who thought likewise. Lastly, Koff asked 'if a boy does not get a secondary place, and cannot repeat Standard VII, what should he do?'. Among rural pupils 44% said one should hunt for work, while 38% thought it best to get down to farming straight away; among urban pupils half thought one should seek further education privately, but 17% thought one should go and farm straight away.

Finally, Heijnen (1967) studied attitudes to jobs among rural and urban pupils in Sukumaland, Tanzania. Uniquely, he only studied jobs which were 'open to primary school leavers'. Pupils were asked: 'please say of each job, whether you like it very much. . .'; to: 'do not like it at all', thus answering on a five point scale. Whether this question got at ideals, or expectations, the astonishing thing is that urban and rural pupils agreed very closely in their rankings of jobs. This means that the two groups are making the same distinction between items like 'petrol pump boy', 'shop assistant', 'shopkeeper', 'hotel servant', etc. In other words, people have a clear, and generally shared idea of the attraction of such jobs.

Heijnen found that 'nation building' was the most common reason for liking jobs; while financial justifications attracted less than half this proportion of replies. Heijnen is aware of the difficulties of interpreting his results, but emphasises the signs of realistic thinking: 'once failed, but not a day earlier, they think it better to turn to farming than to swell the ranks of the unemployed in town. Farming at least means enough food, and in Sukumaland, a very reasonable money income'. In contrast academic critics who now fear the consequences of unrealism and crushing conditions in the towns, may observe a worse dilemma arise. For as we enter the second half of the decade amidst warnings of drought and famine in many African countries, the option of farming as a safe fall-back will be denied to many; and without radical social changes, to remain as 'farmers' may be less realistic than to go to towns.

Conclusions

It would obviously be unrealistic for observers to ignore the attractions of better education and better jobs, and of the dangers if these are not available. At the same time, the spectre of hordes of disgruntled young people, festering with frustration and resentment at being unable to realise their hopes of lucrative careers, leading to uncontrollable delinquency and disruptive political forces, has not really emerged from the attitudes so far surveyed. These cover several West and East African countries. Similar surveys probably exist in other African countries; even if such enquiries produced results opposed to those reviewed here, they would not nullify the results we have seen. The future, however, may hold quite different problems.

Clearly there is a widespread urge for education, less (at lower levels often) for its cultural consequences than for the way it can open up to well paid jobs. The higher that students get up the educational ladder, the higher they want to go, though in some cases (as reported in Kenya, and Francophone West Africa) people do aim in the first place for middle level jobs. This drive for the top is probably reflected in the nature of educational systems, which are not usually designed to deliver people to intermediate destinations. One may liken the educational system to an express bus service. Most people who get on, are interested in getting to the final destination. Those who want intermediate destinations have to jump off, or fall off and make their own way. Thus although there do exist Technical Colleges and Teacher Training Colleges, many students in these are not in the first place interested in intermediate technical and teaching jobs, but want to carry on with more education.

A few leaders of thought and action in Africa, notably President Nyerere of Tanzania (in his *Education for Self Reliance*) have tried to rethink and remodel primary schooling, to make it a relevant experience for a primarily agricultural population. This has been criticised by sociologists, notably Philip Foster (1969) who says that primary schools are an unsuitable springboard for fostering agricultural development; they are the bottom rung of the ladder of knowledge, which leads logically to further schooling. Foster suggests that good farming is best taught by adult education; but he forgets to provide any constructive ideas concerning primary schooling, and what it might do for people who cannot find post-primary education.

Psychological research on attitudes to jobs has served at least two other fields of social scientific interest. One field is that of immigration and urbanisation studies, which are essential for good economic planning, and the provision of services and amenities on a realistic scale. The second topic concerns 'class formation'. Will secondary pupils be recruited proportionately more from already educated families, thus leaving less chance for those from less privileged backgrounds? Though planners may try to combat this by using selection tests, we know that family background influences abilities; thus pupils selected on the basis of tests will include a greater proportion of those from advantaged families. This process will certainly contribute to the formation of an elite class; when this has used up the opportunities the economy offers, children from favoured backgrounds will have to compete for lower level jobs than hitherto. Some of the pressure will be taken up by various devices including displacement of aliens, finding oil, and packing the army and bureaucracy. Psychologists are concerned here with the source of pressure which is a principal provocation of these grave social problems.

Africans have been found to have a view of the prestige ladder of jobs that is basically the same as that in other nations. Those tested have been mostly students, but uneducated youth and adult workers have shown similar results. However older people in rural areas have not been surveyed, and it remains possible that they may not share the same views on job prestige that most other people have. While a good start has been made on studying how prestige is made up, much more remains to be understood why jobs attract prestige, what kinds of personalities are concerned with prestige, and how, if ever, prestige affects whether people will try to get, or to avoid various jobs.

Further investigation is required of attitudes towards middle-level jobs. Most African countries have plenty of unskilled and semi-skilled manpower; after independence, there has been a scramble to take up jobs at the top of the status tree; but a wide range of jobs which offer a balance between satisfying high aspirations and the disappointments of realism, lies in the middle range of technical, skilled and supervisory positions. Any research which points to how people can be encouraged to think primarily in modest terms (such as Somerset's work) could certainly be useful.

Some researchers who deal in generalisations about groups of people, or groups of facts, tend to develop anxious views about a surge of unemployable youth to the towns. Other researchers such as anthropologists, or psychologists who do much of their fieldwork by interview, may develop an affection for their interviewees (certainly no bad thing in itself) and produce a sympathetic account of the ideals and prospects of youth, being reluctant to dramatise disappointments which may lie ahead. There is no point in taking both these approaches as mistaken; rather, the two perspectives have something to contribute to the total picture of the diversity of attitudes towards jobs, and the consequences these attitudes entail.

Future research might usefully integrate work on job attitudes, with themes dealt with in the next two chapters. It would be useful to know how patterns of attitudes develop in individuals, and how attitudes to other important issues in life, including attitudes to oneself may affect — or remain separated from — attitudes towards jobs.

CHAPTER VII

SOME BASIC STRUCTURES
OF ATTITUDES

Introduction

In this chapter we move from the *contents* of peoples' opinions in a particular important area, to explore the *structures* which may underlie patterns of attitudes in a variety of fields. This idea of structure should become clearer in the discussion that follows. Two guidelines have been used in selecting material for study from the wealth available. One principle has been to examine mostly that material which has been put forward by its authors as systematic psychological research. A great deal else in anthropological works, novels, and other sources, tells us about attitudes more profoundly, more sensitively, or more usefully in other ways than those we need here; but it is not organised in a way systematically to explore structure.

A second selection guideline concerns the border area (no clear line exists) between the notions of attitude and of personality. If attitudes are currents of thought and opinion that are reasonably consistent for any one person, then we seem to be describing something characteristic of that person, or part of his 'personality'. The distinguishing marks between attitude and personality material may be at least two: attitudes constitute a smaller part of the wider concept of personality; and methods of measurement and study of what are called attitudes on the one hand, or personality on the other, have been different in the literature. Nevertheless, the two fields are closely linked; we recognise this, and also that other psychologists might well decide to divide up, or even unify these fields in a different way from that which has been chosen here.

It is fairly clear that the major theme which underlies attitudes research in Africa concerns the social change going on in the continent. Certain attitudes will run parallel with traditional forms of society; other attitudes correspond to western social forms. The situation in between is where the search for existing, and new structures has caught the attention of social scientists. Social change has interested historians, sociologists, political scientists, geographers, and economists. But psychologists consider that historical, economic and political processes are all expressed in, and work through the minds of individual people, and attitudes of mind are thus the focus of this chapter.

The research here has been arranged into three rather loose groups of studies. The third concerns inter-group attitudes (or what is colloquially known as the questions of tribalism and nationalism). This does link with the theme in the other two sections, of the emergence of 'modern' attitudes; but researchers have mostly treated the two issues separately, so inter-group attitudes can form a separate section.

The main part of the material can be arranged in two sections. These do not correspond to two self-consciously separate schools of thought or of procedure. Rather, things seem just to have grown in the way they have done. First, we can identify a 'cross-cultural' group of studies. In this, researchers have more or less clearly distinguished between 'western' attitudes (the attitudes associated with western cultures — even though these differ between themselves, and over time) and 'modern' attitudes in Africa. Modern attitudes have been influenced by western ones, but are not necessarily identical with them.

The second group of studies I have called 'centri-cultural'. This is because in them, the researchers uses the idea that western attitudes clearly set the pattern to be followed by new attitudes in Africa. Some researchers have even gone further, and implied that western attitudes are good, and traditional ones by contrast, less good. This kind of attitude among non-Africans in Africa, resembles that of the early missionaries (whether Muslim or Christian). Such people arrive with a conviction of what is good or bad, and where a traditional culture does not meet their criteria of goodness, they recognise this, and try to change the situation. Anthropologists in the first quarter of the century questioned such an absolutist stand, and put forward the idea of 'cultural relativism'. This studies the workings of a culture without trying to judge it morally according to external standards, or to change it. The centri-cultural approach, usually unintentionally, is more absolutist than relativistic. It would be a mistake, however, to think that absolutism is entirely bad and relativism right. Moral innovators such as the prophets of the Bible and Koran, were absolutists, as are modern doctrinaire politicians and revolutionaries. But the researcher had best be relativistic while seeking his facts, otherwise his bias may falsify the picture he reports. A few methodological studies on bias have been done in Africa, and these are now reviewed.

Methodology

In Africa as elsewhere, it has been shown that different experimenters can derive different results from the same field; and such differences may relate to experimenters' own biases. Marwick (1956) reported a survey done in 1947 among the Cewas of Northern Rhodesia with two African assistants, Walter and Bruce, who collected separate interviews. Answers to questions about social change differed greatly according to the interviewer. In answer to 'what will happen to an African who gets rich?', 7% told Bruce 'we can't get rich — we're black', but 27% told this to Marwick. Response did not depend only on interviewer's race; 64% told Bruce there were more witches 'nowadays than there were long ago', but 96% said this to Walter. Though he reported many such differences, Marwick unfortunately did not indicate why the three interviewers had got such varied results.

Mitchell (1968) had five people interview 600 people in Ibadan, Western Nigeria. The questionnaire included 45 items on traditional and western values, and people were given the same interview twice. Among 1,402 first replies, 795 favoured western views; of these 795, 141 favoured the traditional views when asked a second time. An even larger switch, to western responses, occurred among those which were initially traditional. Though Mitchell's own statistical procedures are methodologically incorrect, the sizes of the changes do suggest that very probably there is considerable instability in responses. Reasons may include badly explained questions, and unpredictable elements in the relationship between the interviewer and the interviewee.

The possibility that a researcher may miscalculate his results in ways which reflect his attitudes has been shown by Wober and Cohen (1972). Ugandan students added up figures they were told represented exam results from various districts of the country. Significant errors were not made where figures were thought to represent the observer's own region, but were found to the detriment of results supposed to come from other regions.

These studies suggest that answers in attitude research are not 'objective', but relative to the interviewing situation. If the observer has biases, these may influence him to make his own errors, or in other ways to affect people he questions. It is perhaps best therefore to develop research along cross-cultural, or culturally relativist lines, where the researcher tries to bury any biases he has. As an individual, he might want to act morally or politically on the basis of his findings; but any results on which action is based ideally should faithfully reflect subjects' views, and be free of influence from researchers' bias if possible.

Attitude studies which tend to be cross-cultural

An early pointer to a morally detached approach to research was provided by Sir Frederic Bartlett (1946). He suspected that certain features of traditional culture and associated attitudes would resist change; he called these 'hard' features, in contrast to 'soft' features, which new cultural forms and attitudes would more easily replace. Bartlett suggested that psychologists should distinguish such hard and soft features, and help understand how changes occur.

One of the first to follow Bartlett's direction was Biesheuvel (1955). A preface in fine print inserted by the editor tells us much:

> 'This is the first of a series of papers to appear in this Journal on the nature and measurement of African attitudes towards the standards of conduct that Africans are expected to observe in the Union of South Africa'.

In the mid-fifties, white researchers were still moving hesitantly towards a view that Africans were autonomous individuals, who held opinions that were worthy of study. In South Africa, this interest evidently had to appear in the guise of a moral inquisition. But the method Biesheuvel devised was subtle enough to allow surveying that could be detached from an absolutist standpoint. In fact, Biesheuvel's fieldwork had begun in 1937, and its influence stretches as many years after publication, as its roots predate it.

Five Africans, Tom, Peter, William, Jack and Alfred are reported as discussing various topics, making statements reflecting any one at a time, of eight 'attitudes'. Biesheuvel called these attitudes: ethico-legal, religious,

expediency, traditional, fear, non-complaint, compliant, and pleasure. For
example, in a situation where a passer-by sees a banknote, Peter may say 'the
stranger should pick it up, as he needs the money'; this would exemplify the
'expediency' attitude. Alfred may say 'the stranger should leave the note as a
policeman may be watching, and he would get arrested'; this would illustrate
a 'fear attitude'.

There were 200 such statements and 1,000 young people rated each on a
five point scale, from 'most wise', to 'most foolish'. This is one of the biggest
of such attitude surveys done in Africa. On average, the 'ethico-legal'
statements were rated as wisest overall, and the others less so, in the order
shown above. On this scale the mid point is neutral; above it results denote
wisdom and below it they denote foolishness. Only the first two attitudes fell
in the 'wise' part of the scale. The expediency attitude, presumably
unwelcome to editors who make prefatory comments such as above, fell only
just on the foolish side of the neutral point on average. Feelings were
evidently shared similarly among most people, as there were high correlations
in the ranks of attitudes assessed from sub-groups of different ages.

Later results (Biesheuvel, 1959) with this questionnaire given to 820 High
School pupils were similar to the previous ones, and Biesheuvel stated that
the instrument was a valid one for the study of social attitudes. This refers, of
course, to a psychological consistency rather than to any demonstration that
people's opinions would resemble their actions, which was not shown by
Biesheuvel; nor, indeed, is it ever easily shown elsewhere in attitude studies.
Biesheuvel concludes that people 'wholeheartedly identify themselves with
both ethical and religious values, except in such matters as man's natural
needs and belief in witchcraft, where traditional attitudes tend to persist'.

One must ask further about South African research, whether people
answer as they do because they feel that a whites-sponsored project should be
given such answers. However, the whole project was a very worthy beginning
on technique and in exploring structure (as against just collecting a rag-bag of
scattered opinions). It points to certain 'hard' features of traditional cultures;
in this case, questions of 'man's natural needs', and of supernatural beliefs.
But probably also the ethical values so respected are not a case of some 'soft'
traditional alternative having given way to western principles, but of an
equally durable traditional ethical view simply running parallel to the western
one (eg, on questions of theft, murder, etc).

Another start on attitude research was also made in South Africa, by Elise
Botha (1964) who employed a 'uses' test. This simply consisted of asking
about each of 50 objects, 'what is this for?' Children and adults of four ethnic
groups including Xhosa, were questioned. Answers were classified as
belonging to one of seven categories: sustentative, benevolent, malevolent,
hedonistic, aesthetic, religious, and hierarchical. Xhosa children used many
sustentative and religious themes in their answers (compared with white
children); and Xhosa gave few hedonistic and aesthetic responses. Xhosa
adults scored higher than children on benevolence, hedonism and hierarchical
ideas; while they were lower than children in their frequency of malevolence,
and religious themes. The African adults differed significantly from the

whites on 6 out of 7 categories. This suggests that Africans' ideas current at that time were certainly not identical with western-type ones.

Botha's approach involves open-ended questions, which researchers find it difficult to analyse. Possibly too, the structuring it makes of the material did not appeal to other workers. At any rate, it was Biesheuvel's rather than her type of questionnaire which was being developed by workers elsewhere.

In Ghana, Gustav Jahoda (1961, 1962) reported on fieldwork he had started in 1955. He divided his 501 male and 49 female adult evening class students into a Low group (with elementary education, or less) and a High group (with education above elementary level), and compared attitudes between these groups. The questionnaires dealt with the topics (in Jahoda's terms) of: traditional customs, culture and chieftancy; tribe and illiteracy; employment, family relations and social aspirations; and polygyny and choice of marriage partners. On each issue there were two statements, one expressing a westernised view, and the other representing 'the traditional outlook'. People were to say whether they agreed, or disagreed with each statement. An example of a pair of such statements is:

> Tribalism is bad, and one should put the Gold Coast as a whole before one's tribe.

> One should be loyal and give support to one's tribe, even if sometimes it seems contrary to the interests of the Gold Coast as a whole.

Jahoda points out that with such statements 'agreement or disagreement with both involved a contradication'. The structure of the questionnaire implies that the whole spectrum of opinion lies as it were, somewhere on a straight line between two polar opposites. While this may be true for most people, or with most topics, it is not necessarily true for all, since it is sometimes possible to disagree with both propositions and accept some other which the researcher had not anticipated. As to whether contradictions do occur, Jahoda indicates that they do, when there is a 'lack of any settled views on the issue'. Importantly, he is aware of the effect of exactly how a statement is framed, for 'where opinion on a topic is unstable, the categorical formulation of a point of view tends to tip the scales'. This could be an insight of some political, as well as research psychological importance, for it asserts that when people are unsure on an issue they may accept a firm line, a tendency which may have intuitively been grasped and used by authoritarian rulers.

Jahoda's results showed that the High group supported more western opinion statements; also, there was less inner contradiction among this group. On one topic where opinion was least confused, only 13% of the High group had self contradictory opinions; at the other extreme, for another topic, 58% of the Low group had self contradictory opinions, either agreeing, or disagreeing with both statements.

Jahoda examines his data in contrast with views put forward by two anthropologists; one, Kenneth Little, considered that educated Africans in Sierra Leone are still fundamentally traditional and that their westernisation is in important respects superficial. The other view, held by Clyde Mitchell in Rhodesia is that 'except for their skin colour, educated Africans are effectively Europeans'. Jahoda realises that different countries involve different experiences, and finds his assessment closer to that of Lombard (1954) who did similar research in French–speaking Dahomey. Lombard wrote (my translation) 'acculturative tendencies show most clearly in material and economic life, and less strongly, in demographic matters. In areas which touch a man's private life, his family, social and above all religious affairs, the African seems to keep almost intact his previous personality'. Thus Jahoda's and Lombard's findings agree with Biesheuvel that in family and certain religious matters, traditional attitudes remain strong.

Jahoda next taught in Scotland, where another researcher bound for West Africa, John Dawson, was preparing his materials. Dawson saw that an extension of Jahoda's questionnaire format would be extremely suitable for his task of studying psychological processes occurring alongside social change. Dawson's questionnaire dealt with 18 topics, such as medicine, brideprice, the status of women, and so on. On each topic there were four statements. One each stood for the traditional, western, and also 'semi-traditional' and 'semi-western' points of view. Notably, Dawson did not at first refer to a spectrum ranging from traditional to modern, but from traditional to western views. This leaves open the question of whether a modern opinion is to be found anywhere along this spectrum (if not at the western end), or even off it.

Dawson (1967a) first set out his attitudes theory as a *consistency* one. If a man finds social change presents him with conflicting roles, demands or desires (as for example between polygamy and monogamy) he will experience 'cognitive dissonance'. This dissonance, provided (as Dawson implicitly assumes) that men are rational beings will have to be got rid of. Dawson then believes that one of two things will happen to the cognitive parts of attitudes. Either opinions will swing to one extreme or the other; or there will be some reorganisation of ideas to provide a logical compromise. Dawson later (1969a) repeated his basic argument, but added that there was with certain topics some 'unresolved attitudinal conflict' (UAC). He also insisted again (Dawson, 1969b) that 'lack of achievement of . . . compromises will be maladaptive and result in pressures to reduce or eliminate inconsistency'.

Subjects in Sierra Leone indicated, as with Biesheuvel's five point scale, whether they strongly agreed, agreed, were not sure, disagreed, or strongly disagreed with each statement in Dawson's questionnaire. This gives the extent of group agreement or disagreement with traditional, or with western statements separately; Dawson also subtracted the amount of traditional approval from western approval, and called the result the Range of Variation (RV). Where this is high, people approve western ideas more than traditional ones: when it is negative, they favour traditional ideas overall. Where RV is small, and this is a situation which Dawson has unfortunately ignored in his writing, approval is equally strong or weak for both traditional *and* western items (logically impossible, but as some responses show, *psycho*logically possible).

In one study (Dawson, 1969a) workers from four groups – Creole, Mende, Temne and Fulbe were selected of similar age, education, intelligence test scores, and job grades. While Creoles are urbanised and intermarried with westernised migrants, Mende (Dawson, 1963) have work-oriented traditional values and Temne are traditionally aggressive, and war-oriented. The pastoralist Fulbe are said to be very conservative (though one might question how this applies to men who have broken away from their cattle, to acquire skills and education on a par with those among a group of Creoles).

Dawson found best support for western statements among Creoles, then from Mende, Temne and Fulbe, in that order. Creoles overall rejected traditional statements, while Mende and Temne were relatively neutral towards them. Fulbe showed slight overall support for traditional statements; but awkwardly for Dawson's consistency theory, they also had mild overall support for western ideas. There was probably therefore some discord among these Fulbe minds; Dawson theorises that if people have not decided clearly in favour of one extreme or of the other then there would be strong support for intermediate views. However, Fulbe only had mild support for such intermediate attitudes.

Another adventurous application of Dawson's, was to correlate Range of Variation scores with efficiency ratings for five groups of workers, nurses, labourers, artisans, apprentices and clerks. In all cases the correlations were highly significant. Such a finding, if it meant that certain attitudes promoted work efficiency, could be very useful economically; so in 1965 data were collected in Nigeria to amplify Dawson's findings (Wober, 1971). With a questionnaire very similar to Dawsons's, correlations between RV scores and supervisors' ratings of work efficiency were effectively zero, both for a group of 173 manual workers, and among 50 clerks.

How might we explain the differences between the two sets of results? Several factors may have interlocked to have produced the opposite conclusions we see. If in the Sierra Leonean case occupational selection had not been very efficient, then people of a relatively wide range of educational experience were likely to have been found in each job. Those with better education would be likely to have more approval of western ideas, and larger RV scores. Western supervisors might then have rated the more educated people whom they may have understood better, as more efficient, giving rise to large correlations between rated work efficiency, and the RV attitude measure. In the Nigerian case, if (as observation indicated) educational level corresponded closely to job level, then in any one job there would be workers only of a narrow range of educational experience. Ratings of efficiency would not reflect educational, and hence attitudinal differences. However hypothetical this explanation may be, it remains true that a second attempt to match attitudes with efficiency did not succeed; and if Dawson's discovery is to be of any use, it needs to be readily repeatable.

Dawson wrote (1967a) that illiterate subjects often agreed with both western and with traditional statements, and that where a person made several such 'invalid responses' (Dawson, 1969a), his results were discarded. But even though Dawson rejected the strongest examples of UAC, a considerable amount of it still remained. Dawson defined UAC as approval for both traditional and western items, and at the same time disapproval of the intermediate items by more than a certain amount. With this narrow criterion, he found 6% of 48 apprentices showed conflict in that topic where views were clearest, and 75% conflicting views for the topic where there was most uncertainty. Reflecting Biesheuvel's and Jahoda's results, Dawson found that with topics such as witchcraft, and parental authority, there was the greatest attitudinal conflict. There was also a significant correlation between individuals' levels of UAC, and their scores on a neuroticism scale. Dawson argued (as did two Belgian investigators in Zaïre, Mertens de Wilmars and Niveau, 1960) that unresolved attitudes caused anxiety. It could be argued conversely though, that it is prior constitutional anxiety which hampers clear formulations about attitudes, and that it is the neuroticism which leads to attitudinal conflict, and not vice versa. This is a question it would be extremely difficult to settle, and probably both directions of causation are effective.

One strength of Dawson's work lies in his invention of a questionnaire which enables soundings to be made at four points along a possible traditional-western spectrum. This makes it more possible to realise that what is modern is not necessarily just what is western. For example, Dawson found among university students (in Freetown) 'reaffirmation processes' of support for values which did not meet the full western image. Jahoda (1961) had previously found something similar in Ghana, which he repeated (Jahoda, 1970) a decade later. In Nigeria (Wober, 1971c) a parallel situation emerged; among younger (and more highly educated) clerks there was weaker support for western ideas than could be found among certain less educated manual workers. Thus groups which are sociologically seen as modern (more educated, in more skilled jobs) are examined for their attitudes. In some cases we see that opinions which are 'modern' in their ownership, are traditional in their nature.

In the Nigerian research scores for attitudes on each topic, and for the whole scale, were correlated. Mostly (except for one topic out of 18 for the group of manual workers, and four topics among the clerks) there was substantial correlation between separate topic-, and whole-questionnaire scores. Thus a person with western, or traditional, or intermediate views on any one topic, is consistent to the extent that he may have similar views on the rest of the questionnaire. Notably, as in previous work mentioned, opinions on brideprice, witchcraft, wives' roles, and (a new topic not included in previous research) taste in music were at a more traditional level, even among the more educated clerks.

Next in this sequence of studies is one by the Ghanaian Susan Gilbertson (1971), who later worked as a researcher for her country's television service. She gave children in Accra, aged between ten and twelve, tests of abilities, general knowledge, and a traditional versus western attitudes scale. For children, this combined features of Biesheuvel's more personal, and Dawson's more statistical approaches. There were, for brevity, only seven topics (medicine, children's obedience, women's social status, children's education, girls' education, wives' obedience, and rich men's family obligations), and three statements for each. For example:

Anna is sick. What should her parents do?

A. Her illness is probably due to a witch and therefore it is much better to go to a native doctor as white doctors know nothing about witches.
Agree strongly. Agree. Not sure. Disagree. Disagree strongly.
B. Unless her parents are sure her illness has been caused by a witch they should take her to a white doctor as their medicine is so much better.
Agree strongly. Agree. Not sure. Disagree. Disagree strongly.
C. She should not be taken to a native doctor but straight to the hospital, where a doctor will give her good medicine and put her into bed to be cared for.
Agree strongly. Agree. Not sure. Disagree. Disagree strongly.

It is difficult to devise items that deal purely with a single topic, and this was found by Dawson, Jahoda, and Wober too. Gilbertson compared TV viewers from three social classes (judged by parental occupation) with non-TV viewers of the same social classes. She found that TV viewers in each social class tended to show less agreement with traditional ideas than was found among non-viewers; and among the upper social class, the viewers also had stronger support for western ideas. Such differences may partly have been due to experience in watching TV, or the possibility that even within a relatively narrow range of social class, the TV-owning families had different attitudes from non-owners.

Gilbertson also found that children who agreed with both traditional and western items, also agreed more strongly with compromise items. This seems to support Dawson's theory. But the situation is not so simple. In the order in which statements were answered, a child who agreed with the traditional statement, and then agreed strongly with the Compromise statement, if he then agreed with the western statement as well cannot be described (as Dawson suggested) as 'resolving dissonance'. It is more suitable to say that the logical dissonace has been compounded. This returns to a distinction made (Wober, 1971c) between people who have conflicting attitudes, kept in 'separate compartments' and who are not troubled by the situation; and people who realise the inconsistency of views they hold and feel uncomfortable about it.

As a last example of studies using Dawson's design, we may include some unpublished data collected in 1972-3 in Uganda. The questionnaire covered eleven topics including several previously unexamined, such as ancestral versus municipal burial places, the priority wanted for minority vernaculars, or lingua francas such as English or Swahili, the social or individual nature of intelligence, and birth control. Tested among a group of Kikuyus in Kenya, ranging from uneducated people to undergraduates, and among Ugandan University students, each topic was revealed as having its items designed as intended, since T and W scores correlated negatively and other items appropriately.

Results among 90 undergraduates were revealing. There was not a good consistency *between* topics. That is to say, in some topics(e.g.Medicine, Birth Control) the western view was favoured; in other topics (vernacular languages, the social nature of intelligence) the traditional view prevailed. A factor analysis explored the possibility, hitherto taken for granted, that there was a single prevailing traditional-western attitude dimension, along which at some point the modern view would be located. If this was so we would find one major factor, with which most traditional and western items would be correlated. In fact, this was not found. Instead, there appear to have been at least five factors, each related with two, or three separate topics.

The details of these findings matter less than the new model for thinking about attitudes in the context of social change which they suggest. Instead of the one-dimensional line, we can think perhaps in terms of a wide river, representing a 'current' of personal opinions. Tributaries lead into the river; on one side are fed in traditional currents of opinion; on the other side are fed in western elements. These inputs will lead to a flow of experience that is not necessarily some sort of uniform mixture. Some rivers, like some people, will manifest a well mixed current. For other people, as with other rivers, there will be separate currents and eddies; these represent some topics where the traditional source is still clear, some where the western additions are dominant, other areas or topics where some mixture occurs. Some currents of the river flow alongside each other, different but unmixed; while other currents bordering each other produce conflicts and eddies.

All these studies can reasonably be seen as a connected group. They used questionnaires in which some possible underlying structure linking attitudes which may exist, can emerge. Jahoda (1962) thought that a modern view was not a western one necessarily, but would emerge as a synthesis of old and new elements; the impression existed though, that the modern point of view would be found somewhere along a straight line between the traditional and the western. A new analogy is put forward here however, of a flowing river made up from various tributaries into several currents. In this, the modern view is a composite, across topics; in some, an even blending has occurred, in some areas separate flows or compartments of opinion are found, and between others there may be cross-currents, or eddies of attitude experienced as anxiety or conflict.

The French-speaking world has contributed two studies in this area. Bormans (1968) put ten family problems to children in the Saharan oases of Laghouat and Ghardaia. He found coexistence of traditional and westernised attitudes. In general, he considered that where the topics were principally personal, new outlooks prevailed. However, where changes in social behaviour were at issue, attitudes were more traditional. Thus the changes in outlook so far remained at a 'private' level. The Parisian academics Otto Klineberg and Marisa Zavalloni (1969) questioned students in Ethiopia, Ghana, Nigeria, Senegal, Uganda, Congo and Kenya — though they lost their data from Kenya, in the post. These authors say they found little in the literature on the social psychology of attitudes in Africa, apart from the work of Doob, Jahoda and Van den Berghe (see below). The principal implication of this remark is that the French-language literature has little else to offer, otherwise Klineberg and Zavalloni should have reported it. Even five years later, Armer's bibliography (1974) supports this impression.

The students, mostly in arts and social sciences, were asked whether they agreed with the item 'traditional African culture has certain values but should be modified and integrated with western culture'. This statement drew more agreement (from 44% among the Senegalese to 81% among the Ethiopians) than did a more pro-traditional and a more pro-western statement. In five countries, but not the Congo, students who chose the description of themselves as 'innovators' were just as likely to support this compromise statement, as were people who called themselves 'someone in between'. And in all six countries, by wide margins, innovators were much more likely to support the compromise statement, than the outright pro-western view. This strongly supports the case that more 'modern people' (by their own definition) believe in a synthesis of cultural patterns rather than in more extreme cultural positions.

A group of centri-cultural attitude studies
In the mid-1950s, two American sources financed research on African attitudes. Hortense Powdermaker (1956), supported by the Guggenheim Foundation, went to the then Northern Rhodesia. She started by stating that 'all members of the society can be placed somewhere on a continuum with traditional and modern values at opposite ends'. Here is the identification of 'modern' with 'western', presenting western cultural forms and attitudes as having an overall power of attraction; other systems are seen as facing towards the western system. This is why such studies may be called 'centri-cultural'.

Powdermaker collected essays, some in English, others in Bemba, written by teenage school boys and girls. Each pupil had to describe an African to a stranger in London, a European on return to the village, what job they wanted after school and what kind of person they wanted to be in future. Some virtues, for example of hospitality, were seen as characteristic of Africans but not of Europeans; in others, for example forms of etiquette, European ways were admired. On the 'general attitude' towards Europeans (the personification of western culture and attitudes) 40% of boys and 9% of girls were clearly favourable; none were wholly unfavourable, while 40% of boys and 34% of girls were ambivalent.

This finding of ambivalence led Powdermaker to realise that the one-dimensional model may not contain all the currents of attitude that exist. She wrote 'in these conflicting values . . . are reflected some of the discords of social change . . . we differ from (the view) that opposing value systems in the same individual must necessarily be in conflict . . . the human species appears to have a remarkable facility for rationalising logically incompatible systems, or for not recognising their incompatibility'.

A second fund, the Carnegie Corporation was thanked by Leonard W. Doob (1960) 'for arousing my interest in Africa by means of a red carpet trip in 1952'. Doob writes in an academically witty and personal style; but he did not say why his trip did not start by consultation with Biesheuvel, who could have helped him considerably with methodology. Instead, Doob's fieldwork began in Uganda in 1954 where he says questionnaire 'items were desperately seized when they seemed to fit the problem at hand'.

Doob's book is self-consciously provocative. He write 'civilisation refers to the culture, or way of life, possessed by modern literate and industrial nations in Europe and America'. He insisted that 'the process of becoming more civilised is neither praised or condemned' in his outlook; but it need not take a psychologist to see that this is not how his analysis would be construed by many African students. Doob's perspective is that in the encounter between African and western culture some people remain *unchanged*, others are *changing* and some are *changed*. The people Doob refers to are Africans; though properly in such a model one should enquire equally about members of both cultures. The model is one-dimensional, and as used by Doob is one-directional as well.

If cultural contact had been seen as a two-way process, Doob's book would have acknowledged some influence of Africa on Europeans. This would have had at least two beneficial effects. It would generate interest in the possibility of synthesis, or even points of irresolution between cultures, with the development of new forms to which Dawson, Jahoda and Powdermaker have pointed. It would also give African readers a feeling of dignity, to be perceived as in some sense equals in an interaction. Instead they are shown a view of themselves as takers, rather than as exchangers. A similar loss of dignity is implied in the word 'acculturation' which is commonly used in culture and attitude change studies. This word, from the Latin meaning 'towards culture' implies, as Doob says openly, that people are moving towards culture, hence from a non-cultured condition. A better view however, is that people are moving towards new cultural forms, from old ones.

Doob set out 27 hypotheses concerning psychological aspects of cultural change. Like Dawson, he expects changing people to be more discontented, and aggressive than those who are unchanged, or changed. Like Biesheuvel, Doob expects changing people to 'retain traditional attitudes towards family forms' even when other 'central changes' have occurred in them. Other hypotheses link attitudes with cognitive skills and point to ways in which change processes may occur. His last hypothesis, that 'basic changes in personality are likely to occur as people become adequately civilised' is carelessly provocative; for it is imprecise, and he provides no direct evidence from Africa with which to examine it.

Doob's African data come from interviews among three groups. He listed the Luo (of Kenya), the Ganda (of Uganda), and Zulus (of South Africa) as having, from least to most experience of European forms of behaviour. Like Jahoda, Doob divided his samples into educational 'Lows' and 'Highs' as an index of 'acculturation'. Among a large number of other questions, Doob had 22 statements, mostly of traditional beliefs, to which people were asked simply whether they agreed or disagreed. Traditionalistic items included: 'a cook can put something into his employer's food to get his wages raised'; while western-type items included 'it is better for a man to have his wealth in money than in cattle'. Other items are not easy to distinguish as particularly traditional or western, such as 'the world is a dangerous place in which men are very evil and dangerous'.

In each tribal sample, the High educational group included more who 'claim a European friend' than those with Low education. Among the Luo and Zulu a rating of acculturation 'by competant authorities' (unspecified) was lower for the Low education group. But among the Baganda the difference on rated acculturation between the two educational groups was not a significant one. Education therefore does reflect what observers think of as acculturation; but it is not a clear cut marker in all cases. Another difficulty with Doob's starting concepts of Luo as 'least changed' and Zulu as 'most changed' is that since these are different tribes, we cannot be sure that any differences in attitudes between them are due to acculturation experience, or to differences in the original cultures of these tribes. The Ainsworths (1962a, b, c, see below) did consider in fact, that attitude differences between Luo and Baganda were partly due to their original cultural differences.

Doob provides much good discussion of his material. Like other investigators, he supports the hypothesis that attitudes to family matters die hard . He also discusses how people may contain intellectually differing, or even incompatible ideas. He believes (without discussing any evidence) that 'less civilised people may not compartmentalise their beliefs and categories' but that they show 'faith and absolutism' and 'unity of behaviour'. This implies that such people contemplate each one of their beliefs as part of an integrated cultural whole. It follows from his discussion, that Doob would expect more civilised people to allow some compartmentalisation of their beliefs and attitudes.

Later in his book, Doob deals with the same 'cognitive dissonance' theory that is central to Dawson's work. Like Dawson, Doob expects 'changing' people to reduce their attitude conflicts by devising a 'synthesis based on both'. Here we seem to have an ironic dissonance in what Doob is saying. The very civilised Doob, as he suggests, has evidently kept his thoughts in separate compartments; but in contemplating cognitive dissonance theory he expects more civilised people to be busy producing syntheses. Perhaps they do both.

Doob seems to challenge the reader, in one passage, to judge that his is really a poor book. Regretfully, in spite of its merits of interest and style (the author writes of himself as 'I' and not 'We', as some do), I must accept his implied challenge and say it is a poor book. The internal structure is not clear enough to develop an adequate account of the ways in which attitudes inside individual minds run parallel to and interact with patterns of social change outside the individual. The book scans too great a range of variables (attitudes as well as abilities), peoples, and theories. His groups are also mostly too small to have a chance of showing the differences, or correlations which he is looking for.

A second report by Doob (1967) is this time short, though complex, but still centri-cultural. He wrote 'I have ... striven to be as unoriginal as possible, so that results from Africa could be measured against a base line in the West'. In fact he has borrowed many of his questionnaire items from western sources. This is not misleading in itself; but one should hesitate to judge answers to 'the same' questions in Africa and in America according to the same base line, simply because the cultural contexts — the baselines — are different in the two continents. In this paper Doob published eighty statements based on ideas which 'African leaders *appear* to consider desirable as they define modernisation. . .' (Doob's emphasis). These ideas of 'many (not all) African leaders and their followers for the moment' are used by Doob as a norm of what is 'modern', and embody the following characteristics.

(a) An emphasis on the future, rather than the past or the present.
(b) The belief that the country's present legal government has important beneficial functions to perform for its citizens.
(c) The feeling that life in general is pleasant and that to a significant degree people control their own destiny.
(d) Strong feelings of attachment and loyalty to the country as such.
(e) 'Correct' knowledge from a scientific viewpoint . . . and the . . . conviction that . . . phenomena are intelligible . . . and . . . not . . . completely irrational or capricious.
(f) A non-paranoid, generous, trusting conception of human nature and one's fellow men.
(g) Approval of the country's leaders and of their specific policies.
(h) A tendency to de-emphasise or discredit traditional values and practices.

This list should be extremely controversial, though virtually no discussion of it has come from either Doob himself, or later writers such as Armer and Jahoda. The second and seventh items (b) and (g) are in some contexts very difficult to accept as criteria for modernity. In item (e), the notion that phenomena are completely determinable and not capricious, as Jahoda (1970) pointed out, is typical of many traditional African cultures. Indeed it is the opposite idea, that phenomena sometimes occur 'capriciously' or by statistical chance, which belongs to 'modern western' thought. The implication in item (f) is that traditional ideas expect human nature to be paranoid and non-trusting; this is surely unlikely to find agreement among Africans, or among many social anthropologists.

Doob put this questionnaire to 503 rural people, 955 urban elite, and 425 intermediate individuals (secondary students and police officers) in East Africa. Those sentences with which over three quarters of respondents agreed, Doob labelled 'strongly modern'. Similarly, where 51-75% agreed, statements were 'modern'; likewise he called strongly non-modern any statement to which less than a quarter of each sample agreed. This procedure produces anomalies. Consider statement 43: 'I know quite well what I shall be doing ten years from now'. By Doob's definition, this looks to the future and is a modern sentiment. Yet less than 25% agreed with it; so it is in the 'strongly non-modern' list. There are five such anomalies in the modern and the non-modern sections of Doob's list.

These anomalies arise because the researcher first lays down ideas which he considers to be 'modern'; then he also labels as modern, what the majority of people agree to. There is no necessity that the researcher and the majority should agree. According to Doob's definition of modernity, certain western groups of young people who live for the present instead of for the future, and those who distrust centralised government would be labelled 'traditional'. But sociologically, or in their own minds, such groups would be considered as true modern phenomena. Probably the best way to avoid such tangles is to explore whether a particular set of attitudes exists that can be linked with a cultural tradition; a separate pattern would probably emerge from different kinds of African traditional cultures (such as pastoralists, mixed farmers, and so on); different sets of attitudes might be recognised in various western cultures – French speaking, English and Americanised. The definition of modern attitudes is best taken as the opinions held by whatever group one identifies as modern (probably on sociological criteria); such definitions of modern groups might be; the young; the urban young; educated urban youth; political leadership; the army; or whatever. This way of defining 'modern' attitudes must accept that in many fields 'modern' may be closer to traditional than to western ideas.

Like Doob, Leonard and Mary Ainsworth (1962) were in East Africa in 1954-5. They acknowledge his help, and use his terms to describe students they questioned in Uganda and Kenya, as changing and changed. In this research 'acculturation' and Anglicisation appear to have been treated as the same idea. Four Ugandan schools were chosen to represent four levels of acculturation. A Catholic school where most teachers were 'European' and the regime strict was considered less acculturated than another where 'most teachers were British', and where the regime emphasised self-reliance.

The Ainsworths also assumed that Buganda was more 'acculturated' than North Nyanza (where many Luos live) in Kenya. They say that this 'stems from differences in the *traditional* political organisation of the societies in these two provinces' (my emphasis). This implies that an entirely 'unchanged' Muganda will be labelled as 'more acculturated' (ie more changed!) than an entirely 'unchanged' Luo in Nyanza. In spite of this built-in absurdity however, the Ainsworths' work contained some interesting material.

The Ainsworths hypothesised that because their new attitudes could only be partly fulfilled, the more acculturated people would feel more frustrated. They expected more acculturated people to 'direct more hostility' both to traditional, and to European leaders; but they would also 'have more effective modes of handling frustration and consequent aggression'. They expected more acculturated people to be less rigid in problem solving, to value education more highly, and finally to have ideas closer to traditional ones, on parent-child relations rather than on other topics.

Their papers claim that the evidence 'gives almost complete support to the body of hypotheses' but not all their readers might agree with this. For example they wrote (p.431) 'the more acculturated feel . . . more hostile toward authority figures . . .'; but they also wrote that 'nearly all of the few perceptions of authority as protective (or sympathetic) occurred in the more acculturated groups'. Again, reporting results on the Rosenzweig Picture Frustration Test (see also Leblanc, 1956, 1958) one reads that an 'extra-punitive . . . reaction . . . did not vary significantly with acculturation level', but 'the more acculturated had . . . significantly fewer extra-punitive responses'; and on p.407 the Ainsworths chose a third contradictory conclusion: 'the findings supported the hypothesis. The more acculturated were *more* aggressive than the less acculturated'.

It is a pity that such a muddled presentation has been made. The Ainsworths could have thrown a new perspective on Dawson's and Mertens de Wilmar's theory, that cognitive dissonance and perhaps anxiety and aggression would characterise people caught in the change area between traditional and western social systems. Dawson argued that 'unresolved attitudes' caused anxiety; the Ainsworths implied that 'resolved' new attitudes which could not be fulfilled because people were caught between two systems, would cause anxiety. But though they used elaborate clinical tests of anxiety and aggression, the Ainsworths used no measure of traditional or western trends of individual attitudes.

The next study to examine (Armer & Youtz, 1971) is better designed. Pleasantly (for sociologists) the writers set out to study '*Individual modernity*' (my emphasis) among 591 seventeen year olds in Kano (see Chapter VI). Armer and Youtz saw western schooling as a prime agency for transmitting westernised attitudes. They wanted to explore Bartlett's question — which traditional ideas 'die hard', and which are soft and open to changes.

There was a basic assumption that ten concepts essentially characterise 'modern' thinking, namely, empiricism, secularism, receptivity to change, trust, futurism, independence from family, mastery, openness to new ideas, women's and ethnic equality. Again, this list of 'values' is drawn from an American perspective and runs Doob's danger of being unable to let whatever is the true profile of modern attitudes, as they really are, emerge. However, Armer and Youtz produced a questionnaire, and factor analysed it to find any basic patterns underlying how people answered. One principal factor linked six of the above concepts, and was called a 'traditional versus modern' value orientation. The six concepts they found to be psychologically related were: independence from family, ethnic equality, empiricism, mastery, receptivity to change, and future orientation. It is equally interesting that the four other concepts, secularism, trust, women's equality, and openness to new ideas were evidently not part of the same underlying pattern; the last of these four concepts is perhaps the most conspicuous omission.

Linking scores on the six related 'modernism' concepts showed that amount of education was related to individual modernity. Armer and Youtz claimed it was not family influence which caused both longer schooling, and modern attitudes; rather, schooling itself produced modern opinions. They argued that if family pressure for education lay behind modernity, there would be a great excess of children with modern opinions among those with one year of education, compared with uneducated children; while there would be less contrast between groups with one, two, and more years of primary schooling.

In fact 38% among those without schooling had high modern views, and 42% among those with one year of primary schooling. Boys with seven years of primary school included 65% with modern views. Thus, an average of 3% more boys with modern opinions was added for each added year of schooling, about the same increase as that marking the initial entrance to school. This could indeed reflect educational selectivity, with more modern-minded families having had both the opportunity and the will to have started their sons off earlier and kept them for longer in school by the age of 17. Selection evidently did occur at entrance to secondary school, for those with only one year in secondary school included 75% with highly modern views. It would seem sensible to conclude that probably family background as well as schooling affect attitudes; and research to clarify the issue would need to ask the same attitude questions of the parents. Then, with matched groups on parental attitudes, one could examine any differences between children dependent on schooling.

Next, various other possible modernising influences were examined. These included amount of radio listening, fathers' tribe, income, educational and occupational levels, and literacy in English, ratings of the families' prestige, and the boys' scores on Schwarz's ability test. Little difference in boys' modernity of opinion was found relating to most of these variables. The lack of influence of radio contrasts with Gilbertson's results that less support for traditional points of view was more clearly linked with TV experience. Not only may TV be a more effective medium; but Gilbertson's more sophisticated questionnaire helped to clarify any differences that it might produce. Here, however, while radio experience, and the other possible modernising influences considered were hardly linked at all with amounts of measured modernity, personal educational level and ability test scores did have clear relationships with modern attitude scores.

Armer and Youtz found that on certain topics, receptivity to change, secularism and women's equality, attitudes were least linked with school experience. The last two items again resemble the findings of Biesheuvel and others, that family relationships and beliefs regarding the supernatural are the topics most independent of modernising influences. But this pattern is negated in that 'independence from family' was the topic most closely related to years of schooling. Finally, differences in modernity were found with different types of schooling. Koranic (Islamic) schools produced fewer modern-minded youths; likewise 'grammar'-type schooling was linked with more modernity than was Teacher Training College, and craft, technical or clerical schooling. Among pupils in the highest level of intelligence only, there were still these variations of modernity according to type of schooling. This supports Armer and Youtz's argument that differences in curricula affect attitudes, even though selective entry to these different types of schools could also influence the attitudes found therein.

Subsequently, Armer (1970) explored the links between education, modernity, and alienation among those he tested. Alienation is an idea developed among sociologists, which covers psychological ideas of feelings of anxiety, distrust, and disconnection from one's fellows. Two theories had been put forward to account for alienation. According to one (Doob, 1960, Mertens de Wilmars and Niveau, 1969, and others), people feel lost in a changing society; thus those with more education, moving more from their traditional roots may be expected to show more alienation. A contrary idea emerges from a suggestion by Marshall Segall (1961); this is that people become westernised in a selective way, assimilating new attitudes which suit them. Armer has applied this in a particular way; unlike the Ainsworths, he supposed that people with westernised attitudes, and who have high education, will be able to live the kind of lives they value. They will *not* feel alienated, because they are not frustrated from attaining their goals. People with traditional attitudes will find that if they have considerable education, this may interfere with their overall desire to fit in with traditional ways. Thus alienation should be negatively correlated with educational level for people with westernised attitudes; while alienation should be positively correlated with education among those with traditional attitudes.

After he had pruned those who had conflicting ideas, Armer divided his sample into those who were clearly 'modern' (according to his definitions) and those who were 'traditional'. His scale of alienation used eight questions, which had been shown to relate well together, and his results clearly supported his second hypothesis. Where people had consistently western attitudes, provided they had high education, they had low alienation. Among traditionalist people education and alienation were positively linked.

A centri-cultural approach is found again in a study from South Africa, (Grant, 1969b). Grant focuses on the concept of urbanisation, but assimilates related concepts to it. Thus he combines 'being urbanised . . . westernisation . . . Europeanisation . . . and civilisation . . . although these terms have been used independently they can, to all intents . . . be grouped under the heading of modernisation, a term which is appearing more frequently in the literature'.

We should perhaps realise by now that frequent appearance in the literature is no guarantee of the soundness of a concept. However, Grant follows Smith and Inkeles' (1966) definition of 'attitudinal modernity as . . . a set of attitudes, beliefs, behaviour, etc, especially characterising persons in highly individualised, highly industrialised and highly educated social settings'. Grant is aware that attitudinal modernity is not necessarily similar in every industrialised society. He refers to the idea of 'situational selection' put forward by Mitchell (1960) in Rhodesia. According to this idea a man 'selects behaviour patterns appropriate to the sets of relations in which a situation involves him . . . a man, even while actually in town, can be alternating between rural and urban modes of behaviour'.

Writing from the National Institute of Personnel Research, Grant might have devised attitude scales in the form which Biesheuvel pioneered there and which later workers found so sensitive. However, Grant avoided this. Though fearing that people will fake replies to questionnaires Grant believes 'this can be detected by evidence of internal inconsistency'. Items evoking inconsistent responses 'would not be included in the final scale'. It seems therefore that mistrust evidently rife in South Africa is bound to mislead researchers, who want to iron out results into a consistency which need not naturally be there.

Grant gave 100 Zulu workers in a plywood factory a test of 'conceptual reasoning ability' and a questionnaire. From the latter, 17 items were selected by complex statistical processes to constitute a U-R (Urban-Rural) scale. Scores on this correlated 0.37 with amount of school, and 0.21 with the conceptual test. From this, Grant claims that Doob's hypothesis 'that the more "civilised" individuals become, the better they are at performing abstract tasks' was 'confirmed in a very limited sense'. After a welter of technically sophisticated statistics, Grant thus leaves his reader with a rather lame conclusion. The low correlation tells us that there is a relationship between two measures; but it does not confirm Doob's implication that 'becoming civilised' brings about better abstract ability. Instead, it may be the cleverer people who come to stay in towns and who are influenced by urban society; or both processes more likely happen simultaneously.

Grant factor analysed his questionnaire and found that answers could be separated into different clusters of ideas or attitudes. This finding of more than one principal factor, incidentally, resembles more the new data I have reported from Uganda (see p.145) than Armer and Youtz's finding of one principal factor. Grant listed the most important aspects of urbanisation in order of importance and they included: place of birth; items relating to parents — such as where they live; attitudes towards chiefs; and desires for the artifacts of modern life. Grant missed the opportunity of exploring the cross-currents of 'situational selection', or of how people manage the different, sometimes conflicting strands of their traditional, and newer experiences. His U-R scale is perhaps best thought of as a list of pointers to the condition of the particular workers he studied.

Two Americans who worked in Uganda had also explored the idea Grant used of listing material signs as an index of modernity. The first worker to struggle with this was Marshall Segall (1959) — who later turned to visual illusions (described in Chapter IV). Segall rejected Doob's tripartite scheme of changed, changing and unchanged people. He sensibly declared 'I must abandon the very concept "acculturation" '. Instead, he proposed to study something else: 'let me call that something else the acquisition of a Euro-Cultural Orientation'. Whatever else this is, it is certainly a blinding piece of jargon; it points to the pitfalls of the misuse of words which trap researchers who are not careful enough to distinguish 'modern' from 'western' for example. Segall's new concept has not survived; though his brief work on a checklist of material properties has had some follow-up (see Schiff's work, in Chapter II and Edgerton's in Chapter VIII).

Later in Uganda, Pollnac and Robbins (1972) used Segall's idea. As 'psychological anthropologists' they thought in terms of modernisation, but distinguished two ways in which this could be manifest. One was 'ideational modernisation', or attitudes; the other was 'phenomenal modernisation'; their means to measure this was a 25 item checklist noting possession of western products such as a clock, a radio, etc; and questions bordering on mental attitudes, though ones that are clearly expressed in visible actions, such as 'likes to straighten hair', and 'prefers drinking from glass instead of gourd'. Pollnac and Robbins found a medium-small correlation (0.28) between a person's score on phenomenal modernisation and his answer as to whether he considered himself a 'European-type' African, a 'traditional person' or a 'mixture'. The questions were asked in Luganda, of members of 109 households.

Using Doob's first criterion of modernity, an emphasis on the future, Pollnac and Robbins investigated whether people seemed to prefer immediate, or delayed gratification. Asked what they would do if they received 1,000 shillings, answers were coded as 'deferred' if people said they would use the money for farming (41% said this) or trading (25%) or school fees (17%). These were considered investments in the future. Answers were coded 'immediate' if people said they would spend the money on their house (12%), or on food, or clothes. Clearly, the great majority chose deferred alternatives. Pollnac and Robbins also showed that a complex relationship existed between 'ideational modernity . . . (and) . . . deferred gratification'. Poorer people may spend to satisfy their urgent needs; people of moderate means need to save to better their position, and thus choose to invest a windfall; rich people are secure, and feel they might as well spend a money present straight away.

Another paper published with a young colleague (Robbins and Thompson, 1971) though still using a centri-cultural perspective introduced a new idea to research in Africa. First they defined, in anthropological terms, what they consider modernisation really is: urban living; formal education; commercialisation of land, labour, goods and services; wider social and cultural relationships; mass media, and technological innovations. However, they realise that modernisation is not necessarily the same as westernisation. They said 'In Africa and elsewhere, non-western modernisation and neo-traditionalism is recurring widely and rapidly'.

Their new idea is that every person has an 'optimum stimulation level' – the extent to which the brain needs new stimuli. They also assume that 'modernisation . . . has served to increase the amount of stimulation . . . an individual experiences'. They further reason that urban people, dazzled with the stimulation of their experience would tend to choose the more orderly and straightforward of a pair of 'stimuli'. Their pairs of stimuli each include one orderly pattern or well-known animal, and one chaotic pattern, or a nonsensical animal. Rural people, they supposed, bored with their unstimulating lives, would tend to choose the more weird of the drawings shown them.

With interviews in and around Kampala, Robbins and Thompson did indeed find that rural people tended to prefer the weird designs. Perhaps without full justification, they called choice of weird designs 'exploratory behaviour'. They found that people who had lived longer in town showed less of such 'exploratory behaviour'; while for rural people, phenomenal modernisation scores correlated with 'exploratory behaviour'. Complex statistics also showed that place of residence (rural or urban) was more strongly linked to 'exploratory behaviour' than was either education or age. It could be, for instance, that the more educated, urban people had a better idea of what they thought the foreign researcher would consider 'the correct one' of two drawings, and showed this because they thought he wanted it. The matter cannot be decided at present. But certainly Robbins and Thompson have introduced new ideas for consideration that link mental attitudes, visible signs of modernising life patterns and an unusual, if weird measure of cognitive preference.

Cross-cultural, and centri-cultural studies of attitudes: an overview

By a coincidence, probably, certain researchers of Commonwealth background (Biesheuvel, Dawson, Jahoda, Wober, Gilbertson) have allowed a cross-cultural strategy to underlie their studies. They have set identifiable traditional attitudes on one side, western attitudes on another, and explored how the two meet to produce new patterns in minds which face the task of reconciling both influences. A prescription of what is modern has not been laid down. Rather, whatever emerges is allowed to be called modern, for that group studied.

On the other hand, non-Commonwealth researchers (Doob, Powdermaker, Armer and Youtz, the Ainsworths, Grant), have tended to a firm centri-cultural strategy. They start with a clear idea of what is modern, sometimes equating this idea with westernism, or urbanisation, or civilisation. A joint influence of these schools of procedure seems evident in the work of Tina Wallace (from England) and Sheldon Weeks (from America) who studied attitudes among youth in Uganda (Wallace and Weeks, 1972). Following Mitchell (1960) and Wober (1971c), Wallace and Weeks say '. . . any one actor may play a number of different roles and each of these may be a segment of different institutions and interpersonal situations in which the person moves. . . This view does not force a dichotomy between "traditional" and "modern" roles . . . if they do not perceive a conflict between them why should the outsider impose one?'.

They are saying that humans are not always the relentlessly rational beings that Dawson supposes them to be. As in the simile of the river, suggested earlier, however, both Dawson and Wallace and Weeks may be partly right. In some areas rational balancing and cognitive dissonance in various ways may occur; in other areas, people may suppress their conflicts into their subconscious (an idea that has not really been explored in research in Africa); or they may contrive not to notice potential dissonance. Further research might explore whether some individuals are synthesisers who like to resolve their attitudes, while others may tend to be separators who prefer to keep ideas which might prove inconsistent, comfortably apart. It would also be of interest to discover if such strategies of synthesising, or of separating may correlate with other measures such as of intelligence, cognitive complexity, field independence, and so on.

Studies on inter-group attitudes

One criterion said to characterise western, as compared with traditionalist thinking, is a commitment to national rather than to tribal identity. In one sense the two are psychologically similar, both being loyalty to the largest political grouping which relates regularly to the individual, except that most Africans have faced a new political identity in this century, a challenge unfamiliar to most expatriate researchers. This loyalty usually develops together with some kind of negative feeling for those outside the group. Few studies have explored this sensitive area, since in many African nations 'tribalism' is now considered an evil, and anybody thought to be pointing to signs of tribalism can be strongly resented. Particularly if the researcher is an outsider, sensitivity to the old spectre of 'divide and rule' is close to the surface. Some of the studies have explored relationships between Africans and outsiders (see Chapter VIII); these have their own difficulties, but they are perhaps not so delicate as those attending research on inter-tribal feelings.

An early exploration was by Jahoda (1959) who had Ghanaian undergraduates interview over 200 adults. These were asked about whites living in the country, which nationalities they liked best, and why. Jahoda found that British were liked best, and other nationalities much in an order he might have found had he done the study in England. He supposed that schooling in a British educational atmosphere was probably responsible for transfer of many attitudes held by the British themselves.

At the other end of the continent, Van den Berghe (1962) interviewed 88 African students (as well as others of other races) and asked them to name traits for each of various social groups including City and Rural Africans, Indians and various white groups. He found that the higher people were in the society, the more distant they felt from others; Africans felt least distant from others – though the feeling was not, unfortunately reciprocated. Evidently Africans want more to feel, and be acknowledged as part of a common humanity, while the whites were wanting to reject this. The Africans distinguished between their view of the bluntly oppressive Afrikaners, and the more hypocritically bigoted English-speaking whites. The contrast between Van den Berghe's findings in oppressive South Africa, and results even in late colonial West Africa arose again in comparison with a study by Rogers (1959) who found amoung 200 Ibadan students in Nigeria, basically favourable attitudes towards the British. Attitudes to outsiders obviously depend on current events; thus Ogunlade (1971) showed that undergraduates in Western Nigeria felt better towards foreign nations which supported the Federal side in the civil war, than to those supporting Biafra.

Dawson (1963b) was perhaps one of the first systematically to study inter-tribal attitudes, among workers in Sierra Leone. He showed people a list of adjectives, hopefully covering most of the stereotypes people had of each other, and asked respondents to choose six items only which they thought best described a particular tribe. In this way 'votes' for adjectives built up a 'personality profile' of a particular tribe. This was how he established that Temne had conflict-oriented values (as seen in the eyes of Temne, and non-Temne observers), while Mende had work-oriented values.

The method was repeated in Nigeria (Wober, 1966a, 1967a). Factory employees chose adjectives to describe various Nigerian groups (Ibo, Edo, Hausa, Yoruba, etc) and some non-Nigerian ones (English, Americans, Indians). Not every group had entirely favourable self-attitudes; the Urhobo agreed with some unfavourable descriptions of themselves. Nevertheless, there was broad agreement between people from most tribes on the characteristics of any one particular group or tribe. Attitudes towards Europeans were very favourable. To confirm that this did not reflect the presence of a white researcher in the room, or the fact that the men were employees of a British company, the Nigerian assistant collected data from a Nigerian-run secondary school group, with no white researcher present. Resulting stereotypes closely resembled those from the factory workers. However, the researcher's identity might still influence expressed attitudes, since Opara (1968) found that undergraduates in Eastern Nigeria in 1964 showed closest feelings for Ibo (themselves), American Negroes next, with Arabs least preferred. Members of the then dominant political party – NCNC – were felt socially closer than those of any other party.

A different method of describing intergroup attitudes is that of Bogardus (1968); people are asked to think of an individual of a given group (race, tribe, religion, etc) and to say whether they would agree to have him as a neighbour, a workmate, a friend, a kinsman. These positions are given scores for 'social distance', and average social distance scores can be worked out for how any group is regarded, by members of another. The method was applied by Brown (1967) among over 300 students in Addis Ababa. Ethiopians and 'Negroes' (presumably covering both Africans and Black Americans) had the closest social distance, and Swedes came third. Brown claimed incidentally, that 'most Ethiopians, and especially the Amhara, the dominant ethnic group, had considered themselves Caucasian. . .'. However, Brown's results do not suggest that Ethiopians felt closer to whites than they did to blacks. The English were fifth in social distance providing some support for previous findings, and Turks were last in a list of 31 groups, perhaps because Muslims were perceived as very alien by the Christian Ethiopians. Another study in Ethiopia, by Ziegler, King, King and Ziegler (1972) used the stereotypes approach to measure social distance. They collected the adjectives forming the stereotype of a group, and also found how 'desirable' each adjective was. The average 'desirability' of adjectives applied to peoples' own groups was higher than that of adjectives applied to other ethnic groups.

In Zambia Mitchell (1962) used Bogardus' scale with Lusaka secondary school pupils, and found that social distance was less between people from groups which were both geographically, and culturally close. Thus a Northern Patrilineal group (e.g. Tumbuka) would show smaller social distance to Bemba (who lived close by, though they are matrilineal) than to the Bisa, who are less geographically close. In those pre-colonial times, a military reputation of a group such as the Bemba, might win approval among other Africans who were preoccupied with mustering African feelings vis à vis the colonialists. In independence, inter-African differences might become more apparent.

Later Irvine (1969a) asked 274 primary and training school students who, in their class, they thought 'could choose a team best' or 'I should go away for a holiday with', and thirteen other similar questions. After seven pages of complex statistics and discussion, we learn that 'a general hypothesis emerges . . . that intra-tribal choices will increase with the degree of perceived social distance between tribes'. In other words, if one doesn't like other tribes, one will make friends from one's own. Irvine also says 'a constant reference of individual behaviour to group expectations is essential'; in other words, people look for and respond to guidelines which suggest to them how to behave. One source of such guidelines is 'ethnicity' (or tribal culture and rules, in common language). Ogunlade (1972) pointed to another influence. He gave a Bogardus scale to elite secondary pupils in Western Nigeria, concerning seven ethnic groups. Ogunlade found that 'nearness' was different to 'fairness' in judging groups; interviews suggested that family support for nearness opposed mass media influences or ethnic mixing in schools, whose levelling effects would depend on focussing on likeable behaviour.

In a study in Kenya, Uganda and Tanzania, Brewer (1968) confirmed that cultural and geographical closeness was linked with low social distance. To a smaller extent, westernisation (especially among traditionally similar groups) also linked with social closeness. This points to an added dimension to understanding psychological attitudes between groups, that of emerging levels of status in the new society. In Zambia again, Bethlehem and Kingsley (1973) showed that among University students, tribal background was less important than 'social class' in determining how closely a student might relate to another person. Thus he would sooner have as kinsman another person of similar 'social class' (very similar to westernisation or wealth, since the stimuli were photographs of people wearing either smart western clothes, or poorly clad as labourers or peasants), than another person of similar tribe but of lower social class. Inter-tribal attitudes were largely similar to those found by Mitchell, and tribe was certainly still present as a factor in social distance. Bethlehem and Kingsley considered that even if it was only among University educated people that tribal origin was reducing in importance and social class taking over, this was an encouraging result for Zambian policy, which was trying to remove tribalism as a potentially damaging element in national political life. Nevertheless, the Bemba, most acceptable to the subjects in Mitchell's research, were now lowest of seven groups in popularity. This change possibly linked with their potency having brought them current political success and influence, which was now beginning to be resented.

Elsewhere, Seibel (1967) interviewed over 500 factory workers in ten industries in Lagos and Ibadan, and found 80% said they would prefer a work group of mixed tribal composition. This preference for variety was greater among the more educated workers. Seibel had expected to find people wanting to work with others from their own tribe, and that such groups would be judged more efficient; but the facts ran counter to this. Much earlier, another German Diedrich Westermann (1934) had predicted that when 'the Natives come to the workplace as members of quite different tribes' there could arise 'an entirely new feeling of solidarity'. This he thought would be built upon the workers' common relationship to their white employers. Seibel did not discuss how management nationality might have affected his results; but in situations where African management had predominantly taken over, members of a minority tribal group might want to see a more mixed population of workmates, to avoid domination by one group (the situation where resentment against the Bemba in Zambia was apparently at work). An indication of this possibility is the result Rogers (1959) reported, that 67% of his undergraduate sample agreed that 'some Africans would prefer to work under a European rather than under another African'.

In summary, stereotypes of groups do occur, and are shared among separate sets of observers. While we recognise that many intellectuals now reject the notion of 'tribe' on sociological or on idealistic grounds, this evidence that ordinary people have fairly well-defined attitudes towards certain groups provides a case for arguing that tribes do exist in 'psychological reality'. Not only are such tribes seen as having particular characteristics; people can also agree fairly well on how closely they would wish to have relationships with members of a tribe. Values of social distance, and tribal stereotypes can alter over time, though too few studies in Africa have been done to be able to track such processes well. Presumably the goal for some (say, nationalists) would be to see differences between stereotypes of the tribes within a nation diminish, until all its tribes would have a similar stereotype. Others though, are concerned with the diverse roots of Africa's historic heritage, and work to discover and develop different cultural entities. While stereotypes resemble the cognitive component, social distance corresponds to the affective, or emotional aspect of attitudes; and a long-standing goal in psychology is to understand how these mental aspects of attitudes may link, or not, with peoples' actions in real life.

Miscellaneous studies on attitudes reflecting currents of social change

A number of social scientists have been interested in the ways in which the attitudes of both sexes towards women may be changing in Africa. In 1958 at Lomé, capital of Togo, a conference of women was held; N'Sougan F Agblemagnon (1962) tells us that 'for the first time, women themselves will be asked to play an active part' in research on their attitudes. However, at this stage he gives no fresh data on their attitudes, describing instead the place of women in Ewe society (a tribe overlapping Togo and Ghana). The paper informs us chiefly that before the 1960s, little psychological research can have been done on attitudes in French-speaking Africa, or on women's ideas in Africa as a whole.

Meanwhile, T. P. Omari (1960) had questioned 292 students in 8 Ghanaian secondary schools and Teacher Training Institutions on aspects of attitudes towards marriage. He shows that 8% prefer traditional forms of marriage, 65% want Church marriage and 10% want both; 73% agreed that polygamy was 'definitely backward', 23% thought it a matter of individual choice, and hardly anyone said it was definitely good. The questionnaire appears to have been worded with the message built in, that tradition is 'backward' while modern forms are 'good'; this stands in the way of detecting the true balance of peoples' ideas. It remains quite possible however, that Omari's very pro-Western, or modern results before 1960 may be quite valid, and that Jahoda's evidence of a resurgence of traditional ideas is a more recent phenomenon. Certainly Omari's results contradict the Biesheuvel-based idea that attitude to marriage might be among the traditional forms more resistant to change.

More recently Marjorie Mbilinyi (1970) the American wife of a Tanzanian then based in Dar es Salaam, dogmatically expressed a clear idea of what is good and what is bad. She quoted Marx and Engels, the latter who wrote that 'the degree of emancipation of women could be used as a standard by which to measure general emancipation'. Mbilinyi studied attitudes about women 'as a key to understanding how highly developed a society is, and where it places on a traditional-modern continuum'. She discusses traditional women's roles in Tanzania unsympathetically, and quotes the census to show that fewer women receive schooling than men. Her new data come from 732 girls and 731 of their fathers or household heads from most parts of the country and including members of 38 tribes.

The best data come from projective-test types of items; for example, a girl is forbidden to go to school, but runs away from home to attend; the subject is asked what the girl should have done. The problems ingeniously pit values from western and traditional cultures against each other in contexts with which subjects are familiar. Mbilinyi found that people prefer to educate boys, as they said that boys would bring in money later on; boys were thought to be more intelligent and hardworking, while girls were needed at home. There seems an inconsistency in people's thinking here, as girls would not be needed at home if they were not hardworking and intelligent in bringing up children too. Possibly Mbilinyi's questions had not gone far enough in tapping people's thoughts and attitudes here. People also wanted girls 'kept in' as they feared that by 'going out' to school they would become pregnant, be 'spoilt' by teachers, or even become prostitutes.

Those parents who send their daughters to school, evidently see education as a good experience in itself, and consider that the experience improves the quality of home-loving daughters. Mbilinyi is not happy about her findings and demands legal and political action to ensure full equality in all sectors of society. Her work is applied research, and we could class it with the next studies to be described, even though their aims are less political than technical.

Oscar Ferron (1965) is an educational psychologist who has worked in Northern Nigeria, and Sierra Leone. He believes that 'traditional' ideas among schoolteachers should be replaced by 'progressive' attitudes. Note that 'traditional' here is not specifically African, but is also an older western form. Traditional attitudes are said to approve formal discipline, rely on verbal explanations, use abstract concepts, corporal punishment, and see education as a means to an end. Ferron's idea of the progressive teacher is one who appeals to interest, who uses audio-visual aids, avoids corporal punishment and sees education as an end in itself. Certainly Ferron's idea of 'traditional' attitudes does not correspond to what we have been told about African systems of education, for example by Meyer Fortes (1938) in Ghana and Paul Kibuuka (1966) in Uganda. They both point out that African education in many cultures was traditionally 'informal' and infused all phases of life instead of being disciplined and institutionalised into schooling.

Ferron had four groups of education students at Zaria complete a questionnaire at the start and again at the end of their course. All four groups showed a significant increase in 'progressive' ideas. Such research is useful in that one can see where attitudes are not changing enough as intended in some project, and concentrate efforts to do something about it.

Also in an educational context Jahoda (1970) explored a suggestion that western education produces a 'shattering' effect on superstition. An Index of Supernatural Beliefs (ISB) and various tests were given to 280 male students in Ghana. The ISB includes ideas such as that a person's day of birth influences character (an effect which Jahoda himself has incidentally demonstrated 'scientifically' to be true), and that dwarfs have been reported in the forest. Students still accepted many traditional superstitions, particularly that there is some truth in the power of witchcraft. Those with high superstition scores tended to believe that one had little control over one's fate. Jahoda also found that the younger students had higher ISB scores. The possibility that younger students might lose their traditional beliefs with more years in university, was examined and rejected.

Jahoda used Smith and Inkeles' modernity scale, and found that among older students higher ISB scores related to less modernity. With younger students, ISB scores and modernity were unrelated. Among older students, those scoring higher on a test of cognitive independence tended to be the ones who rejected western ideas, and accepted traditional beliefs. No link between cognitive ability and rejection of westernism was found among the younger students. These findings point to the possibility of successive generations establishing different outlooks, like layers one upon another. In the early colonial years, as writers like Okafor-Omali (1965) point out, independent-minded youth rebelled against traditional attitudes and accepted western innovation; later, the pendulum of independence may have swung against western influence. We see therefore, that western education does not simply open an intellectual window letting in the pure light of 'scientific' fact to banish 'superstition'. As Jahoda (1954, 1969) has made clearer elsewhere, some traditional 'superstitions' are grounded in fact, and there are many western superstitions also.

A final field of attitudes studies we can consider, is that of ideas about family planning. The most significant contribution here is certainly that by Angela Molnos, a social scientist of Hungarian origin, who has worked extensively in East Africa. Molnos (1971) reviews 23 different studies on population problems, of which 10 were psychological in nature. Unfortunately, she reports that 'the outcome was not in satisfactory proportion to the resources invested nor was the resulting information brought to the attention of all those who could have used it to improve their work in family planning'.

Molnos' own work (1970) is not guilty of such defects. She gave incomplete sentences for completion, to 2,648 pupils in 43 schools in East Africa, at primary and secondary levels. Examples included: 'a woman who has many children . . .', 'a woman who has no children . . .', 'in a good marriage the husband. . .', and so on.

Some general themes were distilled from the findings. Childlessness was generally unwelcome, though men and women had different reasons for disliking it. Childless women, labelled 'barren' are in a worse position than men, for whom no such epithet exists. Males apparently want many children, Molnos believes, to secure the future of their line (this theory could well be tested among the matrilineal peoples of Zambia); women need principally to show they are not barren, for which one or two children will suffice. Molnos believes people recognise the difficulties of having large families, but that traditional attitudes on this topic are still strong. Thus the Kikuyu people customarily named a child for each grandparent, so parents wish, or are pressed to go on having children until they have at least two of each sex. Here are echoes of Bartlett's idea, that certain features of traditional culture will be 'hard' and resist change, and Biesheuvel's belief that family matters are a case in point. Molnos's studies and other research she may stimulate usefully indicate how policy makers (if they ever get to know about what has been discovered) can tackle the problems of promoting new attitudes which are compatible with wise population policies.

Conclusion

Most of the systematic attitudes studies in Africa are recent, and reflect a major theme of exploring attitudes which accompany cultural change. Much research has assumed, perhaps wrongly, that traditional cultures would not have changed of their own accord; while western culture has been seen also as relatively static in itself, but an influence for change in Africa. It should be more openly considered however, that what was 'western' in 1940 is not what was western in 1970. More sophisticated work should realise these simplifications in older research, and look deeper for signs of dynamic movement in traditional cultures and attitudes, with currents of reaction to western forms which are themselves often changing in direction.

Some researchers identify westernism with modernism; others do not do this, but simply label as modern the solutions which individuals devise to solve their problems of action and attitude when caught between two major sets of often opposing influence. The one-dimensional, one-direction model of traditional towards western attitude change is almost certainly inadequate in most situations. Influences systematically brought to bear on Africans through colonialism, technology, and travel, are drawn from western cultures which are themselves changing, in part being affected by African attitudes also. This was clear at the beginning of the century in the field of art, and may now be developing through American involvement with concepts of community, and 'soul'.

The links between the concepts of culture and of personality have interested both broad-minded psychologists and anthropologists over the last half century; but this interest has perhaps waned of late. A similar obvious parallel between culture and attitudes, has grown up more recently and is described in this chapter. But the three constructs are clearly all closely related, and the next chapter examines research on personality, in which we should be aware of reflections of what has been explored here of the realm of attitudes.

CHAPTER VIII

PERSONALITY AND IDENTITY

Introduction

Discussing the progress of his science in one particular field, the Oxford psychologist Michael Argyle (1972) regretted that 'the concept of personality has run into serious difficulty . . . due mainly to the failure of tests to predict behaviour . . . and the lack of an agreed conceptual scheme. . .'. As for Africa, Gustav Jahoda (1961) pointed out that 'numerous attempts have been made to generalise about the "African Mind" or "African Personality"', but 'the chastening fact is that our ignorance in this sphere remains almost complete'. Biesheuvel (1961) agreed, specifying more clearly that 'despite much effort, little progress has been made towards the production of satisfactory measuring devices' and 'the core problem is to determine the dimensions of normal personality development'.

Though many Africans object to generalisations being mentioned, or even sought, about 'African' characteristics, other Africans have found merit in talking about 'African Personality'. Psychologists have perhaps generalised less in this way, than have novelists, writers and politicians. We shall, however, survey some of the thoughts of African writers on African personality. These thoughts often serve as goals for personal development and the growth of dignity; they also lead to hypotheses suitable for guiding scientific work on the subject. Westerners have also speculated about African personality, and here perhaps we can trace rationalisation of prejudice, as well as finding another source of hypotheses.

One major orientation of the available research has used psychoanalytic concepts emerging from the perspectives of Freud and his followers. There are two approaches in this field: one concentrates on developing a theory intellectually, loosely relating it to some available facts; the other starts with tests, usually 'projective' ones, and collects a great deal of data, some of which serve to refine the theories being built up. A salient theme in much of this work is the idea of 'dependency', which crops up in the next approach as well.

A second major body of theory relates factors of the physical environment, culture, and cognition. The central measure of individual differences with which this theory is concerned, field independence (or its opposite, dependence) affects so many structural aspects of a person's behaviour, that we can rightly call it a personality variable. The notion of dependency here, though emerging from a different context to the psychoanalytic one, has allowed one or two researchers to explore the possibility of linking the two bodies of theory.

Two smaller and fairly distinct bodies of work have explored how people define their identity, and how phenomena of group behaviour point to personality aspects of the group members. Many of the specifically psychological studies which have been assembled into these four sections could reasonably be placed in one of the other sections. But while it is useful to separate the large amount of material into orderly sections, it is equally good to see the connections between them.

Writers on 'the African personality'

African writers themselves have often gained a perspective of their continent as a whole when they travelled away from it; and perhaps this perspective has been sharpened when there has been contact with West Indians some of whom look to Africa in the search for the roots of their identity. The French-speaking world was the setting for one such meeting of Africans and their distant West Indian cousins. In 1955 in Paris, the Society of African Culture, linked with the journal *Présence Africaine* held a conference which publicised the concept of négritude, a term coined by the West Indian Poet Aimé Cesaire. Léopold Senghor, later to become President of Senegal, wrote approvingly that 'emotion is at the heart of négritude. Emotion is Negro, as reason is Greek. . .'.

Oddly or not, some of these intellectuals were echoing stereotypes about 'African personality' not very different in some respects from those put forward by European writers. Frantz Fanon (1952), another West Indian, quoted Senghor thus: 'rhythm is alive, it is free . . . rhythm affects what is least intellectual in us, tyrannically, to make us penetrate to the spirituality of the object; and that character of abandon which is ours is rhythm'. Fanon also quoted Cesaire's lines:

'Hail those who have invented nothing!

Who have explored nothing!

But they abandon themselves, possessed, to the essence of all things. . .'

Alioune Diop suggests that such lines are quoted in genuine approval and not disdain; in his Introduction to the Belgian Father Tempels' book *La Philosophie Bantoue* Diop wrote: 'the very idea of culture . . . as a revolutionary will is as contrary to our genius as is the very idea of progress. Progress would have haunted our consciousness only if we had grievances against life, which is a gift of nature'.

Unless this has been misunderstood, two themes emerge: that Diop and his colleagues are ready to generalise about African traditional personality characteristics; and that these include a feeling of celebration of the moment rather than of dedication to the future, with an implication (contrary to Doob's idea) that the world is benevolent to innocent man, who accepts his fate within it.

Among Europeans, the Afro-linguist Westermann (1934) generalised about 'the Negro' that 'his self-consciousness is rooted in his compliance with the community; it depends on the security of his daily life as guaranteed by the group, not on the independent action of the individual. . .'; Westermann also remarked that 'although the fact that the Negro is largely ruled by his emotions can be looked on as characteristic . . . we are observing today how he is changing'. Westermann's experience, mostly in Southern Africa and Ghana was echoed by the British administrator from East Africa, Dauncey Tongue (1935) thus: 'the native lived and thought communally . . . his every action was guided and controlled by the sanctions and interests of the social group. . .'. Tongue also believed that modern institutions (of tax, law and religion) forced the person to function as an individual and that these forces were producing personality changes.

Following the Paris conference, President Nkrumah organised an All Africa Peoples' Conference in Accra, in 1958. Here, the South African Ezekiel Mphahlele (1962) described how he was deeply moved on hearing Nkrumah speak of 'The African Personality'. Mphahlele believed that 'The Black man is naturally demonstrative . . . he will look for the most intensive . . . medium of expressing himself . . . there *are* African survivals in American Negro life. You see them in . . . his bodily rhythm in a dance; in his "separatist" religious worship where he is not ashamed to surrender himself to the emotional intensity of the moment. . .'.

Yet Mphahlele recognised dangers in such stereotypes. One is that subconsciously African spokesmen would abandon the kingdom of the intellect (to the Whites?) while claiming the province of personality, or 'soul' in current terms. He distinguished the concept of négritude from that of African personality, preferring the latter 'because négritude wants to peg things'. Yet though the African personality conception 'could express the longings and ambitions, aches and torments, the anger and hunger of our people', on reflection Mphahlele saw that 'African personality' was not an acceptable generalisation for describing the diversity that still exists in Africa. He wrote 'the African personality began to recede' until 'at best it can be but a focus, a coming into consciousness'. Nkrumah's colleague Abraham (1962) having seen 'African personality' problems from an Akan standpoint, had urged that political leaders should base their programmes on attention to and respect for traditional forms. The Nigerian educationist V. O. Awosika (1967) explained 'by African Personality one is trying to bring into a sharp focus what the place of the African is . . . on the world stage. . . Any objective study of the African Personality must assess it as an idealism'.

Researchers must distinguish between target ideals, and what is at present to be found out about personalities of real Africans in towns, farms and countryside. We can now examine what has been discovered, bearing in mind some of the ideas mentioned above to act as hypotheses.

Psychoanalytic theories of personality
1. Developmental theorists
An early contribution here was by the psychiatrist Ritchie (1943, 1944), who had practised in Southern Africa. His theory revolved around the consequences for later personality development, of severe weaning having to occur at a relatively late age (see Chapter I). Ritchie considered that infants, at first allowed to develop feelings of omnipotence, then suffered a terrific rejection inducing a broken feeling of dependence on their parents and ultimately on any external authority of high status. The implication in Freudian jargon, is that the result is an insecure self or a 'weak ego'. In a compact review Crijns (1966) has pointed out that several French and Belgian writers have echoed Ritchie's opinion.

Thus Verhaegen and Leblanc (1955) considered that prolonged early indulgence led to a lack of control in adulthood of selfish behaviour. In Freudian jargon this appears to be a claim that a weak 'superego' results. From Zaïre, Marie-Thérèse Knapen (1962) claimed that after weaning, children are most often punished for 'external misbehaviour', with an accent on a concern for the opinions of others (shame) rather than on developing an inner conscience. Similarly Heuse (1955) referred to the 'externality' of Africans' superego. This seems to imply a distinction between Freudian (and European) superego which is a rebuilding in individual minds of social standards accepted as one's own inner rules of conduct, and Africans' superegos as an account of social rules which are not so fully established or experienced as belonging within. Thus superego may be strong, but felt as attached to external judges; so that if external criteria do not forbid (or if others do not see) then personal demands may be satisfied without offending 'conscience'. Also in West Africa, Parin (1958) referred to the Freudian label of 'oral' personality – a type whose structure allegedly revolves around infant pleasure of feeding or frustration with weaning. Parin claimed that West Africans were dominated by the 'pleasure principle' (giving in to the demands of a strong id), and had a 'clan consciousness' as a counterpart to the superego of European personality structure.

However, weaning and child-raising methods were and are not uniform all over Africa; so these theoretical stereotypes could never have been generally true in the first place. More recently, weaning and child-raising methods have changed somewhat to resemble European practice, so modern African personality development will be affected accordingly. Modern African readers, with youthful training unlike that described above may well resent the resulting descriptions as prejudiced rationalisations by westerners who wanted to justify colonialism. Yet a 'scientific' attitude would try to relax and explore facts and their consequences dispassionately, allowing that there may be some truth in such theories as those above. A perspective which combines an account of African personality structure, and of the interaction with it of colonialist outsiders is provided by the French psychiatrist Octave Mannoni (1956). Though Mannoni derived his ideas from living in Madagascar, he generalised 'my indirect knowledge of other colonial peoples leads me to believe that some of my conclusions are of general applicability'.

Mannoni first observed that when he had done a favour for a young Malagasy, this man did not return gratitude, but expected further favours. Although one simple explanation might be that the man had been encouraged to test out the hypothesis 'ask and it shall be given unto you', Mannoni felt that the man had slipped into a dependent relationship with him. Mannoni felt that the dependency relationship springs into being when 'the white man, even if he is alone, appears in the midst of a tribe, even if it is independent, so long as he is thought to be rich or powerful or merely immune to the local forces of magic'.

The relationship of dependence, according to Mannoni, is developed in cultures where there is an acute sense of spiritual hierarchy, the Malagasy example he observed including what he called a 'cult of the dead'. In this, while youth respects elders, the latter and everybody revere the dead, who are 'the sole and inexhaustible source of all good things: life, happiness, peace, and above all, fertility'. Though perhaps not often to this extent, in many African cultures people are keenly aware that there is a spirit world of some sort, and that communication and even influence is felt from the spirit world, among the inhabitants of our 'living world'.

Evidence on this last claim is provided, for example, by Tettekpoe (1967) who also shows that there existed an African psychoanalytic model very similar to Freud's. Among the Mina people of Togo, personality consists of three structures: the *se* or life force; *kpoli*, which appears at initiation (a possible version of the ego), and *djoto*, the reincarnated ancester found within (the superego). Tettekpoe did not develop the theory of dependence and inferiority. However, Mannoni wrote that 'dependence and inferiority . . . serve to characterise two different types of personality, two different mentalities, two different civilisations'. Whereas 'a European . . . tends to feel . . . an objective position of dependence as a sign of inferiority . . . the Malagasy . . . feels inferior only when the bonds of dependence are in some way threatened. This difference is probably the key to the psychology of the "backward peoples". It explains the long stagnation of their civilisations. It accounts for their belief in magic . . . the ego is wanting in strength . . . the individual is held together by his collective shell, his social mask, much more than by his "moral skeleton" '.

Although Mannoni's theory assumes that Malagasies would dislike feeling inferior (which would happen, he implies, if their protection was withdrawn) it is not at all clear why this dislike should occur. On the contrary, Mannoni implies that Malagasies like to feel dependent and dependence certainly implies an inferiority of power status. Mannoni specified that personality structure in dependency-organised cultures would have weak ego strength; he also referred to the same 'externality' of social control of which other writers have written, which appears to correspond to a qualitative rather than a quantitative aspect of super-ego.

Mannoni also suggested that (white) colonisers are equally prisoners, in a psychological sense, of the colonial relationship as are the colonised. Colonisers need, because they have one kind of inferiority complex, to have somebody to boss about and are incomplete or lost without such colonised people. On the other hand, the colonised people need to have authorities on whom they depend; if this support is abruptly withdrawn 'then clearly the man who finds himself suddenly independent . . . will no longer be able to tolerate guidance, but will yet be unable to guide himself'. According to Mannoni, many colonised people did not develop nationalism in order to attain political independence; instead, they demanded independence as a means to renew nationalism, seen as an intense return to the hierarchical and dependency-protecting systems of traditional cultures.

Mannoni's theory is weak in that it is based on little systematic data, but arises from clinical observation of a few dreams, and personal experiences. Such sources and processing are of course notoriously vulnerable to influence from the personal prejudices of the theorist, which become disguised by him as an account of social reality outside himself. However, Mannoni's work is rich in ideas, some of which can be seen to correspond to what others have observed.

Few researchers have directly tested Mannoni's ideas. But Jahoda (1961) did collect relevant information, from over 500 schoolchildren and adults in Ghana, regarding the impact on their lives of the White Man. Jahoda concluded that 'African attitudes and stereotypes about Europeans are indissolubly linked with African self images . . . normally a person would hardly think of himself as an "African" except in the context of comparison and contrast with Whites'. Jahoda also claimed that formal schooling is 'the most important single influence which has forced the African to look at himself "from the outside" as it were. . .' (See Chapter II). Nowadays, over a decade after independence in most countries, this identity as 'African' principally as a comparison with Whites is probably much less true.

Jahoda found little direct evidence for the existence of either inferiority, or dependence feelings. Some virtues (hospitality, community life) the Ghanaians thought were more characteristic of Africans; other virtues (manners, restraint, honesty) were considered stronger among Europeans. However, 'some 10% . . . expressed anti-African sentiments . . . most . . . phrased in terms of "they" . . . therefore setting themselves apart from the general run of Africans'.

From all his evidence, Jahoda proposed the following classification relating culture, personality, and education:

Value system (culture)	Formal education (schooling)	Personality variable (orientation to Whites)
tribal	nil	dependent
divided	intermediate	inferior
integrated	high	autonomous

This scheme, which Jahoda certainly did not offer as conclusive, differs from Mannoni's in that it puts more emphasis on a situation where Africans stand psychologically on their own feet. The psychologist here must agree with those political scientists who insist that without its political parallels, psychological independence may not prosper. However, these kinds of independence probably interact, and it may be the presence of relatively small numbers of psychologically independent people, who have developed this status through an interaction of personal qualities with some of the challenges posed by the colonial situation, whose demands hastened the arrival of political independence.

For all Jahoda's many criticisms of Mannoni, though, it should be said that the latter did recognise that dependency was not a necessary fate for Africans; he stated that when social conditions existed so that people could deal with one another with 'no emotional reaction to that other . . . the dependency complex can be dissolved and the way is clear for the attainment of a free and independent personality, a scientific approach to reality and a democratic society'. The implication here is that since the basic cultural tradition may not be altered, dependency as a life strategy would grow up in any case but that it could be 'dissolved' in certain conditions; unfortunately Mannoni did not elaborate greatly on this possibility.

At least one African writer, the Ethiopian Haile Woldemikael (1970) supports part of Mannoni's case, when he asserts that dependency is the most important psychological characteristic among Ethiopians. He points out that people do not privately determine important lifetime decisions, such as choice of marriage partners; he says adults do not try 'to achieve material and psychological self-sufficiency'. Further, 'the Ethiopian social system works not towards the emancipation of the individual, but towards his assimilation'. Why then did Ethiopia not succumb to colonial domination, even when assailed by the Italians with guns against swords? Woldemikael argues that Ethiopians shy away from taking, or claiming individual responsibility; for 'in Ethiopia a legend had to be woven into the fact of the battle (of Adwa) . . . in which St. George figures as the hero of the day'. Woldemikael says, though, that Ethiopians also show interdependence, a set of bonds between social equals and that this gave them cohesion in resisting a collapse into domination.

Complicating the problem of personality in Ethiopia, Korten (1971) analysed 129 Ethiopian folktales and suggested that life is seen as a contest providing few opportunities for social co-operation. Instead, there is the feeling that each man fends for himself and resorts to deception or revenge to do so. Korten's view would allow a covertly hostile interdependence, which may describe relations with peers, but it is conceivable that these could coexist with dependency on ancestors.

Elsewhere, Oliensis (1967), a young American teacher, set out to test Mannoni's ideas in Kenya. He used twelve photographs of pairs of people, four where a European was in a dominating position over an African, five in which Africans dominated Europeans, and three where the relationships were equal. Schoolchildren were asked to write stories about each picture. Oliensis found that where racial differentiation (RD) was mentioned, it was in terms of conflict, and in pictures where the white dominated. Among several other differences associated with pupils' tribe, and educational level, when photographs were presented by a white tester there were fewer RD themes than when they were shown by an African.

It is difficult to interpret these results as either favouring, or rejecting Mannoni's ideas. Oliensis made out a picture of 'child-like dependence' among the youngest pupils, replaced by adolescent rebelliousness, which is 'uncertain and unsettling. He is therefore impelled to test himself out through the repeated challenge of authority'. Finally, a mature stage is reached where the young person is 'largely free of the compulsive need to prove or advertise himself'. These interpretations seem but lightly connected with his results, especially since some of his statistical methods are incorrect. Perhaps the work best illustrates a danger with 'projective testing' – where a subject's ideas are said to be 'projected' into a story he writes about some ambiguous photograph or test picture. For the experimenter himself is in effect projecting into *his* analysis his own perspective on people and relationships. Thus the resulting theory, supposed to be of Africans' personality structure, can be contaminated with effects linked with the personality and outlook of the researcher.

2. Projective tests as a key to investigating dimensions of personality

We can turn now to a number of projective test studies, using well-known or adapted tests. The use of a well-known test supposes that the meaning of responses offered by subjects has been well established. However, the same difficulties with assuming that 'intelligence tests' might be culture free (see Chapters III and IV) will be found here. The evidence therefore has to be examined with considerable caution.

One projective test is by the Swiss doctor, Rorschach; it consists of inkblots, which the subject is asked to talk about and say what they look like. Barry Bricklin and Carter Zeleznick (1963) reported on Zeleznick's testing in Ethiopia, of 50 male teacher trainees. Bricklin remained in America, and analysed the materials without knowing much of their background. He must however, have known they were from Africans, and his own ideas on African personality could have flavoured his interpretations accordingly. Bricklin considered that the subjects had 'an ambivalent attitude towards personal achievement. . .; nearly three times as much energy available to the ego is expended on the practical exigencies of life, as on organising, planning and integrating'. Few signs of self-assertiveness were found, while 85% showed evidence interpreted as showing social compliance. Furthermore, the compliant person 'needs to lean on someone psychologically stronger than himself . . . and under whose protective and benevolent wing he can display his full initiative. . .'. Bricklin and Zeleznick fit this observation with that of Ethiopians' deep allegiance to their Emperor, a paternal authority figure.

Bricklin also deduced that Ethiopians 'enjoy the use of the motor system . . . (like) daredevil type persons . . . it is more difficult for the Ethiopian subject to maintain self control'; there is evidence for 'emotions of greater intensity'; and 'aggressiveness among these Ethiopians has a short-lived, non-planned character'. Subjects also tended to stick to one interpretation for each inkblot; Bricklin sees this as 'a naive interpretative realism', inferring that Ethiopians are not used to allowing that things can be seen differently (from one's own view) by other people. Finally, Bricklin deduces that 'in general the parents were seen as sources of supply and as disciplinary forces. They were practically never seen as sources of affection; nor was there any indication that the continued affection of parents was sought'. This suggestion is of great significance. As in Ethiopia, many other African cultures grapple with life at a subsistence level, and have authoritarian ways, and the consequences for personality development of Bricklin's hypothesis, should there be any truth in it, would seem to be extensive.

Another American who used the Rorschach test was Rita Mohr Weinberg (1968) who tested thirty children in Ghana, of mixed ages and tribal origins. Weinberg generalised about a typical Ghanaian child as 'inhibited but realistically oriented, concrete in his thinking, immature, *impulsive*, and sometimes even regressive in his affect. . . His anxiety is free floating and also makes him *cautious*, passive and sensitive. . . The African children are particularly vulnerable to inner misgivings and *sensitised to the reactions of others*. There is a tendency to intense . . . reactions. . . The intrapsychic constriction, *the strong ego*, moodiness related to anxiety, . . . these characteristics . . . most closely resemble an hysterical personality configuration' (emphases mine).

Some of those characteristics seem mutually contradictory (eg impulsive, and cautious); some resemble what other researchers report. Thus sensitivity to reactions of others corresponds to Heuse's 'externality', but the strong ego opposes Mannoni's indications. Weinberg relates her conclusions to Ghanaian children's acceptance of strong parental authority. She suggests that this youthful acceptance of domination produces 'an hysterical pattern of immaturity, constriction, repression of human responses'.

A similar picture was presented by Joel R. Davitz (1970) from Teachers College, Columbia; his results resemble Weinberg's even though they come from the other side of the continent. Davitz asked 107 primary school children in Kampala to write either in Luganda or in English about Happiness, Sadness and Anger. The children's accounts revealed 'extremely violent aggressive impulses when angered by an adult; but these impulses . . . are almost always inhibited . . . with continued unresolved anger'. Most children did not resent strong physical punishment in itself, but dramatised the 'apparent unreasonableness or injustice of the adults' aggression'. As in middle class Victorian Europe, here then are pictures from two African nations of emotionally repressive upbringing, said to result in constricted forms of personality.

French-speaking authors have been even keener than Americans about the Rorschach as a projective test. L.-V. Thomas (1959) praised the Rorschach's 'incredible ingenuity, the thousand and one perspectives which it reveals on the conscious and the unconscious'; it was thus 'one of the most precious instruments for cultural anthropology'. Thomas continued in this eloquent fashion and said that the test had been used by Balandier in Brazzaville, Mlle Barbé and Mme Bardet in Dakar, while he himself had collected about 500 protocols from among Diola people in Guinea.

From this, Thomas (1963) described the Diola as 'particularly sensitive, relaxed with regard to certainties . . . with a predominance of expansive people strongly socialised though suspicious and filled with self regard, but capable of violent reactions and almost of emotional derangement giving the impression of considerable lability'. Thomas likens his results to Senghor's ideas about emotionality characterising Africans, suggesting the possibility that his own preconceptions may have affected his interpretations. Not only does Thomas infer personality characteristics though, he also estimates (with misplaced exactness) that 68.37% of the subjects were of average or above average intelligence. Thomas is thus claiming that standards of intelligence among the Diola are substantially above those in France. In Chapters II and III we have doubted that valid comparisons can be made between the general levels of intelligence among peoples of widely differing cultures, even with tests specially adapted for such a purpose; equal doubt should therefore attach to this comparison made by Thomas. Nevertheless, Thomas has tried to reduce the effects of his own outlook on his interpretation of Rorschach material. He compared his conclusions with those from an independent questionnaire devised by Heuyer-Courthial, and reported close agreement on the picture presented by Diola personality tendencies. This therefore is a reason why Thomas' work should receive attention, though it certainly does not justify either unquestioning belief, or displeased rejection.

Contemporarily, Peiffer (1959) reported Rorschach results among soldiers recruited from all parts of French West Africa, and so generalisations about 'the personality' typical of any one group were not possible. A second, joint paper (Peiffer, Pelage & Pelage, 1963) reported data collected among Bamileke students in the Cameroons. Not surprisingly, the Bamileke results were more similar to those reported among western adults than to the picture that emerged from testing the less educated soldiers in Peiffer's previous study. This merely suggests that formal education, probably as well as differences in traditional culture, can produce noticeable differences in personality development.

Most recently, Tarantino (1970) tried out the Rorschach test with students at Lovanium University, Zaïre. He had little of note to report, other than that from the 'extreme abundance of anatomical and sexual responses ... we may suppose that immediate and vital problems occupy the attention and interests of our subjects'. This is probably not unlike what may be found among many students anywhere.

Other projective tests have also interested French speaking investigators. Two such tests are the Thematic Apperception Test (TAT) developed first in England, and Rosenzweig's Picture Frustration Test (PFT). In the TAT, subjects see rather indistinct pictures and are asked to tell a story about what each picture shows. The PFT is similar, except that the pictures are more definitely of frustrating situations, and it is assumed that the viewer will identify with one of the characters shown, and reflect his or her own personality in this kind of story that is made up.

Ombredane (1954) first adapted the TAT for use in the then Belgian Congo, concentrating on developing the technique of the test. However, he did get drawn into mentioning ideas similar to those of Ritchie, about the supposed effect of harsh weaning in producing a dependent emphasis in adult personality. Maria Leblanc (1958a) criticised Ombredane's work, principally on technical issues, such as the qualities of the pictures he used; she also (Leblanc, 1960) described her own adaptation of the TAT for African testing, but probably her most informative contribution arose out of testing with an adapted PFT, and with sentence completion. Using the latter, in rural and urban locations in Katanga, Leblanc (1958b) showed that in towns women change their views on the traditional role of women quicker than men do. The simple explanation for this is that in traditional society women were more thoroughly used by men, while in towns they found some freedom through wage earning.

For the PFT, Leblanc (1958b) used stories instead of pictures, which had produced extraneous problems in use (see Chapter IV). Primary school children were asked to imagine they were the frustrated person in each story, and write about how they would respond in each case. Responses were examined for signs of any of three types of aggression (extrapunitive, intrapunitive, and impunitive), and 'reactions' (obstacle-dominance, ego-defence, and need persistence); a Group Conformity Rating was also calculated, which expresses the amount of social stereotypes in the expressions among a group of people.

Extrapunitivity, and ego-defensiveness were the most common types of aggression, and 'reaction'. The Congolese children also appeared to show less conformity, and thus socialisation, than was reported in results from

American children. The Ainsworths (1962) also reported PFT data from East Africa, though among secondary school pupils, and their results are similar to those of Leblanc. Leblanc tried to validate her PFT findings by comparison with teachers' overall ratings of children's adjustment. Extrapunitivity was indeed related to ratings of maladjustment; while impunitivity and the score for Group Conformity related to ratings of adjustment.

Leblanc resisted the temptation to characterise these children as extrapunitive, showing low levels of socialisation, impulsive behaviour, etc. She saw cultural alternatives and attitudinal conflict as sources of anxiety ('free floating energy'), which brought her to three ideas which contradict, or extend the thinking of other investigators.

First she suggested that the Congolese concept of *nguvu*, or 'positive sense of external dynamism', is what had cropped up in her test as 'extra punitiveness'. Leblanc asked do we not 'value in western children the traits of obedience and dependence, where the Congolese value independence and vitality'? This may remind us that the concept 'western' is no more unitary than the concept 'African', and French, English and American conditions for comparison with African findings are by no means uniform standards. It may also be argued that obedience and dependence are not related as Leblanc implies; it is true that both refer to external authority; but independence can also produce obedience, or at least conformist behaviour, for reasons determined from within. However, it is interesting to note Leblanc's picture opposite to Mannoni's.

Leblanc also said her subjects were more 'task oriented' than concerned with interpersonal relations. Most interestingly, Leblanc added to the picture developed by Davitz and Weinberg of severe parental control repressing 'human responses', by pointing out that African children in many societies have some relatively unrestrained years until they are brought under very firm adult control when they first enter school. Since discipline does not work upon the child steadily as is the case in western cultures, but is applied strongly though late, Leblanc feels this may explain 'weaker socialisation and the lack of steadiness in superego formation'.

English-speaking authors who have used projective tests have mostly been South Africans and Americans. Thus Gilmour Lee (1953) adapted a TAT for use in Zulu culture, and E. T. Sherwood (1957) devised another adaptation among the Swazi. De Ridder (1961) was less concerned with devising a test, more with describing personality patterns among urban Africans (see below). The American couple M. and L. Ainsworth (1962) used the PFT in East Africa, and devised another interesting projective technique of their own; while L. R. C. Haward and W. A. Roland (1955) represented a lone, and much criticised attempt by English researchers to establish something with a projective test, in this case the Goodenough Draw a Man test.

Using only a few figure drawings collected in Nigeria, Haward and Roland proceeded to generalise (using Goodenough's instructions) not just about Nigerian, but about 'African' personality. Even had their conclusions been flattering, they should not have been accepted; but the picture they developed, of erratic personality structure lacking in integration was too clearly like that of a colonists' stereotype, and received no credit. The

Ainsworths asked school pupils to draw a figure, and then to say if it was an
African or a European. They were then asked to turn over the paper and draw
a person from the continent other than the one already depicted. The sizes of
the drawings for Europeans were greater than those for Africans; but the
Ainsworths refrained from making any sweeeping conclusions from this data.

In Ghana, Lystad (1960) had 94 secondary pupils write down the story
they liked best, and make up their own story of a boy and a girl in the same
town. Best liked stories centered on material needs, which were seldom
satisfied. Invented stories featured needs for social approval, and these were
often satisfied. Relationships described were emotional, group-oriented and
non-hierarchical, setting the scene for the outward-facing superego, but
showing little sign of dependency feelings.

Another projective test which has interested French-speaking writers is
Lowenfield's Mosaic Test. In this, a board is given to the person, with 456
plastic pieces in various colours and geometric shapes. The subject is to make
whatever he likes, and the psychologist has to interpret the results.
Garcia-Vicente (1960) tried this out in Angola; and Kuczynska-Stoffels
(1970) again collected over 600 protocols in Zaire. Little was reported of
note, other than that subjects did not commonly make pictures representing
people, or objects. The episode tells us little except that people with limited
literacy are not accustomed to representing their thoughts in pictures; equally
we should be cautious about anything that has been interpreted from tests
using pictures, or visual material as symbols. This may apply to the Rorschach
as well as the TAT, PFT and tests where subjects draw their own pictures.

One writer who certainly did not observe any such cautions was De Ridder
(1961) who worked for the Public Utility Transport Corporation (PUTCO) in
Johannesburg. He tested over 2,000 Africans from local townships, with his
adaptation of the TAT. The subjects' living conditions were described by De
Ridder himself as 'a landlord's paradise . . . such townships breed misery and
suffering . . . and while they promote vice and crime and disease, have an
atmosphere of individualism, of variety. . .'. Unfortunately De Ridder soon
forgot these premises, and blurred his explanation of hostility in TAT stories,
thus: 'the township African lives in a most aggressive social environment . . .
the Africans as a group appear to be an aggressive people'.

There are further internal contradictions in De Ridder's work. Early on
(p.93) he wrote 'the desire for money is by no means the sole motivating
force moving urban Africans'; but on further consideration (p. 156) he decided
that 'The Position has been reached Today where the Quest for more money
has become the Urban African's Basic Motivation' (De Ridder's capitals).
Frank and aggressive sexual references in stories led De Ridder to claim that
'the id emerges as the dominant personality force — especially in the sex
sphere'. Unfortunately, he failed to show how the hostile social climate of
competition for scarce resources affected superego structure.

After a superficial distinction between 'true humour' and 'the cruder sense
of the comic' (which De Ridder, predictably, assigned to Africans) he
reported that Africans were disenchanted with Christianity, seeing it as a
religion of the oppressive white-dominated state. Thus 'translated into
psychoanalytic terminology, the religious superego of the urban African is

still very strongly tribally conditioned . . .'. Here, he merely used Freudian jargon without clearly explaining whether superego functions were strong in general, or how the superego became weak, as is implied in his conclusion that 'The Urban African is a Personality with Strong Latent Aggression and Insufficient Moderation and Control'.

Other investigators (see below) have used projective testing in wider research strategies, but for the moment this is enough of the material which has rested principally on projective testing for its conclusions. Unfortunately the work has not really improved on Jahoda's original assertion that our ignorance about personality in Africa is almost complete. Research with projective measures has been piecemeal; spread wastefully over the continent, using far too many subjects in some cases, from whom the information has been wasted. It is not at all clear that the investigators have succeeded in applying Freudian concepts which were worked out in Europe, in societies where there is much cultural competition and change. Particularly, it is not clear what kinds of cultural and developmental conditions may produce weak or strong superegos; and whether superegos may differ in their orientation, some being more and others being less externally directed. There is also some confusion about what constitutes a strong ego — whether this indicates simply a childish, self-concerned personality, or more correctly perhaps, a personality able to hold skilfully in balance the forces of id (innate desires and appetites) and superego (the internalised voice of society's norms, rules and standards).

3. Questionnaire tests of personality characteristics

One who has chosen not to work with projective tests, but to develop questionnaires which may not only demonstrate the presence of certain personality traits described by psychoanalysts, but also to measure their strength, is Paul Kline, a psychologist from Exeter University in England. Kline was interested in the so called 'anal character'. Anal traits, of obstinacy, orderliness and miserliness are said to be the result of forcing infants to control their bowel movements. Severe pot training is said by this theory to produce a tight, retentive, obsessive character. (The label 'anal' has no etymological relation to the 'anal' part of the word 'psychoanalysis').

Kline (1969) gave 30 statements to Cape Coast University students in Ghana, including: 'do you keep careful accounts of the money you spend?' and 'do you easily change your mind once you've made a decision?'; 'yes' to the first, and 'no' to the second indicate the orderly, retentive, and obstinate aspects of anal character, respectively. Kline found that people who chose 'anal' answers to some questions, would tend to also answer 'anally' to others. Also, his test scores clustered together in a group with four scales from an American questionnaire by R. B. Cattell, including scales of ego strength, superego strength, and self control. Certainly then, this evidence suggests that those students whose high scores on Kline's questionnaire indicate high superego strength, also have high ego strength.

Two difficulties do, however, exist with these results. One emerges from a link between high scores on Kline's questionnaire, and high scores on what is called the lie scale of Eysenck's Personality Inventory (EPI), which was also given. Kline wrote this 'is accounted for by the fact that many anal characteristics, in this culture at least, are socially desirable – the quality that L is trying to measure as an index of faking'. Here Kline implied that in Ghana it was fashionable to tell lies, but what this might mean for our belief in the rest of his results was not made clear. Also, the Lie scale works by totalling cases where a person agrees with one statement and then agrees with its opposite; so this is a measure of inconsistency, which hardly reflects the meticulous and obsessional aspects of anal character.

The second difficulty with Kline's results is that he has no evidence that Ghanaian potty training was severe (either in absolute terms, or in comparison with English evidence). Instead, Kline tried to explain his high scores by pointing out that students who reach this University must be unusually self-disciplined and persevering. So his sample was not representative of 'normal' Ghanaian personality traits; and though he has found evidence of an identifiable characteristic, it evidently need have nothing to do with its supposed origin in severe bowel training; so it does not really deserve the label 'anal'.

Earlier, Kline (1967) had reported that Eysenck's EPI test did measure real and distinct personality characteristics, namely introversion (with its opposite of extraversion) and neuroticism (with its opposite of non-neuroticism). Kline (1966) also showed that while neuroticism was unrelated to measures of academic performance, the latter was related to introversion. This finding is in line with those from other countries.

To establish the 'validity' of the EPI dimensions Kline merely showed that they correlated well with two similar dimensions (namely anxiety, and extraversion) in Cattell's questionnaire, the so-called 16PF (16 Personality Factor). It is curious though, that while the Cape Coast students scored high on Cattell's measure of anxiety, they were not high on EPI neuroticism. This still leaves us with the question of knowing how anxious/neurotic these students were. Kline described Cattell's anxiety factor as 'sheer timidity of disposition which precludes discussion of the psychological sense of the score'. Perhaps Kline was too timid himself here, since a psychologist must tackle the psychological meaning of dimensions which he is claiming as valid, or on the other hand he should refrain from publishing his results. Certainly Kline's explanation of timidity does not tally with his descriptions of the students as self-possessed, nor does it harmonise with their high scores on Cattell's Self Sufficiency and Unconventionality scales.

Further discrepancies in Kline's results included that the students scored low on Cattell's measures of Ego Strength, Dominance, Surgency and Adventurousness. All this points to the need to do all this testing again, to establish that these results are not the product of random sampling effects, and that Cattell's questionnaire really does describe true structures of personality among such populations. So far, we have found in two of Kline's papers, based evidently on different sets of students at the same University, evidence of high 'anal' characteristics along with ego strength in one group (Kline, 1969) and evidence of low ego strength (Kline 1967) in another group.

Another investigator who has tried out Cattell's 16PF in Africa was

Professor Hamid El-Abd (1971), an Egyptian working in Uganda. El-Abd showed scores from 38 students at Makerere University, on 15 of Cattell's 16 factors; he also showed scores from an unspecified American group as a comparison. However, we can not compare El Abd's scores, which are 'raw', with Kline's, which were transformed by a certain statistical formula. But while El Abd's Makerere students have Ego strength scores only slightly lower than Americans, Kline's Ghanaian respondents had less than one third the Ego Strength of another American comparison group. Unfortunately El Abd does not discuss Kline's results, and the position appears to remain in an unsatisfactory state, since it is not easily credible that Ghanaian and Ugandan University students, who have followed similar careers in competitive educational situations, should have such dramatically different levels of Ego Strength in real terms.

Most recently, Durojaiya (1974a) got 180 Ugandan secondary pupils to list their worries, and to rate how much they were worried by each of 29 such items. Factor analysing the results together with 12 items of personal data suggested that anxiety, far from being a unitary dimension as in Cattell's test, is itself composed of structural parts. These reflect social, personal and philosophical areas, but in this case included a political aspect, reflecting fears of personal security.

4. Dreams as symbolic projections of personality processes and motivation patterns

A third way of exploring personality structures, which as Freud's perspective holds lie rooted in 'subconscious' levels of the mind, is to study dreams. One such study was by Lee (1958) who learned to speak Zulu and extensively analysed 120 women's dreams. As in many African cultures, Zulus consider dreams an important medium through which ancestral spirits communicate with the living. Lee counted mentions in women's dreams of the dead (signifying ancestors), of water and flooded rivers (related to childbirth), and of snakes, spooks and *tokoloshe* (hairy dwarfs — these symbols linked with sexual imagery). The obstetric histories of the women were also compared with dream symbolism. Where women were feeling anxious — if they already had two or more children for example thus proving their fertility, but being under pressure to produce more for their husbands' satisfaction, dreams tended to use symbols; in this case the one of the flooded river (the sated womb) was common. Women not in social conflict, who had not yet given birth and wanted babies, tended to dream directly (without symbols) of babies.

Few dreams related to women's modern economic behaviour, of having to look after cattle while their husbands went to cities to work. Lee explained this as 'cultural lag'; he wrote 'the unconscious minds of individuals would appear to be a very stable repository of the past'. Possibly here (and Lee did not explain this sufficiently) Zulu dream diviners tend to interpret dreams in traditional terms, and this could reinforce women's tendencies to continue to provide dreams with old fashioned symbolism.

A second dream study comes from Buganda, where people also see dreams as links with the dead; dreams are often discussed, and children encouraged to report their dreams to adults. Kilbride (in press) found among nearly 100 respondents that Baganda dream mostly about other people, though a minority of these dreams are about kinsmen. Since social relationships still remain a major pre-occupation of the Baganda, Kilbride's data can neither refute nor support Lee's theory of 'cultural lag'. He found that people living more traditional lives were not better at recalling dreams than those living more modern lives; also that the objects in dreams were more often modern (car, radio, etc) than traditional (panga, cow etc.).

The next study relates to another branch of psychoanalytic theory than that to which most of the above studies are related. While Freud postulated a psychic structure of id, ego and superego and treated these three as though they were separate actors each with a personality of their own, his colleague Adler developed a personality theory using a somewhat different drama. Adler was more interested in how an individual handled his feelings about his place in the social hierarchy. Questions here concerned adjustment to physical, social, or psychological inferiority, and the study of ambition, and patterns of achievement needs.

Okorodudu (1969) used D. C. McClelland's idea that people have a Need to Achieve, or to perform well on a recognised standard of excellence. Different individuals each have their own level, greater or less, of 'Need Achivement' (n Ach for short). The American base for much of this work accepts that meeting a standard of excellence will require the kinds of initiative, or determination to succeed, which are essentially individualistic approaches to a life career; but we should not assume in research outside America, that these are the only possible standards of excellence. Okorodudu found among 27 Kpelle families in Liberia that father absence and mother's marital status together related to the levels of American style achievement motivation in the child. However, this was not related to scholastic success.

R. A. Levine (1966) got Nigerian secondary school boys to write accounts of dreams they remembered, and also to write essays on 'success'. He also advertised nationally for people to contribute ideas on ways ahead for national development, and on personal development therein. He found that dreams reported by Ibo most often contained achievement imagery as he defined it, Southern Yoruba next, then Northern Yoruba and finally Hausa had least. The proportions of people mentioning self-development as a principal ambition were also arranged in the same order of tribal groups. Also, the frequency of social compliance and obedience themes in the essays on success, was in exactly the reverse order of tribes compared with that for achievement imagery.

After excluding explanations such as that Ibo were stung into striving to be best by feeling that their neighbours and colonial rulers considered them 'primitive', Levine comes to a 'status mobility' explanation of his results. This holds that Ibo traditional culture, with its hierarchy of titles that a man could acquire by accumulating wealth, provided an example which Ibo readily followed in terms of hierarchy in a national society. The Muslim Hausa culture discouraged westernisation, thus Hausa might not strive in the same way as Ibo did. Yoruba, Levine claimed, though already familiar with the modern system of status and rewards, were still 'attracted to reliance on modified forms of local clientage'; thus their imagery of n Ach might fall between Ibo and Hausa levels.

Levine's explanations use a version of the idea of psychocultural lag; in this, old cultural forms model child rearing practices, which result in 'certain levels of n Achievement and other personality characteristics' (Levine 1966), and thus old dream imagery will recur in today's dreams. However, it has been shown (Wober, 1966) that public stereotypes in one part of Nigeria included that 'Hausa are traditional' and 'Ibo work hard'; it is possible then that social stereotypes, independently of some inner motivational structure, could work their way into dream reports and even into dreams themselves. Nevertheless, the work shows that wide differences in important personality characteristics can exist between peoples, another reminder of the ideal nature of the concept of 'African personality'.

At least one other large study of n Ach has been done in Africa, this time among the Chagga of Tanzania. Ostheimer (1969) noted that Chagga farmers' per capita income annually was over $280, compared with a national average of $70. Geographic and political reasons certainly favour the Chagga, who live near Kilimanjaro; but personality structure might be important to their success, too. Ostheimer gave various tests including the TAT to over 900 Chagga secondary students; their n Ach score, though not high in terms of the available space on the scale, was nevertheless significantly higher than that of a group from a much less prosperous tribe.

Ostheimer's other tests, though they correlate well enough with n Ach in American research, did not follow the pattern of TAT scores in Tanzania. This suggests that n Ach, measurable in several ways in western countries, was not emerging as such a clearly recognisable personality trait among Tanzanians. Also, while TAT n Ach scores correlated in other research with school exam success, this did not occur in Ostheimer's results. Finally, Ostheimer tested Chagga farmers and compared the better and more prosperous famers with the less good ones. There was no significant difference in achievement imagery between the two groups of Chagga farmers. Ostheimer suspected that real differences did exist between those of 'dynamic personality', and others; but he felt that the unfamiliarity of the testing situation, and the possible irrelevance of McClelland's American-style achievement criteria, might explain the absence of positive results.

5. Other methods of studying motivation patterns

Another approach to studying motivation, is the measurement of 'delayed gratification patterns'. This enquires whether a person prefers to enjoy rewards as soon as possible on the one hand, or to allocate resources for a greater gain later. First Doob (1960) asked Baganda adults if they would rather spend a £5 windfall now, or invest it or get £50 after a year. As hypothesised, the less educated preferred immediate gratification. However, on another question, it was the less educated also who were more likely to say that they 'made plans for a year ahead'. As Robbins and Thompson (1972) pointed out, the highly educated are usually better off, and do not have to hoard a small windfall.

Next Vernon (1969) claimed that delayed gratification choices among schoolboys related to a 'broad perceptual-practical factor' of ability. Pollnac and Robbins (1972) found that rural people were more likely to overestimate the length of a short time interval, suggesting that they were impatient relative to townspeople. They did not, however, test time estimation and gratification preferences among the same individuals to demonstrate a true link. But Wober and Musoke-Mutanda (1972) showed that when the same children were given the two tests, there was no correlation between time estimation and gratification preferences. This research did however extend the idea of patience which underlies the delayed gratification choice, to cover questions of punishment. Here, children were asked if they would prefer a large punishment immediately, or have to wait but get a smaller punishment. Impatience for reward and also for punishment correlated significantly among girls, and very strongly among boys. Particularly upper class boys in an expensive boarding school with its time-marked regime, showed the strongest preference for patience.

Robbins and Thompson (1972), again in Uganda, found no significant correlations between questions on delayed gratification preference and measures of age, education, subjects' own estimates of their modernity, and other variables. The only relationship they could find was that rural people were more likely to prefer delayed gratification. Robbins and Thomspon suggested that town life was more hectic, thus demanding fast living and spending, while villagers had a more contemplative life and were thus used to waiting. This does not harmonise with Robbins' own argument (see Chapter VII) for a *compensatory* process, that villagers bored with their slow pace of life would choose the more 'novel' of two sets of stimuli. Robbins and Thompson tested subjects from various sectors of Kampala without comparing between them; but Wober (1967) distinguished between men who lived in the 'cooler', quieter suburban estate and who tended to be rated as better workers by their supervisors, and men who like 'hotter' life in the more exciting atmosphere of the inner part of the town. There may thus be further distinctions in gratification and personality patterns between town dwellers who gravitate to the different styles of life which occur even within towns.

6. An overview of research emerging from psychoanalytic concepts

Though deferred gratification researchers have not connected their ideas with that of the anal personality, deferment strongly resembles the retentive aspect of the supposed anal character. This realisation opens the way to examining whether the two dimensions correlate, and form part of a broader phenomenon. The task of psychology here is at least twofold; to demonstrate what the phenomena are by describing and classifying personality characteristics; and to explain their origin and development.

The developmental theorists, Ritchie and Mannoni did not substantiate their ideas with any extensive and systematic bodies of data. Neither Jahoda's work in this area, nor Oliensis', was equipped with a wide enough range of suitable questionnaires and projective tests, to be able to substantiate their predecessors theories; in fact their results have tended to cast doubt on the theory that dependency typifies personality. Nevertheless, severe weaning after intense maternal affection, followed by parental withdrawal, are common practices, and it remains possible that they may lead to a dependent personality structure with weak ego strength. There has been some support for this, from Woldemikael, and Bricklin and Zeleznick; oddly, both these studies were from Ethiopia, and Ethiopia is the one African country which, unlike Mannoni's argument that dependent personality styles leave a society open to colonial domination, in fact successfully warded off the colonists.

The idea that weak ego strength would be typical was not supported by evidence from Ghana. Weinberg specifically mentioned strong egos, though she claimed that some 'repression of human responses' resulted from severe parental discipline. This account of repressed anger at what was felt to be arbitrary parental severity was also reported by Davitz from Uganda, though he had nothing to say about ego strength. Also from Ghana, Kline reported both high ego and superego strengh as measured by an Eysenck questionnaire, though low ego strength as measured by a Cattell questionnaire. There was also disagreement on anxiety, Cattell's questionnaire suggesting a high level but Eysenck's suggesting a low level of neuroticism. Further heterogeneity is evident in examining Kline's results where a Ghana-America comparison is made, with El Abd's in Uganda, where a Uganda-America comparison was made. Ugandans appear to have greater ego strength than Ghanaians, though still not as much as Americans.

Theorists and experimenters have also disagreed about expected and measured aspects of superego development. Here the African evidence may offer an opportunity of broadening our theoretical understanding of the superego. To the question of superego strength is added the question of whether the superego has a direction. Thomas reported strong super-ego or at least 'strong socialisation' among the Diola in Guinea, and De Ridder referred both to strong 'religious' superego but also 'insufficient moderation and control', which may be a loose description of strong superego formation. Leblanc referred to lack of 'steadiness' in superego allegedly as a result of severe adult discipline applied after a delay of some years in a child's life during which he receives relatively little adult direction.

All this unfortunately suggests that psychologists have been sketchy in establishing what really happens in childhood to the people they have tested. Instead we have reports from which it is difficult to disentangle the preconceptions of the authors; sometimes the alleged experience in childhood simply does not match what the theory has required, as when Kline had no evidence that severe bowel training produced strong anal characteristics. The way is open for an original theorist who will explore how anal character may relate to superego formation (in its aspect of self control) during childhood in African contexts.

Approaching the motivational structures of personality, Levine claimed clear evidence for the effects of culture on motivational patterns among Nigerians; but the study has not been confirmed in Nigeria; and Ostheimer's attempt to repeat a similar demonstration in Tanzania met with little success. Lee showed that where people had little anxiety their dream content represented their waking interests directly, while themes about which there was anxiety appeared in the disguise of symbols which Lee was able to 'translate'. Levine perhaps neglected a possibility that among some groups achievement imagery may be present, though substantially transformed by the use of symbols.

Studies examining patience have not all supported each other's findings, or been internally consistent. Doob suggested that patience was found more among educated people, and Vernon claimed it was related to a perceptual-practical ability. Wober and Musoke-Mutanda reported patience particularly among boys receiving rigorous boarding schooling, but Robbins and Thompson found it more among rural and not urban dwellers. No researchers have yet recognised or explored a resemblance between patience and that aspect of achievement motivation theory which implies that high achievers would probably follow a policy of deferring gratification.

The evidence has been too widely spread, and awaits an accumulation of repetitive studies which should eventually build up support for one or another theory. Perhaps so far the main lessons are that the political ideal of 'African personality' must deal with a very great deal of variation between different groups in Africa; and that knowledge of most aspects of personality we have so far discussed, is still in a delicate and uncertain condition.

Cognitive theories of personality

To some psychologists this heading may seem a contradiction in terms. However a body of research has arisen which, as Heim (1970) pointed out, has begun to integrate ideas of abilities with others relating to personality. One branch of this research is linked with Witkin's concept of 'field independence' (see Chapter IV). Researchers who used Witkin's ideas in African fieldwork include Berry, Dawson, Wober, Okonji, and more recently Siann, and Baran (see below).

Witkin's theory is that secure affection, rationalised and moderate punishment, and emphasis on individual competence and self reliance (starting with early encouragement for the child to dress himself, play without parental supervision, undertake jobs and assignments, and so on), are likely to produce children who are 'field independent'. Field independence will be detectable by cognitive tests such as the Rod and Frame Test, Embedded Figures, and related tests; in these, field independent people will be able to resist forces of suggestion and context, and stick to their own ideas. At the opposite extreme of what is really a continuum, experience of erratic affection and punishment, overlooking or suppression of individual competence, and subordination of self reliance to social obedience would produce a field dependent individual, who would do poorly on RFT and EFT, and who would be very open to social influence and cognitive contexts set for him. Witkin also showed that field independent people have different patterns in which they may fall prey to mental illness under stress than field dependent people have.

The parallels between aspects of Witkin's concept of dependence, and psychoanalytic concepts of dependence, and between Witkin's ideas on self reliance and those of the need achievement theorists, are clear and invite investigation, a little of which has begun. However, an early exploration of Witkin's ideas in Africa was presented by Berry (1967), who related field independence not only to child-raising styles, but further back, to forms of economy (e.g. hunting, or farming), and even to forms of landscape, which are all interrelated. Thus the Temne of Sierra Leone are farmers and Berry expected them to be conscientious, compliant and conservative. One Temne is quoted thus: 'when Temne people choose a thing, we must all agree with the decision — this is what we call co-operation'. In contrast, their surroundings require Eskimos to be self reliant hunters; so Berry expected Temne to be more socially conformist on a test than Eskimos.

Berry showed people a set of lines, each of slightly different length, and a comparison line equal in length to one of the others. Subjects were told 'Most Temne (or Eskimo) people say *this* line (the experimenter pointed one out) is equal in length to the one at the top. Which one do you say?'. As expected, Temne tended to choose what they thought other people chose, even when the line indicated was not in fact equal to the comparison line. Previously, Berry (1966) had shown that Temne scored lower than Eskimos on the EFT; thus both 'perceptual field independence', and social independence were relatively weak among Temne. We might expect then, that EFT scores and resistance to suggestion scores might correlate; but Berry said that within ethnic groups, correlations between perceptual independence and social independence were insignificant. On the other hand Claeys (1967) using a similar conformity test with Congolese undergraduates found that those who tended to conform were less resistant to stress as indicated by Rorschach responses and the Minnesota Personality Inventory, though they were not, as had been expected, more extrovert or needful of social approval than were non-conformers. Thus the full Witkinian argument that independence spans perceptual, and psycho-social activities, has not been unequivocally supported.

Dawson, Wober and Okonji had each showed that scores among African groups on the EFT, tended to be lower than among Americans (see Chapter IV). However, Wober contended that the RFT, unlike in American research, did not appear to be measuring the same thing among Africans as was measured by the EFT. This was to some extent corroborated by Okonji, and again by Siann. Here again we see that 'field independence' might not develop similarly in perceptual and social 'fields', or even in two different kinds of perceptual field.

In spite of setbacks, though, the theory of field independence is a fruitful one. Evidence has supported it in America and in other cultures; and it provides a unified and meaningful view of ways of bringing up children, of perceptual characteristics of the environment, of the economic conditions determining what people must do to win a living, and of how their society must adapt itself to its local habitat. Quite possibly the most appropriate ways of defining and measuring field dependence may not yet have been developed for use among African populations (other than those who are extensively westernised). If more appropriate ways are found, then assessment of field independence may help in understanding how people adapt to the kinds of social change taking place in Africa, and in linking various theoretical perspectives in psychology. One study has attempted a link-up of field independence with other perspectives, and this is by the South African Sybil Baran (1971).

Baran tested rural people from the village of Mtunzini in Zululand and schoolteachers in the notorious Soweto (South Western) Township of Johannesburg. She explored two theoretical perspectives: Witkin's concept of field dependence, and the ideas of Erikson, an American whose variant of psychoanalytic thinking focuses on the development of a secure, autonomous and independent self. To test field independence, Baran used the RFT, Koh's blocks, and the Draw a Man test; to explore Erikson's ideas a TAT yielded scores on: relations to authority, to parents and to the group; relations with the supernatural; the self concept and other themes. Baran used Grant's measure of 'Acculturation' (see Chapter VI), a questionnaire on emphasis on independence in child raising practices, and measures of n Ach and of 'orientation to work'.

Baran pointed out that 'no attempt was made to match the groups for intelligence. It was felt that intelligence is not a significant factor in determining performance on ... field dependence...'. Her strategy was to factor analyse the results for each subgroup (rural, or urban males or females) and see whether the test results correlated together in clusters, or factors, in the same way for each group, or not.

Some of the results were as expected. Urban males had higher scores than rural males on measures of separate identity, attitudes to child raising practices, on the RFT, on n Ach, orientation to work, but puzzlingly also, on acceptance of authority. Baran is aware that acceptance of authority should not theoretically appear together with high n Ach, but she tried to explain this in a rather unconvincing manner, saying that need Achievement 'may be more indictive of conformity needs than of the achievement motive as understood by McClelland'. But her own scores of need achievement appear to have used McClelland's criteria (which emphasise competition), so they can hardly have indicated conformity needs. Perhaps the explanation of Baran's result may be that answers given by black South Africans on acceptance of authority in a research project promoted by whites may not be valid. They are not likely to say what they really mean about obedience to authority, which is exercised by whites.

The factor analyses, though Baran claimed they support her hypotheses, fail to provide any sign that the personality dimensions developed by different theorists, and which have such superficial resemblances, can be drawn together. Among urban males the chief family of correlated variables (or factor) consists of child raising practice attitudes, sense of separate identity, and the urbanisation score. One might expect that measures of field independence, educational level, or need achievement would belong to this group; but they did not. Instead, need Achievement and Acceptance of Authority appeared with orientation to work, as one statistical factor. Other factor analyses for female groups, and rural males showed similar oddities, and a failure of similar variables to come together in expected ways. Baran pointed out though, that some similarities do exist; same sex groups yield more similar patterns of factors, than two urban, or two rural groups of each sex. This suggests that basic personality structures differ between men and women more than between urban and rural groups. In the end, Baran suggests that field independence 'is more determined by an ability component among the rural group than . . . the urban group where . . . it was essentially comprised of personality variates'. It was perhaps a mistake therefore, for her to have excluded intelligence from her considerations, as she had done at the outset.

Baran also provided some pilot data which link with a small group of studies of some interest. In analysing dream reports she noted a tendency to attribute life to inanimate objects. This she interpreted as a 'field dependent' characteristic, since the self, mankind, and natural objects are said to have been perceived as part of a single continuum.

Jahoda (1958a, b) studied this question among Ghanaian schoolchildren. He asked them about a story concerning a boy who stole an orange and later cut his foot with a cutlass, and about what produced the music in a gramophone. Among late primary classes, only 6% of children showed animistic responses. Curiously, most children who answered animistically about the cut (the cutlass 'knew' the boy had done wrong) did not answer animistically about the gramophone, and vice versa. Later, Poole (1968) found that Hausa village children showed more evidence of animistic ideas (agreeing that the sun, and other objects are 'alive') than did urban children. But the Hausa urban children showed no more or less animistic thinking than a comparison group of English schoolchildren. Earlier, Loves (1957) asked over 1,500 boys in the then Congo about the source of punishment for wrongdoing. Fewer among the older pupils could not specify an origin for punishments (which Jahoda considered an animistic form of response); simultaneously, saying punishment was by God's will, or by simple accident increased to 79% of children at age 16. These results point neither to any great prevalence of animism, nor to any link between this and field dependence.

Research combining features of psychoanalytic and field theories of personality

There is one large study whose theoretical perspectives span most of those which have so far been discussed. R. B. Edgerton (1971) was part of an American team of social scientists and studied among the Pokot of Kenya and the Sebei of Uganda (both Kalenjin groups), and the Hehe of Tanzania and the Kamba of Kenya (both Bantu-speaking groups). Like Berry, Edgerton believed that ecology (savannah, forest, etc) would determine the economy of a people (herding, farming, hunting, etc) and that working conditions would determine social organisation and thereby influence personality patterns.

In all, Edgerton tested 505 people with 85 questions, 10 Rorschach cards, 9 pictures designed to explore 'values', and 22 colour slides. Interviews were in local languages, which Edgerton learned. All responses were categorised by 'manifest content analysis', that is, no subconscious symbolism was read into what was said. Content categories included any mention of adultery, affection, cattle . . . and finally, witchcraft, 31 categories in all. Interviews 'were designed to elicit shared attitudes, beliefs and perceptions . . . by use of an impersonal ("what do the Hehe think?") rather than a personal ("what do you think?") format'. So it is not surprising that he did not find many differences between answers given by men or by women.

Edgerton's impression of personality among these African groups is sadly at odds with the ideals exposed by Diop and others quoted earlier. He saw the elaborate greetings and manners among farmers as a cover-up for real feelings of fear and conflict which derive from competition for scarce land; pastoralists may have less developed enmity, as their mode of life enables them to move away from those with whom they may quarrel. Twelve significant differences between Bantu and Kalenjin respondents (out of the 31 content category comparisons) were found. For example, Bantu showed less respect for certain kinds of authorities than Kalenjins; these differences could not stem from ecological sources either, as both groups contained equal proportions of farmers and of pastoralists.

Edgerton devised an objective measure of 'acculturation' which included data on a person's education, religion, type of footwear, type of roof on the house, experience of travel, and other facts. Overall, farmers were more 'acculturated' on this scale, than were pastoralists. Now Edgerton had to tackle the question of whether any differences in personality characteristics between groups arose from ecological differences, or from differential acculturation.

To test this, Edgerton examined whether links occurred between personality responses and levels of acculturation for individuals within each society, where ecological differences would be relatively minor. Edgerton claimed that few significant, and no systematic links between acculturation and personality patterns arose within societies. However, this neglected the fact that on six out of 31 content categories, there were significant links with acculturation levels. Thus the groups which were more acculturated (Kamba farmers at the head) were 'less affectionate, less concerned with cattle, less independent, less fearful and less depressed'. Here then is one echo of Berry's ideas — that farmers (like the Temne) may be less independent, while the more mobile pastoralists are more independent. Another possible explanation though, for Edgerton's results, which he did not develop, is that it may be personality differences which produce different levels of acculturation.

The finding that Kamba farmers are 'less fearful and less depressed' than others, like Edgerton's Rorschach data, refute his intuitive analysis that farmers are in psychological strife with one another. The Rorschach responses showed high levels of anxiety, high impulsivity and low inner controls (this last being in line with the earlier theorists' ideas about weak ego formation), but 'one of the most striking findings . . . was a lack of hostile responses, and there were still fewer overtly aggressssive ones'. Edgerton felt that Rorschach results had not succeeded in revealing something that he believed was present; and he put it down to the 'low ambiguity tolerance of these Africans' which led them to restrict the fluency of their Rorschach responses. Though Chapter VII examines evidence that there can be tolerance of ambiguity in situations of cultural and attitudinal conflict, another reason for scanty Rorschach responses could be that people unaccustomed to reading messages into visual symbols and displays may easily be bored with blotches on paper and consider brief answers to be quite enough.

One facet of Edgerton's Rorschach findings contradicts a conclusion which Berry offered. Exploring 'cognitive rigidity' Edgerton finds that 'the pastoralists gave more stereotyped responses; the farmers responded . . . more freely and creatively, restructuring (inkblots) and assigning their meaning more flexibly'. This closely resembles Witkin's description of how field independent people perform with the Rorschach. Thus unlike Berry's findings, and his own content analyses, Edgerton found farmers more field independent in their Rorschach results, than were pastoralists. In all, it is perhaps safest to refrain from any conclusions from Edgerton's Rorschach data; perhaps they have not really revealed, as he himself suggests, sufficient psychological truth about the people he tested.

Edgerton's final analysis is also, though massive, unsatisfactory. He correlated results from all the 31 content categories, and many other measures, together, and concluded that 'most of the variables are unrelated'. Unfortunately, he immediately continued with a complex statistical analysis to show how these variables may cluster together in groups. In this way two large 'families' or characteristics were assembled. One includes: affection, brutality, cattle, self control . . . direct aggression, respect for authority etc, and a difficulty with this analysis is that it includes fairly contradictory characteristics (such as brutality and affection) as part of a supposedly connected group.

Another difficulty is more complex to explain. It relates to the point that the sophisticated cluster analysis arranges items together because they are *relatively* close in some respect; but it ignores what the real values are. For example, cluster analysis has separated 'disrespect for authority' and 'respect for authority' into clusters which Edgerton assigned to farmers, and pastoralists respectively. Certainly disrespect for authority is rare among pastoralists' responses (only 0.16 times on average, per person); but nor was it really common among farmers either (4.20 times per person). The ratio between the two rates of prevalence is certainly that farmers show 26 times as much as pastoralists. Now we compare 'direct aggression'. This was mentioned 17.5 times per person among farmers; and pastoralists showed this more, but not more than twice as much. Because of the greater *ratio* in the case of 'disrespect of authority' Edgerton labelled this as a typical farmer's characteristic, though it was mentioned just 4.2 times per person; but 'direct aggression', which farmers showed 17.5 times a person is not grouped among their characteristics!

In spite of such statistical chaos, some merit remains in Edgerton's work. Though he has not much discussed their work, his study does move tentatively to bridge the perspectives of those who have used psychoanalytic ideas, and others who have used cognitive field theory ideas in African research. Out of all his evidence, Edgerton has suggested two personality dimensions, one of which may link up with dimensions suggested by other workers; and the second may turn out to be an original contribution worthy of further investigation. The first dimension he called emotionality; farmers, he said, show 'closed' and pastoralists 'open' emotionality. These concepts resemble Eysenck's ones of extraversion (open versus closed in Edgerton's terms) and neuroticism (emotionality). Edgerton's second dimension is action. Here, he said pastoralists tend towards more 'direct' action and farmers towards more 'indirect' ways. Perhaps the direct action personality is another way of describing Witkin's field independent character. Perhaps it is a new and relevant way of describing personality. Only further research can establish which of these possibilities, or none, may be correct. Indeed, a large study is now under way in the Central African Republic, in which Canadian and other social scientists guided by John Berry are studying social, psychological and even genetic correlates of different ecologies. Results will not only increase our knowledge, but will raise many new questions and ensure that this area of enquiry becomes more actively and fruitfully cultivated.

Studies exploring aspects of self awareness

In Ghana, Jahoda (1954) noted that several peoples customarily named children according to the day of the week on which they were born. Day names have acquired associations of meaning and the one for Wednesday is associated with naughtiness. Possibly reflecting how they thought society perceived them, Wednesday-named boys were more numerous among a group of delinquents than boys with other day-names. Wober (1971a) has pointed out that African cultures are among many world-wide examples where parents give names which remind children of their hoped-for personalities, or positions in society; thus names may function as signposts to directions of personality development.

To explore how children have learned their places in society, Grayshon and Olanlokun (1966) asked Yoruba children to write around large circles drawn on sheets of paper 'the names of persons in your family'. Yoruba children wrote down well over 20 names each on average, compared with just five names each produced by English children. Very few Yoruba children place themselves at the top, while somewhat more English children did so; Yoruba generally placed a male name at the top, possibly recognising a male dominance in status. Barbara Lloyd (1968) asked Yoruba children questions like 'what animal would you like to be', and to rank in order of preference: father, mother, brother and sister. Lloyd considered that age was probably more important than sex in determining recognition of status. She gave the same questions to Gusii children in Kenya, and found the reverse, that there male dominance was more effective a sign of status than was age. But whatever the rules of a society, these studies show that children readily learn them and accordingly know in what directions their personalities have most freedom to develop. In a similar study, Richard Trent (1965) asked 360 Ghanaians aged from 4-21 'who are you?'. Younger children mostly gave their names, but the early teens saw considerable differentiation in the terms of identity, with the crucial characteristics being name, physical attributes, sex and age.

Knowledge of one's society may also affect the scope and direction of personality development. Longton (1955) found that 40% of over 300 secondary schoolboys in Lusaka said that tribal identity had a signficiant influence on social relationships. Edgerton (see above) found that Bantu people liked a photograph of a Bantu girl (not of their own tribe) better than a picture of a Kalenjin; while the Kalenjins' preference was reversed. These studies suggest that feelings of identity can reflect membership of a tribe, or of a wider cultural grouping.

In Uganda, a study of group identification in its formative stages was done by Ndumbu (1972). Children (aged from 4½ to 9½ years old) were shown black and white pairs of dolls, similarly dressed. The children could identify which race the dolls were supposed to represent, and knew which 'race' (black or white) they themselves belonged to. Children were then asked to point to which doll 'you want to play with', which 'looks bad', which is 'a nice doll' and which 'is a nice colour'. Whereas half the European children pointed out the white as 'bad', three quarters of black children in a racially mixed school pointed to the black doll as 'bad', and about 90% of poor children in an all-Ugandan school did likewise. The other questions on preference showed similar patterns of results. It seems that children are aware of signs of race, and associate colour with status. A low preference for one's own kind may relate to awareness of low status, and was certainly greater among the children from the lower status school than among those in the elite, racially mixed school; but signs of it were present among the latter as well. In South Africa, Meij (1966) showed that pre-school Tswana children had made some choice between dolls that represented racial distinctions, though some choices did not. Also, Gregor and MacPherson (1966) found that in a perceptual task of choosing between two pictures, black children seemed to prefer and try to identify with whites; rural blacks however, were less confused by status and race than were their urban brethren.

Another early study, by Leonard Bloom (1960), focused on self concepts rather than inter-group attitudes. Students in Durban, South Africa, were asked questions like 'in what way would you like to change' and 'what sort of person do you most despise/admire'? While white students looked for changes in personal qualities (like intelligence), and admired an intelligent man, black Africans hoped, not unnaturally, for social status changes, and admired a humanitarian man. These models of ideal personality are fully in line with Powdermaker's and Jahoda's findings on attitudes elsewhere in Africa and with Irvine's, Wober's and Serpell's investigations on the concept of intelligence (Chapter III).

A more complex study of self concepts was done with Xhosa men in South Africa by Du Preez and Ward (1970). They defined groups of 'modern' (more educated, and in literate or skilled jobs) and traditional men. Men were shown photographs of a wide range of African figures, three at a time, and were asked to say in what way two pictures were similar and the third was different. This procedure discovered men's own 'constructs', such as 'this man does dangerous work/these men do easy work'. Men were then asked to rank photographs from the one most like one extreme of the construct, to that most resembling the other extreme. Finally subjects rated each photograph on two constructs given by the experimenter, namely like oneself, and like one would like to be.

Modern men were more likely than traditional men to see themselves in terms of educational level. The modern men used fewer adjectives in their picture of what was 'like oneself', than did traditional men; but these adjectives were at a more superordinate, or general level (like educated/uneducated). Overlapping with this finding was a distinction between urban and rural men. Rural men used more constructs which are called 'impermeable' or indivisible. Whereas educated/uneducated is a construct that can be further divided (e.g. into been to school, knows languages, etc.) an 'impermeable' construct can not be much further divided (e.g. 'wears a uniform', or 'has a bad complexion').

Finally Du Preez and Ward examined how people ranked photographs as 'like myself', and 'like I would like to be'. While signs of disharmony between actual and ideal self were not more common among rural than among urban people, the traditional men (whether they lived in country or town) were more at odds with themselves than were the modern men. The upshot of all this is that people seem to want to be more modern, and are more pleased with themselves if they are more modern. It remains to be said that traditional rural men were less at odds with themselves than traditional urban men. It is less unsatisfying being a peasant if one is uneducated than being an unskilled worker in the town, where the examples of the rewards of being educated and in a better job are very visible.

A simpler study than Du Preez and Ward's, was done in Nigeria (Wober 1971a). Subjects were all young men in Lagos, some employed in clerical or semi-skilled jobs and others unemployed and looking for similar kinds of jobs. Each person was asked to describe how 'most people I know' would describe a person they liked, and a person they respected. Subjects next chose from the list of criteria they had mentioned, the two which they themselves felt were most important. Finally, they each rated themselves, on the extent to which they exhibited the qualities they had indicated as important. Adjectives were classified into groups of those that were 'consensual' (i.e. – need the presence of others to make them real – e.g. popular) and those that were 'subconsensual' (criteria which can operate without the presence of others – e.g. rich or happy).

Employed people had better self esteem than the unemployed, in that more of them claimed to have the characteristics which they found important. Levels of self esteem seemed to relate to the type of criteria on which they were based. People who had consensual criteria of esteem, especially if they were employed, had higher levels of self esteem. It appears that in the culture of urban Lagos in which these young men lived, people expected self esteem to be based on social criteria, like 'friendly', 'generous' and so on. A change in social predicament, in this case to unemployment, may have made people more aware of their personal qualities, and thinking of themselves in these terms was not good for their personal adjustment.

These few studies merely begin to show that people do learn the rules of their culture, and of the kinds of personalities they are expected to develop in order to fit into society, surprisingly early. We are beginning to discover how the ideal self comes to be thought of, and of conditions in which self esteem, or the extent to which one's perceived self is like one's ideal, is more or less fulfilled. Great scope remains here, for exploring how dimensions of self esteem which spring from peoples' own perspectives (e.g. sociable, modern) may relate to other personality dimensions (e.g. dependence, emotionality) which have been derived more from the perspectives and theories of research psychologists.

Personality characteristics as revealed by studies of group behaviour

Some group phenomena, like games, have been anthropologically studied as of interest in themselves; but it has been realised, as by Hopkins and Wober (1973) that a study of the diversity of African games that exist, and of the ways in which they reflect social values, could shed light also on modes of socialisation and of 'cognitive style'.

One such study was by Meeker (1970) among the Kpelle of Liberia. She used a variant of some traditional Kpelle games and compared strategies used by traditional and Westernised players. Results suggested that Westernised subjects were more competitive than traditional subjects; but the evidence was not clear cut. But though there are many African board games and others, psychologists have so far preferred to use imported, laboratory-devised games.

One such 'game' is that of discussion of 'choice dilemmas'. For example, a story is presented that a businessman needs a serious heart operation; without it, he would have to retire to a quieter life, duller than he previously had, but without immediate risk of death. With the operation, the man might be restored to the full style of life he was enjoying, though on the other hand it could fail and he might die. Individuals are asked to say at what level of risk, expressed in terms of chances out of ten of a success, they would advise one to take such an operation. In America it had been found that during group discussions, people tended to take riskier joint decisions, and also made riskier private decisions after the discussions than they had offered before joining in discussion. The phenomenon became known as the 'risky shift'. One of the best theories to account for this was that American culture favoured boldness, and people exposed to each other in 'public' groups, did what was valued in their society. Psychoanalysts might say that the phenomenon reflected high superego strength.

Clive Davis (Carlson and Davis, 1970) ran group discussions with Ugandan secondary students using the standard American problems. He found that Ugandans before discussion showed less risky levels of decision than Americans; they did not shift in discussion to more risky levels but became more cautious on two out of eleven problems. Wober (1971d) devised a locally relevant problem, and repeated one of the American problems, with undergraduate subjects; no shift, either to safer, or more risky decision levels occurred.

Next, Wober and Bukombi (1973) devised two locally relevant problems. The first concerned whether a student should change from Arts to Science, risking a difficult new subject for the chance of a better career. The second problem concerned birth control and family size; a man with four children, and family pressures to have more, could risk having more and being able to cope financially with their education; or he could be cautious and use birth control. With both of these problems, undergraduates showed significant shifts to caution. If caution is a traditional value, then possibly students with more traditional attitudes would shift more to caution, while those with more westernised opinions might even shift towards risk. However, there was no correlation between changes in individual level of risk after group discussions, and attitude scores.

In terms of personality, cautious group behaviour might relate in certain economic conditions (e.g. of security) with deferred gratification preferences. Caution might otherwise link (e.g. in insecure economic situations) with an intention to immediate realisation of resources. Other links to be investigated could be with ego or superego strength.

Another American laboratory game was used by Tedeschi *et al* (1971) among Akan late primary schoolchildren in Ghana. This game, called the Prisoners Dilemma, involves two people: both simply choose one out of two possible actions at each 'play'. How much they win, or lose, depends on what both players do. When the experimenter said 'go', players either faced a wall, or turned to face away from it. By co-operating, and facing the same way as the other player, one could get small gains. By acting on one's own, one could gain more − provided the other player happened to do one thing, but if he did the other thing one would lose. The amounts each can win or lose are shown to players before each episode and the odds can be varied. Token money is used, exchanged for sweets at the end of the whole game.

Akan children were found to be more competitive, or risk taking, than Americans. Boys were more competitive than girls; but there was no relation between the size of the possible gain compared to possible loss, and inclination to co-operative behiaviour. This suggests that players may not have understood the instructions well, and chose the biggest possible option even when that was risky. The authors theorised that the results show genuine competitiveness, possibly stimulated by the very competitive educational system. They speculated that children in a transitional cultural situation would be more competitive than those in a securely traditional culture; on the other hand, competitiveness might disappear among children in a secure, bureaucratic society as in America, where rewards appear to be virtually assured in life. The same explanation could have applied to the Ugandan undergraduates who showed little risk in group discussions. However, Davis has recently obtained results from Kampala workers and traders open to competitive conditions in life, which show that they still have low levels of risk-taking readiness.

Recent support for Tedeschi's position is provided by Bethlehem (1973) who had Zambian and white boys in Zambia play the Prisoners Dilemma game. The white boys were rich, and the Zambians poor, yet there were no significant differences between the groups with respect to overall average scores. Bethlehem pointed out there was little evidence in either group of altruism or co-operativeness. The Zambians however, showed a larger range in sizes of scores, which suggested to Bethlehem that 'there is a conflict among Zambians − traditional norms adjuring co-operation in conflict with town-induced competitive tendencies'.

A third game offers yet another context in which personality may be expressed, and studied. Paul Hare (1969) conducted 'communication network' experiments among Ibadan undergraduates. In these, participants either sit in a *circle* and can communicate only by passing notes to their neighbours; or they sit around one man in the centre (a *wheel*) and can pass notes only to and from the central man. Hare characterised the Yoruba as more 'authoritarian' and Ibo as more 'democratic'; he expected the wheel network to be better suited to people accustomed to an authoritarian atmosphere in discourse, and that Yoruba would solve problems more efficiently with the wheel than Ibo.

In fact Yoruba passed more messages and took longer to solve problems than did Ibo on the wheel arrangement. Hare said that in a society where people enjoy 'palavers', they do not try for speedy solutions of problems. Ibo did, however, press home a determination to reach a solution and this could be said to be an outcome of the same drive which was manifest as competitiveness in Tedeschi's study. Hare certainly takes a great deal for granted; why a circle arrangement should be termed 'democratic' is not clear, and whether this communication structure would be best used by individualistic or participatory people is not clear either. Another personality dimension which Hare implied has an effect here, might be the difference between people who are more interested in the 'expressive' aspects of tasks (ie they enjoy doing things) and others who prefer an 'instrumental' outlook (i.e. they like achieving results).

Though the available evidence from games is scant, when ideas and methods have been refined, the approach will be a useful one for studying personality. People enjoy games, and will express themselves naturally in playing them, while questionnaires and projective tests have less appeal. This then, is an area in which interesting developments may well occur in the future.

An overview of the research on personality in Africa

In the early 1960s, the best informed observers were pessimistic about the state of knowledge about personality in Africa. Researchers did not know exactly what 'dimensions' they were looking for, and they did not have appropriate means of searching, since it was not known how suitable existing foreign tests would be. Over a decade later, there is still chaos in the field, albeit a richer and more complex chaos. Various research methods have been explored; and it is realised that they do point to ways in which ecology, economy, culture, socialisation, cognitive style, personality, and social life are all interrelated.

Two schools of generalisation about 'African personality' can be discerned. There were intuitive psychologists, seeking perhaps to rationalise some of the stereotypes about Africans that had sprung up during approximately a century of colonial interrelationships. There were also the Pan-African idealists whose ideas linked both political and psychological aspects of a drive for independence. Most of the experimental and survey work has, however, failed to support the ideas of these generalists. One reason is because 'African personality' is not a unitary concept, but varies over the continent, with cultural, economic and social variety. Another reason may be because to some extent the generalists' ideas were derived not wholly from a dispassionate respect for the processes of personality as they really are, but sprang also from the personalities, and relationships of the theorists themselves.

   The available research can be examined first within the broad perspective of psychoanalytic theory. Here one includes studies which use ideas such as the id-ego-superego structure of personality, or of the subconscious revealed in projective tests or in dreams, and of anxiety. The whole question of dependence can be related to the idea of ego strength; and the question of personality in cultures where social norms are very strong may be discussed in terms of superego construction and strength. Currently, a very important contribution could be made by psychologists in Ethiopia, who should be able to help in understanding how people might react in the course of a revolution which is trying to replace the old, vertical hierarchy which fostered psychological dependency (and which was represented and propagated in the cultural matrix of folk tales and metaphors which are difficult to change rapidly) with new, more horizontal schemes of human relationships in which status and power may be more evenly distributed. A second perspective arises from the 'cognitive psychology' of Witkin and workers interested in the idea of field-independence. Finally, attempts to let subjects define their own terms of self measurement, and group behaviour studies both serve as windows on personality, which could be used to link up either with psychoanalytic or with field theory perspectives.

CHAPTER IX

PSYCHOLOGICAL ADJUSTMENT TO SOCIAL CHANGE

Introduction

The material we have so far covered has been rooted in academic perspectives, and while it is inadvisable to leave these if we want to consider work which is sound in conception and in method, we need also to explore regions in which the concerns are more directly linked to the need to understand and alleviate human problems. Such problems can be conveniently surveyed in this chapter under two principal headings.

First we can deal with the problems of normal psychological functioning, which must cope with situations of social change that are by definition abnormal, at least to the perspectives of traditional societies. This whole area can then be divided up into two sections; first there is research on psychological adjustment to urban life; and secondly there is the question of industrialisation, where processes of psychological adjustment to new forms of work are explored.

The second principal heading covers the huge field of abnormal psychological functioning. Here the available research is perhaps even more fragmentary and beset by problems of definition than is research in any of the areas so far covered in this book. Yet the problems posed are extremely important in at least two ways. One is that we must understand psychological stress and collapse in its new causes and contexts, to begin to know how to alleviate a major section of human misery. Secondly, good research on patterns of abnormal psychology will help in answering wider questions about human nature.

What then are some of the background facts of urbanisation in Africa? Safier (1969) estimates that in 1885 at the beginning of the major colonial era not more than 1% of the population lived in towns; 70 years later nearly 30 million (or about 10%) lived in towns. Smith and Blackler (1963) wrote that 'if Africa repeats in the second half of the twentieth century trends in urbanisation in the first half, about 20% of the population of the continent will be living in towns of 20,000 or more by the year 2000'. One reviewer of their book thought that this could even happen by 1980.

Urbanisation does not necessarily mean industrialisation. Thus on the one hand cities like Ibadan and Benin in Nigeria and Mombasa in Kenya existed for centuries without industrialisation in its present forms. Again, disasters such as droughts in the countryside sometimes precipitate large population increases in cities without producing industrialisation. However, very often industrial development is the key to urban expansion and the two processes go together. Here we come to our first problem that has had political as well as theoretical relevance. For in colonial times, and in many places even now, men were considered to be rooted in non-urban life; though welcome in towns as workers, only minimal residential facilities were allowed, and so the development of true generations of town-dwellers was hampered.

Nevertheless, industrialisation has taken root where there were material resources to exploit (e.g. mines and the timber industry) during colonial times. The administrative machinery of modern societies has also led to the growth of urban populations. Mitchell (1951) said the Copperbelt of Zambia developed in 25 years from being a sparsely populated bushland, to supporting an industry-based population of 170,000. A similar phenomenon occurred in the adjoining Katanga area of Zaire. Gonidec (1963) estimated that in French Equatorial Africa in 1955 there were 155,000 salaried employees who formed 13% of the eligible male population; comparison figures were 8% in French West Africa (now Mali, Niger, Mauretania) and 85% in Europe. Safier (*op cit*) estimated that while over Africa the population was growing by 2-3% per annum, in urban areas it grew by 4-5% and the largest cities grow by 6-7% per annum. Overall, the industrial sector is still small, but growing; while the urban sectors of some African countries are growing faster and already rival the cohesive social significance of traditional, principally rural, population groupings.

Psychological aspects of urbanisation

An early milestone in the study of urbanisation is the study by Hellman (1948). The actual fieldwork was in Rooiyard, an urban slum in South Africa; but following the academic perspectives of that time the place where she implied that town-dwellers really belonged was in the country area they originally came from. Hellman examined criteria by which she would analytically consider a worker 'detribalised' and thus settled as a townsman.

These criteria included: a complete break in a man's relations with his chief; a permanent residence away from the chief's place; thirdly, some financial independence from rural relatives for support during sickness or unemployment; and finally independence from rural relatives in carrying out ceremonies marking the major milestones of life. In some countries however, many workers were prevented by law from having permanent residence near to their work-places in towns, so they were forced to rely psychologically for many of the social supports which give meaning to life, on links with their rural kinsmen.

At a similar time Gluckman (1945) set up a research centre in Rhodesia intending to consider 'the major social developments in the region . . . and . . . the most important social problems confronting the Government, . . . by a study of the problems of labour migration'. One academic influence certainly felt at that time, both in terms of research and Government policy-making perspectives, was that of anthropologists who concentrated on rural fieldwork. This work is certainly important, and even urgent for its own reasons of describing traditional culture before it is too eroded; but its perspective led workers to be seen as *men* in their rural traditional society, and as economic units when living in industrial towns.

An example of this implied dehumanisation is shown by McGregor (1956) who referred to workers as 'our human resources'; social scientists, McGregor believed, should be employed to find out the 'most practical' system of motivating such workers to work more efficiently. Previously, Burrows and Scully (1950) did ask South African workers if they would want to bring their wives to live in towns, or if they would prefer to work in factories, if such existed, in the countryside. Since urban housing was known not to comprise decent family accommodation, 80% naturally replied they would prefer to stay away from town. The book reflects a view of men as complete men in the countryside, but assumes only a partial and temporary existence when it refers to notions such as the 'distance of dormitory to factory' in towns.

Burrows and Scully wrote five years after a Commission of Enquiry (Jones, 1945) had recommended that policy should accept the permanent presence and full life of workers in towns, to replace the previous policy of 'repatriation' of workers after a spell of life in town. However even ten years after Burrows and Scully wrote, Kilby (1961) still had to say that 'a clearly definable . . . construct of the African workers [exists]. The universality of the image is so great . . . as to rank it as a major tenet in the folklore of modern Africa'. The image was of a migrant who came only for a short spell to town, who worked inefficiently partly because he was not interested in a permanent town life, but wanted to fulfil some rural goal, for example to raise money for a bride-price or to buy cattle or build a house.

A variant of this theme was put forward by Gugler (1968). He suggested that among some peoples the 'externalisation' journey from home had come to stand for a form of adult initiation process. A salient point was also made by Peter Lloyd (1967), in effect giving detail to one of Hellman's broader criteria. This was that among the so-called 'target workers' in Eastern Nigeria 'all men state that they wish to return to their home communities before their death so that they may be buried in their traditional compounds'. In Western Nigeria too, Amachree (1968) wrote of ageing workers that 'they are beginning to think of retirement and are starting to root themselves more firmly with their kin in the villages'. However, research from Makerere (Chapter VII) shows that even though it was done in a society far from Nigeria, and more importantly among people several decades younger, some people do agree with the notion of being buried in a new urban setting.

Clifford (1964) has pointed out that to live in town after retirement requires a pension, or some source of income. Clifford acknowledges that pension schemes are scarce in Africa, but suggests that governments could help towards the costs of these, and mentions that Kenya, Nigeria and Tanzania had made moves in this direction. From Francophone Africa Hervo-Akendengué (1967) described a pension plan devised by the Gabon government, and Songuemas (1967) reported similar schemes in Ivory Coast, Niger, Mauretania, Mali and the Malagasy Republic.

Adequate pensions for people wanting to live in towns are an expensive commitment for governments, and it will take long to be at all effective in replacing ties men have with their families who live outside towns. Furthermore, towns like Kampala or Ibadan, where there are entire extended family groups who have lived in their town for generations, are only few in Africa. Many towns are like Sapele in Nigeria, a timber-industry centre, where several surveys on industrialisation and urbanisation have been done. In one (Wober, 1967a) very few manual workers valued their company's pension fund (many more men liked the medical clinic). Even among clerks and supervisors only 11% valued the provision of pensions; some of these also said they would prefer to have a lump sum on retirement, so they could build a house 'at home'.

Thus colonial policy, independent governments' shortage of resources, and the momentum of traditional cultures have led town workers in Africa to look back to their rural roots, and away from a permanent existence as townsmen. Nevertheless, for important parts of peoples' lives, towns exert a very strong attraction (Chapter VI). More recently social scientists whose focus has been on town- rather than rural-based development of identity, have found evidence that in many ways there is a powerful motive for urban life, and in some places people also see this in an extended perspective.

Pfefferman (1968) asked 188 workers in Dakar a range of questions and found that 62% said they would stay in town on retirement. Half wanted this for family reasons, but one quarter said they just preferred town life, even for their old age. The anthropologist Kenneth Little (1965) has found that not only does urban life have attractions, but also that urban societies and associations have sprung up to offer mutual financial and psychological support. This kind of evidence has perhaps been more forthcoming from West than from East Africa where for example the Sofers (1956) claimed that the young Uganda town of Jinja had a dearth of associational life.

Another study in Sapele was done by the Nigerian social scientist, S. O. Imoagene (1967a, b) who looked in detail at associations as an aid to developing identity as town dwellers. Unlike Gluckman, who saw rural and urban lives in terms of an 'alternation' model in which men moved between two distinct social systems, with their identities somehow changing to reflect the different contexts, Imoagene proposed a 'dynamic' version of Hellman's 'change' model. In this, following Little, he suggests that membership of clan or village-based associations in the town will promote adjustment to urban life which will be expressed in a greater satisfaction with life there.

While villagers showed better personal adjustment than those who had moved to towns, those townspeople who belonged to associations of people from the home village were indeed more adjusted to town life than those who did not belong to such associations. Simple length of stay in town did not relate to better adjustment therein. While these findings do not absolutely prove that membership is the cause of better adjustment, this must nevertheless be true for many town dwellers. For some, however, it is possible that abnormal personalities may have related to poor adjustment either in village or in town, and may have stood in the way of belonging to an association. More complex research is needed to examine how extreme personality difficulties may hinder a satisfactory adjustment to town life.

Imoagene further suspected that among those with higher education, clan association membership was less important in promoting adjustment. Nevertheless, he concluded that 'clan associations have . . . replaced the extended family within whose tradition of social co-operation Ego was brought up'. The parallel studies Imoagene conducted in nearby villages led him to conclude that 'the reasons people leave the rural community may not always be economic'. That is, though they do not have to go to town to earn money (or be unemployed), and though they may not be fundamentally disaffected with village life, nevertheless curiosity and adventure are motives which do influence people's desire to move to town.

Studying timber factory workers in Sapele, Wober (1967c) looked at different styles of town life among these urban dwellers, and at possible personality correlates of different life styles. Men were interviewed in a company housing estate, where there was spacious layout and published norms of conduct, and compared with a matched sample of factory workers. Most of the latter lived in the main town with much denser population and a more hectic atmosphere of motor and social traffic. Estate dwellers were found to want to get ahead with their career plans, were in relatively higher jobs and had more children towards their intended family size at a younger age than workers living in the main town. There was some slight evidence that estate dwellers were rated as better at their jobs, than a group of other workers living elsewhere.who were matched for age and level of job. One estate dweller stated 'we have to learn to live like gentlemen', and a town dweller referred to the estate as for 'those cool people'. Wober tentatively suggested that a consciousness of self-discipline, some desire for apartness and privacy needed for such pursuits as reading rather than social interaction may have characterised the estate dwellers both in their choice of where to live (the estate was no more expensive than the town) and in their adaptation to work.

These distinctions had been sensed by previous researchers elsewhere in Africa. Thus Marris (1961) reported that many slum dwellers in Lagos found them economically suitable as well as socially lively places to live in. They did not want to be rehoused in Surulere, (then) a more spacious government-built housing estate. One Lagos dweller said 'the condition of the houses [there] doesn't suit me ... in this yard you see people coming and going ... but out there it's just empty ... it's not the kind of place for people used to communal life'. In South Africa, Reader (1961) also described slum dwellers who did not want to move to new municipal accommodation. As well as reluctance among Africans to comply with any government action, there may, nevertheless, also be some psychological truth in what Reader called 'satisfactions derived from the way of life associated with or tolerated in the shacks — dancing ... etc'.

In the Cameroons, Ardener et al (1960) noted 'the remarkable degree of overcrowding that the ordinary labourer will tolerate', though 'artisans, clerks and workers with high standards have been more quick to complain'. More recently. Draper (1973) stated that !Kung bushmen in the Kalahari desert of South West Africa, though they have considerable space in which to build, nevertheless seemed to crowd together more densely by choice. Nevertheless the 'biological indicators of stress' that western scientists expect to find when people with personalities conditioned by western cultural patterns have to live in high densities, were absent.

Finally, Butcher (1965) noted a distinction between amenities of space, and of other services, when studying an estate at Tema, Ghana. He reported that 'people thought much more highly of the services which had been provided (latrines, etc) than they did of their houses which were often large. . .'. None of these researchers believe that people should be left to live in unhealthy slums, because they seem to prefer them to spacious estates. Rather, a more complex question is being raised. This is, that while certainly every effort should be made to improve water supply, power services and sanitation, these need not perhaps be done in a way which explodes the geography of spatial relations to which people have grown accustomed. Sometimes these densities and patterns will turn out to have been imposed by lack of resources, in which case people from such conditions would more easily adapt to new spatial patterns. Sometimes however, high densities and spatial patterns may accord with traditional social structures and preferences for closer social relationships. In such cases, people might wish for better services, but not for the dispersed housing patterns which appear to be the preference of the westernised middle and upper classes.

Psychological adaptation to industrialisation
    Occupational psychology usefully develops two perspectives for examining men's adaptation to working lives in a modern industrial society. One examines how men can be selected for and trained in jobs so that men will be 'right' for the jobs in the sense that they will work more efficiently and show less accidents, waste, or absenteeism. The emphasis here is on selection tests and on training procedures. The second perspective revolves more around the worker himself. Here we study if the job is 'right' for the worker, and investigate his job satisfaction.
    It seems that more studies done so far in Africa concentrate on the first perspective, for several reasons. Psychologists are usually employed by, or for the industrialists, and thus tend to serve the broader, economic view exemplified in the attitudes of McGregor (above) and others. Also strong 'behaviourist' traditions in Western psychology, and the concentration of much effort in developing tests of abilities and intelligence, produced techniques and attitudes among psychologists which fitted them well for work on techniques of selection. Far fewer studies deal with job satisfaction. This is partly because the attitudes of many people in power during colonialism, and even in some places after independence, did not and do not give primacy to the interests of the African individual. Nevertheless, several studies do exist on satisfaction, and we will examine some of them. First, however, we can deal with applied research on selection and training of workers.
    One of the most widely used tests for selecting manual workers, and potential supervisors from among recruits fresh from their country areas was devised in South Africa. This is the General Adaptability Battery, described in many articles, as far back as the early 1950s (Biesheuvel, 1952a). The instructions are by mime shown on a silent film, and there are seven subtests, involving considerable amounts of apparatus: washers, nails and screws to be sorted, metal pegs of different shapes to fit into a board, and items such as a tripod to be assembled from parts provided. The test does not attempt to assess 'intelligence'; it is merely devised so that on the basis of past experience

with it, candidates who do well, or produce a certain pattern of results on the subtests, are likely to do well in supervisory, mechanical, or labouring jobs. Even so, Biesheuvel noted differences in test performance between candidates from different areas, and offered hypotheses to account for such variation.

Biesheuvel (1952b) saw tests as a useful asset towards understanding Africans' difficulties in adapting to industrial life. Thus he suggested that Africans in general had a 'preference for slow, modulated action, rather than for speed. . . Production is now so dependent on speed . . . that the African may be at a disadvantage in meeting its requirements'. Further, 'to raise his standard of living . . . he must shed his tribal ways. With them he inevitably sheds his tribal code of conduct as well. . . Herein lies the crux of most of his troubles'. However, we have seen in Chapter VII that Biesheuvel suggested later that traditional attitudes in important social and moral matters have more endurance then he earlier feared. This may, in turn, have implications for peoples' attitudes to speed at work.

Biesheuvel (1954) initially hoped that his test would be used all over Africa, since it is 'independent of language'. Thus he cited hopes that the tests would be used in Uganda to study the psychological effects of kwashiorkor; it was being tried out in Ghana, and in Sudan and Tanganyika for the selection of apprentices. However, the weight of apparatus was one disincentive to using the GAB; so also was one study by Mkele (1953) which studied selection of winch drivers for gold mining. Mkele tested over 1,500 men, and found that the GAB results correlated very well with the criterion assessment of performance at winch driving. But the 'screening' preliminaries to the GAB (sorting nuts and bolts, before the test proper) were almost equally efficient as a predictor of winch driving performance.

After the main GAB, further tests can be used for selection of supervisors. Hudson and Konger (1958) described a 'leaderless group' test being used in South African mines and the building industry. In this a small group of men tackle a practical problem, such as to get a heavy barrel over a fence using only certain supplied tools; assessors observe how leadership emerges and rate each participant. The need to evaluate performance on the increasingly more complex jobs Africans were doing, meant that these jobs had to be analysed into component parts and functions. Each of these could serve as a yardstick to assess how well an individual was doing at it. This 'job evaluation' also — and perhaps primarily — served as a way of relating wages more accurately to the level of job complexity being tackled. Hudson and Murray (1958) explain one study of this kind of job evaluation, which also had goals of giving management a wages system which would be easy and economical to operate. It is unfortunately, not clear whether a goal was also to make the scheme easy to understand by the workers, and one which would provide them with incentives which might help them feel enthusiastic about working harder or more efficiently.

The value of various incentives had occasionally been studied. Esther Hayes (1952) tested 240 goldminers in South Africa with several tests of manual dexterity and co-ordination. Some were given incentives to better performance and learned their tasks better than those without incentives. The effect was more marked where the tasks were more difficult. This was perhaps encouraging, but though it was done with workers as subjects, their tasks were in the laboratory instead of in the real work situation with real rewards.

Van der Walt (1952) also showed that workers would work faster with incentives on a test, even though this did entail making more mistakes. Much later on, Cook and Molomo (1971) found among Malawian schoolchildren that several incentives they tried, failed to increase performance on tests; in fact in one case of an 'incentive', performances decreased. Possibly this was because children were already working to their limit even without incentives, so the latter could only perhaps confuse and impede performance. However, pupils would probably behave differently from adult workers who were not working flat out, and who therefore had scope for increasing their output.

Wage incentives cannot be applied mechanically to increase work performance among western workers, and nor would this result among Africans, as Biesheuvel (1955) explained. He quoted Hudson's (1958) study which showed that workers had clear ideas of which mines they preferred to work on. These preferences did not reflect differences in wage bonus rates which existed, but did accord with their ideas of how they considered management behaved, and the interest management took regarding complaints, requests for information and the like. However, in another study men said they would prefer to work in industrial, rather than mining jobs, primarily because of better wages on the former. Most likely where wage differences (especially when linked with a totally different work context) are big enough, people would give wages as a reason for preferring the more desirable job situation.

Additional complexities affecting Africans' work performance might include climate and diet. Biesheuvel (1952b) considered it possible that natural selection will have contributed to a development of physique and temperament that must function in hot and humid climates, and which is therefore more measured in its pace. However, informal observation of Africans relaxing, able to keep up strenuous physical activity at speed in sports and dancing, discourages too ready an acceptance of Biesheuvel's view. Biesheuvel and Milcenzon (1953) described an experiment in which workers were retested four months after starting employment; they showed significant weight gain, attributed to improved diet, but no increase in retest scores. This failed to link diet with improved performance; and even if performance had improved, it need not necessarily have been diet, but any of several other changes in psychological experience on entering work that could have been responsible.

An early survey of performance by Africans in industry in several countries was made by Hudson (1955). Some statistics he gathered were encouraging: thus on East African Railways 34% of Asian trainees failed but only 14% of Africans. Unfortunately though, most of Hudson's 'evidence' was a hearsay collection of European employers' opinions. Among his impressions was one that African workers tended to value leisure more than wages, which they used for exceptional purposes or luxuries. From the French-speaking countries Dormeau and Latouche (1955) concluded somewhat differently, that among younger people in urban centres the acquired attitudes to work are much the same as in western societies, where salaries are seen as the source of basic sustenance. Reader (1961) came to the same conclusion in South Africa.

A variety of attempts were made to develop rather more precise tests of visual coordinated with manual skills. Mkele (1955) tested urban bus drivers and winch drivers working in rural mines on a two-hand co-ordination test, in which a steel ball has to be manoeuvered on a tilting tray through a complicated pathway marked on it. Performance correlated reasonably well with that on winch driving. Hudson, Lake and Mbau (1957) gave a test where subjects had to add numbers displayed as sets of dots, to men who had only four months industrial work experience, compared with others who had not yet worked. This showed that even a small amount of industrial experience enabled men to know how to tackle such a test, while rural subjects had little idea of how to do so. It follows as a caution, that many rural subjects who might 'fail' such tests would be wasted if turned away from employment, since poor performance might very likely be due to unfamiliarity with the whole idea of the test, rather than to a fundamental lack of ability.

Building on this, Hudson, Mokoatle and Mbau (1958) set out to show that training could be a more fruitful procedure in which to invest, than selection. Though the performance of men with intial poor scores improved with training and practice, so also did that of others with good initial scores. Hudson *et al* were forced to acknowledge that selection can be important, though training was also.   They also found that incentives improved performance gain, and concluded that workers' attitudes were important in determining their performance.

Several workers in South Africa (Bradley, 1960; Hector, 1960; Hector, Dlodlo and Duplessis, 1961; Fridjohn 1961) experimented with a 'seven squares test' and a 'pattern completion' (Patco) test as possibly useful for testing illiterate recruits to industry. The seven squares test consists of seven card squares which can be arranged together to form more or less representative 'pictures', and subjects are asked to recognise what these might be, or even to make their own pictures. The Patco test involves simply continuing a regular pattern that has been started, and noting how well subjects can reproduce it and maintain continuity. Hector (1960) showed medium-sized correlations for the Patco test with the General Ability Battery, but the literature is short of evidence that the test ever was widely applied industrially if at all.

Finally, Bennett (1970) presented some evidence from Zambia of the usefulness of a test in which subjects are asked to bend wire into a complex pattern supplied, and the accuracy of their copies is then scored with a marking system that itself requires some learning by the tester. Satisfactory correlations were shown between test scores and performance in training courses among several groups of Zambian trainees for mechanical jobs. Nevertheless, good correlations did not always emerge and the reasons governing when this test will, and when it will not predict work performance are complex and need to be unravelled.

As these studies above got under way, it became clear that men's attitudes affected their performance in tests, and at their jobs. Partly prompted by this, studies of job satisfaction began to emerge. An early study was by Yette Glass (1960), and many of the subsequent studies of job satisfaction were also by women. Glass reported on 1,200 workers in 18 separate firms; she showed that their absenteeism rates compared very favourably with British, American or Australian rates in comparable jobs, and they were better than 'a group of white South African operatives'. Workers' attitudes were measured on a variety of topics; they included that between 60 and 88% of workers in ten firms rated their supervisors favourably. On companies' 'firing policies' these ranged from 15 to 92% approval. Though it is difficult to be certain how to interpret some of these workers' attitudes within the overall South African political context, Glass's work has merit as an approach to the worker as a human being, whose base of existence is acknowledged as being in the town.

Glass (1962) comments that companies were often authoritarian, and researchers too often accepted the idea that their enquiries should not digress from the company-centered point of view. As a woman, perhaps Glass managed to take a more unusual view, which was more responsive to the workers' outlook. An example of earlier reluctance to respond to workers' feelings was shown by Gussman (1952) who studied labour turnover; he wrote 'Africans say they leave jobs because they have worked long enough to qualify for a rise' (and then do not get one). Gussman then admitted 'these allegations were not investigated'. It was only a decade later that psychologists did begin to conduct their studies more openly and fully.

Another woman, Rae Sherwood (1956) interviewed Africans working in professional jobs; later (Sherwood, 1958) she compared how clerks saw their jobs with how white supervisors viewed them, but job satisfaction directly was not reported. Cortis (1962) compared 78 African workers' opinions of their jobs with the opinions of a white group. The white employees were more satisfied, but Cortis carefully avoided quoting actual levels of scores of satisfaction. Further north, Mrs Evelyn Bell (1963), retired from social work in the UK, asked Rhodesian workers about their jobs. The questions were not psychologically elaborate, but the impression emerged that men were principally interested in their pay.

This was not what other researchers often found. In Francophone Africa Nelly Xydias (1960) asked drivers, clerks and unskilled workers which of six characteristics they would most like jobs to have. They all agreed in ranking first the idea that work should be enjoyable, with pay further down in rank. Hauser (1963) explored the reasons for absenteeism among 2,600 industrial workers in Dakar, but realised that satisfaction was the principal measure of work attitudes that related to absenteeism; the quality and nature of supervision (strictness of company rules) was also related to absenteeism, viewed comparatively across several companies. Labour turnover was high in companies with poor working conditions, and where workers had unfavourable attitudes to the management and to their jobs.

Further details of how workers vary considerably in their opinions depending on the nature of the companies they work for, are provided by Biffot (1963). He studied several hundred workers in three companies in Gabon. Opinions ranged from 3% to 43% agreeing that 'the company pays me well'; only 9% in the worst company, but 69% in the best company would recommend it to an unemployed brother as a work-place. Even in the best company 35% disagreed that 'the company treats us well', but in the worst company 87% had a similar opinion. Biffot emphasises that management behaviour and workers' perceptions of human relations are extremely important in determining satisfaction. The lesson from the Francophone studies is clear, that lower absenteeism and turnover are related to job satisfaction, which in turn may depend as much on the quality of human relations developed by the management as upon pay levels. This conclusion is expanded in an essay by Delbard (1962) based on interviews with several hundred personnel at a phosphate mine in Togo.

The English-speaking African world also saw studies elaborating issues of workers' opinions, in the later 1960s. Sheila van der Horst (1964) led the way in South Africa, and offered no less than forty-two tables on workers' opinions and reasons for their opinions. Among 431 workers, 32% disliked their jobs and one fifth of these did so because their work was unskilled, but three quarters were dissatisfied with their wages. Though only 2% said the reason for choosing to work where they were was that the foreman was 'congenial', once in the job, 65% said they liked their foreman. Out of 631 answering, 53% said they would prefer European foremen, and 22% would prefer African.

This last result may reflect a reluctance to answer truthfully to white researchers in South Africa, though workers can find it awkward if they work under African foremen of another tribe, whom they sometimes suspect of favouring others. Similarly, it may be awkward to have a foreman of a man's own tribal or cultural background; for example, more educated younger men can be in supervisory jobs, over less educated older men, thus reversing the common expectation that authority should flow from older to younger people. Such problems will obviously be overcome in time, but they can underlie such results as van der Horst's. Evidently they did not occur among 520 workers in Nigeria whom Oloko (1970) had interviewed in 1963-4. He found that commitment to the job was greater among men working in firms with Nigerian managers than among those working under Europeans.

Another extensive study in Sapele, Nigeria (Wober, 1967a) investigated opinions as well as tested abilities among workers. Among manual workers job satisfaction did not relate to any of the tests given, nor with rated job efficiency. Nor did satisfaction correlate with attitudes towards traditional or western ideas (see Chapter VII). Among a group of clerks, job satisfaction correlated with age, and thus with a variety of other measures that also associated with age.

Among clerks and a sub-group of skilled manual workers, satisfaction was related to the quality of relationships between workers and supervisors, which was also reflected in the supervisors' ratings of employees' job efficiency. Most employees reported good relationships with African and European supervisors alike; however, a group of younger, more educated 'radical' clerks had poorer job satisfaction and supervisor-relationships. Overall, it was clear that workers derived an element of satisfaction from association with a modern and technically advanced company. They appreciated the scope for gaining mastery over complex tasks and processes, and they valued the status their employment gave them in the town. The same point was made by Alverson (1969) who showed that high job satisfaction did not always occur with high 'industrial commitment'. Some committed men were not satisfied; high satisfaction was found principally among well committed men who had complex and challenging jobs. At Magburaka in Sierra Leone, Dorjahn and Hogg (1966) found that workers in high prestige jobs valued prestige, while those in low prestige positions found a good boss most important. Good wages and easy work were not the most important reasons given for valuing jobs.

Several observers have noted how migrant workers come to new industries which have often failed to attract the immediately local population who have initially preferred the status of home-based landowners, but later industrial prosperity has enabled the migrants to acquire wealth and status. Wober (1966a) reported workers' own stereotypes concerning which tribespeople were harder workers and more industrious than others. Such stereotypes certainly existed; but there was little sign that men from tribes stereotyped as hard workers were rated as more efficient by their supervisors than men from tribes not stereotyped as hard workers. To some extent this is because industrial selection operates to keep in men who are reasonably efficient, whatever tribe they come from; so measurement of efficiency within a company, of men from different tribes should not show any differences; this is a function of management's own efficiency in its training, job allocation and selection procedures.

Psychological distress and failure in adaptation

Wallace (1961) pointed out that two major schools of thought exist in this field. One focusses on biochemical sources of harm; these include congenital, dietary or inflicted disorders of body chemistry which affect psychological functioning. Thus behaviour can be affected by physical conditions such as pellagra, senility, syphilis or trypanosomiasis, among a host of other causes. A second school of thought takes disorder to spring from social, cultural and psychological conflicts. There is no doubt much of value to be gained from the knowledge offered by both schools of thought and enquiry.

The psychocultural school of thought is one where the cross-cultural problems of non-equivalence of concepts of intelligence and of personality, already encountered in Chapters III and VIII, crop up again. Basically, certain types of behaviour occur commonly in one culture while in another they are taken as evidence of psychological abnormality. An example is a belief in witchcraft as a widespread and real phenomenon affecting the self. This is common in African traditional societies, but not in Western ones, where a person who becomes hampered by a fear of being controlled by outside agents such as witches (or radio beams, or divine voices) may be labelled 'paranoid'. This kind of cultural difference is full of pitfalls for social scientists and students; sometimes entire cultures have been called 'sick', as when Ruth Benedict (1943) described the North American Indian Kwakiutl society as 'megalomaniac paranoid'. It is essential to realise however, that such cultures are not abnormal to the people who belong to them, but only to outsiders from cultures with very different standards. Nevertheless, if we accept that different cultures have different methods of child care, and styles of typical personality, then it is reasonable also to expect that there will be different patterns of mental ill health.

While most of this review will deal with questions of cultural influences on mental health, two works can serve as convenient summaries for biochemical and physical phenomena which relate to psychological abnormalities. Carothers (1972) describes how throughout Africa many endemic infections cause damage to the brain and thus to normal psychological functioning. Certain infections like syphilis and yaws were once more common, but have to some extent been curbed by the use of drugs. Trypanosomiasis, transmitted to man by the bite of an infected tsetse fly has been blamed by Tooth (1950) as 'probably the commonest cause of mental derangement throughout large areas of West Africa'. This is an affliction in which both biological and cultural factors have to be considered, since control of trypanosomiasis would require control of the sources of water (where flies breed), of ecology (in Uganda trees and bushes have been felled over wide areas, since tsetse flies apparently need to perch on them within a certain range of flight) or of human migration.

Malaria is also important in tropical psychiatry, for two reasons. It causes general debility, and a depressed state of physical health is a fertile ground for mental ill-health to take root; it also causes high fever which may overheat and damage the brain. Schistosomiasis or bilharzia, encephalitis, meningitis and other infections are all too common, and contribute to psychological ill health in both the ways described above.

Nutrition affects psychological health in several ways. Cultures in which people depend on hunting and food-gathering account for a minority of African populations, but most African peoples have diets based heavily on starchy carbohydrate foods. Minerals, proteins, vitamins and fats are often lacking, and in many cases at important stages in individual and brain growth, such as at the transition from breast feeding to solid foods. Certainly kwashiorkor which afflicts young children has been shown to have harmful effects on aspects of psychological development (Hoorweg, 1972) though it is not clear whether this has any direct effect on later psychological ill health. Davies (1949) has suggested that cirrhosis of the liver can lead to sex hormone disturbances, and arises in the first place from chronic malnutrition. Among the effects can be feminisation, which is manifest in some cases in gynaecomastia, or enlargement of the male breasts; Dawson (1963a) has suggested that gynaecomastia among the Temne may be responsible for their field dependent or 'female' cognitive style; and Witkin *et al.* (1962) have evidence that differences in cognitive style may be related to differences in psychological disorders, when these occur.

One aspect of these hypotheses on feminisation that has not been adequately investigated, if at all, is that the same dietary forces would presumably affect women, enhancing their biological feminity, with consequences for their patterns of mental health. Also, men would probably become more drawn to homosexual needs, though there are very few reports of such phenomena in Africa. Presumably the cultures effectively discourage active homosexual behaviour, which must set stresses upon feminised men which would again contribute to particular patterns of psychological disorder.

In one of the few cross-cultural studies of causes and incidence of psychological disorders, Leighton (1969) reported comparison of data from two locations in Western Nigeria and from Stirling County in Canada. Twice as many people were rated as 'psychologically impaired' (on each society's own local criteria) in Canada as in Nigeria. Further, while 81% of villagers, and 95% of urban people in the Nigerian samples had 'symptom patterns' which were psychophysiological, only 59% of the Canadians had symptoms of this source. This reflects the point that biochemical sources of weakness and disease are certainly important in African patterns of mental ill-health.

Physical sources of mental damage are probably manifest in signs of abnormal electrical activity in the brain. These are measured by the Electro Encephalo Graph (EEG), a machine which senses electrical impulses and activity in the brain, and prints out a record of this activity. The most prominent worker in this area in Africa has been Mundy-Castle (1970) who explains much of the research done on the topic. Originally the French workers Gallais, Corriol and Bert (1949) tested soldiers from Guinea Coast, and found that 58% of otherwise apparently healthy men had 'abnormal' (as they were then called) EEG patterns of a certain kind ('theta rhythm'). Mundy-Castle tested African neuropsychiatric patients, who perhaps more than healthy soldiers might be expected to show abnormal EEG patterns. However, such were not found.

Mundy-Castle then compared normal African and European adult EEGs in South Africa, and found no differences in abnormal symptoms between the samples. There were, however, some differences (Africans showed 'alpha rhythms' further forward in the brain, and tended not to react to a flickering light). Both Nelson (1964) in South Africa and Verhaegen (1956) in Katanga confirmed Mundy-Castle in failing to support Gallais' original finding. All these workers, Gallais included, considered that Gallais' subjects had probably suffered impairment of their nervous systems, possibly from dietary deficiencies or infections, early in life. Nelson (1959) had supported this idea with data from Kampala showing that kwashiorkor sufferers had brain rhythms on EEG records which suggested retarded development.

Mundy-Castle's newest evidence was from Ghana, where he had tested well over a thousand people including normals and others suspected of epilepsy. The first point was that certain patterns which might be considered signs of abnormality in Euroamerican groups (pi waves and slow alpha variant rhythms) were so common among normal people as to be of no clinical significance. This is like saying that a very dark skin among Europeans would be considered abnormal, but is normal among tropical peoples. Mundy-Castle considered it possible that Gallais *et al.* had diagnosed as 'abnormal', EEG patterns which were simply typical of the general population in West Africa. Nevertheless, over and above the particular nature of normal patterns found among Ghanaians, Mundy-Castle found other signs that were common and would be considered abnormal both among Europeans, and among Ghanaians who were suspected of having fits. This points to the possibility that there are large sections of the population who have suffered mild brain injury in early life, perhaps as a result of malnutrition. Much more research would be needed to confirm this, and to explore how such damage would affect the development of abilities and of personality. It is obvious however, that the EEG work has pointed to phenomena which could underlie all aspects of psychological development.

The psychocultural line of enquiry explores disorders in behaviour and ideas of what is considered abnormal. The World Health Organisation (1953) initially reported that there was 'little exact information on the extent of psychiatric morbidity' in Africa; later (WHO, 1960) they had advanced in knowledge and could assert that most African societies recognised and considered abnormal what in western terms are called epilepsy, mania, florid schizophrenia, acute confusion, marked dementia, agitation and severe mental defect. Nevertheless, there was a 'lack of a common classificatory system of mental disorders' which appeared to hamper analysis and understanding. Within the next decade, Ellenberger (1968) summarised the second Pan-African Psychiatric conference in Dakar and was able to report a broad conclusion that biological predispositions to health or ill health were probably distributed similarly among all men, but that cultural factors determined symptom patterns in neurotic and reactive conditions. There was much reference to a condition resembling acute paranoid schizophrenia, and the possibility that certain early autistic children were considered 'marvellous' for their ethereal, socially detached quality.

Three interesting issues can be discerned in the literature on psychocultural explorations of mental disorder. One is that cultural change will entail psychological stresses (e.g. see Chapter VII) which will produce more cases of psychological disorder. Second is that different cultures are likely to result in different patterns of disorder among those who do succumb to stress. Third is whether local healers should be recruited in the treatment of the mentally ill, or whether therapy should focus first on the biochemical changes which accompany mental disorder, and accordingly follow a standard and universal approach to therapy based on drugs.

Several workers have held that cultural stresses stimulate mental ill-health or breakdown. Lambo (1960) reported that 85% of a sample of 1,300 Nigerian school pupils had used traditionally prescribed medicines to help with school progress, or to ward off evil effects of other medicines they believed were directed against them. This shows where some stresses lie, and suggests that collapses would be interpreted by patients and traditional healers alike as in some cases concerned with the task of adapting to modern life. One well-known term for psychological disorders in this field is indeed 'brain fag'. Eken (1972) supported this with a study of dreams from Hausa, Ibo and Yoruba students in Nigeria which suggested that academic performance standards were related to what he called 'examination dreams'.

Fortes and Mayer (1966) report comparisons among the Tallensi of Northern Ghana, based on Fortes' original fieldwork data published in 1937. The later survey found much more psychosis; since important social structures were still functioning, the authors attributed psychoses possibly to changes in individual value systems. Two Dutch workers Giel and van Luijk (1969/70) explored the occurrence of psychological disorders in two places in

Ethiopia. They found that 'psychoneurotic illness and personality disorder are no less common in a rural and rather remote area, than in an urban society'. This might discourage the view that social and cultural change (to which the Ethiopian town dwellers would have been more exposed) would cause much of the mental illness to be found. However, Leighton (1969) introduced a distinction that could help to resolve the matter. Discussing his broader study (Leighton *et al.*, 1963) he reported that 'in socioculturally disintegrated Yoruba villages, the mental health of the women is, if anything, worse than that of the men'; and 'it is the disintegration, and not cultural change in and of itself that is damaging to mental health'.

Unfortunately, it is not clear why some villages have become 'socioculturally disintegrated' while others have not. Sampling or chance fluctuations may have caused biochemical factors (heredity, infections, poorer ecology and diet) to act together with cultural stresses to produce social disintegration in certain villages only. Further, Leighton's data on women's roles in different Yoruba and American villages, and their mental health in these villages does suggest that cultural stresses may directly contribute to mental ill health.

The first way of exploring how culture may affect patterns of mental ill health deals with individual cultures' concepts of mental functioning and failure, and three studies can be mentioned in this connection. Leighton (1969) reported that Yoruba healers know most western 'symptom patterns', but not phobic or obsessive-compulsive patterns; and not depression as a unified pattern (though they did recognise constituent parts as occurring separately, including crying, worry, withdrawal, etc.). On the other hand, Yoruba healers did not report any symptom patterns that were not known to western psychiatry.

The English psychiatrist Orley (1970) studied concepts of mental illness among the Baganda. He reported that Baganda think of illnesses according to three sets of dichotomies. These are illnesses which come by themselves, as against those that are sent; there are those that are strong rather than weak; and those that are Kiganda as against others that are foreign. Madness and epilepsy are 'strong' illnesses, based on the trouble and suffering they entail. Orley says that to cope with madness 'an explanatory model (paranoid in nature) is formulated by the family, which . . . absolves them from blame and opens up a course of action'. Orley means by 'paranoid' that the cause of trouble is attributed to an outside malign agency rather than to a person or a family's own weaknesses.

Orley shows how Baganda relate behavioural to biochemical events. Epilepsy, madness, drinking to excess and smoking hemp are all considered to 'spoil the brain'. People who start any such behaviour are socially isolated, which especially with children will lead to social impairment, 'so that the brain appears spoilt'. The role in which patients find themselves is a difficult one from which to improve themselves, as 'all too often patients seem quite demoralised and become resigned to their lot of having a "spoilt brain"'. This description shows that the Kiganda system of thinking about behavioural and mental disorders differs from western ideas.

In French-speaking West Africa, Bisilliat and his colleagues (1967) investigated the concept of 'lakkal', a word evidently related to an Arabic word for intelligence, but which in the Muslim culture of Djerma-Songhai extends to an idea of proper mental functioning; it also entails aspects of proper social behaviour, and thus extremely abnormal behaviour will be bound up with a negation of 'lakkal'. Again, this is a well-organised, but different way of thinking about mental ill-health than is found elsewhere.

A second way of investigating whether cultures influence patterns of mental disorder is to track down all those in a community who are considered disordered, and to try and classify their cases. Comparison is then made between the incidence of different types of disorder in separate cultures. Some researchers give figures based on people who are brought to hospitals. But others (e.g. Wallace, Orley) point out that certain kinds of ailments may be better tolerated by the community, and such patients rarely brought to hospital.

Carothers (1972) reports that many writers say that depression is rare in African societies. He reports hospital entry classifications gathered from separate researchers in Kenya, South Africa, the Congo, Tanzania, and Uganda, showing that about 6% of nearly 3,000 admissions were described as cases of depression. The incidence of depression is much more common among Europeans. However, Collomb and Zwingelstein (1961) reported that 16% of 580 admissions in Dakar were cases of depression. Leighton *et al.* (1963) found that psychoneurotic depression was more common in their Nigerian fieldwork than in Canada, though depression carried to the extreme of a psychotic condition was less common in Nigeria. Margaret Field (1955) claimed that 'depression is the commonest mental illness of Akan women' in Ghana and linked this with her observation that depressed women went to shrines with 'spontaneous self-accusations of witchcraft'.

Against this, Diop (1967) maintained that the notable aspect of melancholic illnesses among Africans was the rarity of delirium involving self-accusation or suicide. He said that ideas of possession and persecution often mask depression, and with this Field (1968) later agreed, saying that attitudes are 'paranoid' even among healthy, intelligent people. Over 85% among 900 patients she referred to were afraid that someone was trying to kill them. Lambo (1962) had made a similar claim, that fear of bewitchment was the commonest cause of acute anxiety states among detribalised, semi-literate Africans. The position is therefore quite open as to whether depression is more, or less common in Africa than in western societies, particularly since the symptoms are not the same in all the societies being compared, and because methods of counting cases in Africa have varied so much.

Finally, it is worth mentioning what Carothers terms 'unclassified psychoses' which do not fit into Western diagnostic criteria. Evidently, many of such cases show a clinical picture of what Carothers calls 'frenzied anxiety', leading soon to dangerous violence. Other names for this condition, which appears to resemble the 'running amok' originally described in South East Asia, are 'periodic psychosis' and in French, 'bouffée délirante' or paranoid reactions. Collomb (1965) reported that such cases were the most frequent syndrome in hospital admissions (no doubt, as Orley pointed out, because in a well policed society such disturbing people are immediately captured and taken in). The Egyptian psychiatrist Tewfik (reported in Carothers, 1972) placed over 80% of 304 hospital admissions in such a category when he referred to 'sudden onset of confusion, persecutory delusions, vivid hallucinations. . .' and 'in the more educated African this syndrome of restlessness, violence and hallucinations is . . . often absent . . . the rural African, whenever his sanity is threatened, responds in a stereotyped, dramatic way'.

Evidently most writers consider that sufferers from such disorders usually recover quite quickly. Carothers felt that such states are precipitated by a variety of physical and psychological stresses. He considered that biochemical factors probably underlay the trouble in the more lasting cases, while emotional factors played a larger part for those who could recover more quickly.

Regarding therapy there is little controversy, merely a concern to know in what way to integrate the work of traditional healers with that of western medicine. The position is slightly complicated in that traditional healers are sometimes found to be using (and sometimes misusing) herbal and other drugs which correspond to medicines developed in western science. Lambo (described in Leighton, *et al.*, 1963) is the best known exponent of the idea that patients from traditional backgrounds should be treated in a context with which they are familiar. Orley (*op. cit.*) is perhaps one of the psychiatrists who has been most cautious about such ideas. He points out that traditional healers are expected by their patients to effect cures, and they often understand the cultural and family context within which mental ill-health is precipitated. It is known in western medicine that a 'placebo effect' exists, where patients improve with blank 'medicines' which really contain no active drugs, but which work by raising expectations of cure. Such effects must occur with the activities of African traditional healers.

However, as African traditional medicine has not until recently had the benefit of written records, standardised knowledge of locally derived drugs is lacking. Sometimes people set up as healers who have insight into psychological problems, and charisma to project trust in therapy, but who have uncertain knowledge of drugs and biochemical therapies even though they try to use the latter, sometimes with harmful effects. The outcome is that western knowledge of biochemical causes and therapies for disorders should be used, together with traditional knowledge of social and cultural forces which act upon and sometimes make people mentally ill.

Zempleni and Collomb (1968) see many disorders as affecting the personality superficially; people who develop personalities especially conscious of their identity in a group may experience their conflicts at a relatively external level. Thus social and collective methods in psychiatry may be particularly successful in treating such troubles. Much attention has been given to the therapeutic role of such phenomena as 'zar' in Ethiopia, in which people are 'possessed' by other forces, or 'dispossessed' of their self-control temporarily, and the mentally cleansing practices of the Cherubim and Seraphim religious groups in Nigeria, and similar cults all over Africa.

However, these ways of setting about the problems of mental or social ill-health need not exclude aspects of treatment based on western drugs.

Concluding remarks

This chapter has briefly ranged over such a wide scope, that it is not particularly meaningful to try and distil any one integrated picture from it. Nevertheless, some overview is beneficial as a conclusion for this chapter, as for the book as a whole.

In the colonial years when traditional cultures were still very much linked to their roots and flourishing, African social scientists who might truly understand the scene were in a tiny minority. Recently, traditional cultures have been much disrupted by forces of western influence, migration, and the apparatus and needs of modern statehood; now, when more and more people are 'modernised', western social scientists are withdrawing from universities and institutes of research, and African scientists are stepping into these fields. To some extent, there is a re-search for traditional roots and cultural values; but much of this is bound to be from a viewpoint that has been externalised.

African social scientists are thus in a good position to act as cross-cultural researchers. They know the external influences through educational experience and of Africa, from family background and tradition. They may thus avoid the narrowness of the 'centri-cultural' view, which sees phenomena as abnormal or deficient when they do not resemble what is normal in the observer's own parent culture. A danger which African social scientists are also equipped to avoid is one of adopting an absolutist view based in some western culture with which that person is most familiar. Thus in understanding problems of child development, of the measurement of abilities, of personality patterns and of the causes and treatment of psychological disorder, African social scientists can become more modern by not being just western. They can use the knowledge developed in the west, particularly in the fields of biochemical aspects of medicine; but it is sad that it is not they themselves who could have been fully involved in exploring psychology in Africa over the last half century, and helping to avoid some of the mistakes which the expatriate social scientists, for all their effort and goodwill and partial success, have made.

REFERENCES

Abiola, E.T. The nature of intellectual development of Nigerian children. *Teacher Education*, 1965, 6, 37-57.

Abiri, J.O.O. The educational attitudes of some Nigerian adolescent grammar school pupils. *West African Journal of Education*, 1966, 10, 118-121.

Abraham, W.E. *The Mind of Africa.* Chicago: University of Chicago Press, 1962.

Abrahams, R. *The People of Greater Unyamwezi, Tanzania.* London: International African Institute, 1967.

Agblemagnon, N'S.F. Research on attitudes towards the Togolese woman. *International Social Science Journal*, 1962, 14, 148-156.

Ainsworth, L.H., & Ainsworth, M.D. Acculturation in East Africa, I. Political awareness and attitudes towards authority. *Journal of Social Psychology*, 1962, 57, 391-399; II. Frustration and aggression: 401-407; III. Attitudes towards parents, teachers, and education: 409-415; IV. Summary and Discussion: 417-432.

Ainsworth, M.D. The development of infant motor interaction among the Ganda. In B.M. Foss (Ed.), *Determinants of Infant Behaviour: Vol II.* London: Methuen, 1963.

Infancy in Uganda: Infant Care and the Growth of Love. Baltimore: Johns Hopkins Press, 1967.

Akim, B., McFie, J., & Sebigajju, E. Developmental level and nutrition (a study of young children in Uganda). *Journal of Tropical Pediatrics*, 1967, 2, 159-165.

Albino, R.C., & Thompson, V.J. The effects of sudden weaning in Zulu children. *British Journal of Medical Psychology*, 1956, 29, 177-197.

Allan, M.B. A practical plan for occupational selection from Zambia. 1st African Regional Conference of the International Association for Cross Cultural Psychology. Behavioural Sciences Research Unit, University of Ibadan, 1973.

Allport, G.W., & Pettigrew, T.F. Cultural influence on the perception of movement: The trapezoidal illusion among Zulus. *Journal of Abnormal and Social Psychology*, 1957, 55, 104-113.

Almy, M., Davitz, J.R., & White, M.A. *Ugandan Children in School: Four Experimental Studies in Psychology.* New York: Teachers College Press, 1970.

Alverson, H.S. The social and organisational antecedents of job satisfaction among Black South African industrial workers: A multivariate analysis. PhD Dissertation, Yale University, 1969.

Amachree, I.T.O. Reference groups and worker satisfaction: Studies among some Nigerian factory workers. *Nigerian Journal of Economic and Social Studies*, 1968, 10, 229-238.

Angi, C., & Coombe, T. Training programmes and employment opportunities for primary school leavers in Zambia. *Manpower and Unemployment Research in Africa*, 1969, 2, 1-12.

Ardener, E.W., Ardener, S., & Warmington, W.A. *Plantation and Village in the Cameroons.* Ibadan: N.I.S.E.R., 1960.

Argyle, M. *The Social Psychology of Work.* London: Allen Lane, 1972.

Armer, J.M. Intersociety and intrasociety correlates of occupational prestige. *American Journal of Sociology*, 1968, 74, 28-36.

Formal education and psychological malaise in an African society. *Sociology of Education*, 1970, 43, 143-158.

African Social Psychology. A Review and Annotated Bibliography. New York: Africana Press, 1974.

Armer, J.M., & Youtz, R. Formal education and individual modernity in an African society. *American Journal of Sociology*, 1971, 76, 604-626.

Ashem, B. Cultural and social class differences in maternal communication and teaching strategies of the Nigerian mother. Prepublication Ms. Department of Psychiatry, University of Ibadan, 1972.

Augusto, A. The intellectual development of Negro children of Mozambique. *Criança Portuguesa*, 1949-50, 9, 407-429.

Awosika, V.O. *An African Meditation.* Lagos: African Literary and Scientific Publications, 1967.

Babalola, J., & Szajnzicht, E. Ocular characteristics in West Africans and Europeans: A comparison of two groups. *British Journal of Physiological Optics*, 1960, 17, 27-37.

Bakare, C.G.M. Social-class differences in the performance of Nigerian children on the Draw-a-Man test. In L.J. Cronbach & P.J.D. Drenth (Eds.), *Mental Tests and Cultural Adaptations.* The Hague: Mouton, 1972.

Balandier, G. The French tradition of African research. *Human Organisation*, 1960, 19, 109-111.

Daily Life in the Kingdom of the Kongo from the Sixteenth To the Eighteenth Century. London: Allen & Unwin, 1968.

Bam, E.E. Aspects of child rearing techniques in Lesotho. University of East Africa Social Sciences Conference, Nairobi, 1969.

Baran, S. *Development and Validation of a TAT-type Projective Test for use among Bantu speaking people.* Johannesburg, N.I.P.R., 1971.

Barbé, R. Psychologie. In: Rapport No I de l'Organisme d'Enquête pour l'Etude Anthropologique des Populations Indigènes de l'A.O.F., 99-113; Psychologie. In: Rapport No 3, 23-33. Direction Générale de la Santé, Dakar, 1946.

Bardet, C., Massé, G., Moreigne, F., & Senecal, J. Application du test de Brunet-Lezine à un groupe d'enfants Ouolofs de 6 mois à 24 mois. *Bulletin de la Société Medicale d'Afrique Noire de Langue Française*, 1960, 5, 334-356.

Bardet, C., Moreigne, F., & Senecal, J. Application du test de Goodenough à des écoliers Africains de 7 à 14 ans. *Bulletin de la Société Medicale d'Afrique Noire de Langue Française*, 1959, 4, 255-270.

Barrett, J.H.W. Pre-natal environmental influences on behaviour. In G.N. Batstone, A.W. Blair, & J.M. Slater (Eds.), *A Handbook of Pre-natal Pediatrics.* Philadelphia: Lippincott, 1971.

Bartlett, F.C. *Remembering: A Study in Experimental and Social Psychology* Cambridge: Cambridge University Press, 1932.

Psychological methods for the study of 'hard' and 'soft' features of a culture. *Africa*, 1946, 16, 145-155.

Bekombo, M. Note sur le temps: conceptions et attitudes chez les Dwala. *Ethnographie*, 1966-1967, 60/61, 60-64.

Bell, E.M. 'Polygons'. A survey of the African personnel of a Rhodesian factory. Occasional Paper No 3 of the Department of African Studies, University College of Rhodesia and Nyasaland, 1963.

Benedict, R. *Patterns of Culture.* Boston: Houghton Mifflin, 1934.

Bennett, M. The wire-bending test applied to apprentice selection in Zambia. *Psychologia Africana*, 1970, 13, 240-247.

Berlioz, L. Etude des progressive matrices faites sur les Africains de Douala. *Bulletin du Centre d'Etudes et Recherches Psychotechniques*, 1955, 4, 33-44.

Berry, J. W. Temne and Eskimo perceptual skills. *International Journal of Psychology*, 1966, 1, 207-229.

Independence and conformity in subsistence-level societies *Journal of Personality and Social Psychology*, 1967, 7, 415-418.

Ecology, perceptual development and the Muller-Lyer illusion. *British Journal of Psychology*, 1968, 59, 205-210.

Ecology and socialisation factors in figural assimilation and the resolution of binocular rivalry. *International Journal of Psychology*, 1969, 4, 271-280.

Bethlehem, D.W. Co-operation, competition and altruism among schoolchildren in Zambia. *International Journal of Psychology*, 1973, 8, 125-135.

Beti, M. *Mission to Kala.* London: Heinemann, 1964.

Beveridge, W.M. Racial differences in phenomenal regression. *British Journal of Psychology*, 1935-36, 26, 59-62.

Some racial differences in perception. *British Journal of Psychology*, 1939-40, 30, 57-64.

Biesheuvel, S.   *African Intelligence*. Johannesburg: South African Institute of Race Relations, 1943.

Personnel selection tests for Africans. *South African Journal of Science*, 1952a, 49, 3-12.

The occupational abilities of Africans. *Optima*, 1952b, 2, 18-22.

Manpower and Productivity in Africa South of the Sahara. Johannesburg: National Institute for Personnel Research, 1954a.

The measurement of occupational aptitudes in a multi-racial society. *Occupational Psychology*, 1954b, 28, 189-196.

Incentives and human relations in industry. *Industrial Review of Africa*, 1955a, 2, 1-7.

The measurement of African attitudes towards European ethical concepts, customs, laws and administration of justice. *Journal of the National Institute of Personnel Research*, 1955b, 6, 5-17.

Further studies on the measurement of attitudes towards western ethical concepts. *Journal of the National Institute of Personnel Research*, 1959a, 7, 141-155.

Race, Culture and Personality. Johannesburg: South African Institute of Race Relations, 1959b.

Personality tests for personnel selection and vocational guidance in Africa. *Bulletin of the Inter-African Labour Institute*, 1961, 8, 37-49.

Biesheuvel, S., & Milcenzon, S. The effect of diet on the test performance of African mine labourers. *Bulletin of the National Institute of Personnel Research*, 1953, 5, 173-175.

Biffot, L-M. *Facteurs d'Intégration et de Désintégration du Travailleur Gabonais à son Entreprise.* Paris: Office de la Recherche Scientifique et Technique Outre-Mer, Cah. ORSTOM, Sciences Humaines, No 1, 1963.

Bisilliat, J., Laya, D., Pierre, E., & Pidoux, C. La notion de Lakkal dans la culture Djerma-Songhai. *Psychopathologie Africaine*, 1967, 3, 207-264.

Bloom, L. Self concepts and social status in South Africa: A preliminary cross cultural analysis. *Journal of Social Psychology*, 1960, 51, 103-112.

Bogardus, E.S. Comparing racial distance in Ethiopia, South Africa and the United States. *Sociology and Social Research*, 1968, 52, 149-156.

Bonté, M. The reaction of two African societies to the Muller-Lyer illusion. *Journal of Social Psychology*, 1962, 58, 265-268.

Bormans, M. Contribution à l'étude des mentalités sur la famille: ce qu'en pensent les jeunes Sahariens. *Revue Occident Musulman*, 1968, 5, 15-39.

Botha, E. Some value differences among adults and children in South Africa. *Journal of Social Psychology*, 1964, 65, 241-248.

Bradley, D.J. The ability of Black groups to produce recognisable patterns on the 7 squares test. *Journal of the National Institute of Personnel Research*, 1960, 8, 142-144.

Brewer, M.B. Determinants of social distance among East African tribal groups. *Journal of Personality and Social Psychology*, 1968, 10, 279-289.

Bricklin, B., & Zeleznick, C. A psychological investigation of selected Ethiopian adolescents by means of the Rorschach and other projective tests. *Human Organisation*, 1963, 22, 291-303.

Brimble, A.R. The construction of a non-verbal intelligence test in Northern Rhodesia. *Rhodes-Livingstone Journal*, 1963, 34, 23-35.

Brown, R.L. Social distance and the Ethiopian students. *Sociology and Social Research*, 1967, 51, 101-116.

Burrows, H.R., & Scully, G.C. (Eds.) *The African Factory Worker.* London: Oxford University Press, 1950.

Butcher, D.A.P. Social Survey. In *Volta Resettlement Papers*. Accra: Volta River Authority, 1965.

Callaway, A. Unemployment among African school leavers. *Journal of Modern African Studies*, 1963, 1, 351-371.

Cameron, V.L. *Across Africa*. London: Dalby, Isbister & Co., 1877.

Carlson, J.A., & Davis, C.M. Cultural values and the risky shift. A cross cultural test in Uganda and the United States. *Journal of Personality and Social Psychology*, 1971, 20, 425-429.

Carothers, J.C. *The African Mind in Health and Disease: A Study in Ethnopsychiatry*. Geneva: World Health Organisation, 1953.

The Mind of Man in Africa. London: Stacey, 1972.

Chaplin, J.C. Some methods of analysing picture perception: with special reference to Ugandan children. Unpublished MA Dissertation, University of East Africa, Makerere, 1969.

Claeys, W. Conforming behaviour and personality variables in Congolese students. *International Journal of Psychology*, 1967, 2, 13-23.

La structure factorielle de l'intelligence des enseignants au Congo. In L.J. Cronbach & P.J.D. Drenth (Eds.) *Mental Tests and Cultural Adaptations*. The Hague: Mouton, 1972.

Clarke, J.D. Performance tests of intelligence for Africa. *Overseas Education*, 1948, 20, 777-787; and 1949, 20, 822-826.

Clifford, W. Social security in Africa (with special reference to Northern Rhodesia). *Bulletin of the Inter-African Labour Institute*, 1964, 4, 370-380.

Clignet, M.R. Education et aspirations professionelles. *Tiers Monde*, 1964, 5, 61-82.

Clignet, M.R., & Foster, P. La préeminence de l'enseignement classique en Côte d'Ivoire: Un exemple d'assimilation. *Revue Française de Sociologie*, 1966, 7, 32-47.

Cole, M., Gay, J., Glick, J.A., & Sharp, D.W. *The Cultural Context of Learning and Thinking*. London: Methuen, 1971.

Collomb, H. Bouffées délirantes en psychiatrie Africaine. *Psychopathologie Africaine*, 1965, 1, 167-239.

Collomb, H., & Zwingelstein, J. Les états dépressifs en milieu Africain. First Pan-African Psychiatric Conference, Abeokuta, Nigeria, 1961. *L'Information Psychiatrique*, 1962, 6, 515-528.

Cook, P.F., & Molomo, M.R. The effects of incentives on the test taking behaviour of Botswana primary school children. In L.J. Cronbach & P.J.D. Drenth (Eds.) *Mental Tests and Cultural Adaptations*. The Hague: Mouton, 1972.

Cooper, W.H. Usability of American tests with African students. *West African Journal of Education*, 1961, 5, 86-91.

Cortis, L.E. A comparative study in the attitudes of Bantu and European workers. *Psychologia Africana*, 1962, 9, 148-167.

Cowley, J.J., & Murray, M. Some aspects of the development of spatial concepts in Zulu children. *Journal of Social Research*, 1962, 13, 1-18.

Cox, D.R. Child rearing and child care in Ethiopia. *Journal of Social Psychology*, 1971, 85, 3-5.

Crijns, A.G.J. African intelligence: A critical survey of cross cultural research in Africa South of the Sahara. *Journal of Social Psychology*, 1962, 57, 283-301.

African basic personality structure: A critical review of bibliographical sources and of principal findings. *Gawein*, 1966, 14, 239-248.

Culwick, A.T., & Culwick, G.M. Religious and economic sanctions in a Bantu tribe. *British Journal of Psychology*, 1935, 26, 183-196.

Cureau, A.L. *Savage Man in Central Africa. A Study of Primitive Races in the French Congo*. Translated by E. Andrews. London: Unwin, 1915.

Dalby, D. An investigation into the Mende syllabary of Kisimi Kamara. *Sierra Leone Studies, New Series*, 1966, 19, 119-123.

d'Andrade, R.G. Sex differences and cultural institutions. In E.E. Maccoby (Ed.) *The Development of Sex Differences*. Stanford: Stanford University Press, 1967.

Davidoff, J. The effect of colour distraction on a matching task in Ghanaian children. A methodological note. *International Journal of Psychology*, 1972, 7, 141-144.

Davies, J.N.P. Sex hormone upset in Africans. *British Medical Journal*, 1949, 2, 676-679.

Davis, C.M. Education and susceptibility to the Muller-Lyer illusion among the Banyankole. *Journal of Social Psychology*, 1970, 82, 25-34.

Davis, C.M., & Carlson, J.A. A cross-cultural study of the strength of the Muller-Lyer illusion as a function of attentional factors. *Journal of Personality and Social Psychology*, 1970, 16, 403-410.

Davitz, J.R. Two reports of research in child growth and development. In M. Almy., J.R. Davitz., & M.A. White. *Studying School Children in Uganda*. New York: Teachers College Press, 1970.

Dawson, J.L.M. Psychological effects of social change in a West African community. D.Phil Thesis, Keble College, Oxford, 1963a.

Traditional values and work efficiency in a West African mine labour force. *Occupational Psychology*, 1963b, 37, 209-218.

Traditional versus western attitudes in West Africa: the construction, validation and application of a measuring device. *British Journal of Social and Clinical Psychology*, 1967a, 6, 81-96.

Cultural and psychological influences upon spatial-perceptual processes in West Africa. Parts I and II. *International Journal of Psychology*, 1967b, 2, 115-125; and 171-185.

Attitudinal consistency and conflict in West Africa. *International Journal of Psychology*, 1969a, 4, 39-53.

Theoretical and research bases of biosocial psychology. *University of Hong Kong Gazette*, 1969b, 3 (supplement), 1-10.

Delbard, B. Etude de quelques déséquilibrés créés par l'industrie au Togo: Contribution à l'étude socologique des problèmes du travail en Afrique noire. Paris: Ecole des Psychologiques Praticiens, 1962 (mimeo).

Dent, G.R. *Investigation of Certain Aspects of Bantu Intelligence*. Pretoria: National Bureau of Education and Social Research, 1949.

Deregowski, J.B. The horizontal-vertical illusion and the ecological hypothesis. *International Journal of Psychology*, 1967, 2, 269-273.

On perception of depicted orientation. *International Journal of Psychology*, 1968a, 3, 148-156.

Difficulties in pictorial depth perception in Africa. *British Journal of Psychology*, 1968b, 59, 195-204.

Pictorial recognition in subjects from a relatively pictureless environment. *African Social Research*, 1968c, 5, 356-364.

Perception of the two-pronged trident by two- and three-dimensional perceivers. *Journal of Experimental Psychology*, 1969, 82, 9-13.

A note on the possible determinants of 'split representation' as an artistic style. *International Journal of Psychology*, 1970a, 5, 21-26.

Effect of cultural value of time upon recall. *British Journal of Social and Clinical Psychology*, 1970b, 9, 37-41.

Responses mediating pictorial recognition. *Journal of Social Psychology*, 1971, 84, 27-34.

The role of symmetry in pattern reproduction by Zambian children. *Journal of Cross Cultural Psychology*, 1972a, 3.

Reproduction of orientation of Kohs-type figures; a cross cultural study. *British Journal of Psychology*, 1972b, 63, 283-296.

Effects of symmetry upon reproduction of Kohs-type figures: An African study. *British Journal of Psychology*, 1974, 65, 93-102.

Deregowski, J.B., & Byth, W. Hudson's pictures in Pandora's box. *Journal of Cross Cultural Psychology*, 1970, 1, 315-323.

Deregowski, J.B., & Ellis, D. Symmetry and discrimination learning. *Acta Psychologica*, 1974, 38, 81-91.

Deregowski, J.B., Muldrow, E.S., & Muldrow, W.F. Pictorial recognition in a remote Ethiopian population. *Perception*, 1972, 1, 417-425.

Deregowski, J.B., & Munro, D. An analysis of "polyphasic pictorial perception". *Journal of Cross Cultural Psychology*, 1974, 5, 329-343.

Deregowski, J.B., & Serpell, R. Performance on a sorting task: A cross cultural experiment. *International Journal of Psychology*, 1971, 6, 273-281.

De Ridder, J.C. *The Personality of the Urban African in South Africa. A TAT Study.* London: Routledge & Kegan Paul, 1961.

Devauges, R. Eléments pour une sociologie de l'enseignement en Afrique indépendente. *Civilisations*, 1965, 15, 404-419.

Diop, M. La dépression chez le Noir Africain. *Psychopathologie Africaine*, 1967, 3, 123-194.

Doob, L.W. *Becoming More Civilised.* New Haven: Yale University Press, 1960.

Psychology. In R. Lystad (Ed.) *The African World.* London: Pall Mall Press, 1965.

Scales for assaying psychological modernisation in Africa. *Public Opinion Quarterly*, 1967, 31, 414-421.

Dorjahn, V.R., & Hogg, T.C. Job satisfactions, dissatisfactions and aspirations in the wage labour force of Magburaka, a Sierra Leone town. *Journal of Asian and African Studies*, 1966, 1, 261-278.

Dormeau, G. L'oeuvre Africaine du Professeur Ombredane. *Bulletin du Centre d'Etudes et Recherches Psychotechniques*, 1959, 8, 5-10.

Dormeau, G., & Latouche, G. Quelques aspects particuliers des problèmes humaines du travail en Afrique Equatoriale Française. *Bulletin du Centre d'Etudes et Recherches Psychotechniques*, 1955, 4, 347-362.

Draper, P. Crowding among hunter-gatherers: The !Kung bushmen. *Science*, 1973, 182, 301-303.

Duncan, H.F., Gourlay, N., & Hudson, W. *A Study of Pictorial Perception among Bantu and White Primary School Children in South Africa.* Johannesburg: Witwatersrand University Press, 1973.

Dunn, J.S. Fante star lore. *Nigerian Field*, 1960, 25, 52-64.

Du Preez, P.D. Social change and field dependence in South Africa. *Journal of Social Psychology*, 1968, 76, 265-266.

Du Preez, P., & Ward, D.G. Personal constructs of modern and traditional Xhosa. *Journal of Social Psychology*, 1970, 82, 149-160.

Durand, R. Formation et adaptation professionelle du jeune africain. *Travail Humain*, 1960, 32, 81-92.

Durojaiye, M.O.A. Psycho-cultural constraints on formal education of the African child. Universities of East Africa Social Sciences Conference, Dar es Salaam, 1970.

Is the concept of African intelligence meaningful? *East Africa Journal*, 1971, 8, 4-12.

Introduction to Educational Psychology for Teachers in Africa. Department of Educational Psychology, Makerere University, Kampala, 1972a.

Conservation in Six African Cultures. 20th International Congress of Psychology, Tokyo, August, 1972b.

The role of non cognitive factors in school learning of Ugandan secondary school pupils, 20th International Congress of Psychology, Tokyo, August, 1972c.

Psychology for a Changing Africa: Paths and Booby-Traps. 1st African Regional Conference of the International Association for Cross Cultural Psychology.

Behavioural Sciences Research Unit, University of Ibadan, 1973a.

Early childhood child-rearing practices in two African urban communities: Ibadan and Kampala. An Inter-African cross cultural study. 1st African Regional Conference of the International Association for Cross Cultural Psychology. Behavioural Sciences Research Unit, University of Ibadan, 1973b.

Patterns of anxiety among Ugandan adolescents. 2nd International Conference of the International Association for Cross Cultural Psychology, Kingston, Ontario, 1974a.

Cognitive abilities of pupils of African and European origins in an international secondary school. 2nd International Conference of the International Association for Cross Cultural Psychology, Kingston, Ontario, 1974b.

Du Toit, B.M. Pictorial depth perception and linguistic relativity. *Psychologia Africana*, 1966, 2, 1-10.

Edgerton, R.B. *The Individual in Cultural Adaptation*. Berkeley: University of California Press, 1971.

Ekandem, M.J. The use of plants as symbols in Ibibio and Ibo country. *Nigerian Field*, 1955, 20, 53-63.

Eken, P.D. Examination dreams in Nigeria: A sociological study. *Psychiatry*, 1972, 35, 352-365.

El Abd, H. *Readings in Educational Psychology in East Africa*. Kampala: Department of Educational Psychology, Makerere University, 1971.

Ellenberger, H.F. Impressions psychiatriques d'un séjour à Dakar. *Psychopathologie Africaine*, 1968, 4, 469-480.

Endemann, T.M.H. The intelligence of the native in the light of pedagogical findings at the Bothsabelo training school for natives. M.Ed. Thesis, Pretoria University, 1927.

Erny, P. La perception de l'espace et du temps dans l'Afrique noire traditionelle. *Revue de Psychologie des Peuples*, 1970, 25, 64-74.

Erpicum, D. Tests mentaux et résultats scolaires chez des enfants congolais. *Revue de Psychologie Appliquée*, 1959, 9, 11-21.

Etienne, P. Les Baoulé et le temps. *Cahiers de l'Office de la Recherche Scientifique et Technique d'Outre-Mer*, 1968, 5, 17-37.

Evans, J. *Children in Africa: A Review of Psychological Research*. New York: Teachers College Press, 1970.

Evans, J., & Segall, M.H. Learning to classify by colour and by function: A study of concept-discovery by Ganda children. *Journal of Social Psychology*, 1969, 77, 35-53.

Faladé, S. *Le développement psychomoteur du jeune Africain originaire du Sénégal au cours de la première année*. Paris: Foulon, 1955.

Le développement psychomoteur de l'enfant Africain du Sénégal. *Concours Médicale*, 1960, 82, 1005-1013.

Falmagne, J.C. Etude comparative du développement psychomoteur pendant les six premiers mois de 105 nourrissons blancs et 78 nourrissons noirs. *Mémoires de l'Academie Royale des Sciences d'Outre-Mer. Classes des Sciences Naturelles et Medicales*, 1962, XIII, 5.

Fanon, F. *Peau Noire Masques Blancs*. Paris: Editions du Seuil, 1952. translated by C.L. Markman, as *Black Skin White Masks*. New York: Grove Press, 1967.

Ferron, O. A comparative study of the attitudes of West African students and teachers towards the modern approach in teaching. *British Journal of Educational Psychology*, 1965, 35, 294-299.

Fick, M.L. Intelligence test results of poor White, native (Zulu), Coloured and Indian schoolchildren and the educational and social implications. *South African Journal of Science*, 1929, 26, 904-920.

The Educability of the South African native. Research Series No 8. Pretoria: South African Council for Educational and Sociological Research, 1939.

Field, M.J. Witchcraft as a primitive interpretation of mental disorder. *Journal of Mental Science*, 1955, 101, 826-833.

Search for Security: An Ethnopsychiatric Study of Rural Ghana. Evanston: Northwestern University Press, 1960.

Chronic psychosis in rural Ghana. *British Journal of Psychiatry*, 1968, 114, 31-33.

Fisher, O. Ridicule: A potent form of social control. 1st African Regional Conference of the International Association for Cross Cultural Psychology. Behavioural Sciences Research Unit, University of Ibadan, 1973.

Fjellman, J. The myth of primitive mentality: A study of semantic acquisition and modes of categorisation in Akamba children of South Central Kenya. PhD Dissertation, Department of Anthropology, Stanford University, 1971.

Flavell, J.H. *The developmental Psychology of Jean Piaget*. New York: Van Nostrand, 1963.

Fontaine, C. Notes sur une expérience d'application de tests au Mali (1962-1963). *Revue de Psychologie Appliquée*, 1963, 13, 235-246.

Fortes, M. Social and psychological aspects of. education in Taleland. *Africa*, 1938, 11, (Supplement to No 4).

Fortes, M., & Mayer, D.Y. Psychosis and social change among the Tallensi of northern Ghana. *Cahiers d'Etudes Africaines*, 1966, 6, 5-40.

Foster, P.J. *Education and Social Change in Ghana*. London: Routledge & Kegan Paul, 1965.

Some remarks on education and unemployment in Africa. *Manpower and Unemployment Research in Africa*, 1968, 1, 19-20.

Education for self-reliance: A critical evaluation. In R. Jolly (Ed.) *Education in Africa*. Nairobi: East African Publishing House, 1969.

Foster, P.J., & Clignet, M.R. *The Fortunate Few: A Study of Secondary Schools and Students in the Ivory Coast*. Evanston: Northwestern University Press, 1966.

Franke, E. *The Mental Development of Negro Children*. Leipzig: Voigtlander, 1915.

Fraenkel, P. *Wayaleshi: Radio in Central Africa*. London: Weidenfeld & Nicholson, 1959.

Fridjhon, S.H. The Patco test, symmetry and intelligence. *Journal of the National Institute for Personnel Research*, 1961, 8, 180-188.

Gachuhi, J.M., & Kinyanjui, P.E. Utilisation of cultural information for population planning in East Africa. University of Nairobi, Institute of African Studies Conference Report, 1973.

Gallais, P., Corriol, J., & Bert, J. Etude préliminaire des rhythmes éléctroencephalographiques chez le noir. *Médecine Tropicale*, 1949, 5, 687-695.

Gamble, D.P. Occupational prestige in an urban community (Lunsar) in Sierra Leone. *Sierra Leone Studies*, 1966, 19, 98-108.

Garcia-Vicente, J. Le mosaic Lowenfeld test parmi les noirs de l'Angola. *Revue de Psychologie Appliquée*, 1960, 10, 77-91.

Gay, J., & Cole, M. *The New Mathematics and an Old Culture: A Study of Learning among the Kpelle of Liberia*. New York: Holt, Rinehart & Winston, 1967.

Geber, M. The psychomotor development of African children in the first year, and the influence of maternal behaviour. *Journal of Social Psychology*, 1958, 47, 185-195.

Problèmes posés par le développement du jeune enfant Africain en fonction de son milieu social. *Travail Humain*, 1960, 1-2, 97-111.

L'environnement et le développement des enfants africains. *Enfance*, 1973, 3, 145-174.

Geber, M., & Dean, R.F.A. The state of development of newborn African children. *Lancet*, 1957a, 272, 1216-1219.

Gesell tests on African children. *Pediatrics*, 1957b, 20, 1055-1065.

Psychomotor development in African children: the effects of social class and the need for improved tests. *Bulletin of the World Health Organisation*, 1958, 18, 471-476.

Le développement psychomoteur et somatique des jeunes enfants africains en Ouganda. *Courrier*, 1964, 15, 425-437.

Giel, R., & Van Luijk, J.M. Psychiatric morbidity in a rural village in South-Western Ethiopia. *International Journal of Social Psychiatry*, 1969/70, 16, 63-71.

Gilbertson, S. Television attitudes and cognitive dissonance phenomena in Ghana, MSc Thesis, University of Bristol, 1971.

Glass, Y. *The Black Industrial Worker. A Social Psychological Study*. Pretoria: National Institute for Personnel Research, 1960.

Gluckman, M. The seven year research plan of the Rhodes-Livingstone Institute. *Rhodes-Livingstone Journal*, 1945, 4, 1-32.

Goldberg, S. Infant development in Zambia: Measuring maternal behaviour. University of East Africa Social Sciences Conference, Nairobi, 1969.

Infant care, stimulation and sensori-motor development in a high density urban area of Zambia. Human Development Research Unit, Report No 15, University of Zambia, 1970.

Gonidec, P.F. The development of trade unionism in Black Africa. *Bulletin of the Inter-African Labour Institute*, 1963, 10, 127-156.

Gonzales, V.B. *Capacidad mental del Negro*. Madrid: Consejo Superior de Investigaciones Cientificas, 1952.

Gordon, H.L. The mental capacity of Africans. *Journal of the Royal African Society*, 1934, 33, 226-242.

Grant, G.V. *The Organisation of Mental Abilities of a Venda group in Cultural Transition*. Johannesburg: National Institute for Personnel Research, 1969a.

The Urban-Rural Scale: A Socio-Cultural Measure of Individual Urbanisation. Johannesburg: National Institute for Personnel Research, 1969b.

Grayshon, M.C., & Olanlokun, J.O. Authority patterns in the Yoruba family. *West African Journal of Education*, 1966, 10, 113-117.

Graves, N.B. Child rearing patterns and maternal perceptions of locus of control. American Anthropological Association Conference, San Diego, 1970.

Greenfield, P.M. Equivalence grouping in Senegal, In J.S. Bruner, R.R. Olver, & P.M. Greenfield (Eds.), *Studies in Cognitive Growth*. New York: Wiley, 1966a.

On culture and conservation. In J.S.Bruner, R.R. Olver, & P.M. Greenfield (Eds.), *Studies in Cognitive Growth*. New York: Wiley, 1966b.

Gregor, A.J., & MacPherson, D.A. Racial preference and ego-identity among White and Bantu children in the Republic of South Africa. *Genetic Psychology Monographs*, 1966, 73, 217-253.

Griffith, W.J. On the appreciation of African music. *Nigerian Field*, 1951, 16, 88-93. Jillawol and Dare. *Nigerian Field*, 1956, 21, 122-124.

Griffiths, J.McE. Development of reflexes in Bantu children. *Developmental Medicine and Child Neurology*, 1969, 11, 533-535.

Gugler, J. The impact of labour migration on society and economy in sub-Saharan Africa. Empirical findings and theoretical considerations. *African Social Research*, 1968, 5, 463-486.

Gutkind, P.C.W. Tradition, migration, urbanisation, modernity and unemployment in Africa: The roots of instability. *Canadian Journal of African Studies*, 1969, 3, 343-366.

Han, K. Evidence of the use of pre-Portuguese written characters by the Bini? *Bulletin de l'Institut Français d'Afrique Noire*, 1959, 21 Ser.B, 109-154.

Hare, A.P. Cultural differences in communication networks in Africa, the United States and the Philippines. *Sociology and Social Research*, 1969, 54, 25-42.

Hart, K. Small scale entrepreneurs in Ghana. In R. Apthorpe (Ed.), *People, Planning and Development Studies*. London: Cass, 1970.

Hauser, A. *Facteurs Humaines Affectant la Productivité des Travailleurs Industriels du Cap-Vert*. Dakar: Institut de Science Economique Appliquée, 1963.

Haward, L.R.C., & Roland, W.A. Some inter-cultural differences in the Draw-a-Man test: III. Conclusion. *Man*, 1955, 55, 40-42.

Hayes, E.E. A preliminary study of an experimental investigation of psychomotor learning in African natives employed underground in certain goldmines of the Witwatersrand. *Bulletin of the National Institute for Personnel Research*, 1952, 4, 43-53.

Head, S.W. (Ed.), *Broadcasting in Africa. A Continental Survey of Radio and Television*. Philadelphia: Temple University Press, 1974.

Hector, H. Results from a simple gestalt continuation test. *Journal of the National Institute for Personnel Research*, 1960, 8, 145-147.

Hector, H., Dlodlo, M.S., & Duplessis, C.F. An experiment on silhouette recognition and projection with Bantu children of different ages. *Journal of the National Institute for Personnel Research*, 1961, 8, 195-198.

Heijnen, J.D. Results of a job preference test administered to pupils in Standard VIII, Mwanza, Tanzania. In J.R. Sheffield (Ed.), *Education, Employment and Rural Development*. Nairobi: East African Publishing House, 1967.

Heim, A. *Intelligence and Personality*. Harmondsworth: Penguin, 1970.

Hellman, E. Rooiyard. *Rhodes-Livingstone Papers No 13*, Livingstone, 1948.

Heron, A. Studies of perception and reasoning in Zambian children. *International Journal of Psychology*, 1968, 3, 23-29.

Heron, A., & Simonsson, M. Weight conservation in Zambian children. A non-verbal approach. *International Journal of Psychology*, 1969, 4, 281-296.

Herskovits, M.J. *Man and His Works.* New York: Knopf, 1950.

Hervo-Akendengué, A. Social security in Gabon. *African Social Security Series No 1*, 3-50. Geneva: International Social Security Association, 1967.

Heuse, G. Personnalité du Noir et relations inter-ethniques. *Encyclopédie Mensuelle d'Outre-mer*, 1955, 63, 453-457.

Etudes psychologiques sur les noirs Soudanais et Guinéens. Essai de standardisation technique en psychologie racial. *Revue Psychologique des Peuples*, 1957, 12, 35-68.

Heyns, O.S. *Abdominal decompression.* Johannesburg: University of Witwatersrand Press, 1963.

Hicks, R.E. Occupational prestige and its factors. *African Social Research*, 1966, 1, 41-58.

Similarities and differences in occupational prestige ratings. *African Social Research*, 1967, 3, 206-227.

The relationship of sex to occupational prestige in an African country. *Personnel and Guidance Journal*, 1969, 47, 665-670.

Hill, P. *Rural capitalism in West Africa.* Cambridge: Cambridge University Press, 1970.

Hoffman, M. Research on opinions and attitudes in West Africa. *International Social Science Journal*, 1963, 15, 59-69.

Holmes, A.C. *Health Education in Developing Countries.* London: Nelson, 1964.

Hoorweg, J.C. Africa (South of the Sahara): Review of psychological literature. In V.S. Sexton, & H. Misiak (Eds.), *Psychology Around the World Today.* Monterey: Brooks Cole, 1974.

Hoorweg, J.C., & Stanfield, J.P. The influence of malnutrition on psychological and neurological development. Seminar on Malnutrition in Early Life and Mental Development, Paper. Kingston, Jamaica: Pan American Health Organisation, 1972.

Hopkins, B., & Wober, M. Games and Sports: Missing items in cross cultural psychology. *International Journal of Psychology*, 1973, 8, 5-14.

Hudson, W. Observations on African labour in East, Central and West Africa. *Journal of the National Institute for Personnel Research*, 1955, 6, 18-29.

Psychological research on the African worker. *Civilisations*, 1958, 8, 193-203.

Pictorial depth perception in sub-cultural groups in Africa. *Journal of Social Psychology*, 1960, 52, 183-208.

Pictorial perception and educational adaptation in Africa. *Psychologia Africana*, 1962a, 9, 226-239.

Cultural problems in pictorial perception. *South African Journal of Science*, 1962b, 58, 189-195.

The study of the problem of pictorial perception among unacculturated groups. *International Journal of Psychology*, 1967, 2, 90-107.

Hudson, W., & Konger, C.F. Selection of African supervisors by leaderless group tests. *Bulletin of the Inter-African Labour Institute*, 1958, 5, 10-26.

Hudson, W., Lake, R.M., & Mbau, G.G. A study into the application of a counting test designed to obtain work curves for illiterate Africans. *Journal of the National Institute for Personnel Research*, 1957, 7, 71-73.

Hudson, W., Mokoatle, B., & Mbau, G.G. The influence of training and practice in the test and work performance of a small sample of African workers. *Journal of the National Institute for Personnel Research*, 1958, 7, 88-94.

Hudson, W., & Murray, C.O. A methodology for job evaluation studies of tasks performed by Africans in four industrial enterprises. *Journal of the National Institute for Personnel Research*, 1958, 7, 83-87.

Hunkin, V. Validation of the Goodenough Draw-a-Man test for African children. *Journal of Social Research*, 1950, 1, 52-63.

Ikua, P.N.M. Children's understanding and interpretation of pictorial material (at ages 5-13) with special reference to Kikuyu children of Central Kenya. Occasional Paper No 1, Social Psychology Section, Sociology Department, Makerere University, 1971.

Imoagene, S.O. Mechanisms of immigrant adjustment in a West African urban community. *Nigerian Journal of Economic and Social Studies,* 1967a, 9, 51-66.

Psychosocial factors in rural-urban migration. *Nigerian Journal of Economic and Social Studies,* 1967b, 9, 375-386.

Irvine, S.H. Ability testing in English-speaking Africa – an overview of comparative and predictive studies. *Rhodes-Livingstone Journal,* 1963, 34, 44-55.

Adapting tests to the cultural setting: A comment. *Occupational Psychology,* 1965, 39, 13-23.

Towards a rationale for testing attainments and abilities in Africa. *British Journal of Educational Psychology,* 1966, 36, 24-32.

Exams and the economy: An African study. In *World Yearbook of Education.* London: Evans, 1969a.

The dimensions of vocational preference and prestige in an African elite group. In *World Yearbook of Education.* London: Evans, 1969b.

Factor analysis of African abilities and attainments: constructs across cultures. *Psychological Bulletin,* 1969c, 71, 20-32.

Degrees and dimensions of social interaction in tribal groupings. *International Journal of Psychology,* 1969d, 4, 27-38.

Irvine, S.H., & Sanders, J.T. (Eds.). *Cultural Adaptation Within Modern Africa.* New York: Teachers College Press, 1972.

Irvine, S.H., Sanders, J.T., & Klingelhofer, E.L. *Human Behaviour in Africa: A Bibliography of Psychological and Related Writings.* Department of Education, Brock University, St Catherines, Ontario, 1969.

Irwin, M.H., & McLaughlin, D.H. Ability and preference in category sorting by Mano schoolchildren and adults. *Journal of Social Psychology,* 1970, 82, 15-24.

Irwin, M.H., Schafer, G.N., & Feiden, C.P. Emic and unfamiliar category sorting of Mano farmers and U.S. undergraduates. *Journal of Cross Cultural Psychology,* 1974, 5, 407-423.

Jahoda, G. A note on Ashanti names and their relationship to personality. *British Journal of Psychology,* 1954, 45, 192-195.

Assessment of abstract behaviour in a non-western culture. *Journal of Abnormal and Social Psychology,* 1956, 53, 237-243.

Child animism: II. A study in West Africa. *Journal of Social Psychology,* 1958a, 47, 213-222.

Immanent justice among West African children. *Journal of Social Psychology,* 1958b, 47, 241-248.

Nationality preferences and national stereotypes in Ghana before independence. *Journal of Social Psychology,* 1959, 50, 165-174.

White Man. London: Oxford University Press, 1961.

Aspects of Westernisation: A study of adult-class attitudes in Ghana: I. *British Journal of sociology,* 1961, 12, 375-386; and II. 1962, 13, 43-56.

Geometric illusions and environment: A study in Ghana. *British Journal of Psychology,* 1966, 57, 193-199.

Scientific training and the persistence of traditional beliefs among West African University students. *Nature,* 1968, 220, 1356.

Cross-cultural use of the perceptual maze test. *British Journal of Educational Psychology,* 1969a, 39, 82-86.

The Psychology of Superstition. London: Allen Lane, 1969b.

Supernatural beliefs and changing cognitive structures among Ghanaian university students. *Journal of Cross Cultural Psychology,* 1970, 1, 115-130.

Retinal pigmentation, illusion susceptibility and space perception. *International Journal of Psychology,* 1971, 6, 159-208.

Jahoda, G., Deregowski, J.B., & Sinha, D. Topological and Euclidean spatial features noted by children. A cross cultural study. *International Journal of Psychology*, 1974, 9, 159-172.

Jahoda, G., & Stacey, B. Susceptibility to geometrical illusions according to culture and professional training. *Perception and Psychophysics*, 1970, 7, 179-184.

Jones, S.C. review of: The Report of the Commission Appointed to Enquire into the administration and finance of native locations in urban areas. *Rhodes-Livingstone Journal*, 1945, 3, 82-84.

Kaplan, B. Malnutrition and mental deficiency. *Psychological Bulletin*, 1972, 78, 321-334.

Kamoga, F.K. Future of primary school leavers in Uganda. *Inter-African Labour Institute Bulletin*, 1965, 12, 5-18.

Kasimbazi, A., & Wober, M. The pre-school environment and cognitive ability. Occasional Paper No 10, Social Psychology Section, Sociology Department, Makerere University, 1972.

Kaye, B. *Bringing up Children in Ghana*. London: Allen & Unwin, 1962.

Kellaghan, T. Abstraction and categorisation in African children. *International Journal of Psychology*, 1968, 3, 115-120.

Kemigisha, B. A re-investigation of Deregowski's experiment on time-perception among rural and urban women. Occasional Paper No 22, Social Psychology Section, Sociology Department, Makerere University, 1966.

Kidd, D. *The Essential Kaffir*. London: A. & C. Black, 1925.

Kilbride, J.E. The motor development of rural Baganda infants. MA Thesis. State College, Pennsylvania State University, 1969.

The influence of socio-environmental factors on Ugandan infants' motor development. In M.C. Robbins, P.L. Kilbride, & R.B. Pollnac (Eds.), *Nkanga*. Kampala: Makerere Institute for Social Research, 1972.

Kilbride, P.L. Individual modernisation and pictorial perception among the Baganda of Uganda. PhD Dissertation. University of Missouri-Columbia, 1970.

Modernisation and the structure of dream narratives among the Baganda. In M.C. Robbins, P.L. Kilbride, & R.B. Pollnac (Eds.), *Nkanga*. Kampala: Makerere Institute for Social Research, 1972.

Kilbride, P.L., & Robbins, M.C. Linear perspective, pictorial depth perception and education among the Baganda. *Perceptual and Motor Skills*, 1968, 27, 601-602.

Pictorial depth perception and acculturation among the Baganda. *American Anthropologist*, 1969, 71, 293-301.

Kilbride, P.L., Robbins, M.C., & Freeman, R.B. Pictorial depth perception and education among Baganda schoolchildren. *Perceptual and Motor Skills*, 1968, 26, 1116-1118.

Kilbride, J.E., Robbins, M.C., & Kilbride, P.L. The comparative motor development of Baganda, American white and American black infants. *American Anthropologist*, 1970, 72, 1422-1428.

Kilby, P. African Labour productivity reconsidered. *Economic Journal*, 1961, 71, 273-291.

King, K. J. Education and ethnicity in the Rift Valley: Maasai, Kipsigis and Kikuyu in the school system. Institute for Development Studies, Staff Paper No 113, Nairobi, 1971.

Kingsley, P. The development by Zambian children of strategies for doing intellectual work. 1st African Regional Conference of the International Association for Cross Cultural Psychology. Behavioural Sciences Research Unit, University of Ibadan, 1973.

Kingsley, R.C. Reversal and extra-dimensional shifts by Ugandan children using one-dimensional and two-dimensional discrimination problems. University of East Africa Social Sciences Conference, Dar es Salaam, 1968.

Kline, P. Extraversion, neuroticism and academic performance among Ghanaian university students. *British Journal of Educational Psychology*, 1966, 36, 92-94.

The use of Cattell's 16PF test and Eysenck's EPT with a literate population in Ghana. *British Journal of Social and Clinical Psychology*, 1967, 6, 97-107.

References 229

References 229

The anal character: A cross cultural study in Ghana. *British Journal of Social and Clinical Psychology*, 1969, 8, 201-210.

Klineberg, O., & Zavalloni, M. *Nationalism and Tribalism among African Students. A Study of Social Identity*. Paris: Mouton, 1969.

Klingelhofer, E.L. Occupational preferences of Tanzanian secondary school pupils. *Journal of Social Psychology*, 1967, 72, 149-159.

A note on language, school and examiner effects on the performance of Tanzanian schoolchildren on Raven's Standard Progressive Matrices Test. *Journal of Social Psychology*, 1971, 83, 145-146.

Knapen, M-T. *L'enfant Mukongo. Orientation de Base du Système Educatif et Développement de la Personnalité*. Louvain: Publications Universitaires, 1962.

Koff, D.R. Education and employment perspective of Kenya primary pupils. In J.R. Sheffield (Ed.), *Education, Employment and Rural Development*. Nairobi: East African Publishing House, 1967.

Konner, M.J. Aspects of the developmental ethology of a foraging people. In N. G. Blurton-Jones (Ed.), *Ethological Studies of Child Behaviour*. London: Cambridge University Press, 1974.

Korten, D.C. The life game: survival strategies in Ethiopian folktales. *Journal of Cross Cultural Psychology*, 1971, 2, 209-224.

Kubik, G. Xylophone playing in Southern Uganda. *Journal of the Royal Anthropological Institute*, 1964, 94, 138-159.

Kuczynska-Stoffels, M.J. Responses figuratives Congolaises au Lowenfeld mosaic test. *Revue de Psychologie Appliquée*, 1970, 20, 27-40.

Lambo, T.A. Mental health in Nigeria. *World Mental Health*, 1959, 11, 131-138.

Malignant anxiety: a syndrome associated with criminal conduct in Africans. *Journal of Mental Science*, 1962, 108, 256-264.

Laroche, J.L. Effets de répétition du Matrix 38 sur les résultats d'enfants Katangais. *Bulletin du Centre d'Etudes et Recherches Psychotechniques*, 1959, 8, 85-99.

Recherches sur les aptitudes des écoliers du Katanga industriel (Congo Belge). *Travail Humain*, 1960, 23, 69-80.

Langton, E.A.C. Some observations on infants and young persons in Bunyoro, Uganda. *East African Medical Journal*, 1934-5, 11, 316-323.

Leblanc, M. Adaptation Africaine et comparaison interculturelle d'une épreuve projective: Test de Rosenzweig. *Revue de Psychologie Appliquée*, 1956, 6, 91-109.

La problématique d'adaptation du TAT au Congo Belge. *Revue de Psychologie Appliquée*, 1958a, 8, 265-274.

Acculturation of attitude and personality among Katangese women. *Journal of Social Psychology*, 1958b, 47, 257-264.

Personnalité de la Femme Katangaise: Contribution à l'Etude de Son Acculturation. Louvain: Publications Universitaires, 1960.

Lee, S.G. *Manual of a Thematic Apperception Test for African Subjects: Set of 22 Pictures*. Pietermaritzburg: University of Natal Press, 1953.

Social influences in Zulu dreaming. *Journal of Social Psychology*, 1958, 47, 265-283.

Leiderman, P.H. Some contributions of child development research to African Psychiatry, In A.L. Raman (Ed.), *Proceedings of 2nd Pan African Psychiatric Workshop*. Mauritius: Government Printer, 1970.

Leighton, A.H. A comparative study of psychiatric disorder in Nigeria and rural North America. In S.C. Plog, & R.B. Edgerton (Eds.), *Changing Perspectives in Mental Illness*. New York: Holt, Rinehart & Winston, 1969.

Leighton, A.H., Lambo, T.A., Hughes, C.C., Leighton, D.C., Murphy, J.M., & Macklin, D.B. *Psychiatric Disorder among the Yoruba*. New York: Cornell University Press, 1963.

Levine, B.B., Nyansongo. In B.B. Whiting (Ed.), *Six Cultures: Studies of Child Rearing*. New York: Wiley, 1963.

Levine, R.A. Africa. In F.L.K. Hsu (Ed.), *Psychological Anthropology*. Homewood, Illinois: Dorsey Press, 1961.

Dreams and Deeds: Achievement Motivation in Nigeria. Chicago: University of Chicago Press, 1966.

Liddicoat, R. Development of Bantu children. *Developmental Medicine and Child Neurology*, 1969, 11, 821-822.

Liddicoat, R., & Griesel, R.D. A scale for the measurement of African urban infant development: Preliminary report. *Psychologia Africana*, 1971, 14, 65-75.

Liddicoat, R., & Koza, C. Language development in African infants. *Psychologia Africana*, 1963, 10, 108-116.

Little, K. *West African Urbanisation*. Cambridge: Cambridge University Press, 1965.

Littlejohn, J. Temne space. *Anthropological Quarterly*, 1963, 36, 1-17.

Lloyd, B.B. Choice behaviour and social structure: A comparison of two African societies. *Journal of Social Psychology*, 1968, 74, 3-12.

Antecedents of personality and ability differences in Yoruba children. In R. Jolly (Ed.), *Education in Africa: Research and Action*. Nairobi: East African Publishing House, 1969.

The intellectual development of Yoruba children: A re-examination. *Journal of Cross Cultural Psychology*, 1971a, 2, 29-38.

Studies of conservation with Yoruba children of differing ages and experience. *Child Development*, 1971b, 42, 415-218.

Perception and Cognition. Harmondsworth: Penguin, 1972.

Lloyd, F., & Pidgeon, D.A. An investigation into the effects of coaching on non-verbal test material with European, Indian and African children. *British Journal of Educational Psychology*, 1961, 31, 145-151.

Lloyd, P.C. *Africa in Social Change*. Harmondsworth: Penguin, 1967.

Loades, H.R., & Rich, S.G. Binet tests on South African natives – Zulus. *Journal of Genetic Psychology*, 1917, 24, 373-383.

Lombard, J. Cotonou, ville africaine. *Bulletin de l'Institut Français d'Afrique Noire*, 1954, 341-377.

Longton, J. Tribal distance in a secondary school. Ninth Conference of Research Officers. Lusaka: Institute for Social Research, 1955.

Loram C.J. *The Education of the South African Native*. London: Longmans Green, 1917.

Loves, H. Ancestral beliefs and Christian catechesis. *Lumen Vitae*, 1957, 12, 353-376.

Lusk, D., & Lewis, M. Mother-infant interaction and infant development among the Wolof of Senegal. *Human Development*, 1972, 15, 58-69.

Lystad, M.H. Traditional values of Ghanaian children. *American Anthropologist*, 1960, 62, 454-464.

MacCrone, I.D. Preliminary results from the Porteous maze tests applied to native schoolchildren. *South African Journal of Science*, 1928, 25, 481-484.

MacDonald, A. Selection of African Personnel. Report on the work of the Selection of Personnel, Technical and Research Unit, M.E.F. Ministry of Defence, London, 1944-1945.

MacLean, C.M.U. Blood donors for Ibadan. *Community Development Bulletin*, 1960, 11, 26-31.

Maistriaux, R. Reflexions sur l'intelligence des Noirs et des Blancs, à propos d'une épreuve simple de classement. *Problèmes Sociaux Congolais*, 1955a, 31, 29-56.

L'unité de l'intelligence humaine établie par les 'Progressive Matrices' de J.C. Raven. *Problèmes Sociaux Congolais*, 1955b, 31, 6-28.

Les methodes actives en terre d'Afrique. *Problèmes Sociaux Congolais*, 1960, 49, 7-56.

Mannoni, O. *Prospero and Caliban: The Psychology of Colonisation*, translated by P. Powesland, New York: Praeger, 1956.

Marais, H.C., & Hoorweg, J.C. Psychology in Africa: A bibliographical survey. *International Journal of Psychology*, 1971, 6, 329-335.

Marris, P. *Family and Social Change in an African City*. London: Routledge & Kegan Paul, 1961.

Marwick, M.G. An experiment in public opinion polling among preliterate people. *Africa*, 1956, 26, 149-159.

Mbilinyi, M.J. Traditional attitudes towards women: a major constraint on rural development. Universities of East Africa Social Sciences Conference, Dar es Salaam, 1970.

Mbiti, J.S. *African Religion and Philosophy.* London: Heinemann, 1969.

McFie, J. The effect of education on African performance on a group of intellectual tests. *British Journal of Educational Psychology, 1961, 31, 232-240.*

McGregor, H.H. *Wage incentives raise productivity. Industrial Review of Africa,* 1956, April, 25-27.

McLuhan, M. *The Gutenberg Galaxy.* New York: Wiley, 1962.

McQueen, A.J. Aspirations and problems of Nigerian school leavers. *Inter-African Labour Research Bulletin,* 1965, 12, 35-42.

Education and marginality of African youth. *Journal of Social Issues,* 1968, 24, 179-197.

Unemployment and future orientation of Nigerian school leavers. *Canadian Journal of African Studies,* 1969, 3, 441-461.

Meeker, B.F. An experimental study of co-operation and competition in West Africa. *International Journal of Psychology,* 1970, 5, 11-19.

Meij, L.R. The Clark dolls test as a measure of children's racial attitudes: A South African study. *Journal of Social Research,* 1966, 15, 25-40.

Mertens de Wilmars, C., & Niveau, L. L'influence de l'acculturation sur l'équilibre psychique. Théorie de l'information culturelle fragmentaire. *Bulletin du Centre d'Etudes et Recherches Psychotechniques,* 1960, 9, 385-398.

Miller, A., & Bibby, J. Aspirations and expectations of fifth form pupils: some implications for policy and research. *Ghana Journal of Education,* 1969, 1, 17-27.

Mitchell, J.C. A note on the urbanisation of Africans on the copperbelt. *Rhodes-Livingstone Journal,* 1951, 12, 20-27.

The anthropological study of urban communities. *African Studies,* 1960, 19, 169-172.

Some aspects of tribal social distance. In A.A. Dubb (Ed.), The Multitribal Society: Proceedings of the 16th Conference of the Rhodes-Livingstone Institute, Lusaka, 1962.

Measuring social attitudes. *African Urban Notes,* 1968, 3, 4-15.

Mitchell, J.C. & Epstein, A.L. Occupational prestige and social status among urban Africans in Northern Rhodesia. *Africa,* 1959, 29, 22-40.

Mitchell, J.C., & Irvine, S.H. Occupational prestige and aspirations in some Southern Rhodesian African schools. Mimeographed Report, African Studies Department, University College, Salisbury, 1962.

Social position and the grading of occupations. *Rhodes-Livingstone Journal,* 1965, 38, 42-54.

Mkele, N. Validation of aptitude tests for the selection of winch drivers on the Witwatersrand goldmines. *Bulletin of the National Institute for Personnel Research,* 1953, 5, 100-109.

The two-hand co-ordination test. Quality of performance as a test variable. *Journal of the National Institute for Personnel Research,* 1955, 6, 30-33.

Molnos, A. *Attitudes Towards Family Planning in East Africa.* Munich: Weltforum Verlag, 1970.

The sociocultural background to fertility and family planning: analyses of 23 studies conducted in East Africa, 1952-1970. *Rural Africana,* 1971, 14, 63-81.

Moreigne, F., & Senecal, J. Résultats d'un groupe d'enfants africains au Terman-Merrill. *Revue de Psychologie Appliquée,* 1962, 12, 15-32.

Morgan, R.W. Occupational prestige ratings by Nigerian students. *Nigerian Journal of Economic and Social Studies,* 1965, 7, 325-332.

Mphahlele, E. *The African Image.* New York: Praeger, 1962.

Mundy-Castle, A.C. Pictorial depth perception in Ghanaian children. *International Journal of Psychology*, 1966, 1, 290-300.

Epilepsy and the electroencephalogram in Ghana. *African Journal of Medical Science*, 1970, 1, 221-236.

Mundy-Castle, A.C., & Nelson, G.K. A neuropsychological study of the Knysna forest workers. *Psychologia Africana*, 1962, 9, 240-272.

Munro, D. Pre-school environments and intellectual development: a selective survey of the literature, with particular reference to Africa. Human Development Research Unit, Report No 5, University of Zambia, 1967.

Munroe, R.H., & Munroe, R.L. Reading pictures: A cross cultural perspective. Claremont Reading Conference, California, 1969.

Infant care and childhood performance in East Africa. Unpublished Conference Draft Paper, 1974.

Household density and infant care in an East African society. *Journal of Social Psychology*, 1971a, 83, 3-13.

Munroe, R.L., & Munroe, R.H. Effects of environmental experience on spatial ability in an East African society. *Journal of Social Psychology*, 1971b, 83, 15-22.

Obedience among children in an East African society. *Journal of Cross Cultural Psychology*, 1972a, 3, 395-399.

Munroe, R.L., Munroe, R.H., & Levine, R.A. Africa. In F.L.K. Hsu (Ed.), *Psychological Anthropology: Second Edition*. Cambridge: Schenkmann, 1972b.

Murray, C.O. The structure of African intelligence: A factorial study of the abilities of Africans. MA Thesis, University of Natal, 1956.

Musgrove, F. Uganda secondary schools as a field of culture change. *Africa*, 1952, 22, 234-249.

Myambo, K. Shape constancy as influenced by culture, western education and age. *Journal of Cross Cultural Psychology*, 1972, 3, 221-232.

Nadel, S.F. A field experiment in racial psychology. *British Journal of Psychology*, 1937, 28, 195-211.

Ndumbu, A. Prospects of tailoring racial harmony. A study of racial preference and identification in an unpolarised African setting. Occasional Paper No 9, Social Psychology Section, Sociology Department, Makerere University, 1972.

Nelson, G. K. The electroencephalogram in kwashiorkor. *Electroencephalography and Clinical Neurophysiology*, 1959, 11, 13-84.

Race, Culture and Brain Function. Johannesburg: Institute for the study of Man in Africa, 1964.

Nerlove, S.B. Trait dispositions and situational determinants of behaviour among Gusii children of Southwestern Kenya. PhD Dissertation, Stanford University, 1969.

Nerlove, S.B., Munroe, R.H., & Munroe, R.L. Effect of environmental experience on spatial ability: A replication. *Journal of Social Psychology*, 1971, 84, 3-10.

Newton, N. The effect of psychological environment on childbirth: combined cross cultural and experimental approach. *Journal of Cross Cultural Psychology*, 1970, 1, 85-90.

Nissen, H.W., Machover, S., & Kinder, E.F. A study of performance tests given to a group of native African Negro children. *British Journal of Psychology*, 1935, 25, 308-355.

Nketia, K. *African Music in Ghana*. Accra: Longmans, 1961.

Occitti, J.P. Growing up in Acholi, In H.A. El-Abd (Ed.), *Readings in Educational Psychology in East Africa. Book Two*. Department of Educational Psychology, Makerere University, 1971.

Ogunlade, J.O. National stereotypes of university students in Western Nigeria. *Journal of Social Psychology*, 1971, 85, 309-310.

Ethnic identification and preference of some school children in Western Nigeria. *Sociology and Social Research*, 1972, 56, 195-201.

Okafor-Omali, D. *A Nigerian Villager in Two Worlds*. London: Faber, 1965.

Okonji, O.M. Differential effects of rural and urban upbringing on the development of cognitive styles. *International Journal of Psychology*, 1969a, 4, 293-305.

A grass-root approach to 'Revolution by Education' in Africa. *Mawazo*, 1969b, 2, 11-16.

The effect of special training on the classificatory behaviour of some Nigerian Ibo children. *British Journal of Educational Psychology*, 1970, 40, 21-26.

A cross cultural study of the effects of familiarity on classificatory behaviour. *Journal of Cross Cultural Psychology*, 1971a, 2, 39-49.

Independence training and the development of cognitive style in Uganda. Universities of East Africa, Social Sciences Conference, Kampala, 1971b.

Culture and children's understanding of geometry. *International Journal of Psychology*, 1971c, 6, 121-128.

The development of logical thinking in pre-school Zambian children: Classification. Human Development Research Unit, Report No 23, University of Zambia, 1972.

Socio-economic background, race and audio-visual integration in children. In J.L.M. Dawson and W. Lonner (Eds.), *Readings in Cross-Cultural Psychology: Proceedings of the Inaugural Meeting of the International Association for Cross Cultural Psychology*. Hong Kong: Univ. Hong Kong Press, 1974.

Okorodudu, C. Achievement training and achievement motivation among the Kpelle in Liberia: A study of household structure antecedents. *Dissertation Abstracts*, 1967, 29 (A), 1527-1529.

Oliensis, D. Some aspects of inter-racial attitudes of Kenya secondary school students. *Race*, 1967, 8, 345-355.

Oliver, R.A.C. The comparison of abilities of races: With special reference to East Africa. *East African Medical Journal*, 1932a, 9, 160-204.

The musical talent of natives of East Africa. *British Journal of Psychology*, 1932b, 22, 333-343.

Mental tests in the study of the African. *Africa*, 1934, 7, 40-46.

Oloko, O. Effects of demographic variables on worker commitment to industrial employment in Nigeria. *International Review of Sociology*, 1971, 1, 98-121.

Omari, T.P. Changing attitudes of students in West African society toward marriage and family relationships. *British Journal of Sociology*, 1960, 11, 197-210.

Ombredane, A. Principes pour une étude psychologique des Noirs du Congo Belge. *L'Année Psychologique*, 1951, 30, 521-547.

L'exploration de la mentalité des Noirs Congolais au moyen d'une épreuve projective. Le Congo TAT. *Mémoires de l'Institut Royal Colonial Belge. Section des Sciences Morales et Politiques*, 1954, 37, 1-243.

Etude psychologique des Noirs Asalampasu. I. Le Comportement intellectuel dans l'épreuve du Matrix-Couleur. *Mémoires de l'Academie Royale des Sciences Coloniales. 1re Classe*, 1956, 6, fasc. 3.

Ombredane, A., Bertelson, P., & Beniest-Noirot, E. Speed and accuracy of performance of an African native population and of Belgian children on a paper and pencil perceptual test. *Journal of Social Psychology*, 1958, 47, 327-337.

Ombredane, A., & Robaye, F. Le problème de l'épuration des résultats des tests d'intelligence étudiés sur le Matrix-Couleur. Comparaison des techniques de reduplication et d'explication. *Bulletin du Centre d'Etudes et Recherches Psychotechniques*, 1953, 32, 3-17.

Ombredane, A., Robaye, F., & Plumail, H. Resultats d'une application répétée du matrix-couleur à une population de Noirs Congolais. *Bulletin du Centre d'Études et Recherches Psychotechniques*, 1956, 6, 149-160.

Ombredane, A., Robaye, F., & Robaye, E. Etude psychotechnique des Baluba. Application experimentale du test d'intelligence Matrix 38 à 485 noirs Baluba. *Memoires de l'Academie Royale des Sciences Coloniales, Ire Classe,* 1957, 6, fasc. 5.

Etude psychologique des Noirs Asalampasu. II. Analyse du comportement dans le test des relations spatiales de Minnesota. *Mémoires de l'Academie Royale des Sciences Coloniales, Ire Classe,* 1958, 6, fasc. 6.

Opara, P.A.U. Social distance attitudes of Nigerian students. *Phylon,* 1968, 29, 13-18.

Orley, J. *Culture and Mental Illness.* Nairobi: East African Publishing House, 1970.

Ostheimer, J.M. Measuring achievement motivation among the Chagga of Tanzania. *Journal of Social Psychology,* 1969, 78, 17-30.

Otaala, B. Performance of Ugandan African children on some Piagetian conservation tasks: An exploratory investigation. In H.A. El-Abd (Ed.), *Readings in Educational Psychology in East Africa. Book Two.* Department of Educational Psychology, Makerere University, 1971.

Owoc, P.J. On culture and conservation once again. *International Journal of Psychology,* 1973, 8, 249-254.

Page, H.W. Concepts of length and distance in a study of Zulu youth. *Journal of Social Psychology,* 1973, 90, 9-16.

Parin, P. Some character traits of 'Primitive Africans'. *Psyche,* 1958, 11, 692-706.

Parkin, J.M., & Warren, N. A comparative study of neonatal behaviour and development: differences at birth between Europeans and Africans, and between Africans from widely differing social levels. University of East Africa, Social Sciences Conference, Nairobi, 1969.

Paulme, D. *Women of Tropical Africa.* London: Routledge & Kegan Paul, 1963.

Peiffer, E. Données obtenues au test de Rorschach chez les noirs d'Afrique Occidentale Française. *Bulletin de l'Institut Français d'Afrique Noire,* 1959, 21, 20-60.

Peiffer, E., Pelage, S., & Pelage, M. Quelques résultats obtenus au test de Rorschach, chez les Bamilekes du Cameroun. *Bulletin de l'Institut Français d'Afrique Noire,* 1963, 25, 454-457.

Peil, M. Aspirations and social structure: A West African example. *Africa,* 1968, 38, 71-78.

Pettigrew, T.F., Allport, G.W., & Barnett, E.O. Binocular resolution and perception of race in South Africa. *British Journal of Psychology,* 1958, 49, 265-278.

Pfefferman, G. *Industrial Labour in the Republic of Senegal.* London: Praeger, 1968.

Pillner, A.E.G. Objective testing in West Africa. Report to the British Council, 1964.

Pinard, A., Morin, C., & Lefebvre, M. Apprentissage de la conservation des quantités liquides chez les enfants Rwandais et Canadiens-Français. *International Journal of Psychology,* 1973, 8, 15-23.

Pollnac, R.B., & Robbins, M.C. Gratification patterns and modernisation in rural Buganda. *Human Organisation,* 1972, 31, 63-72.

Poole, H.E. The effect of urbanisation upon scientific concept attainment among Hausa children of Northern Nigeria. *British Journal of Educational Psychology,* 1968, 38, 57-63.

The effect of Westernisation on the psychomotor development of African (Yoruba) infants during the first year of life. *Journal of Tropical Pediatrics,* 1969, 15, 172-176.

Poortinga, Y.H. Relative proficiency on simple auditory and visual experiments: A comparison between African and European students. In L.J. Cronbach & P.J.D. Drenth (Eds.), *Mental Tests and Cultural Adaptations.* The Hague: Mouton, 1972.

Porteus, S.D. *Intelligence and Environment.* New York: Macmillan, 1937.

Powdermaker, H. Social change through imagery and values of teen age Africans in Northern Rhodesia. *American Anthropologist,* 1956, 58, 783-813.

Price-Williams, D.R. A study concerning concepts of conservation of quantities among primitive children. *Acta Psychologica,* 1961, 18, 297-305.

Abstract and concrete modes of classification in a primitive society. *British Journal of Educational Psychology,* 1962, 32, 50-61.

Ramarasaona, Z. Psychomotor development in early childhood in the Tananarive region.

Report of the CSM Meeting of Specialists on the Basic Psychological Structures of African and Madagascan Populations. London: CCTA/CSA Publication No 51, 1959.

Rattray, R.S. *Ashanti.* Oxford: Oxford University Press, 1923.

Read, M. *Children of their Fathers: Growing Up among the Ngoni of Nyasaland.* London: Methuen, 1959.

Reader, D.H. *The Black Man's Portion.* Cape Town: Oxford University Press, 1961.

Rérat, G. La crise des cadres Africains: quelques faits concernant l'Afrique Noire Francophone. *Travail Humain,* 1963, 26, 219-228.

Richards, A. *Hunger and Work in a Savage Tribe.* London: Routledge, 1932.

Richelle, M. Contribution à l'étude des mécanismes intellectuels chez les Africains du Katanga. *Problèmes Sociaux Congolais,* 1959, 45, 3-70.

Ritchie, J.F. The African as suckling and as adult. A psychological study. Rhodes-Livingstone Institute Paper No 9, 1943.

The African as a grown up nursling. *Rhodes-Livingstone Institute Journal,* 1944, 1, 55-60.

Robaye, F. Propos inédits du Professeur Ombredane sur les niveaux de compréhension du film par les noirs congolais. *Bulletin du Centre d'Etudes et Recherches Psychotechniques,* 1959, 8, 15-24.

Robaye, E., Robaye, F., & Falmagne, J.C. Le testing de l'éducabilité dans un groupe de noirs congolais. *Bulletin de l'Académie Royale des Sciences d'Outre-Mer, Nouvelle Serie,* 1960, 6, 295-321.

Robbins, M.C., Kilbride, P.L., & Bukenya, J.M. Time estimation and acculturation among the Baganda. *Perceptual and Motor Skills,* 1968, 26, 1010.

Robbins, M.C., & Thomason, R.W. Modernisation and exploratory behaviour: An Example from Buganda. Symposium on Modernisation, University of Rhode Island, Kingston, Rhode Island, 1971.

Robbins, M.C., & Thompson, R.W. *Socio-cultural Bases of Gratification Patterns.* Bethesda: Public Health Service, 1972.

Rogers, C.A. A study of racial attitudes in Nigeria. *Journal of the Rhodes-Livingstone Institute,* 1959, 26, 51-64.

Roloff, B. The concept of conservation in a sample of Zambian children. Mimeographed Report, Institute of Education, University of Zambia, 1970.

Roscoe, J. *The Baganda.* London: Macmillan, 1911.

Safier, M. Some thoughts on planners and planning for urban development in Africa. In M. Safier & B.W. Langlands (Eds.), *Perspectives in Urban Planning for Uganda.* Kampala: Makerere Institute for Social Research, 1969.

Salamone, F.A. Further notes on Hausa culture and personality. *International Journal of Social Psychiatry,* 1969, 16, 39-44.

Salber, E.J. The effect of different feeding schedules on the growth of Bantu babies in the first week of life. *Journal of Tropical Pediatrics,* 1956, 2, 97-102.

Sasieni, L.S. *The Principles and Practice of Optical Dispensing and Fitting.* London: Hammond and Hammond, 1962.

Schepers, J. Pictorial depth perception in a group of black industrial workers: the efficacy of linear perspective in conjunction with a gradient of texture. XXIst South African Psychological Association Conference, 1969.

Schiff, M.R. An analysis of reported caretaker behaviour correlates of manifest curiosity among Ganda pre-school children. PhD Dissertation, Syracuse University, 1970.

Schmidt, W.H.O. School and intelligence. *International Review of Education,* 1960, 6, 416-432.

Schwarz, P.A. *Aptitude tests for use in the Developing Nations.* Pittsburgh: American Institute for Research, 1962.

Adapting tests to the cultural setting. *Educational and Psychological Measurement,* 1963, 23, 673-686.

Schwitzgebel, R. The performance of Dutch and Zulu adults on selected perceptual tests. *Journal of Social Psychology,* 1962, 57, 73-77.

Scott, G.C. Measuring Sudanese intelligence. *British Journal of Educational Psychology,* 1950, 20, 43-54.

Scribner, S., & Cole, M. Cognitive consequences of formal and informal education. *Science*, 1973, 182, 553-559.

Segall, M.H. A preliminary report on psychological research in Ankole. East African Institute for Social Research, Kampala, 1959.

A psychological view of changing Africa. *Antioch Review*, 1961, 3, 270-280.

Segall, M.H., Campbell, D.T., & Herskovits, M.J. *The Influence of Culture on Visual Perception*. New York: Bobbs-Merrill, 1966.

Seibel, H.D. Some aspects of interethnic relations in Nigeria. *Nigerian Journal of Economic and Social Studies*, 1967, 9, 217-228.

Serpell, R. Cross-cultural differences in the difficulty of copying orientation; a response organisation hypothesis. Human Development Research Unit, Report No 12, University of Zambia, 1969a.

Cultural differences in attentional preference for colour over form. *International Journal of Psychology*, 1969b, 4, 1-8.

The influence of language, education and culture on attentional preference between colour and form. *International Journal of Psychology*, 1969c, 4, 183-194.

Discrimination of orientation of Zambian children. *Journal of Comparative Physiological Psychology*, 1971, 75, 312-316.

How perception differs among cultures. *New Society*, 1972, June 22, 620-623.

Serpell, R., & Deregowski, J.B. Frames of preference for copying orientation: a cross cultural study. Human Development Research Unit, Report No 20, University of Zambia, 1971.

Shapiro, M.B. The rotation of drawings by illiterate Africans. *Journal of Social Psychology*, 1960, 52, 17-30.

Sherwood, E.T. On the designing of TAT pictures with special reference to a set for an African people assimilating Western culture. *Journal of Social Psychology*, 1957, 45, 161-190.

Sherwood, R. Motivational analysis: a comparison of job attitudes among African and American professional and clerical workers. Proceedings of the South African Psychological Association, 1956-1957, Nos 7/8, 37-38.

The Bantu clerk: A study of role expectations. *Journal of Social Psychology*, 1958, 47, 285-316.

Siann, G. Measuring field dependence in Zambia: A cross cultural study. *International Journal of Psychology*, 1972, 7, 87-96.

Silvey, J. Testing ability tests: The measurement of ability among African schoolboys. East African Institute for Social Research Conference, Dar es Salaam, 1963a.

Aptitude testing and educational selection in Africa. *Rhodes-Livingstone Journal*, 1963b, 34, 9-22.

The occupational attitudes of secondary school leavers in Uganda. In R. Jolly (Ed.), *Education in Africa*. Nairobi: East African Publishing House, 1969.

A longitudinal study of ability and attainment from the end of Primary to the end of Secondary school in Uganda. In L.J. Cronbach & P.J.D. Drenth (Eds.), *Mental Tests and Cultural Adaptations*. The Hague: Mouton, 1972.

Smith, T.E., & Blackler, J.C.C. *Population Characteristics of the Commonwealth Countries of Tropical Africa*. London: Allen Lane, 1963.

Smith, D.H., & Inkeles, A. The O.M. scale: a comparative sociopsychological measure of individual modernity. *Sociometry*, 1966, 29, 353-377.

Sofer, C., & Sofer, R. *Jinja Transformed*. East African Studies No 4, Kampala, 1956.

Somerset, H.C.A. *Predicting Success in School Certificate*. Nairobi: East African Publishing House, 1968.

Educational aspirations of fourth form pupils in Kenya. Universities of East Africa Social Sciences Conference, Dar es Salaam, 1970.

Songuemas, N. Social security and indigenous institutions in African societies. African Social Security Series No 3, 18-27, Geneva, 1967.

Stanier, M.W. The blood of the Karamojong. *Uganda Journal*, 1953, 17, 173-177.

Stewart, V.M. Tests of the 'carpentered world' hypothesis by race and environment in America and Zambia. *International Journal of Psychology*, 1973, 8, 83-94.

Stoch, M.B., & Smythe, P.M. The effect of undernutrition during infancy on subsequent brain growth and intellectual development. *South African Medical Journal*, 1967, 41, 1027-1030.

Suchman, R.G. Cultural differences in children's colour and form preferences. *Journal of Social Psychology*, 1966, 70, 3-10.

Super, C.M. Cognitive changes in Zambian children during the late pre-school years. Human Development Research Unit, Report No 22, University of Zambia, 1972.

Talbot, P.A. *In the Shadow of the Bush*. London: Oxford University Press, 1912.

Tarantino, O. Réponses banales congolaises au test de Rorschach. *Revue de Psychologie Appliquée*, 1970, 20, 181-201.

Taylor, A., & Bradshaw, G.D. Secondary school selection: The development of an intelligence test for use in Nigeria. *West African Journal of Education*, 1965, 9, 6-11.

Tedeschi, J.T., Smith, R.B., Gahagan, J.P., & Elinoff, J. Economic development and social conflict. A cross cultural study of Americans and Ghanaians. *Human Relations*, 1972, 25, 65-76.

Tekane, I. An error analysis of responses to the PATCO test by Bantu industrial workers. *Journal of the National Institute for Personnel Research*, 1961, 8, 189-194.

Symmetrical pattern completions by illiterate and literate Bantu. *Psychologia Africana*, 1963, 10, 63-68.

Tettekpoe, R.D. Some aspects of the self among the Mina of Lower Togo. *Bulletin d'Enseignement Superieur de Benin*, 1967, 1, 35-40.

Theunissen, K.B. A preliminary comparative study of the development of motor behaviour in European and Bantu children up to the age of one year. MA Thesis, Natal University College, Durban, 1948.

Thomas, L-V. De l'usage de quelques tests projectifs pour la compréhension de la personnalité noire (aperçus méthodologiques). *Bulletin de l'Institut Français d'Afrique Noire*, 1959, 21, 1-19.

Le test de Rorschach comme mode d'approche de la psychologie noire. Aperçus sur la personnalité Diola. *Bulletin de l'Institut Français d'Afrique Noire*, 1963, 25, 288-350.

Thomas, L-V., & Sapir, D. Le Diola et le temps. *Bulletin de l'Institut Français d'Afrique Noire*, 1967, 29, 331-424.

Tongue, E.D. The contact of races in Uganda. *British Journal of Psychology*, 1935, 25, 356-364.

Tooth, G. *Studies in Mental Illness in the Gold Coast*. London: HMSO, 1950.

Trent, R.D. A study of the self concepts of Ghanaian children utilising the 'Who are You' technique. *Ghana Journal of Science*, 1965, 5, 78-91.

Uka, N. *The Development of Time Concepts in African Children of Primary School Age*. Ibadan: Institute of Education, 1962.

Underwood, L. *Bronzes of West Africa*. London: Tiranti, 1949.

Van den Berghe, P. Race attitudes in Durban, South Africa. *Journal of Social Psychology*, 1962, 57, 55-72.

Van der Horst, S.T. *African Workers in Town*. Cape Town: Oxford University Press, 1964.

Van der Walt, N. The influence of incentives on the performance of African native mine-workers on a psychomotor test. MA Thesis, Pretoria University, 1952.

Van Rensburg, J.A. The learning ability of the South African native compared with that of the European. *Research Series No 5*. Pretoria: South African Council for Educational and Sociological Research, 1938.

Verhaegen, P. Utilité actuelle des tests pour l'étude psychologique des autochthones congolais. *Revue de Psychologie Appliquée*, 1956a, 6, 139-151.

L'éléctroencephalogramme de l'autochthone congolais et les différences raciales. *Acta Neurologica et Psychiatrica Belgica*, 1956b, 56, 842-852.

L'Enfant Africain. Paris: Fleuris, 1960.

Possibilité d'une orientation scolaire basée sur les épreuves psychologiques chez des enfants africains. *Revue de Psychologie Appliquée*, 1962, 12, 123-133.

School-readiness as a function of age among Congolese African children. *Psychologia Africana*, 1967, 11, 151-156.

Verhaegen, P., & Leblanc, M. Some thoughts on the pre-school education of the black child. *Revue Pedagogique Congolaise*, 1955, 2, 17-28.

Vernon, P.E. *The Structure of Human Abilities*. London: Methuen, 1950.

Administration of group intelligence tests to East African pupils. *British Journal of Educational Psychology*, 1967a, 31, 282-291.

Abilities and educational attainment in an East African environment. *Journal of Special Education*, 1967b, 1, 335-345.

Intelligence and Cultural Environment. London: Methuen, 1969.

Vincent, M., & Hugon, J. L'insuffisance pondérale du prémature africain au point de vue de la santé publique. *Bulletin of the World Health Organisation*, 1962, 26, 143-174.

Vouilloux, P.D. Etude de la psychomotricité d'enfants africains au Cameroun. Test Gesell et réflexes archaïques. *Journal de la Société des Africanistes*, 1959, 29, 11-18.

Wallace, A.F.C. *Culture and Personality*. New York: Random House, 1961.

Wallace, T., & Weeks, S.G. Youth in Uganda: Some theoretical perspectives. *International Social Science Journal*, 1972, 24, 354-361.

Warren, N. African infant precocity. *Psychological Bulletin*, 1972, 78, 353-367.

Weeks, S.G. A preliminary examination of the role of minority students at a day secondary school in Kampala, Uganda. East African Institute for Social Research Conference, Kampala, 1963.

Weinberg, R.M. Personality characteristics of African children: A projective analysis. *Journal of Social Psychology*, 1968, 83, 65-77.

Welbourn, H.F. The danger period during weaning among Baganda children. *East African Medical Journal*, 1954, 31, 147-   .

Wells, F.A., & Warmington, W.A. *Studies in Industrialisation*. London: Oxford University Press, 1962.

Werner, E.E. Infants around the world: cross cultural studies of psychomotor development from birth to two years. *Journal of Cross Cultural Psychology*, 1972, 3, 111-134.

Westermann, D. *The African Today*. London: Oxford University Press for I.A.I., 1934.

The African Today and Tomorrow. London: Oxford University Press for I.A.I., 1939.

Whiting, J.W.M., Kluckhohn, R., & Anthony, A.S. The function of male initiation ceremonies at puberty. In *Readings in Social Psychology*. New York: Holt, 1958.

World Health Organisation. Expert Committee on Mental Health, 3rd Report. Geneva, 1953.

Expert Committee on Mental Health, 8th Report. Geneva, 1960.

Wickert, F.R. *Readings in African Psychology from French Language Sources*. East Lansing: African Studies Center, Michigan State University, 1967.

Winter, W. The perception of safety posters by Bantu industrial workers. *Psychologia Africana,*, 1963, 10, 127-135.

Winterbottom, J.M. Can we measure the African's intelligence? *Rhodes-Livingstone Journal*, 1948, 6, 53-59.

Wintringer, G. Considerations sur l'intelligence du Noir Africain. *Revue Psychologique des Peuples*, 1955, 10, 37-55.

Witkin, H.A. A cognitive style approach to cross cultural research. *International Journal of Psychology*, 1967, 2, 233-250.

Witkin, H.A., Dyk, R.B., Faterson, H.F., Goodenough, D.R., & Karp, S.A. *Psychological Differentiation*. New York: Wiley, 1962.

Wober, M. Under Nigerian Eyes. *New Society*, 1966a, May 26, 19.

Sensotypes. *Journal of Social Psychology*, 1966b, 70, 181-189.

Recognition of pictures of animals in unusual settings. *Nigerian Field*, 1966c, 31, 70-74.

Psychological factors in adjustment to industrial life among employees of a firm in South Nigeria. PhD Thesis, University of London, 1967a.

Adapting Witkin's field independence theory to accommodate new information from Africa. *British Journal of Psychology*, 1967b, 58, 29-38.

Individualism, home life and work efficiency among a group of Nigerian workers. *Occupational Psychology*, 1967c, 41, 183-192.

The meaning and stability of Raven's Matrices test among Africans. *International Journal of Psychology*, 1969, 4, 229-235.

Confrontation of the H-V illusion and a test of 3-dimensional pictorial perception in Nigeria. *Perceptual and Motor Skills*, 1970, 31, 105-106.

What's in a name. *Science Journal*, 1971a, September.

Explorations on the concept of self-esteem. *International Journal of Psychology*, 1971b, 6, 147-155.

Adapting Dawson's traditional versus western attitudes scale and presenting some new information from Africa. *British Journal of Social and Clinical Psychology*, 1971c, 10, 101-113.

A cautious note on the risky shift, and some risky speculations on further relevance in research; with new information from Uganda. Occasional Paper No 5, Social Psychology Section, Sociology Department, Makerere University, 1971d.

Horizons, horizontals, and illusions about the vertical. *Perceptual and Motor Skills*, 1972a, 34, 960.

Genes and the politics of intelligence. *Transition*, 1972b, 40, 11-26.

Towards an understanding of the Kiganda concept of intelligence. In J.W. Berry and P.R. Dasen (Eds.), *Culture and Cognition: Readings in Cross Cultural Psychology*. London: Methuen, 1974a.

Polyphasic picture perception: a phenomenon demonstrated in Africa. In J.L.M. Dawson and W. Lonner (Eds.), *Readings in Cross Cultural Psychology: Proceedings of the Inaugural Meeting of the International Association for Cross Cultural Psychology*. Hong Kong: University of Hong Kong Press, 1974b.

Wober, M., & Bukombi, S. The shifty risk phenomenon, and changing attitudes to birth control in Uganda. Occasional Paper No 20, Social Psychology Section, Sociology Department, Makerere University, 1973.

Wober, M., & Cohen, E. L'influence de l'attente de l'experimentateur appliquée à une étude sur l'identité nationale en Ouganda. *International Journal of Psychology*, 1972, 7, 119-120.

Wober, M., & Musoke-Mutanda, F. Patience, and gratification preferences among Ugandan schoolchildren. *Journal of Social Psychology*, 1972, 87, 141-142.

Woldemikael, H. Social dependency in Ethiopia. *Ethiopian Journal of Education*, 1970, 4, 4-15.

Xydias, N. Un test de situations appliquées en Congo Belge. *Travail Humain*, 1955, 18, 109-123.

Les Africains du Congo Belge: Aptitudes, attitudes vis à vis du travail. *Travail Humain*, 1960, 23, 41-54.

Etude comparative des populations Sahariennes. *Travail Humain*, 1963, 26, 57-90.

Yoloye, E.A. The effect of schooling on the performance of bilingual students in tests of intelligence. *Research in Education*, 1971, 5, 25-34.

Zahan, D. Pictographic writing in the Western Sudan. *Man*, 1950, 50 (219), 136-138.

Zempleni, A., & Collomb, H. On the functions and substance of social psychology in Africa. *Journal of Social Issues*, 1968, 24, 57-67.

Ziegler, M., King, M., King, J.M., & Ziegler, S.M. Tribal stereotypes among Ethiopian students. *Journal of Cross Cultural Psychology*, 1972, 3, 193-200.

INDEX

For Product Safety Concerns and Information please contact our EU
representative GPSR@taylorandfrancis.com Taylor & Francis Verlag GmbH,
Kaufingerstraße 24, 80331 München, Germany

Printed and bound by CPI Group (UK) Ltd, Croydon, CR0 4YY
11/04/2025
01843979-0006